BOOM CHICAGO

PRESENTS

THE 30 MOST IMPORTANT YEARS IN DUTCH HISTORY

BOOM
CHICAGO

PRESENTS

THE 30 MOST IMPORTANT
YEARS IN DUTCH HISTORY

ANDREW MOSKOS & PEP ROSENFELD
WITH MATT DIEHL AND SASKIA MAAS

BROOKLYN, NEW YORK

Published by Akashic Books
©2023 Andrew Moskos, Pep Rosenfeld, Matt Diehl, and Saskia Maas

ISBN: 978-1-63614-104-6
Library of Congress Control Number: 2022947077
All rights reserved
First printing

Photographs courtesy of Boom Chicago except where noted.

Akashic Books
Brooklyn, New York
Instagram, Twitter, Facebook: AkashicBooks
info@akashicbooks.com
www.akashicbooks.com

To all the actors who ever cowboyed
their way through a Boom Chicago show.

And to Odette Taminiau from the Amsterdam tourism
office, who told us our plan would never work.

TABLE OF CONTENTS

WELCOME TO THIRTY YEARS OF BOOM CHICAGO

It was when we—Andrew Moskos and Pep Rosenfeld, old friends since childhood—were traveling through Europe after graduating college that we fell in love with Amsterdam. And no, it's not for the reason you think . . .

It was for the drugs.

In our stoner haze, we thought we'd found a hole in the market there. See, we were fans of comedy who'd grown up visiting Second City, Chicago's improv and sketch institution. We remember when we were finally old enough to stay for Second City's after-show improv sets, which started at ten thirty p.m. And in our early twenties, on our first trip to Amsterdam in the early 1990s, we were on improv teams at ImprovOlympic (now iO). Like many young, aspiring comedians in Chicago, we were also taking improv classes. Lots of improv classes . . .

Performing improv wasn't just not paying the rent—it was actually costing us money. But what if we turned it around? What if we skipped the classes and just put on a show? And what if we tried to make a business of it? Hey, what if we left Chicago and did it somewhere else? What about Amsterdam? Why not? The Dutch, global traders for over five hundred years, were historically open-minded to foreign ideas. There was no serious anti-Americanism permeating the Netherlands; plus, everyone spoke great English there. With a base of locals plus expats and tourists, we figured we'd be able to find enough of an audience to make this concept work.

So we faxed the City of Amsterdam with our big idea: open an English-language theater that puts on smart shows good enough to be reviewed, but fun enough that you actually want to see them. "Your idea won't work," the City of Amsterdam faxed back with a healthy dose of Dutch skepticism, and an even healthier dose of Dutch bluntness. "Dutch people do not want to see a show in English, and tourists don't want to see a show at all. You will need a subsidy to do theater in the Netherlands, but you won't get a subsidy. Think twice about your plans."

We framed the fax (1993, baby!), and decided to do it anyway. With a mix of American optimism, hard work, and a small amount of savings, we—along with our childhood pal, former Boy Scout–turned–Boom's first technical director, Ken Schaefle—started performing in the back of a salsa bar just off the Leidseplein.

Meanwhile, Saskia Maas was studying in Amsterdam after spending a year abroad in America. That was in Muncie, Indiana, of all places, at Ball State University—the school where David Letterman studied. In 1993, with him hosting the innovative *Late Night with David Letterman* on NBC, these were quite cool credentials. Saskia brought *stroopwafels* and Sinterklaas to Muncie, and in return she got Wendy's hamburgers and baseball. She also liked Americans, as they were optimistic and upbeat. While in America, Saskia met Andrew's brother, Peter. He gave her phone number to Andrew, and they met and hit it off. She learned about our plans for Boom Chicago, and was naturally drawn to the project. Saskia was soon Boom Chicago's Dutch representative, translator, and coconspirator.

The show in the salsa bar finally opened, and we performed five nights a week. We did funny shows at night, then hustled selling tickets on the street during the day. We filled the house *and* even got a really good review in the left-leaning *de Volkskrant* the first year. (Thank you, Hein Janssen.) We learned two things from that experience. The first was, judging by every Dutch friend's reaction, it was hard to get a good review in *de Volkskrant*. The second was that the Dutch love an underdog.

Boom Chicago's first show, "Get off the Bike Path," was

aimed at tourists, but soon we wanted to make shows for the locals too. We wondered just what was so crazy about Dutch people and modern life. And what made people laugh? Over the next three decades, we created almost sixty shows, getting many great reviews and continuing to learn by doing. Our luck ran out in 2017, just in time for our twenty-fifth anniversary. When we premiered our latest show, "FaceTime Your Fears," the Amsterdam newspaper *Het Parool* gave it one star. The review's two internal section headings, highlighted in bold, read "*sporadische lach*" ("occasional laughs") and "*mislukking*" ("failure"). It ended with a clear message: "Boom needs to reflect."

Okay, maybe the show wasn't our best, but come on. One star? Was it really one of the worst shows of the year in Amsterdam? Why so extreme? Maybe because in Holland, there's a desire to bring down those who are ahead. Dutch people teach it to their kids as a warning: "The tall tulip gets cut down." So upon the suggested reflection, maybe it was actually a *great* review. Perhaps that one star implied we were a tall tulip that needed to be cut down. After so many years, we'd finally arrived!

With one foot in the Netherlands, another in America, and with an eye toward Europe, we were in a unique position to comment on international and local affairs over the years. We spent guilders. Then we spent euros. Then we converted euros into guilders in our heads and complained: "Can you believe this meal cost eighty guilders?" Since arriving, we've lived through five American presidents and ten Dutch governments. We enjoyed hearing English newscasters mispronounce the name of Wim Kok, Holland's prime minister from 1994 to 2002: "In the Hague, Wim *Cock* leads the 'purple' coalition. Yes, *Cock* is the purple head."

In local politics, Boom Chicago watched the rise of Dutch agitator Pim Fortuyn, followed by Dutch populist Rita Verdonk, who led directly to right-winger Geert Wilders. We lived through Donald Trump, who put America (and also comedians) first. We saw England vote for Brexit and put the UK last. We experienced the fast-fashion rise of Zara and the equally fast fall of V&D, both replaced by Shein on the high street. The coffee "haves" upgraded to George Clooney and Nespresso, while the "have-nots" stuck with *onze eigen* Senseo. *(Onze eigen,* which means "our very own," celebrates local heroes with small-p pride. It's like shouting, "USA! USA!" at a sports game, but without making too many in the world cringe.)

The Internet accelerated everything from zero to one hundred in only ten years. Cell phones went from being used by doctors to drug dealers, and then everyone. Phones got smart, and went from big to small to big again. Videotapes turned into DVDs, and DVDs turned into . . . nothing. Music got free, concerts got expensive. Netflix appeared, revolutionized TV, peaked, and then became more like good ol' HBO. Bodies got fitter and underwear got sexier—but public nudity on beaches retreated.

In many areas, the Netherlands has led the world. Take water management, for example. The Dutch are the first people to visit if you want to build an island. *[Cue mafia music]* "Hey, Singapore, this Sentosa is a real nice island that you started building here. It'd be a shame if it sank . . . I'm just sayin'. Look, you need to see *de Godvader* about this." The Dutch tackled tough problems head on. Euthanasia rules were humane. Drug laws were an inspiration. Gay rights were the strongest in the world. Holland was the first country to legalize same-sex marriage; it was also the first to have a federally funded monument for gay people. And Amsterdam was the first city to have a full-time, G-string-wearing Rollerblader. He was tireless. (And surprisingly tan, considering the weather.)

These past thirty years were not only important to Holland— they were also important to comedy. We witnessed the Dutch comedy revolution, and became a part of it. Until the early 1990s, Holland had "cabaret"—comedy programs created for the country's state-subsidized theaters. Cabaret was rather literary, occasionally funny, and at times dull. Music was a part of cabaret, and the songs were clever . . . sometimes.

Then came Dutch stand-up comedy. It was a fresher, hipper, and funnier (and less subsidized) comedy beast. By the Dutch definition, stand-up comedy was everything funny that wasn't classic cabaret. As such, there were two leaders in Holland: Toomler and Boom Chicago. Toomler—named for the Yiddish word meaning "creator of comic tumult"—was hands down the most influential force in Dutch stand-up comedy, serving as performance home for the beloved Comedytrain troupe. The members of Comedytrain are a who's who of performers and writers on the funniest shows on Dutch TV. To this day, Toomler offers the crème de la crème of the Dutch-language comedy scene, launching careers for many of the most successful comedians under the direction of Raoul Heertje and later Jan Jaap van der Wal. (Yes, "Yan Yahp" is a real Dutch first name. And yes, Jan's first name plus last name equals *five words*.)

About the time Comedytrain launched Toomler, Boom Chicago opened its place on the Korte Leidsedwarsstraat, just off Amsterdam's Leidseplein nightlife district. Although the Dutch called whatever Boom Chicago did stand-up comedy, by the US definition we weren't stand-up at all. To most English-speakers, stand-up comedy was one person with a microphone telling jokes. What we did at Boom, though, was sketch and improvisation comedy—not better or worse, just different.

Boom Chicago's improv meant five people working together onstage. Stand-up by comparison was mere tennis to Boom Chicago's football, or as the Dutch say, *voetbal*. (A note: to maintain our European credentials in this book, when we say football, we mean "soccer." When we mean NFL-style football, we will specify *American* football. This deft command of local Dutch vocabulary was key to us being accepted in the early years.) The first year, Pep, Andrew, and three other comedians from the Chicago improv community (Mirjam Tolan, Lindley Curry, and Neil Mc-

Namara) performed a show that mixed sketches and short-form improvisation. While we've had occasional stand-up events and debuted a longer-form improv show in 2018, the sketch/improv combo would become the primary Boom Chicago style for our entire run.

In our three decades of existence, Boom Chicago's shows have sold millions of tickets, and many of our actors and collaborators have gone on to be influential in the comedy world—from television and film to Broadway and that thing known as the Internet. Boom alumni have written and performed on *Saturday Night Live*. Former Boom actor Seth Meyers went from "Weekend Update" to hosting his own acclaimed talk show, *Late Night with Seth Meyers*. Along the way, Seth became the leading edge of topical, politically focused comedy—de facto taking the mantle from Jon Stewart when he retired in 2016 (and Trevor Noah had not yet found his footing). Seth was becoming a most trusted and beloved source of both laughs and non-fake news in his own right. He would also open doors for fellow Boom alums like Amber Ruffin, whose historic *Late Night* hiring made her the first African American woman to work on a late-night talk show writing staff—paving the way for Amber to shatter another glass ceiling in becoming the first Black woman to host her own late-night talk show, *The Amber Ruffin Show*.

Another famed alumnus, Jordan Peele, went straight from Boom to being cast in the *MADtv* ensemble before he and Keegan-Michael Key created the groundbreaking sketch show *Key & Peele*. Jordan then pretty much retired from acting to concentrate on his directing and producing projects, emulating his role model, Steven Spielberg. This move seems to have worked out. For his second directorial effort, 2017's *Get Out*, Jordan was nominated for three Oscars, and actually won one; since then, everything Jordan does becomes a major pop-cultural event. Meanwhile, Boom grad Kay Cannon wrote the smash *Pitch Perfect* franchise after an award-winning stint on *30 Rock*, ultimately leading to a major career as a writer-director of films like the 2018 hit *Blockers* (also starring Boom's Ike Barinholtz). Oh, and Boom OGs Jason Sudeikis, Brendan Hunt, and Joe Kelly went on to create the culture-defining hit show *Ted Lasso* for that newfangled Apple TV+ in 2020—based largely on the love of football they developed during their shared Amsterdam comedy pilgrimage.

Likewise, what do *A Black Lady Sketch Show, Parks and Recreation, Community, Russian Doll, Late Night with Conan O'Brien, Jimmy Kimmel Live!, The Office, Breaking Bad, The Tonight Show with Jimmy Fallon, Nope, The Colbert Report, Inside Amy Schumer, The Daily Show, Rick and Morty, Horrible Bosses, Portlandia, Girls5eva, It's Always Sunny in Philadelphia, Suicide Squad, Superstore, How I Met Your Mother, Wicked, The Pee-wee Herman Show, Brooklyn Nine-Nine, Broad City, Urinetown, Grey's Anatomy, Freestyle Love Supreme,* and *Veep* all have in common?

Yes, they all feature writers, creators, directors, or actors who got their start at Boom Chicago. And—*ahem*—that's a partial list. Back in the early days (daze?) of Boom Chicago, we had no idea any of this would happen. We just thought the likes of Seth, Jordan, Amber, Brendan, Jason, Ike, and so on were funny as hell. We had no idea they'd be the funniest, most important voices of a comedy generation. Lucky us!

We would also have a sizable impact on the comedy scene in our adopted Holland. Boom Chicago directly influenced the huge TV improv show *De Lama's* with our improvisation games, and even trained one of the show's stars, Ruben van der Meer, in our improv style. Our own *Comedy Central News* was the highest-rated show on Dutch Comedy Central from 2007 to 2008. Anchor Greg Shapiro was also the voice of Trump in Arjen Lubach's 2017 viral video hit, "America First, the Netherlands Second." Meanwhile, with more than 100 million views, Boom Chicago's "SpongeBob SquarePants in China" remains the biggest Dutch YouTube comedy video of all time. It even caught the attention of the Chinese embassy, who asked us to remove the video, which lambasted the Chinese government for censoring free speech. Um, we declined.

Over the years, Boom Chicago's community of 120 actors has grown to share a unique bond. They've all gone through our comedy boot camp, in a foreign country no less, where they didn't speak the language. They would go on to form close ties with each other, Amsterdam, and the people who live here. The actors' connection to Boom, comedy, and each other would continue long after they left. Many Boom alumni still work with each other in writing, performing, and directing onstage, television, and in the movies. Others have started their own successful theaters in Los Angeles, London, Pittsburgh, Austin, and Providence. And when World Cup season rolls around every four years, soccer parties in Los Angeles erupt, with Boom alumni spanning the decades donning orange shirts and meeting in bars at seven a.m. to watch Oranje play.[1]

Still, dwelling on our own success as we like to do, we find ourselves sometimes wondering, *Just why are so many Boom Chicago alumni so successful?* Of course it's because they're good. *Really* good. But also because the Boom Chicago experience itself is great for one's post-Boom career (and not just because of the alumni network). From a comedy perspective, Boom is where a lot of actors have learned how to write and play for strangers, night after night. Before they came to Boom, many of our performers were big shots at improv institutions like iO, Upright Citizens Brigade, and the Free Association. But the audiences there are passionate improv fans, and often students or aspiring performers themselves. They understand the structure, take the same improv classes, know the same improv games, and get the same references. Sometimes a "move" on-

---

1 Well, okay, not for World Cup 2018. The Dutch couldn't even qualify in that cursed year . . .

stage is rewarded with supportive laughter from the approving insiders who make up the audience. Off nights, meanwhile, can be forgiven based on the comedians' greater body of work. In that context, sometimes it's hard to tell what's actually funny—especially as you might only get onstage once or twice a week, max.

In the Chicago comedy scene, ultimately you find yourself playing for your peers. At Boom Chicago, however, our audience gets babysitters, parks their cars, and they might not even speak perfect English. They certainly don't know your reputation in the "scene," and they don't get your US-centric references, either. CVS Pharmacy? Baseball? High school? Philly cheesesteaks? Tom Brady? *Everybody Loves Raymond?* Chicago-style hot dogs? All to which the Dutch give a collective *Huh?* Dutch audiences are by their nature less enthusiastic, anyway. If you tell an American audience to make some noise, they yell, "Woo-hoo!" and pump their fists. Dutch audiences, meanwhile, remain seated with arms crossed: "So, tell me why exactly I should make some noise?"

If Boom's talented actors can unlearn what they have learned and connect to new audiences—a Dutch audience, an international audience—then they will become stars on our stage. They often find that the experience of connecting to these strangers gives them a leg up in getting future creative jobs. Their next project, like writing for TV, will also be about connecting to an audience that doesn't know them. By taking these creatives out of improv's closed ecosystems in LA, New York, Chicago, and London, and putting them in front of DGAF Dutch audiences five nights a week, they ultimately can't help but improve their funny game.

English-language comedy in general has also gotten bigger in the Netherlands. The Internet has given visibility to so many international comedians who would otherwise have gone unnoticed outside their home countries. Thanks to Netflix and YouTube, comedians don't even have to star in big movies or be on

Dutch TV to sell out venues in Holland. Jim Jeffries fills Amsterdam's 17,000-capacity Ziggo Dome; Ricky Gervais and Gabriel Iglesias bring crowds to AFAS Live. Bill Maher packs them in at the Meervaart, and Whitney Cummings sells out Boom Chicago. Hardly a Netherlands household name, Jimmy Carr tours multiple Dutch cities, including international hot spots Eindhoven and Tilburg. Yes, Tilburg. If it's Thursday, it must be Tilburg!

Which brings us back to our true subject: the thirty most important years in Dutch history.

For centuries, philosophers have wondered, *If a tree falls in the forest, but no one is there to hear it, does it make a sound?* Similarly, if a country exists for centuries, but no satirical outsiders have moved there to make fun of it, can you truly say it ever existed? No way! History only starts once we're there to joke about it. So pinpointing the thirty most important years in Dutch history was easy: Boom Chicago did our first Amsterdam comedy show in 1993. Let's face it—that's when things started getting really interesting in the Netherlands, okay? Everything that came before—that was just practice for the arrival of Boom Chicago's innovations. Holland's golden era? The East India Trading Company? Tulip mania (and the tulip crash)? The German occupation? Thorbecke's constitution? "Radar Love" by Golden Earring?

Meh. All that took place BBC (Before Boom Chicago). When future historians look back at the years spanning 1993 to 2023, they will see clearly what we are only beginning to appreciate now: we're living in a *new* golden age—making history faster than ever before. Each year since Boom has been in Holland, there has been exactly one earth-shattering event that has influenced the Netherlands and defined the country—even in parts of the country that need their Dutch subtitled into Dutch as if they are Belgians. Actually, what other country besides the Netherlands puts subtitles on movies where the characters *speak the same language* the audience also speaks? And before some

Dutch nerd says, "Well, Belgium does it too"—just think of how ridiculous you sound, Daan!

In the end, we're so happy to have been a part of Amsterdam life these last glorious three decades, and to have been part of so many game-changing talents' origin stories. We love it here, and feel lucky to feel loved in return. Well, except for that one-star review in *Het Parool*. Fuck that guy.

But we do love you. No, really. So please enjoy our—and your—history . . .

—Andrew Moskos & Pep Rosenfeld

FOREWORD
by Seth Meyers

As ideas go, Boom Chicago should never have worked. It should have ended up on the scrap heap of "Terrible Ideas Americans Have Had While Stoned in Amsterdam," a scrap heap likely higher than the tallest building in the Netherlands. (So five stories? Six?) Honestly, have you ever seen two American tourists talking loudly in front of a bar at three a.m. in Amsterdam and thought, *You know what I bet they're doing? Business planning.* But for them, it worked out that way and here we are, three decades later: Boom Chicago, the English-language improv comedy theater, is still alive and kicking. So who can we thank for this success?

Well, let's start by thanking the aforementioned Americans, Andrew Moskos and Pep Rosenfeld. The first rule of improv is "Yes, and . . ." You agree with what your scene partner says, and you add to it in order to make it better. This runs counter to the first rule of Dutch commerce: "No, go away." And yet, when the "Yes, and-ers" came face-to-face with the "No, go away-ers," they stood their ground and insisted this idea could work. Why? Because Andrew and Pep are stubborn romantics, and when you stubbornly love one thing (comedy) as much as another thing (Amsterdam), you just believe they should be together.

But that wasn't the most important union. The most important union was when Andrew and Pep found Saskia Maas, because this journey needed the wise input of an actual Dutch person. And she was the perfect match for this job, as Saskia is both no-nonsense and a lover of nonsense; a shrewd business mind who thought business could use a little silliness, and the owner of the best laugh this side of the IJ. So thank you, Saskia!

As funny as the three of them are, they still needed a cast, so thanks also to those who have graced the Boom stage not just for their humor, but also for embracing adventure. There is no surefire path that guarantees success as a comedian. But for those of us who try to plan, it would look something like this: *Take classes, join a theater, get an agent, go to Hollywood.* No one, in any plan before 1993, had *Move to the Netherlands* on their list. So for everyone involved, Boom Chicago was a change of plan. Then why did so many of us make the leap? Well, for one thing, Amsterdam was a huge draw. With all due respect to the rest of the Randstad, we probably weren't leaving our family behind for Boom Utrecht. Though I have nothing against Utrecht. I'm a huge fan of the (googling it . . .) Dom Tower. But the other, more important thing was the love of the unknown. When an improviser walks onstage, they have to think, *I don't know what this is going to be, but I bet it's going to be fun.* Over the years, so many different kinds of performers walked through the doors of Boom, with so many different styles. But the one thing we all had in common was, when we heard about Boom Chicago, we thought, *I don't know what that's going to be, but I bet it's going to be fun.*

And were we right? My God, yes. Outside of the lifetime friendships, hours of laughs, and triumphant shows, here is just a short list of things I now love thanks to my time in that Amsterdam: bicycles, house music, Heineken on tap, the shade of blue in the KLM logo, narrow-ass stairwells, Schiphol-bought cheeses, three kisses, Febo *bitterballen*, girls with *k*'s in the *middle* of their name, KNVB, the word *doei,* and King's Day. Also, it should be noted that I lived in Amsterdam so long ago, there are things I love that are gone now: tulip glasses, Queen's Day, and your goofy paper guilders. So thank you, Amsterdam. Despite fighting the idea at first, Boom would not have been Boom anywhere else.

So I hope you enjoy this book. Just remember as you read it that comedians are truth tellers, but they will also lie if it makes a story better.

FORE-AND-A-HALF-WORD
by Ruben van der Meer

I f you're reading this book in English, you might recognize *Ruben van der Meer's name from the credits of TV shows like* Atlanta, *where he inevitably stars as some variation of "the Dutch guy." But if you're reading it in Dutch, you already know this native Amsterdammer is a massive star in the Netherlands. In Holland's comedy world, Ruben is like Bill Burr meets Will Ferrell—but with a thick Dutch accent, doner kebab grease stains on his Ajax jersey, and his own crazy versatility—making him a popular presence on small-screen shows, big-screen films, and Holland's biggest stages alike. A true titan and innovator on the national comedy scene, Ruben found fame starring in the smash TV hit* De Lama's—*the first Dutch show to successfully bring improv to the Netherlands's airwaves and audiences. Meanwhile, a 2019 reunion show by* De Lama's *sold out Amsterdam's 17,000-capacity Ziggo Dome four freakin' nights in a row, proving Ruben remains as relevant as ever—a destiny in no small part inspired by (wait for it) his experience with Boom Chicago . . .*

I've been into comedy since I farted in my friend Horace's face. He was four years old, and I was a mature five and a half. It was pretty funny. A fart joke always works. Everyone farts, so everyone gets it, wherever you are.

Dutch comedy, though, is a very specific thing. There's a very terrible type of Dutch comedy where someone enters a room, slams the door, and is like, "Here I am." As if just them being there is funny enough. They don't have to work at it, or earn it. I mean, it's fine if you like them already—but it's no fart joke.

Dutch people didn't know about true improv comedy for a long time, either. We do have something called *theatersport* in Holland, which is competitive improvisational theater. Two teams compete using improvisation games to score points with the audience. One team does a scene, then the other. The crowd throws roses for those they like, and whoever has the most roses at the end of the night wins. It's still around, *theatersport*. I shouldn't call it terrible, but . . .

So when Boom Chicago first started performing in Amsterdam, the Dutch naturally claimed to have been there first. But it was Boom Chicago that impacted the local and then national comedy scene. The Dutch were living in the Paleolithic era before Boom Chicago came to save us with American-style improv. It's not so much that Boom created a new Dutch style of comedy, it was more like how America added the hamburger to our national diet, and then it became a Dutch tradition. Boom Chicago is to the Netherlands, in a way, like the hamburger.

The Dutch are very critical. Some Dutch comics think I've never done "true" comedy in my entire career. Some audiences think so too. Here in the Netherlands, improv is not considered "real" theater—or even real humor. Basically, you're considered less of a comedian if you do improv than if you write your jokes in advance.

For a long time, the Dutch tradition of written comedy was *kleinkunst*, or "small art," but everyone called it "cabaret." Cabaret was always performed in a theatre (and only in the classy kind ending in "re"). The program was stand-up comedy, interspersed with performances of very serious songs about incest or racism or something. The songs added the socially conscious message for cultural credibility, in case the show offended anyone with its humor. Even in comedy, we have Dutch tolerance.

Cabaret in a nutshell was this: here's a hilarious joke—now

we're going to bum you out about the existential crisis of your human existence. The audience must come out of the theater not only laughing, but also having learned something important. Now it's enough to hashtag *#MeToo* on social media at a cabaret show, but frequently you'll still find someone singing depressing songs about how terrible men are, or the government, or human trafficking. It just wouldn't be real Dutch humor unless a song ended in tears. Stand-up comedy and Boom Chicago helped change that.

I would become known in the Netherlands for improv comedy. In 2004, I was a member of *De Lama's*, the prime-time hit TV show that clued a lot of Dutch people into improv. When we won the Gouden Televizier-Ring for Best Television Show (basically the Dutch Emmy Award), where did we go to party?

Boom Chicago, of course. Where it all began . . .

The first time I saw Boom Chicago was at what is now the Sugar Factory, off the Leidseplein. I was working in the kitchen there, being paid cash under the table,[2] so I had to keep things low-key. But that's really where I discovered true improv comedy for the first time.

I remember walking into the theater after I finished my kitchen shift during a Boom show. I had no idea what they were doing onstage. People were laughing their asses off.

What they were doing was definitely not standard Dutch humor. At first I was like, *Is this even funny? Why are there so many people on the stage? Why is the audience yelling at the actors?* I didn't get it. I didn't know anything like that existed here in Amsterdam.

It went one joke after another. It was hard to keep pace, but I got caught up in it. I loved how they played off suggestions from the audience. The cast was great, and it blew my mind: I wanted to do that. I worked there for a couple more weeks, and then

2 *Paid cash under the table?* That can't be true. Oh Ruben, what a kidder you are.

they fired me because I was too slow with the salads. That was how I started my relationship with Boom Chicago.

Years later, Horace and I had successful shows on TV with *Live Opgenomen* and *Frøland,* and Andrew, Pep, and Saskia were fans. They invited us to join them onstage as guests. Right away we said yes, and we just kept coming back. That's where we honed our unique comedy style. But we kept the farts.

During the era I call "AB" (After Boom), I would always say in interviews how Boom Chicago is where I really learned improv. Having them teaching me the rules and when to break them helped me and *De Lama's* a lot to create our own thing.

The cool thing about improv is that, when you first see it, it's so spontaneous you're like, *I can do that.* And then you realize you have to study it. I got super lucky in that area. Before he created *Key & Peele* and directed the Oscar-winning film *Get Out,* Jordan Peele was in the Boom Chicago cast. He was one of the most incredible performers I'd ever seen. You couldn't believe how funny he was. Then I found out he taught weekend improv workshops. Taking those classes with Jordan—and later Amber Ruffin, another great TV writer/performer, and the ever-infamous Brendan Hunt—that's how I got started.

Learning how to do improv is like learning a language, and I wanted to be fluent. It wasn't easy. At first, I was the worst. I had no idea what I was doing. I'd be sitting there sometimes thinking, *Oh my God, how stupid. My choices are terrible. My characters are lame. The other performers must hate me!*

There were so many lessons . . . I learned to always say yes when my instinct was to say no. I learned to not just stand there, but to walk around the stage and do something. Start by sweeping the floor, maybe. Then listen, and react. One of the big improv rules, of course, is to start off by defining who you are—or even funnier, defining who the other actors onstage are: "Hello, Mayor. I see you're walking around naked again . . ." Now he has something to start from. Why is he naked? Even if it's absurd, you have to convince the audience that what they're seeing is possible.

After doing one scene, and then another scene, and then another, and then another, I was like, *Okay, maybe I've got the hang of this now.* And the rest, as they say, is history . . .

Today, true improv exists here in the Netherlands, and it's flourishing—and not just with American expats. That's indisputable now. People know what improv is, and that's largely thanks to Boom Chicago. Whenever I talk to my fans after a show, I tell them, "If you're ever in Amsterdam, go to Boom Chicago. See the original and experience it for yourself."

Or go home and do comedy the old-fashioned way: sing a song to yourself about incest and have a good cry.

I'll take farts and improv!

MEET THE CAST
by Rob AndristPlourde and Greg Shapiro

So many wonderful people have been a part of Boom Chicago over the years (and really only a few jerks—lookin' at you, Canale). We've compiled the biographies of these brave souls whose voices appear in this book—adding some bonus salacious details and ridiculous nicknames.

Rob AndristPlourde (1996–present). Rob has appeared in Dutch and American TV and films like *Sint, A Small Light,* and *Harold & Kumar 2.* He directed the full-cast short-form improv show "Late Night" for years, and developed "Late Night Massive" with Horace Cohen and Ruben van der Meer. He cocreated Boom Chicago's improv hip-hop game "Yo! Here We Go." He once gave a TED Talk on how to beatbox.
Boom nickname: RAP
Rap name: MC Slow
Favorite anecdote: Rob's last name combines his given name "Plourde" with his wife's surname "Andrist." Giving her top billing shows his unparalleled commitment to the improv rule: *Always make your partner look good.* As director of "Late Night," Rob would rally the actors by reading from the Wynton Marsalis book *Jazz in the Bittersweet Blues of Life.* He set up the pizza-for-barter ticket deal with the Melkweg, where he's seen many of the more than a thousand concerts he's attended—chronicled in his solo show, *Legends of Rob.*

Ike Barinholtz (1999–2002). Ike's career quickly went from

Boom Chicago to *MADtv*; his television work includes *The Mindy Project, Eastbound & Down*, and *The Afterparty*. Ike's best work can be found in the film *Blockers* (directed, natch, by Boom alum Kay Cannon), and he has also appeared in *Suicide Squad, Snatched*, and *Bad Neighbors*. Ike debuted as a writer-director with 2018's *The Oath*.

Boom nickname: I-kers

Rap name: The I

Favorite anecdote: When Ike announced he was going on a juice cleanse, Seth and Josh Meyers sent him a box of smoked sausage. When Ike broke down and devoured it, he suddenly had to pull off the road. His orifices exploding, Ike realized he'd stopped in front of a school surrounded by kids saying, "Look—it's the guy from *MADtv!*"

Suzi Barrett (2003–2005, 2007). Suzi is known for *Kirby Buckets, Drunk History,* and the half-improvised Disney sitcom *Just Roll with It.* She is the writer/creator of *Affirmators!*— a line of humorous self-help cards and books. An improviser at Upright Citizens Brigade, she produces the show "PDQ: Pretty Darn Queer," and is also a regular guest on *Comedy Bang Bang*.

Boom nickname: Suz

Rap name: Lil Humpy/Scary Mary Poppins

Favorite anecdote: For the 2003 Boom Chicago/Second City swap, Suzi designed an entire book of puzzles to keep us entertained on our flight to Chicago.

Dave Buckman (1999–2002). After Pep took a few years off as artistic director in 1997, Bucky stepped in to help create some of Boom's best work, including 2000's game-changing show "Live at the Leidseplein." After a spell directing/training/recruiting for Second City, he helped turn Austin, Texas, into a comedy destination as the creative force behind ColdTowne Theater, Aus-

tin Sketch Fest, the Out of Bounds Comedy Festival, and the award-winning troupe the Frank Mills, founded with his wife, Rachel Madorsky.
Boom nickname: Bucky
Rap name: n/a
Favorite anecdote: Buckman was our director when 9/11 happened, and he was part of the decision to not cancel the show that night.

Liz Cackowski (1999–2000). Liz came from Northwestern University straight to Boom Chicago. Post-Boom found Liz writing for *Saturday Night Live*. Liz went on to write/produce for *Community*, *Last Man on Earth*, and *Girls5Eva*. You may have also seen her onscreen in *Forgetting Sarah Marshall*, *Speechless*, and the *Neighbors* movies.
Boom nickname: Tattlina (given to her by Joe Canale "because I always told on people—especially him")
Rap name: n/a (though she did marry a comedy rapper from the Lonely Island, so clearly she's down)
Favorite anecdote: The Cackowski name was already heralded in Chicago improv circles, due to Liz's older brother Craig Cackowski's work with Second City, *Drunk History*, *Community*, and *Veep*.

Heather Anne Campbell (2003–2005). Heather's film career began in 2005 at Boom Chicago with her role as "Newscaster" in *Deuce Bigalow: European Gigolo*. Since then, she's been killing it on *Rick and Morty, Corporate, Whose Line Is It Anyway?, Saturday Night Live, ADHD TV, Key & Peele,* and Upright Citizens Brigade LA's *The Midnight Show*. The Chicago native started improvising at age fourteen at iO, and has had her photography chosen for *National Geographic*.
Boom nickname: H-bomb
Rap name: MC Beverly Hills

Favorite anecdote: Heather once had ten deep-dish pizzas flown from Chicago to Amsterdam for her birthday so we could all watch the dystopian Japanese film *Battle Royale*.

Joe Canale (1999–2000). Perhaps Boom Chicago's greatest en- fant terrible shit-stirrer, Joe was a New Yorker before blowing up in the Chicago improv world en route to Amsterdam. After Boom, Joe returned to Chicago to join Second City's mainstage. Now Los Angeles–based, Joe writes and directs, along with ap- pearing in *The Mindy Project* and frenemy Ike Barinholtz's feature-film directorial debut, *The Oath* (tellingly cast as "Most Annoying Pundit Number One"). Joe currently hosts the Second City alumni podcast, *Second Citizens*.
Boom nickname: Canale
Rap name: n/a
Favorite anecdote: Canale was notorious for making strange noises during preshow sound checks. This annoyance culmi- nated into an irate crew member[3] hurling a box of nine-volt bat- teries at Joe—his noggin saved from being turned into tapioca by mere millimeters.[4]

Kay Cannon (2000–2001). Kay is the writer/director of the 2021 smash *Cinderella* reboot, and also directed *Blockers* (one of the funniest movies to star Ike Barinholtz); she had a big hand in all the *Pitch Perfect* films too. She's also written for *New Girl, Girlboss,* and *30 Rock*.
Boom nickname: Kay Kay
Rap name: n/a
Favorite anecdote: Kay was such a dedicated director and writer

---

3 We can neither confirm nor deny said crew member was Ken Schaefle, as he would sue the bejeebus out of us if we did. And he's a doctor now, so he has the cash to at least hire Rudy Giuliani, wherever he's still able to practice law. So we'll put it like this: this incident happened clearly before Ken took the Hippo- cratic oath . . .
4 Yes, it's the metric system. Get used to it—it's better.

at Boom, we once discovered her in the business office sleeping with her face on the computer keyboard.

Horace Cohen (guest performer). Horace is a star in Dutch TV and films, and *De Lama's* homey. He is also a cocreator of "Late Night Massive."
Boom nickname: Horatio
Rap name: n/a
Favorite anecdote: Like Boom Chicago, Horace was born in America and raised in the Netherlands.

Tarik Davis (2004–2006). Tarik currently stars as Amber Ruffin's cohost on *The Amber Ruffin Show*, after numerous appearances on *Late Night with Seth Meyers*. Before starring in Lin-Manuel Miranda's Broadway smash *Freestyle Love Supreme*, Tarik appeared as "Weed Guy" in *Harold & Kumar Go to Amsterdam*. His award-winning short film *Page One* is about the Black character who gets killed off in every horror movie.
Boom nickname: T
Rap name: n/a (but in *Freestyle Love Supreme*, he's known as Tardis Hardaway)
Favorite anecdote: While in Amsterdam, Tarik learned how to ride a bike as a faster way to get hit by cars. (Three times. No lie.)

Michael Diederich (1993–present). Michael is well known in the world of Dutch musical theater, especially as DJ Monty in *Saturday Night Fever*. (But we love him most as Frank N. Furter in his self-written *Rocky Horror/Wizard of Oz* mash-up, *Rocky Over the Rainbow*.) He has contributed music and choreography to *The Amber Ruffin Show*. In 1995, Michael made a name for himself in the Netherlands with a dynamite rendition of "Pinball Wizard" on the TV show *A Star Is Born*, and also appeared in Boom Chicago's *Comedy Central News* as "Super Catty Celebrity Bitch."

Boom nickname: Mike D
Rap name: Notorious F.A.G.
Favorite anecdote: Michael is so gay, he's caused homophobia in women who are afraid he'll steal their boyfriends during the show. (He does try.)

Colton Dunn (2002–2005). An Emmy-nominated writer and producer for *Key & Peele*, as well as an actor/writer on NBC's hit *Superstore*, Colton was once described by Tarik Davis as "total chaos inside a human body."
Boom nickname: Febo
Rap name: MC (whatever prop Colton picked up backstage)
Favorite anecdote: Colton and fellow Boomers Randall Harr and Rob AndristPlourde performed as the beatbox crew Three Little Birds in front of an audience of five thousand during Dutch DJ Marcello's ten-hour set at Club Escape. He still can't wash off the glitter.

Peter Grosz (1997). Pete was among the first Boom alumni to win an Emmy Award for his writing on *The Colbert Report* (where he's performed as "McGnaw the Gluten-Free Beaver"). He went from HBO's *Veep* to playing actual vice president Mike Pence on Comedy Central's *The President Show*. Pete was also one of the original writers on *Late Night with Seth Meyers*, starred in those famous Sonic commercials, and remains a mainstay on NPR's *Wait, Wait . . . Don't Tell Me!* In 2022, he appeared as a mysterious sommelier in *The Menu*.
Boom nickname: Groszie
Rap name: n/a
Favorite anecdote: Pete and Seth are still working on a screenplay for *Super Computer Colossus: I'm Going to Take Over the World* (as they have been since 1997).

Carice van Houten. Carice is probably Holland's most famous

film star, thanks to her roles in *Game of Thrones, Valkyrie, Black Book, Minoes,* and *Alles Is Liefde.* But our personal favorite is her cameo on *The Simpsons* as a cousin prone to excoriating Bart with Dutch insults like *"Jullie kunnen de pot op"* and *"Jullie kunnen de boom in."*
Boom nickname: Jelke's sister
Rap name: n/a
Favorite anecdote: Carice reprised her role of Minoes in Boom Chicago's "Tittyshirt" video.

Brendan Hunt (1999–2005, 2006, 2008 . . . Brendan never really left). Brendan found fame as hirsute Coach Beard on *Ted Lasso*—which he cocreated with Boom homies Joe Kelly and Jason Sudeikis, winning hella Emmy Awards. Brendan wrote and performed the award-winning plays *Absolutely Filthy, Five Years in Amsterdam,* and *The Art Couple.* He was also head writer for Boom Chicago's *Comedy Central News,* and has appeared on *Key & Peele, Girlboss,* and *Community.*
Boom nickname: Brando
Rap name: MC Squared
Favorite anecdote: In the 2013 Boom reunion show photo, Brendan appears naked, dangly bits tucked between his legs, wearing a pope hat and a hockey mask. He is also a rock star, having served as frontman for notorious Boom-associated band Granville Waiters.

Ruben van der Meer (guest performer). A founding member of Dutch improv legend *De Lama's,* Ruben is a big star in the Netherlands—appearing in TV and films including *Papadag* and *Plan C.* He was notably voted off *MasterChef* for not taking it seriously enough.
Boom nickname: Gozer—which has wonderfully different meanings in Dutch ("cool dude") and English ("evil villain from *Ghostbusters*")

Rap name: Supergabber
Favorite anecdote: Ruben once repaired a stranded tourist's bike chain, explaining, "My father would be very upset with me if he saw that I didn't help." You may now blame Ruben for all the extra tourists in Amsterdam.

Seth Meyers (1997–2001). Seth is the host of *Late Night with Seth Meyers* and former head writer on *Saturday Night Live*, as well as organizer of many softball games on Museumplein.
Boom nickname: Soof
Rap name: MC Suburban Dad
Favorite anecdote: Seth and Jill Benjamin's show "Pick Ups & Hiccups" received five stars in the *Scotsman*—despite the reviewer's description of Seth's "scary American teeth."

Josh Meyers (1998–2001). Josh kicked off his post-Boom career at *MADtv* before appearing on *That '70s Show*, *Red Oaks*, and *Pee-wee Herman on Broadway*. He is also Seth's younger brother.
Boom nickname: Posh
Rap name: MC Fa-Shawn! (pronounced "fashion")
Favorite anecdote: While working in Amsterdam, Josh was *this* close to dating Brigitte Nielsen—but instead dated Carice van Houten. He holds Boom's records for Longest Hair for a Male Actor and Best Euro Style.

John O'Brien. John is one of the first Americans to have a starting position in a major European football team, Ajax Amsterdam. He has a doctorate in clinical psychology, working with athletes around mental health. Befriended by football fanatic Brendan Hunt, John was roped into performing at Boom's "Late Night" show.
Boom nickname: John
Rap name: n/a

Favorite anecdote: John is as tall as Rob AndristPlourde and half as tall as Greg Shapiro. So John is half-a–Greg Shapiro.

Josie O'Reilly (1994, 1996–2000). The only Australian cast member, Josie was discovered during the (very) brief window when Boom Chicago was thinking of expanding to Sydney. Joining the cast for the 1994 season, she returned as artistic director from 1997–1999, and would direct Boom Chicago's first shows at the Edinburgh Festival Fringe. Josie later went on to perform globally with the musical comedy group the Nualas.
Boom nickname: Jo
Rap name: MC O'Reilly
Favorite anecdote: Josie introduced influential Aussie terminology to the Boom Chicago creative process, such as "daggy," "Bob's your uncle," and "no flies on me."

Nicole Parker (2000–2002). A prolific actress, singer, writer, and voice-over artist, Nicole served time as a cast member on *MADtv*, starred in *Martin Short: Fame Becomes Me* and *Wicked* on Broadway (and then across America), and provides the voice of Penelope Pitstop on *Wacky Races*.
Boom nickname: Nickel Bag
Rap name: The Nickel Bag
Favorite anecdote: A master of impressions, Nicole once impersonated everyone at Boom Chicago in under three minutes.

Jordan Peele (2000–2004, 2009). Jordan won an Oscar for Best Original Screenplay for *Get Out*. He is also a cocreator of *Key & Peele* and a star of *MADtv*. He made lots of other dope, critically acclaimed, cultural game-changing shit, like *Nope* and *Us*.
Boom nickname: (briefly) Cobra
Rap name: MC Nigga Please
Favorite anecdote: In 2003, following a Boom corporate show

in Berlin, Jordan was at a bar where he found himself in a rap battle with actor Danny Hoch (*Seinfeld*)—and lost.

Amber Ruffin (2004–2005, 2008–2011). Joining NBC's *Late Night with Seth Meyers*, Amber became the first-ever African American female to join a late-night comedy writing staff; in creating and starring in *The Amber Ruffin Show,* she became the first Black woman to host a late-night show. She hosted the 2018 Writers Guild Awards and rocked the Golden Globes the year Seth hosted too. Amber also wrote a best-selling book with her sister Lacey, *You'll Never Believe What Happened to Lacey: Crazy Stories about Racism,* as well as its 2022 sequel, *The World Record Book of Racist Stories.*
Boom nickname: AmBam
Rap name: MC Fresh Outta Jail
Favorite anecdote: Amber was the first customer at the opening of Starbucks on Leidseplein. Famous for her sweet tooth (and resulting cavities), she haunts every cotton candy booth everywhere.

Ken Schaefle (1993–2006). Ken was a cofounder of Boom Chicago, and its first technical director. Then he left Boom to become a doctor. No, really: now he's board certified for internal medicine and works at the Montefiore Medical Center in New York. Ken has seen the Grateful Dead thirty-nine times, and Bob Dylan eighteen times.
Boom nickname: Shaflee
Rap name: n/a
Favorite anecdote: A much-awarded Eagle Scout, whenever Ken (frequently) needed help with some literal heavy lifting, he was known for saying, "Hey, fellas, you look like a couple of big, strong guys . . ." (And when Jordan Peele put that line into his 2022 film *Nope*, it was not an accident.)

Greg Shapiro (1994–present). Greg is best known as the voice of Donald Trump in the viral video "Netherlands Second" and as the host of the Boom Chicago TV show *Comedy Central News: Because Dutch News Is News, Too.* He is a published author of titles including *How to Be Dutch: The Quiz* and *The American Netherlander.* Greg is also a cocreator of Boom's famous game "Yo! Here We Go."
Boom nickname: Shappy
Rap name: Papa G
Favorite anecdote: Greg has been described by castmates as "a horse on roller skates" and "most likely to buy stacks of pizza after 'Late Night.'"

Tim Sniffen (2004–2005, 2018). Tim is a writer, performer, graphic designer, and voice-over artist whose contributions can be seen and heard on Showtime's *Work in Progress,* the *New Yorker, McSweeney's, Hello from the Magic Tavern,* and legendary video game *You Don't Know Jack.*
Boom nickname: Timothy
Rap name: MC Delicious
Favorite anecdote: Tim wrote the long-running Boom sketch "Love Song," featuring himself as a homeless street performer who bizarrely knows too much about random passersby. One of the lines in his song is, "*I've got a master's degree in English, and I write for the* New Yorker." To which Andrew replied, "Not enough people know the *New Yorker*—can we make it the *Wall Street Journal*?" Tim objected, but was overruled. So it gave Tim great satisfaction when he was indeed published in the *New Yorker.*

Jason Sudeikis (2000). After his six-month Amsterdam stint, Jason departed Boom Chicago for Second City Las Vegas and ended up crushing it on *Saturday Night Live.* He then went on to star in movies like the *Horrible Bosses* films and *We're the Millers,* as well as TV including *Last Man on Earth* and

30 Rock. Oh, Jason also currently stars as the titular character in *Ted Lasso*, which he cocreated with Boom homies Brendan Hunt and Joe Kelly.
Boom nickname: Suds
Rap name: n/a
Favorite anecdote: Jason developed his love for pinball from Andrew while at Boom, and now has multiple pinball machines in his basement.

Steven Svymbersky (1998–2016). Steven went from Boom Chicago street promoter to its longest-serving technical director. Like Boom cofounder Ken Schaefle, Steven is also an Eagle Scout. He founded two independent bookstores, both named Quimby's, and both (against all odds) still in existence.
Boom nickname: The Wizard.
Rap name: n/a
Favorite anecdote: Steven remains one of the most beloved technicians at Boom Chicago for his tattoos, an uncanny John Waters impression, and his embrace of the Dutch philosophy *That is not possible*. When he left, no one knew where to find anything.

Holly Walker (1998–2001). Holly became renowned in her career as a writer/performer on *A Black Lady Sketch Show*, *The Amber Ruffin Show*, and *The Nightly Show with Larry Wilmore*. She was also a writer on *Full Frontal with Samantha Bee*.
Boom nickname: Holly Walker (sung like a six-year-old—you hear it now?)
Rap name: MC Double D
Favorite anecdote: In an improv scene during her last show at Boom, Holly and alumnus Brendan Hunt competitively made out for more than a full minute onstage. It got hysterically awkward.

CHAPTER 1
1993

FLEVOLOLLAPALOOZA: THE YEAR
THE MODERN MUSIC FESTIVAL—AND
BOOM CHICAGO—ARE BORN

In the Netherlands, compromise is central to the national psyche—indoctrinated into the core of every human social interaction. In the most hilariously Dutch way, this can result in some awkward contortions, or it can produce utter genius. Out of the Dutch tradition of compromise, in fact, both the acclaimed Lowlands Festival and Boom Chicago were born into most unlikely homes.

Both Chicago and Amsterdam also claim to have, if not invented, then perhaps refined and perfected the contemporary music festival. Both cities proved early developers of the genre, continuing to stay relevant in this space so many years later. As a concept, large music festivals proved slow to take off in the US—but today, they're considered part of life across North America. The famed Pitchfork and Lollapalooza fests, for example, now take place in Chicago annually—the latter enjoying the cultural luster of its picturesque location on the shores of Lake Michigan, in the heart of Chicago's urban pulse.

But what about Woodstock, that granddaddy of music festivals that defined a generation and has nothing to do with either Chicago or Amsterdam? Woodstock, Shmoodstock. It was really Europe where the big festival format and culture took off. And yes, Holland was there first. While the UK's Glastonbury event has been rocking since 1970—evolving into an annual British coming-of-age tradition—the Dutch music festival Pinkpop beat Glasto by a year.[5] And while Coachella is enmeshed inside the California desert, and Lollapalooza takes place next to Lake Michigan, Holland's Lowlands has them both beat by being the first multiday music and performing arts festival that was built *underwater*. Well, at least under where water used to be . . .

Most of Holland's livable acreage is set below sea level, and it's a pain in the ass. This compelled Dutch society to collectively work to figure out better ways to make this seemingly impossible situation more viable on a day-to-day basis. If Amsterdam already sits below sea level, the area forty-five miles east of Amsterdam is *really* below sea level. Tell Sebastian the Crab to start singing, because this place is literally under the sea: to live comfortably in the Lowlands before it was all stopped up, you pretty much needed to be born with gills or a mermaid.

But why take on such a major pain-in-the-ass proposition? Well, Holland needed space. It needed farms. It needed greenery, and most of all, it needed land—ideally near desirable urban centers like Amsterdam. Otherwise, experts predicted, land prices in Amsterdam would just continue their rise to astronomical levels. (Funny how this happened anyway.)

With this mission, a brain trust of Dutch engineers, scientists, and urban planners pumped all the water out of the Zuiderzee bay fed by the North Sea—creating a sophisticated drainage and damming system to keep the land dry enough to build on. As a final coup de grâce, elite Dutch marketing minds were put to work to rebrand the area and introduce it to *Nederlanders* as an entirely new province.

They came up with "Flevoland."

I know: *Flevoland*. But that's what you get when you've got

---

5 Technically there were earlier editions of Lowlands in Utrecht in 1964 and 1968, but the modern Lowlands began in Flevoland in 1993. And just how *low* are the *lands* in Utrecht, really?

to *polder* everything from the ground up. To build places to live in the most uninhabitable place in all of Holland, the Dutch inevitably turned to the *polder* model. Cue the announcer voice from black-and-white newsreels: "Sixty percent of the Dutch population lives on the *polder*, which is below sea level. How did we get rid of the water? By pumping. Pump your water and your neighbor's water. Only by working together did the Dutch keep their feet dry." That's why Dutch people are the tallest people in the world.[6] Because the short ones drowned. That's the original *polder* model: grow tall or die.

Polder is the Dutch philosophy of compromise that underpins all life in Holland. Living in close quarters to each other makes Holland a nation of negotiators and compromisers. Amsterdammers may not be allowed to, say, bring their bikes into their apartment stairways, but chaining them to the fence out front remains permitted. Others may play music, but not after ten p.m. Restaurants and bars dance a delicate ballet with their neighbors with demands, promises, and rules about sidewalk seating, garbage, and the perennial: noise. The end result of all this *poldering* is that things are slow to change in Holland— and when they do, they're slow to change back. Before anything happens, first there needs to be a seemingly limitless series of nuanced compromises, built on top of each other like a *Tetris* game. Everybody stays in the room until the group hammers out a compromise that the majority grudgingly accepts.

In full-on *polder* sessions, opposing parties face each other in leather chairs, drink coffee together, maybe knock back a glass of jenever (gin). And then they talk. And talk. And *talk*. And then they agree to talk more. Eventually a solution is hatched that no one would've come up with individually, and no one is

---

6 It's true. Next to the Dutch, Danes look like mere giants. What about tall Africans? While the nation-state of Wakanda might be able to use sophisticated nanotechnology to make that killer suit for the Black Panther, by all metrics the Dutch remain taller. And they're getting taller with every generation, so the Dutch need more space on a purely practical level too!

100 percent happy with, either—which is then implemented everywhere. Rehabbing the Zuiderzee is a textbook-perfect *polder* setup: *This idea is crazy, and impossible to execute. How do we get everyone on board to agree to it?*

Actually, reaching consensus was the foundation on which the Netherlands was built. A very long time ago, Dutch dealmakers presented a series of contracts to drain the water: "We'll use this windmill to pump the water to here, and from there pump the water out into the bay, where it will be safely dammed by a series of dikes and levees . . ." The developers, local community, government, and workers all had to agree before any water was diverted *anywhere*. And yo, this was 1400!

As a direct result of these agreements, almost six hundred years later, Flevoland was invented. But once it was built, there was another problem all the *poldering* hadn't caught. Why would people *want* to move there? Now the powers that be had to reach what we now call "early adopters" to sell the hard-to-sell concept of Flevoland. The first slogan proved unsuccessful: *At least it's not Lelystad.*[7] In the proto-Internet, pre–social media era, Flevoland's progenitors struggled to get the word out to urban pioneers about this exciting new province in what was once considered no-man's-land. Or more accurately, no-*land*-land? In the United States, to polish up a real-estate turd, we typically open up a brewery in an old warehouse and throw up a sign that says, *Arts District*. Once again, Holland's top marketing minds were put out to *polder*. This time, they came up with a great solution that would impact Dutch culture forever: *We can get people to come to this shitty area by throwing the coolest music festival ever.*

---

7 A quick word to the people of Lelystad: sorry you live there. Think about it: your dull town was deliberately built as far as possible from anyplace you might actually want to be. When the new airport finally comes on line in Lelystad, passengers can thank you for being the "before" picture of their vacation. Each and every passenger on every plane can smile as they take off, knowing that they are flying to a place better than Lelystad.

And that's how the Lowlands festival came to be in the summer of 1993. Au courant alternative rockers like Smashing Pumpkins, the Breeders, Stone Temple Pilots, and Rage Against the Machine headlined that first Lowlands—sharing stages with maverick legend Iggy Pop, indie-pop forefathers Big Star, and noisier, challenging sounds from Alice Donut, The Jesus Lizard, and Cosmic Psychos. Just six years later, Boom Chicago would join the Lowlands lineup too.

In fact, it was the cultural moment that gave birth to Lowlands that also spawned the first incarnation of Boom Chicago. Like Lowlands, Boom Chicago made its public debut in the summer of 1993—and is now enjoying its thirtieth anniversary as a Dutch cultural institution as you read these very words. Well, unless you're reading these very words on your grandpa's dog-eared copy of this book, in which case we might be celebrating our fiftieth anniversary.[8] Or maybe you're Charlton Heston, discovering this tome amid the rubble while wandering the Planet of the TikTok-scrolling Apes. Yes, Charlton, we did it. We blew it all to hell.

But we digress. On with the show!

Andrew Moskos: In 1993, yours truly and my friend Pep Rosenfeld started Boom Chicago, a name chosen to mean the same thing in every language: nothing. "Chicago" was chosen because that was where improv comedy came from, and "boom" suggested something fun and exciting, like an explosion. Of course in Dutch, boom was not *boem* (rhymes with "room"), but *bohm* (which rhymes with "foam"). Boom in Dutch means "tree," and as such our early *Boom Paper* was sometimes mistaken as an environmental-activist leaflet.

Pep Rosenfeld: We'd graduated three years earlier from Northwestern University in our hometown of Evanston—a suburb

---

8 A more likely scenario is, "What's a *book,* Grandpa?"

that directly borders Chicago. Andrew and I both grew up with parents who worked as Northwestern professors.

Andrew Moskos: In the early 1990s, Pep and I had risen to the middle of the improv comedy scene in Chicago, epitomized at that time by the irreverent iO. Del Close, the father of long-form improv, was still alive and teaching, and we both studied with him (and made sure he ended up with hash from Amsterdam. It was a symbiotic creative relationship).[9] iO was the leader in long-form improv, while ComedySportz was a player in short-form improv. The future founders of the Upright Citizens Brigade were still members of "The Family," the iO house team, with UCB's influential New York and LA theaters still just a glint in their eyes.

Pep Rosenfeld: Hands down, Chicago's most established comedy institution was (and remains) Second City. From its 1950s beginnings to today, Second City was considered to be the true breeding ground of American improvisational comedy and many comedic icons. Generations of groundbreaking household names would make the leap from Second City to *Saturday Night Live*, including Dan Aykroyd, John Belushi, Stephen Colbert, Tina Fey, Mike Myers, Bill Murray, and Amy Poehler. Before he starred in *The Office* (or was ever a forty-year-old virgin), Steve Carell was a Second City regular. And many of Boom Chicago's illustrious alums like Amber Ruffin, Kay Cannon, Peter Grosz, and Jason Sudeikis jumped straight from Amsterdam to Second City as a stepping stone to future Hollywood success.

In 1993, though, Andrew and I felt the cutthroat competition of Chicago's comedy scene wasn't conducive to, well, making it in comedy. There were great shows every night, but they were happening in an improv-community bubble—and this bubble

---

9 Pep and Andrew brought Close hash after the first summer of Boom in Amsterdam. *Dude was stoked!*

wasn't paying its performers. Neither Andrew nor I had found our calling in our day jobs, either. Andrew worked as an expert in early childhood literacy, while I ended up with the familiar role of actor-waiter.

Andrew Moskos: So we took our meager savings and—instead of blowing it on tuition for more Second City and iO improv classes—blew it on a vacation to Europe. Like many young Americans before us, we made our first stop in Amsterdam. Also like many before us, Pep and I quickly found ourselves in Rookies, a coffeeshop (i.e., a café where you can legally buy and smoke weed) near the Leidseplein—ironically, not far from Boom Chicago's future home.

Pep Rosenfeld: There we had what we still refer to as "the greatest stoner idea in history." Why not do a comedy show in Amsterdam? The place seemed relaxed and beautiful. There was a great mix of English-speaking natives, expats, and tourists. And we liked the danger of it. This was a city, after all, where trams ran right down the middle of the street with no American warning signs, fences, or lawsuits. Safety has slowed down trams in the interceding years, but back then trams rang their bell and get out of the way or get hit. The rules were crystal clear. Strangely, it worked.

Andrew Moskos: Some perspective on how insane an idea this was: we were talking about opening a Second City–style institution in a European city where English was the second language, with absolutely zero tradition of American-style improv comedy—let alone comedy performed by Americans. This was the classic American dream, enabled by cannabis and youthful ambition. *Fuck it*, we thought, *get out of the way or get hit*. If the Dutch could hold a music festival underwater, maybe a pair of Chicagoans could make visitors to the Netherlands laugh—and maybe even some natives. And, well, we had the market to ourselves.

Pep Rosenfeld: So that's how in 1993, both Boom Chicago and the Lowlands Festival were born—cultural brothers to different international mothers.

Andrew Moskos: We thought Boom's initial audience would be tourists, so we looked for a place for the summer season from late June to late August. Since this was traditionally the quiet time for Dutch theaters, we thought it would be easy. Looking at the expected locations near the Leidseplein or Rembrandt-plein, we were shocked—*shocked*—to receive a chorus of no's. Most theaters, comfortably subsidized, preferred to just close in the summer. Then we saw a sign on a building a few steps off the Leidseplein, across from what's now the Jimmy Woo club. It didn't look like much from the front, and it was hard to see inside through the dark, dirty windows. But the bar had a sign out front replete with tragedy and comedy masks above the joint's name: *Theater Bar Iboya.*

Pep Rosenfeld: Returning that night when the Iboya was open, we immediately took a liking to it. It was this dive bar that was kind of falling down; the ceiling actually collapsed at one point during our run there. But it had a desirable eight p.m.–to–three a.m. nighttime liquor license. This was fortunate, because this place didn't look or smell good during the day; but at night, in a haze of indoor smoke, it all kind of worked. Yes, indoor smoking was still a thing back then, and didn't seem weird.

In the back, past the old, leaking toilets, was our potential venue. A bar on one side left half the space available for tables, chairs, or a dance floor. With seats, it could hold eighty-five people. There was a small dressing room to the side of the stage that you could only access from the stage, which was *just* big enough for a band . . . or a small comedy show.

Andrew Moskos: The venue was owned by a dysfunctional music family who ran it equally dysfunctionally. The children and stepchildren barely spoke to each other. The clan's daughter, Heddy Lester, a moderately famous singer appreciated by Dutch people of a certain age, was the family's claim to fame. She didn't come by often, however. On Sundays, Heddy's son Frank would play "Easy" by the Commodores over and over on a beautiful grand piano that took up 20 percent of the tiny bar. The patriarch, sixty-something Coen Affolter, was an ostensibly functioning alcoholic who perched at the end of the bar most nights. Stepson Pieter ran the venue with the less successful daughter, the black sheep of the family. Friendly bartender Gerda worked most nights, the middle-aged listening ear all bars used to have before the young and better looking took over nightlife.

Iboya's main tenant was a Saturday salsa night, the venue's main moneymaker. Other nights, the back was empty, and let's be honest, so was the front—an older person's piano-bar sanctuary amid the noise, youth, and energy that was Leidseplein. Iboya offered a choice of two jenevers. This was a place where a woman could order a sweet white wine without getting a funny look. On the wall hung the oldest of old-school rotary phones, which served as both the bar phone and a public pay phone. Even in 1993, this was an antique: the headset was very heavy, and would have looked at home on a Gestapo officer's desk: *Guten tag, is this Das Vaterland Oven and Furnace Repair?* Using this phone required dropping guilder coins into a slot and watching them roll down a tiny ramp behind the glass, lining up next to each other. After twenty-five cents' worth of time had elapsed, another coin dropped into the cashbox, giving us the Dutch expression still used today when you finally understand something: *Now the quarter falls*. This was the phone Gerda answered when we made our appointment with Coen.

Pep Rosenfeld: When we met Coen to discuss our lucrative business proposition, he moved from his perch to the bar's slightly raised booth, a semicircular six-seater where junior mafiosos might discuss business. Per Gerda's wise suggestion, we held the meeting "early in the evening" when Coen would be more, uh, focused.

Andrew Moskos: I think Coen went for it because he saw something of himself in us—reminding him of a younger, more glamorous era of the Iboya. He didn't know much about comedy or improvisation, but he liked the theater part. Coen agreed to five shows a week, Wednesday to Sunday, for two months—against the wishes of stepson Pieter, who had no desire for new ideas. But with his green light, Coen got to help us young creatives, double his bar's turnover, and poke his least favorite son-in-law in the eye. Win-win.

Pep Rosenfeld: Venue in place, the two of us returned to Chicago to make preparations for Boom Chicago's summer Amsterdam debut. We managed to convince our technically savvy friend Ken Schaefle and three other actors to accompany us. A two-month paid stint in Europe was not that hard to sell.

Greg Shapiro: I first heard about Boom Chicago in 1992, at Mardi Gras with Andrew and Pep. While we were wearing beads and partying our asses off, they told me, "By the way, we're going off to Amsterdam to start an improv comedy theater." I didn't know if they were serious or if that was just the mint juleps talking. A year later, I was in New York City going very broke following my acting dream and paying my rent with credit cards when I got the call from Pep: "Hey Greg, we're doing a summer's worth of shows in Amsterdam. Wanna give it a shot?" Having nothing else going on, I said yes. What did I have to lose? I'd already lost my virginity and my dignity—but would Amsterdam also take my pride?

Pep Rosenfeld: Around the same time, Andrew got the phone number of Saskia Maas, a Dutch acquaintance of his younger brother Peter. When we returned to Amsterdam for the shows, Andrew asked Saskia out on a date. Soon they were mixing business and pleasure: it might've been a #MeToo moment, but they eventually got married, so the story ended romantically. Having a smart Dutch person help actually turned out to be a vital ingredient to move our vision forward, especially in the less international days of the early 1990s.

Andrew Moskos: Those simpler days meant Amsterdam was ripe for two American innovations that Boom Chicago exported to Amsterdam that year: the table tent and the pitcher. The table tent was an upright piece of plastic into which you could slide a paper menu. Now, of course, table tents are everywhere, but then you couldn't buy them in the Netherlands. We had to smuggle them in our luggage from America. Our first ten table tents we, uh, *liberated* from tables at Second City; we snuck them out in a backpack.[10] Our table tent offered our drink specials: the Michael Jordan and the Oprah Winfrey, named for the two best-known Chicagoans of the time.

The other improvement was the pitcher. Beer company representatives were not impressed at first. "Dutch beer should only be served in small glasses," a Heineken deliveryman announced one day, twirling his unironic handlebar mustache as he spoke. Breweries not only didn't sell pitchers to bars, they discouraged us from using ours. Naturally, thirty years later, Heineken put out an ad campaign called "Big Bigger Biggest" where the "biggest" was a massive Heineken-branded pitcher. But back then there were only twenty pitchers in Holland—smuggled in by Boom Chicago, all residing at the humble Theater Bar Iboya.

---

10 Thank you and sorry, Second City. You influenced us in more ways than you could ever realize.

Ken Schaefle: Boom Chicago opened for business on June 11, 1993. Our first audience comprised seventeen people in total—fourteen of whom were from a bachelor party who left early when the groom puked. Those early years would grow into something really magical, though.

Andrew Moskos: It was only up from there. In time, our mix of comedy and beer proved a hit. Audiences were laughing at our mix of improv games and sketches about Amsterdam. Our operation, however, was not yet developed. Financially, we were still under the radar and using the First National Bank of Pep's Boot. As in cowboy boot. Back then, Pep's "look" was nonstyle "I'm just starting to grow it out" hair, jeans with gaping crotch holes, and cowboy boots. Luckily, his Kurt Cobain party-casual vibe was conducive to our unbanked status. We kept all the money Boom made then in Pep's right boot. And before every show, while Ken was setting up the house and the other three actors were getting ready, Pep and I flipped into entrepreneur mode. I'd be roaming the square looking to reel in the last ten people for the audience before showtime, while Pep stood out front selling tickets.

Ken Schaefle: Andrew was really serious about this idea at a time in our life when nothing was serious. He was a real student of Chicago's improv economy. On the improv scene in Chicago, the last thing you ever heard about was money—because there was none. Literally, the same five bucks changed hands over and over: you'd pay five dollars to go see your friend's show, and then he'd pay five dollars to see yours. But by the end of college, Andrew had become the manager of the Fine Arts movie theater, which is pretty prestigious. Andrew always had his eye on crowds and tickets—things like figuring out how long intermission should be to sell the most popcorn. Andrew was obsessed with tickets as a unit of income: the box office as a potential revenue generator was in his DNA. We'd sit on the couch and debate for hours how much you could charge for a ticket, what the expenses would be, and so on.

Pep Rosenfeld: I never stopped selling tickets until I saw Andrew leading a motley parade of people he'd persuaded to see the show across the Leidseplein. He'd quickly turn "So, what are you doing tonight?" into "Whatever your plan is, forget it, you're coming to see Boom Chicago." Andrew always scored at least six last-minute takers. Once stragglers were accounted for and seated, I'd stuff the cash into my boot, then run and tell Ken to start the show. Afterward, I'd count the money and get the information to our accountant. And by accountant, I mean the spreadsheet on my organizer, a Psion 3c.

Andrew Moskos: During our first summer we lived in this tiny apartment near Centraal Station in the old, old, *old* part of Amsterdam. It was in a very narrow building, in classic Dutch style. Our sweet landlord made the mistake of renting her dainty, delicate place to us. It had five rooms all stacked on top of each other: kitchen, living/dining room, two bedrooms, and an attic crawl space best suited for serial-killer storage. Naturally, six of us were living there. Neil and Ken took the *slaapkeuken,* or "sleeping kitchen." Ken built a bunk bed behind the refrigerator: they had to get to sleep before the refrigerator compressor switched on and woke them up.

Pep Rosenfeld: I had to climb a ladder up to the attic where I slept. I mean, it wasn't an actual ladder—more like stairs that were 90 percent vertical, so you had to use your hands too. It was a typical Dutch execution of stair design. I eventually learned that *trap* meant both "ladder" and "stairs" in Dutch. That totally made sense.

Andrew Moskos: One night after a show, Pep knocked on my door. He whispered, "Hey man, I brought someone home, and I don't know if I can trust her with the boot." He then gave me the boot, so to speak, and continued hands-and-feeting it up the ladder-stairs.

Pep Rosenfeld: Hey, business is business.

Andrew Moskos: Just because you trust someone with your naked, unconscious body doesn't mean it's a great idea to have the company bankroll next to the bed.

Pep Rosenfeld: Heavy is the head that wears the boot. Or the foot. Or something.

Andrew Moskos: The first year we mainly drew tourists, but that changed over time. It felt like Boom Chicago had truly been accepted by Dutch audiences when we were first asked to play the Lowlands Festival six years later, in 1999.

Ruben van der Meer: With the arrival of Lowlands, it meant Dutch people could now use drugs and go camping while watching excellent bands and, eventually, great comedy. In terrible weather, of course. It's a rite of passage.

Pep Rosenfeld: Lowlands became one of the many initiations into Dutch culture that Boom Chicago cast members undergo. This increased after Lowlands launched the new Juliet Tent—a showcase for nonmusical comedy and performance art.

Andrew Moskos: We played Lowlands many times after that, but it was an especially big deal for Boom to perform the first year Lowlands had a dedicated comedy tent. We helped create a comedy tradition at the festival, a format that influenced US festivals like Bonnaroo, where they'd attempt to mix music, humor, and muddy camping too. I couldn't believe how much fun it was to actually play at Lowlands.

Greg Shapiro: Lowlands already had ten music tents and stages by that point, so they figured it was a good time for an all-comedy tent.

Andrew Moskos: We drove to the location to check it out. It was a big top–style tent, with a real stage, real sound, and real lighting, with capacity for 1,500 people. It felt like when the Blues Brothers arrived at their final huge venue: "It's a barn. We'll never fill it." At least we'd get paid and receive all-access backstage passes to Lowlands, so we told them, "We think we can do this." They were like, "Great! You're on Sunday morning at ten a.m."

Um, *ten a.m.*? As it turned out, we didn't know about the rhythm of Lowlands's schedule. Little else was happening at ten in the morning, and everyone was up. It's a camping festival: the audience gets up when the sun rises, if they sleep at all. When we started the show, there were extra people standing in the back and in the aisles, going wild and yelling out suggestions. They were so into it. It was a great crowd, and one of the best shows I've ever done. That was Boom's biggest audience up to that point.

Rob AndristPlourde: Playing that first show to a tent filled to capacity at ten a.m. . . . *wow.* I mean, people were lined up to get in there. I filmed a video of the thousand people waiting outside the tent and thought, *Well, fuck—look at us now!*

Dave Buckman: This continued for many years. I was with Boom when we played Lowlands in 2001. That year we played a sketch that always killed, based on Brendan Hunt's real experience with a Dutch girl. The protagonist goes to the birthday party of a girl he likes; there, her Dutch friends mock his inability to speak Dutch properly. By the end, he manages to express his feelings in spotty, vaguely obscene Dutch—and finally in the lyrics of "Zij Gelooft in Mij" by Andre Hazes.[11] The lights would go out in midchorus while the track played, and every single night the entire audience would raise the candles off their tables and sing along. It was powerful. I'm not a good singer, but leading 1,500 people in a tent at Lowlands, I nailed every note and Dutch word, which is shocking.

Rob AndristPlourde: After the show, we watched the Stone Temple Pilots's main-tent set from above, where we could see both the stage and the backstage area. They were great, leaving the audience chanting, "We want more!"

Did you ever wonder what happens backstage during those few minutes before a huge rock band's encore? It turns out: nothing. They just stand there shooting the shit and drinking water. Except in this case, once Scott Weiland got backstage, he took off all his clothes, grabbed his signature megaphone, and wrapped himself in a Dutch flag before going back onstage. So not only did I sing for 1,500 people perfectly that day, I got to see a rock star naked.

Andrew Moskos: Our '93 season was supposed to finish by the end of August, but the audiences kept growing. Two cast members had to return to Chicago, so we flew out replacements for a two-week extension into September. The last performance was our biggest audience yet. Capacity was eighty-five people, but we rarely hit that. That last night, we broke a hundred.

---

11 A Dutch translation/adaptation of the Kenny Rogers song "She Believes in Me" that has become an enduring Dutch anthem.

Pep Rosenfeld: We always thought Boom Chicago would make it, but didn't know what exactly that meant. We planned to return to Amsterdam the following year, yet couldn't quite see the future. We thought we'd have a good run for a summer or two, but never imagined how it would turn out. We certainly didn't expect that this journey would become our entire lives. Furthermore, we never imagined Boom Chicago would become a springboard for talented people who'd make important things after leaving. We just worked together and kept pumping to keep our feet dry . . .

CHAPTER 2
1994

ROYALE WITH CHEESE? YES, PLEASE!
PULP FICTION GOES BOOM IN AMSTERDAM

Jules: Okay, so tell me again about the hash bars.
Vincent: Okay, what you wanna know?
Jules: Hash is legal there [in Amsterdam], right?
Vincent: Yeah, it's legal, but it ain't 100 percent legal . . .

1994 had a lot going for it, movie-wise, but nothing like Quentin Tarantino's *Pulp Fiction*. That year featured many influential films: *The Lion King* turned Shakespeare's *Hamlet* into a Disney classic (and never-ending stage show). *Forrest Gump* divided the world between those who considered it '94's best picture and those repulsed by the "wisdom of an idiot" theme. *Dumb and Dumber*, meanwhile, cemented the celebrity of Jim Carrey—lovingly referred to by the *Onion* as a "rubber-faced fartsmith."

1994 was even a World Cup year, hosted in the US, no less—some games even in Chicago. Alas, the delightful irony of the Dutch team playing our hometown during Boom Chicago's second summer was not to be, as Brazil eliminated Team Oranje in the quarterfinals. At least they got knocked out by the winner of the tournament, right? But nothing dented culture like *Pulp Fiction* following its volcanic debut at Cannes. Tarantino's sophomore film following his cult breakout *Reservoir Dogs* gave him the name recognition of, say, Steven Spielberg. Its impact was perhaps felt most locally in Amsterdam.

When it came to *Pulp Fiction*'s most memorable moment, many—especially Boom Chicago's cofounders—recall the scene where John Travolta's hit-man character Vincent Vega gives his partner in crime Jules (played by eternal badass Samuel L. Jackson) a quick lesson in the Netherlands's famously relaxed policy toward cannabis. Travolta-as-Vega never says the word *gedogen*—the Dutch term for "tolerating something that's maybe illegal, but not that big of a deal"—but he ends up describing it perfectly:

> *Vincent: I mean, you can't just walk into a restaurant, roll a joint, and start puffin' away. I mean, they want you to smoke in your home or certain designated places.*

> *Jules: And those are hash bars?*

> *Vincent: Yeah. It breaks down like this: Okay, it's legal to buy it, it's legal to own it, and if you're the proprietor of a hash bar, it's legal to sell it. It's legal to carry it, but that doesn't matter, 'cause . . . get a load of this: if you get stopped by the cops in Amsterdam, it's illegal for them to search you. I mean, that's a right the cops in Amsterdam don't have.*

> *Jules: Oh man, I'm goin'. That's all there is to it: I'm fuckin' goin'!*

Jules's response evokes that of Boom Chicago founders Andrew and Pep after their first summer in the Dutch capital: "We're goin' back. That's all there is to it: we're fuckin' goin' back!" With *Pulp Fiction* becoming an instant '90s classic, there was surely a major post–*Pulp Fiction* uptick in stoner tourism. The movie shook up attitudes about Amsterdam amid the hype surrounding *Pulp Fiction. The violence! The comeback! The dialogue! The nonchronological storytelling! The dancing! The music! John Travolta stabbing Uma Thurman with a syringe! Samuel L. Jackson saying, "Motherfucker!"* Amsterdammers' reaction to *Pulp Fiction* captured the typical Dutch response to their hometown shout-out in an era-defining cinematic event—a mix of modest pride and *"Dat is gewoon Amsterdam"* ("That's just Amsterdam").

For locals, *Pulp Fiction* cemented Amsterdam's innate identity crisis—a love-hate relationship with its reputation for sex and drugs, intensified by cheap *Pulp Fiction*–related memorabilia in souvenir shops. On the side the Netherlands Board of Tourism likes, there's Rembrandt, the Anne Frank House, and delft-blue tiles purchased by aging German tourists decrying the Holocaust *just a bit too much* on their way to the tulip fields. (To paraphrase *Get Out*, "Und I vould've voted against Hitler three times if I could.") On the *Pulp Fiction* side are seedy stereotypes of stoned backpackers puking outside the Bulldog, squatters throwing raves in abandoned warehouses, and the Red Light District's legal prostitution. To a big part of the world, Amsterdam is perceived as tulips and windmills, or prostitutes and coffeeshops. It's a marketing nightmare, but that paradox represents the heart of Amsterdam.

Tarantino introduced something else truly Dutch to international audiences, and perhaps even more shocking: mayonnaise on french fries—though if he'd gone deeper into weird Netherlands fast food, he would've hit *oorlog*, oddly named after the Dutch word for "war." While there might be some geezers who remember life in Holland during World War Two (endlessly explaining what you have is not "hunger," but "appetite"), most Dutch only think of war when ordering a *patatje oorlog*—that is, fries with mayo, peanut sauce, *and* onions.

The battle between pro-and-con *oorlog* factions is real. You can tell society has forgotten what war is actually like when one's choice of condiments gets likened to combat. It's easy to imagine a wizened old alcoholic explaining it from a chair at Café Heuvel, dramatically gesturing with one hand and precariously swinging a tiny Dutch beer glass in the other:

> Oorlog *is like the war. The french fries, that's the Netherlands during the Second World War. And the mayonnaise, you see, represents the Dutch people. The peanut sauce, meanwhile, symbolizes the foreigners who lived here peacefully during the war. And then the German onions come. The onions occupy the french fries, ruining the taste of everything. And then the Dutch mayonnaise is like, "Hey, German onions, check out the peanut sauce hiding up in the attic with Anne Frank."*

As *Pulp Fiction*'s homage to Dutch potato condiments entered the conversation, Andrew and Pep returned to Amsterdam for a second summer of living and working to make people laugh. What impressed them was how much Tarantino got *right* about Amsterdam. As Vinnie notes to Jules, the funniest things a newcomer experiences living in Europe are "the little differences. I mean, they got the same shit over there that they got here. But it's just, there, it's a little . . . different." We were shocked that Dutch people paid for ketchup at McDonald's, paid to use the toilet, and didn't pay for the tram, thanks to an honor system without much honor.

Legend has it that in 1993, Quentin Tarantino concocted *Pulp Fiction* during a stoner writer's retreat to Amsterdam, filling notebooks in longhand in local coffeeshops. Again, 1993 was also the year Boom Chicago was birthed in the backrooms of seedy Amsterdam drinking establishments. Coincidence? Or further evidence that Boom Chicago had in fact been keenly instrumental, à la *Pulp Fiction*, in dragging Amsterdam out of its cozy, *gezellig* hiding place and into the cultural zeitgeist? Why, pray tell, did it take young, witty, highly verbal Americans to finally communicate what a paradise Amsterdam is?

We soon realized that if Boom Chicago was to spend another summer in paradise, we needed more seats (and ideally a less-drunk landlord). Around the corner from Iboya on Lijnbaans-grach, we came upon a theater looking for a summer tenant. It was unsubsidized, so money meant something to the landlord, who liked us and our show and rented us the space.

This move resulted in three major changes. Capacity doubled to 180, which meant if we sold tickets, we'd have a real business. The second was that now we had our own bar—we could pour our own Michael Jordans and Oprah Winfreys. The third was the most painful: our days running an all-cash business were over. We would need a *KvK* number. We would need to pay taxes. Worst of all, we would be retiring Pep's boot. Our entire bookkeeping system remained Pep's Psion, but we'd outgrown the boot.[12]

We got two new apartments where no one had to sleep next to a loud refrigerator. Pep, Andrew, and Ken found a place in East Amsterdam by the Amstel, while new actors moved into a flat in the north. Saskia had a spot near the Concertgebouw that today would command ten times her rent from an Airbnb guest. Considering how hot these neighborhoods became, we were true urban-hipster pioneers years before the concept existed!

Andrew Moskos: With a new cast including Pam Gutteridge, Greg Shapiro, Emilie Beck, and Josie O'Reilly, Boom Chicago returned for a three-month season in the summer '94, around when *Pulp Fiction* hit cinemas. Of course, whenever Amsterdam gets a nod from global pop culture, residents are flattered. But *Pulp Fiction* was next level! Quentin Tarantino was so American— *so cool.* For many young male travelers in Boom's audience, everything they knew about Amsterdam, they learned from *Pulp*

---

12 Cue "Cat's in the Cradle" . . .

Fiction. And I think Tarantino learned a lot about Amsterdam from Boom Chicago. He saw a show. I remember that.

Pep Rosenfeld: You remember it?

Andrew Moskos: Well, I don't *remember* remember, but come on. I must've handed Quentin a *Boom Magazine* in front of Rookies once.

Ken Schaefle: Boom's magazine was the coin of the realm of our promotional effort until 2009—about the same time *Time Out New York* disappeared.

Josie O'Reilly: Andrew never stopped talking about *kranting*—handing tourists our free *Boom Chicago Guide to Amsterdam* while simultaneously offering them discounted tickets to the show that we were also acting in. I found this mortifying. This was equivalent to me knocking on people's doors and trying to convert them to Catholicism. (I come from a long line of failed nuns.)

Ruben van der Meer: Quentin was definitely around. He'd always check out LaserDiscs[13] at the artsy-fartsy hipster video store Cinecenter—then write for hours at the Pi Kunst and Koffie coffeeshop, where he wrote *Pulp Fiction*. Then again, every place Tarantino walked into in Amsterdam claims that he wrote *Pulp Fiction* there.

Andrew Moskos: *Someone* must've given Quentin a *Boom Magazine*. He has it in a shoebox somewhere, next to an original VHS version of *Spetters*, I'm sure. That's how, in the time he spent in Amsterdam from 1992 to 1993, Quentin came to see

---

13 Another Dutch invention, courtesy of Amsterdam-based electronics giant Philips . . .

Boom. It feels true. I remember this very intense, weird-looking American in the front row, with greasy, thinning hair and crazy eyes, checking out our feet . . .

Pep Rosenfeld: Jerking off to our feet . . . No, wait, that was when Ron Jeremy visited Boom.[14] If Greg Shapiro had been with us in '93, *he* could've gotten Tarantino into a show with the bounce shoes, of which he was a virtuoso. Greg was not only great onstage, he also turned out to be a key marketing tool. See, when I lived in Chicago, I'd get high late at night, watch TV, and then order products advertised on infomercials. During one late-night shopping spree, I bought these shoes that had springs on the bottom. In theory, you could jump over a fucking car in this footwear. In reality, you could leap maybe three feet: not a lot, but hey, Greg's very tall. So that spring, Greg would put on a cape and bounce around on these shoes, handing out Boom Chicago flyers. *Boing!* "Excuse me, miss—do you speak English?" *Boing!* "Would you like to see a comedy show?"

Andrew Moskos: I would've run like hell from Super-Bouncing Man, but Greg proved surprisingly effective in this role.

Greg Shapiro: When I came to Amsterdam in 1994, I did have a little bit of culture shock. I'd seen this documentary, *Sex, Drugs & Democracy*, about the contrast of individual liberties in America and Holland. According to the movie, Holland was *really* tolerant. I was sure Amsterdam was going to be this run-down Red Light District: liberal but old world, unpolished, maybe a little tacky.

Ruben van der Meer: In other words, Greg got it right.

---

14 While Tarantino coming to Boom Chicago remains hotly disputed, disgraced porn star Ron Jeremy and his sad mullet did indeed attend one of our shows.

Greg Shapiro: But I found I *liked* the slightly tacky liberal old world. I liked the Tarantino-esque little differences. Take movies opening on Thursdays, not Fridays, with sneak-preview screenings on Tuesday nights at the Kriterion theater. Unlike America, you didn't know what Kriterion's movie was going to be. Sometimes it would be a meditation on basket-weaving, sex-crazed mermaids by an obscure Greek filmmaker—in Greek, with Dutch subtitles, of course. We didn't understand anything, but at least there was nudity. One time Andrew made us go to the Kriterion sneak preview, and it turned out to be *Pulp Fiction*. We were already huge *Reservoir Dogs* fans, but now we were in a movie theater in Amsterdam drinking beer while watching John Travolta talk about drinking beer in a movie theater in Amsterdam: "And I don't mean just like an old paper cup. I'm talking about a *glass* of beer." We couldn't get enough of that.

Andrew Moskos: Back then they had intermissions too: the *pauze*. During the *pauze*, you could smoke a joint, have another beer—and once refreshed, keep watching the movie. That's still a great idea. Too bad they stopped the *pauze*.

Liz Cackowski: I miss the *pauze* too. It was a great tradition.

Greg Shapiro: It also became Boom tradition to go to the movies and cause a scene while ordering tickets.

Pep Rosenfeld: This was when you actually had to line up at the box office to buy tickets. We'd always roll up with four or five people: everyone had to prepare a one-liner bit about the movie we were about to see—then you hype it up and outdo the person before you. So you'd start with something easy: "I vould like von ti-cket . . . to *Bram Stoker's Dracula*. Ah-ha-ha-ha!" Once the bar was set, everyone else had to do better.

Greg Shapiro: Joe Canale's bit became infamous: he'd buy two boxes of popcorn, one of which he intended to eat, the other to use as a prop. Joe would wait until the most boring moment during previews—and then go right down to the front row, stand in front of the screen, looking confused. He seemed like he was searching for his date: "Honey, I have your popcorn—where are you?" Just when everybody was now watching him, Joe would suddenly pratfall—sending the popcorn skyward. That got the biggest laugh; it was magnificent. Amsterdam audiences eventually caught on, though: you'd hear people say in Dutch, "Here comes the popcorn dickhead again."

Andrew Moskos: Sometimes we went too far. Once the ticket seller called the manager on Pep.

Pep Rosenfeld: I totally freaked her out. When we went to see *The Dark Knight,* I locked eyes with the woman selling tickets. I paraphrased the original Batman comic where Bruce Wayne says, "Criminals are a cowardly and superstitious lot." So instead of "Two for *The Dark Knight,* please," I go crazy intense: "People who would deny me a ticket to see Batman in *The Dark Knight* are a cowardly and superstitious lot. I swear on the grave of my dead parents who, like Thomas and Martha Wayne, were murdered right before my eyes, I *will* see *The Dark Knight.*" Never broke eye contact.

Greg Shapiro: And then she called the manager?

Pep Rosenfeld: Immediately. Still proud of that one. Actors had to commit to their bits, and I led by example. Andrew had a great one when we went to see *The Time Machine.*

Andrew Moskos: Shitty movie.

Pep Rosenfeld: But what a bit! Andrew walks up to buy tickets, normal as can be: "One for *The Time Machine,* please." Then he asks, "How many micro-credits will that be?"—then whips out a wallet full of blue "future money" that he made at home. When she responds, "Seven euros, please," he yells, "Euros? What year is this?"

Andrew Moskos: We made enemies at the cinema, but we made friends at the Melkweg. In 1994, Boom's space was across from Amsterdam's coolest live music venue. Back then we would just stumble onto new stuff. They would have a drum-and-bass night at the Melkweg, and we'd just pop over: "Who's playing tonight? Dreadzone?" We'd send pizza to the bouncers and DJs, and invite Melkweg's staff to our shows. They loved us, and always let us in for free. People we met at the Melkweg then still come to Boom Chicago shows. A bouncer actually hired us to perform at his wedding.

Greg Shapiro: People were starting to know us in Amsterdam. In Chicago or LA . . . not so much. Amsterdam was a blip on the international comedy scene. Pep and Andrew had their hands full trying to convince actors to join the Boom cast. If you were looking at up-and-coming comedians in Chicago, they were trying to get cast at Second City, or be discovered by an agent so they could go to Los Angeles for TV-pilot season. Chicago's comedy scene was the springboard for that trajectory—but not one that led to *Amsterdam.*

Pep Rosenfeld: Talking international blips—heck, we convinced Josie O'Reilly to join us from Australia.

Josie O'Reilly: I was appearing in a comedy show called *Gilligan's Island Improvised.* I played both Mary Ann *and* Mrs. Howell. It was in a six-hundred-seat theater on downtown Sydney's main street. No one came. Well, except Andrew Moskos and Pep Rosenfeld. I thought they were such dags [an Australian term for sheep shit caught in wool].

Andrew Moskos: I told you: spending our hard-earned profits on an Australia trip was an *investment* in our future.

Pep Rosenfeld: Yes, you did. With Josie, it proved money well spent. She taught us to ask the most important question: *[cue terrible Australian accent]* "What does the show *need?*"

Andrew Moskos: Josie introduced the principle of F-U-N to Boom: don't be too smooth and have fun—because when audiences *see* we're having fun, they'll have fun.

Josie O'Reilly: F-U-N was about having a genuine laugh *with* an audience—quick, unpretentious physicality providing a cheeky connection with the crowd. It was a departure from intellectual snobbery. We were far less up our own arseholes than the too-cool-for-school improv I sometimes saw in Chicago's comedy scene.

Greg Shapiro: Joining Boom Chicago was at best a career tangent. But in 1994, that changed. It was clear we weren't going back to Chicago, and Boom Chicago wasn't leaving Amsterdam.

Ken Schaefle: '94 was also the year when computers and video equipment became cheap, so we started incorporating video and early Internet stuff before anyone else.

Andrew Moskos: Audiences kept growing. The hipper tour operators like Contiki brought busloads of young Australians to Boom Chicago, and now we had capacity for them.

Josie O'Reilly: Contiki's tour groups of eighteen-to-thirty-five-year-olds from the southern hemisphere were known for drunkenly vomiting their way across Europe.

Nicole Parker: Those Australians would get so wasted, they'd even come up onstage. One thing significantly unique about Boom is that I don't know any performance space where the audience is different every single night. I've never played anywhere else where the audience is such a factor in terms of the unpredictability of what the show's vibe would be. Each night, you didn't know what to expect: Boom's stage was as no-safety-net Wild West as it gets.

Liz Cackowski: When I did Second City, I never thought to ask, "What's the crowd like tonight?" It was the same show, and pretty much the same type of audience, every night. But at Boom, one show might have a crowd that's 60 percent Dutch and 40 percent drunk Contiki Australians. Those stats changed how you played.

Andrew Moskos: These crowds revealed new cultural frames of reference in the suggestions they shouted out during our improv games. Like, "What the fuck is Vegemite?"

Pep Rosenfeld: Toward the end of '94, Boom Chicago was visited by a local Leidseplein cop checking our liquor license. Saskia explained that we just rented the space and our landlord had all the necessary paperwork. "Uh, that's not how it works," the cop responded. "You're running a bar: you need proper hygiene papers—and more importantly, a liquor license."

Andrew Moskos: On the one hand, this cop knew we were causing no real trouble. But on the other hand, rules are rules. "How much longer is your season?" he asked. Saskia said three weeks.

The cop thought a bit more. "I'm going to let you finish your season," he said, "but I'm not going to let you open for a single day next year if you don't get your paperwork sorted." We quickly agreed.

In Chicago, cops would've shut us down immediately. If we were shut down three weeks early, we wouldn't make enough money to return the following year, and this would've been a much shorter book. Luckily, we were in Amsterdam. We finished the season with three very busy weeks, making enough to come back. That winter, Saskia took a hygiene course and set up the liquor license. When the Leidseplein policeman returned in the spring, everything was in order.

The policeman's read of the situation—no bad will on our part, plus no immediate problem—combined with his willingness to bend the rules for the greater good allowed him to get what he wanted (i.e., correct paperwork). It's a perfect illustration of *gedogen*, the Dutch "blind-eye" tolerance of technically illegal but low-urgency situations. *Gedogen* impressed Vincent Vega in *Pulp Fiction*, and it saved Boom Chicago from being a two-summer footnote.

CHAPTER 3
1995

AJAX WINS THE CHAMPIONS LEAGUE: ACTORS GET SOCCER FEVER

There's a great joke about the Dutch national football team of 1998. Oh wait—it's *our* joke.

As Dutch fans need no reminding, in the World Cup semifinals that year, a nail-biting 1–1 result ended with Holland losing to Brazil on penalties. Or, as we translated for Americans: "In Europe, two soccer teams ran around for two hours and couldn't score more than one goal each . . . *[hold for laughs]* Finally, they put the ball right in front of the net and said, 'See if you can kick it in now.' *[bigger laughs]* Unfortunately, Holland. Could. Not." *[The crowd goes wild!]*

The Dutch national team is always the bridesmaid, never the bride when it comes to actually winning championships. We re-purposed our joke in 2000 after Oranje lost on penalties against Italy, and again in 2014 versus Argentina. Holland had the miserable chest-kicking loss to Spain in 2010's World Cup. Before that, it had been around four decades since the Netherlands had a serious shot at a title: in 1974 and again in 1978, Oranje ultimately lost in the finals. Football remains the country's obsession, even though these days, the Dutch expect to be brokenhearted in terms of winning games—an ingrained masochistic quirk in the national psyche.

At least in Amsterdam, we have Ajax (pronounced, in contradiction to everything in the English language, "EYE-ax").

If the national team can't deliver, Ajax certainly does. It's the Netherlands's most successful club, notching thirty-three Dutch national league titles and eighteen KNVB Cups. Ajax has an enduring nickname too—enduringly weird with a capital "W." Local fans and opponents alike refer to the team and its players as what sounds like "YO-da," especially with an Amsterdam accent. They're not referring to *Star Wars*'s beloved green Jedi master, though: they're saying *Joden*—the Dutch word for Jews.

As Amsterdam's historically a Jewish city, rival-team fans gave Ajax its beloved yet loaded nickname, *Joden*. Ajax supporters took it as a badge of honor—in perhaps the only example of gentiles calling other gentiles Jews as a compliment (and relating to athletic prowess, no less). Like Judaism itself, our *Joden* show tenacious underdog strength in the face of opposition on the pitch. Ajax's nickname allegedly also refers to Amsterdam's famous resistance movement against the Nazis—though let's be real, Amsterdam is also famous for ratting out Anne Frank.

Opposing-team fans were happy to use improv's most basic tool and say, "Yes, and . . ." to Ajax's Jewishness. They ratcheted up the slur on the terraces by making a hissing noise evoking the sound of Jews being gassed in Auschwitz. Classy, right?

We're from Amsterdam, and we love our Jews.[15] In Holland, every socioeconomic/cultural group seems somehow linked in their shared obsession with football. During big games in Amsterdam, you can find junkies in back alleys debating Ajax's best penalty kicker while shooting up. Dutch people of Moroccan descent scream when Ajax scores a goal, as do bankers checking *onze Joden*'s scores on their iPhones while chasing deals in the boardroom.

In our native Chicago, athletics prove as socially divisive as they are unifying. You're either a "jock" who only dresses in team colors, or a "freak" whose rejection of sport represents bohemian intellectual superiority. It's some real John Hughes shit.

---

15 Or as we say in Dutch, *onze Joden*.

Ajax crosses social strata more easily, especially apparent when tragedy struck the club's beloved star, Abdelhak "Appie" Nouri. After Appie suffered a dramatic cardiac arrest on the field in Germany in 2017, all manner of race, age, and socioeconomic status represented when Ajax fans arrived en masse at his house to show support.

Boom Chicago creatives have long embraced this identity crisis. In 2006, Boom's biggest football fan/future *Ted Lasso* co-creator Brendan Hunt, Boom's most sports-averse nerd Pep, and Andrew (somewhere in between) created "Kick This, a World Cup Comedy with Balls."

Saskia Maas: The idea was to do our show first, and then the audience stays to watch World Cup games in the theater. Great plan, right? Unfortunately, theater fans don't want a show about football, and football fans don't want comedy shows at all. Go figure.

Andrew Moskos: Still, there was something familiar about it all. Chicagoans and *Nederlanders* are used to disappointment. While Chicago teams have eked out occasional championships, like Dutch teams, they're often the semifinalist, never the finalist—even if they make it to the finals. Holland's national team didn't even qualify for World Cup 2018 (nor in 2002), resulting in protracted periods of national mourning.

Pep Rosenfeld: In both Chicago and Amsterdam, sports fans go on destructive rampages when their teams win (or lose) big games. In both cities, the response to either outcome is: drink more alcohol and wreck shit. And this, of course, attracts a police response. 1995 is often remembered fondly by Boom alumni as "tear-gas summer," referring to Amsterdam police gassing rowdy, vomitous football fans outside Boom's Leidseplein theater when Ajax won the European Championship League.

Armed with tear gas and water cannons, the blue-clad ME riot police easily put down Amsterdam's scrappy football hooligans.

Ruben van der Meer: True Amsterdammers grow up with *voetbal*. It's in your blood, informing every aspect of coming of age—school life, throwing up from drinking beer for the first time in front of your friends and family . . .

Horace Cohen: It's like basketball for Americans, and ice hockey for Canadians. All Dutch kids want to grow up to be pro footballers—and every Amsterdam kid wants to play for Ajax.

Andrew Moskos: North America only embraced football in the 2010s, with the rise of women's soccer and Olympic victories. The Dutch, however, loved football pretty much since its inception. As with so many things, the Dutch punch above their weight football-wise. This tiny country of [then] fifteen million produced many great players and teams, the whole world coming to respect the Dutch "total football" playing style.

For example, I was in Portugal in 2012 when the Portuguese eliminated the Dutch team in the group stage. And this was right after the 2010 World Cup where Holland got to the finals. So we're the only people wearing orange on the street. But instead of rubbing it in, the Portuguese were all saying, "Oh, it's really too bad. We know the Dutch team should've done better."

As Boom Chicago slid into our third year of existence, Ajax was dominating, and as a coowner of a small business, I learned some crucial things about the Dutch work ethic. When the weather gets nice, everybody says, "Peace out—I'm just going to enjoy the sunshine today, not coming to work." It's the same whenever there's a big game. Whenever the World Cup rolls around, we anticipate losing a whole month of productivity. In 2022, due to stupidly holding the tournament in Qatar, we lost a month before Christmas.

Greg Shapiro: In 1995, Ajax won the Champions League—not easy to do! Ajax stepped up and beat Italian strongholds Juventus and AC Milan *silly*. As a recent American expat, it was pretty exotic walking to work through tear gas and smoke to find soccer fans rioting in Leidseplein square. I'm still partially deaf from all the explosions that summer. I learned the hard way that while the Dutch love football, their passion for fireworks—a habit picked up from trading with the Chinese in Marco Polo days—is a close second. Well, third after alcohol.

Pep Rosenfeld: Ah, tear-gas summer. I remember showing up at Boom for a rehearsal the day after a riot. Normally, the Leidseplein teems with delivery trucks unloading at restaurants and bars, but it was remarkably quiet that morning. Businesses were closed, and I was dodging glass from broken windows. As I got closer to the theater, I noticed this funny chemical smell, and my eyes started watering. I was like, *Oh, so* that's *what tear gas feels like*. That's Ajax winning the Champions League for me: not tears of joy—tears of tear gas.

Greg Shapiro: Crowds from all over flocked to the Leidseplein to celebrate holidays like King's Day, but also whenever Ajax won. The area became not only a magnet for foreign tourists, but also for Dutch visiting from the provinces—in New York, we'd call them "bridge-and-tunnel."

Ruben van der Meer: They're not from the New Jersey shore, but North Holland: "Who are those obnoxious drunk assholes? Oh, it's a bachelor party visiting from the north." Any Ajax game provides an excuse for Amsterdammers to party—but the Champions League means nuclear-level partying. I was at the 1995 Champions League game when Ajax won against AC Milan. Amsterdam city flags were on every seat, so half of the stadium waved them whenever Ajax scored a goal.

Horace Cohen: Only one person was doing that, and it was Ruben. His drunken enthusiasm made up for everyone else, though.

Ruben van der Meer: I still have that flag, actually. It's right here on my desk. *[Picks up flag and starts waving it]* "*Joden! Joden! Joden!* Fuck AC Milan! Fuck Berlusconi!"

Brendan Hunt: Everybody in Amsterdam has their personal favorite era of Ajax. They were always better in the past, and you're always apologizing for the present, no matter how good the current team is. Gerbrand van Kolck, Boom's musical director at the time, always knocked some small beers back after the show—launching into epic oratories about how we'd *just* missed the true good ol' days of Ajax. Gerbrand took me to my first football match in Holland, along with Ike Barinholtz and Kay Cannon. It was a nonqualifying friendly between Oranje and Romania. Later, I found out friendlies weren't as exciting as the matches that qualified a team for the finals. Fans, though, reacted like every Oranje game was the World Cup.

We left early, missing a Romania goal that actually paid tribute to Johan Cruyff. They did Cruyff's move where, instead of taking a penalty, he'd tap the ball left so the charging player can score. I haven't left a soccer game early since.

Ike Barinholtz: To this day, when a Dutch soccer game is on, I will watch it, and that's strictly from my Boom Chicago days.

Saskia Maas: Whenever Holland plays, Boom alumni all over gather, dressing in orange to cheer the games. In 2014, Holland made it to the semifinals against Argentina. Seth, a huge Oranje fan, postponed his *Late Night with Seth Meyers* taping until after the game. Unfortunately, it went into thirty minutes of over-time, and then into penalties, so the end of the game happened during the show. Seth got the result on his iPad in front of the studio audience; upon learning that Holland lost, he threw his iPad across the studio! That story made the Dutch papers.

Seth Meyers: As a Red Sox fan, I was so drawn to the romantic failures of Dutch football. Dutch teams, they get *so* close . . .

Peter Grosz: When Seth and I joined the Boom cast, we'd spend off nights watching British shows, which introduced us to football culture. That a team was called "Tottenham Hotspur" was completely hilarious to us. Seth and I actually created a sketch called "Tottenham and Hotspur" where we played old, pompous Brits arguing and boasting about old war stories. We really had fun with that.

Heather Anne Campbell: When *Rick and Morty* needed someone to write a soccer commercial around the World Cup, they were like, "Heather should do it—she lived in Amsterdam."

Andrew Moskos: Her commercial even includes a herring joke.

Brendan Hunt: Before I came to Boom Chicago, I'd never watched football, never heard of Ajax. I vaguely knew about the World Cup, and there was the Chicago Sting—Chicago's first pro soccer team from 1974 to 1988, who were more of a local curiosity. Now, as FIFA disintegrates before our eyes, soccer's finally getting its due stateside. When you're in a country that really cares about the World Cup and European football championships, it's just so different. On game day, everyone wears orange and team shirts and excitement permeates the streets. That, and puke.

Horace Cohen: It's a big deal for Amsterdammers. We're fortunate to be from a generation that witnessed our national team win the European championship, and then Ajax win the Champions League, football's most important prize. We'd always celebrate with fellow fans on the Museumplein.

Pep Rosenfeld: As a dude who lives near there, I must correct you: you'd celebrate with fans by pissing on and destroying the Museumplein.

Brendan Hunt: When I got to Amsterdam, I started watching football a little bit—emphasis on *little*. Then I moved into this crazy apartment above McDonald's on the Leidseplein, which pretty much sealed the deal with me and football. There, I lived with nine Dutch guys who knew each other from university, and we had the whole floor. By May 2000, I'd lived in the McDonald's crib for less than a year.

One day, there was all this lumber piled high in the living room—along with a huge new video projector. For the Euro 2000 season, my roommates decided to build bleachers in our living room. They wanted the full arena experience without, well, leaving their living room. These were responsible fans: they did a sensible weight analysis, figuring out the precise capacity of drunk Dutch lunatics these bleachers could safely hold without imploding. Access was limited—I couldn't just invite anyone over anytime to watch a game. There was a sign-up sheet, and once filled, that was it; otherwise, the bleachers would be over capacity and self-destruct.

This was a very Dutch thing, engineering everything down to the last kilo—even for watching football with your friends. Building those bleachers to add game-day vibes to the living room was just so fucking cool. I mean, they built goddamn bleachers.

Ruben van der Meer: When Holland made it to the 2000 semifinals, it was like watching the famous matches I heard about growing up. It was a great team.

Brendan Hunt: Dennis Bergkamp, Patrick Kluivert, Edgar Davids, Edwin van der Sar—all great Dutch legends. Alas, it ended in heartbreak in the semis, losing on penalties.

Andrew Moskos: Cue our joke!

Horace Cohen: It still hurts.

Brendan Hunt: Ajax had this popular American player, John O'Brien, and we eventually became friends.

John O'Brien: I met Brendan and Jason Sudeikis at a bar in the Red Light District that played American football. We were there to watch a playoff game, and we ended up playing pool with them. Brendan was super intense, but also really poignant. He knew I'd just gotten back from the Olympics, and was really specific with his praise—neurotically precise. It was nice meeting Americans who could talk about soccer on a deeper level, and we went from there.

Brendan Hunt: John hung out at Boom quite a bit. We actually got him onstage for a "Late Night" show.

John O'Brien: I was just trying to keep my wits about me, but I managed to get a laugh right away. When I first saw a Boom Chicago show, I was like, *Man, why wasn't I connected with this earlier?* I mean, American guys who live in Amsterdam, making jokes about Dutch culture? I should've been there from day one. Brendan would get me tickets to Boom Chicago shows, and I'd get him tickets to Ajax games. Soon, things got debaucherous in all the good ways, and this whole world got introduced to me. Brendan had keys to Boom Chicago, so I'd bring friends and players and we'd all hang out there after hours.[16] A friend of mine from LA named Alex Jimenez came to stay with me, and he even got a job with Boom passing out flyers in front of the Heineken brewery.

Rob AndristPlourde: After winning a big match, John asked if he and some of the Ajax players could take the Boom boat around the canals to party in.

Brendan Hunt: That was after Ajax took the Eredivisie title in 2004. After Ajax won the final game, John called me late that night and asked, "Hey, man, do you still have that boat?" We had the boat all right, and I was happy to captain it.

For some reason, we took the boat to Cooldown Café—a particularly terrible decision. Cooldown is this awesomely desperado party spot where you walk in and someone rushes up and says, "Welcome. Here, have some shots." And you're like, "Oh, wow! That's so generous and *gezellig.*" And then after you drink the shots and realize anywhere else in Amsterdam would be a cooler place to be, you're handed the check: "That will be sixty euros, please."

As we pulled up on the canal next to Cooldown, one of the Ajax players was getting cold, so I gave him my jacket. We had to go through metal detectors to enter the club. After the beloved soccer player puts my jacket through, suddenly this big gnarly bouncer yanks two Rookies prerolled joints from it and starts giving the soccer player a hard time. The player was like, "Dude, it's not my jacket. It's the boat captain's." I almost got an Ajax player kicked out of a nightclub for drugs—glad it didn't make the papers.

---

16 Saskia Maas: "What? After hours? I don't recall approving that . . ."

Andrew Moskos: Today, some boat captain would be getting "Coach Beard" thrown out of a club.

John O'Brien: It's so funny: that player didn't even smoke pot—a lot of them didn't. When I first got to Holland when I was seventeen or eighteen years old, none of the players on my youth team had ever smoked—so I introduced them to weed. I was like, "C'mon, guys—we're in *Amsterdam*."

Brendan Hunt: After the jacket incident, we weren't going to be at Cooldown Café long . . .

Pep Rosenfeld: *No one* can be at Cooldown Café for long.

Brendan Hunt: So we boated away, and the party raged on all night.

John O'Brien: One player wanted to throw a bike into a canal—so he did. Going from one spot to the next, we ended up at a bar where they had a jam session going. Brendan got up with the band and just killed Stevie Wonder's "Superstition," and everyone was blown away. The other Ajax players were like, "God, this guy can really do this!" Just seeing that part of Brendan come out was really cool.

Brendan Hunt: By the end of the night, the party crew got down to me, John, and Christian Chivu, probably Ajax's best player then. We were in the Jordaan on the Herengracht canal, and it was so beautiful: that special gray version of sunrise you only get in Amsterdam, with cold drizzle and lightning added. John and Christian stood at the front of the boat, processing the moment with this dazed "fuckin' A, man!" expression, enjoying Amsterdam the best way: from a boat traveling the canals. It was cool to see these guys humbly loving the city as much as we did. Ajax in that era really was a phenomenal team. They won all the trophies . . . and then it was over. Weirdly, I felt like I'd already lived through this with the Chicago Bulls.

John O'Brien: I grew up in the '80s in LA, when the Lakers were such a successful dynasty with Kareem Abdul-Jabbar. For me, Ajax was always the Lakers of football: a Hollywood team that has a national movement behind it, with people supporting it who aren't even from the team's city.

Pep Rosenfeld: Can we get back to the fact that everybody calls Ajax "the Jews"? Nobody thinks that's weird when you cheer Ajax at home, jumping up and down yelling, "Our Jews are winning!"?

Brendan Hunt: Seeing a whole stadium scream, "Jews! Jews! Jews!" at each other for the first time? I'm not even Jewish, and it still weirds me out to hear that at every game.

Rob AndristPlourde: If *Joden* wasn't offensive enough, there's the *shhh*-ing noise opposing teams' fans make at Ajax games. They're emulating the sound of gas being turned on in the chambers where millions of Jews were killed during the Holocaust. Like, you know, Anne Frank.

Pep Rosenfeld: That's really the implication—it's absolutely a single entendre.

John O'Brien: That was bad—just nastiness. I stayed focused, but I didn't like that as a player. As a psychologist, that just speaks of trauma in people's lives—trying to hurt others so they can feel seen. Putting it into perspective, I thought I was the first American player for Ajax, but then a journalist told me an American named Eddie Hamill played for the club right before World War Two—and then was killed in a concentration camp.

So the *Joden* tradition really goes back to Ajax's founders and a culture that's obviously been through so much.

Ruben van der Meer: It's a cultural, historical thing: because Amsterdam took in a lot of Jews back in the day, everyone started calling Ajax *Joden*. It's like Anne Frank and football—two great tastes that go great together.

Rob AndristPlourde: Ajax hooligans actually started wearing Stars of David and waved them on banners during the game. So that's kind of *funny* weird, right?

Horace Cohen: I get the nuances because I'm from Amsterdam and I'm Jewish. It's like Ajax is always the underdog persecuted and destroyed by these Axis powers. *We haven't forgotten, Germany!* So when other teams call us *Joden*, we're like, "That's right—we're all Jews here."

Ruben van der Meer: Owning it takes out the sting, and the slur isn't a slur anymore.

Pep Rosenfeld: Brendan wrote a great sketch about Americans experiencing this for the first time at an Ajax game—showing how bewildering it is for everyone who doesn't speak Dutch to hear people screaming "Yoda" at each other, like, "That's so cool Ajax has a *Star Wars* thing!"

> *Brendan: So you just chant the word "Jews" over and over?*
>
> *Ajax Fan: It's my favorite part.*
>
> *Brendan: Jesus Christ.*

Ajax Fan: Probably not.

Brendan: Actually, Jesus was the king of the Jews.

Ajax Fan: No, the king of the Jews was Johan Cruyff.[17] *Cruyff wasn't Jewish, but sometimes sounds like Yoda when he says things like, "Every disadvantage has its advantage."*

Brendan: Um, I'm Jewish . . .

Ajax Fan: Me too. We all are!

Andrew Moskos: Brendan went through the most extreme Eurofication of all cast members. Loving Ajax is a big part of becoming a true Amsterdammer.

Brendan Hunt: Coming to Amsterdam for Boom Chicago taught me things you don't learn performing in Chicago. It's like summer camp for enlightenment; away from things in your everyday life, you get to . . . explore. There's football, but also dancing in clubs and taking Ecstasy too. The night of my first Boom show, I had my first one-night stand. Amsterdam was another planet, sure, but one I was in no hurry to leave. My coming of age began then.[18]

Ike Barinholtz: Boom Chicago is like another version of the college experience. You can lay back in ways you don't get chances to later as an adult, doing work that's going to help you succeed after. You'll never have this moment again, so enjoy it and get

17 Johan Cruyff was voted European Player of the Century in 1999, and ranked only behind Pelé in the World Player of the Century poll.
18 Boom's class of '95's coming-of-agers comprised Sue Gillan, Lesley Bevan, Scott Jones, Tami Sagher, and Lillian Frances.

the most out of it. It's impossible to live in Amsterdam without comprehending a whole universe outside your world you didn't even know existed. I was lucky to be there at that moment in time. Now I tell everyone, "Get out of your shell and see the world, whether it's Boom Chicago or the Peace Corps."

Andrew Moskos: Well, if that's the choice, I would definitely join Boom Chicago. Unless you're not funny. Then, hello Peace Corps!

Pep Rosenfeld: A tear-gas summer seems less likely in the Peace Corps.

Andrew Moskos: Ajax is back on top, and we were optimistic about Holland's World Cup chances—but Dutch enough to know things go in cycles. Seven years of famine follow seven years of plenty, or something. We're more *Jesus Christ Superstar* than *Joseph and the Amazing Technicolor Dreamcoat* people.

Seth Meyers: Of all the drugs that I was introduced to in my time in Amsterdam, I would say soccer is the one I'm still addicted to.

Ruben van der Meer: *Joden! Joden! Joden!*

CHAPTER 4
1996

VILLA VOLTA: THE RIDE OPENS AT THE BEST THEME PARK ON EARTH (WITH EXPAT COMEDIANS SHOCKED TO DISCOVER HOLLAND HAS SUPERIOR THEME PARKS TO AMERICA)

In 1996, new actors arrived to Amsterdam, with Rob AndristPlourde, Jason Meyer, Karin McKie, Jeremy Hornik, Shane Oman, and Spencer Kayden all joining Boom's cast. Spencer would go on to win multiple Tony Awards for her roles in Broadway hits like *Urinetown*. Rob, meanwhile, would set records as Boom Chicago's most senior actor—serving in full-time capacity for more than two decades, and still frequently onstage as a regular Boom performer.

We needed more help. As Boom Chicago continued selling out shows, we expanded into Amsterdam's comedy community—hosting the Comedy Explosion promoted by Frans and Franco Ruhl, who'd later go on to open the Comedy Theater on the Nes; MC Bob McLaren (aka Kiwi Bob) would later coach *De Lama's*.

1996 also represented one of the most momentous events in Dutch history: the opening of Villa Volta. What is this Villa Volta, you say? And why does it have an Italian name—especially if it's supposed to be something so awesomely Dutch? The Villa Volta would soon be revealed as the most groundbreaking ride at Holland's beloved amusement park, the Efteling. But friends, trust us when we say that, when it comes to the Villa Volta, nothing is quite as it seems.

Let's flash forward a bit. By 2004, Boom Chicago, comfortably installed at the Leidseplein theater, was now regularly invited to swanky local events like the grand reopening of the Heineken Tour. By the 2000s, the public flagship of Holland's most iconic brand found itself at a crossroads. On one hand, it was famous and successful: few college students, Andrew and Pep included, visited Amsterdam without stopping at the former brewery. The Heineken Tour combined historical interest, civic pride, and corporate tourist entertainment—with a finale of forty-five minutes of power drinking, and all for only two guilders. That was the equivalent of $1.50—less than what a beer in a bar cost. Not too many unsatisfied customers stumbled out after that deal. Unsatisfied neighbors? Perhaps a few.

The biggest problem with the Heineken Tour, however, was its aging content and production values. Entering into the post-Internet era of Tupac holograms and virtual reality, the beer behemoth knew the time had come for a revision. Company bigwigs decided to remodel the tour completely, renaming it the Heineken Experience. Multimedia was in, and everything was made livelier—more *now*. Capacity increased, with flesh-and-blood guides replaced by self-guided tours. Tech was upgraded, branding increased, the price of admission shot up to twenty euros, the infamous drinkathon climax was cut—and strangely, no one complained.[19]

At the Heineken Experience grand reopening, the Boom contingent rolled in to encounter a team of Americans having a good ol' time drinking, laughing, and talking in thick Texas accents. They were the "imagineers" who'd worked on the project. Sparing no expense, Heineken hired the world's most elite imagineers—famed for transforming many of the most beloved theme parks with new attractions that were as thrilling as they were innovative. Their creations showed you the world anew

---

19 For the next upgrade of the Heineken Experience, I, your coauthor Andrew Moskos, was actually hired to rewrite the tour, completing the circle . . .

in unexpectedly breathtaking and vivid ways. As attraction and amusement park fanatics, we were excited to pick their brains—coyly asking, "So, what's your favorite attraction in the world?"

"My favorite ride is Spider-Man at Universal Florida," the alpha imagineer said, sipping a beer glass topped with two perfect fingers of foam. In the Spider-Man ride, guests sit in twelve-person vehicles which move through the story—but unlike similar rides, the vehicles could now twist and pivot. Spider-Man's budget soared into the millions—money spent to make riders feel they really were inside a superhero movie. The Texan confessed they were working on something even more incredible involving Harry Potter. "But right now, Spider-Man remains the best ride in the world," he concluded authoritatively.

I mentioned that Holland has a great amusement park, the Efteling, with a most magical attraction called the Villa Volta. Did he know it? The imagineer's eyes lit up. In his barbeque-sauced twang, Mr. Imagineer Alpha Dog proclaimed, "Villa Volta is the *second*-best ride in the world."

An intellectual friend on drugs called Villa Volta the essence of European surrealism—"like going inside a Magritte painting in the middle of a cosmic earthquake." Indeed, Villa Volta was something you didn't know you wanted to experience, but then found it astonishing when you did.[20] Villa Volta was in fact the first ever "Madhouse/Crazy Room" attraction—a new genre of theme-park ride conceived by a renowned and imaginative Dutch attraction producer, *onze eigen* Vekoma.[21] Villa Volta's setup proved simple but deceptively nuanced: in it, two rows of high-backed wooden pews faced each other in a swing ride—not

---

20 Kind of like Utrecht . . .

21 Who knew that many of the world's most famous roller coasters were designed and built by the Dutch? In addition to Bird Roc at the Efteling and five roller coasters at Walibi in Flevoland (!), Vekoma created Space Mountain at Disneyland Paris, Everest at Disney World, and Tron—the flagship attraction at Disney World and Disneyland Hong Kong. Incredibly, the company is based in Vlodrop, a town of two thousand in the most unsexy province of Limburg.

unlike, say, a pirate ship attraction, but wider and shallower. The room's walls could either rotate with or separately from the swinging seats, which didn't necessarily match the gravity your body felt. You couldn't tell which way you were spinning—or if you were upside down or right side up. As the ride progressed, it was hard to believe you were experiencing what your eyes were telling you. Because you weren't.

As the Villa Volta room returned to normal at the end of the ride, the audience always burst into applause. What other ride inspired that kind of reaction? In 2004, eight years after it opened, Villa Volta remained the best ride at Efteling—and perhaps the second-best ride in the world too.

Efteling opened back in 1953—pretty much becoming the closest thing to Hogwarts for generations of *Nederlanders* growing up with it. A truly immersive and unique experience, Efteling became part of nearly every Dutch person's childhood, and subsequently a place to return to feed one's inner child. Not surprisingly, it also became a requisite destination for Boom Chicago expats to commune on (mostly legal) psychedelic substances. Efteling pilgrimages grew into a classic Boom Chicago team-building tradition—and nothing epitomized the place's enduring magic than the opening of the storied, mind-altering phantasmagoria of Villa Volta in 1996.

Unlike most American amusement parks, Efteling keeps branding to a glorious minimum. Instead of heavily marketed superheroes or movie characters, Efteling attractions draw on Northern European folk-fantasy, mythology, and lore—making their narratives instantly familiar and iconic to anyone who's ever read classic fairy tales. While some Efteling rides remain refreshingly old school, using simple effects like smoke and even smells, many are ultra-advanced technologically—not surprising coming from a culture of engineers like the Dutch. But the Efteling experience ultimately becomes less about tech wizardry and more the astounding imagination on display. Can you picture a donkey that shoots collectable coins out of its ass? Nope, we couldn't; Walt Disney never did either. But at Efteling, it's ass coins for everyone! And don't be surprised if giant mushrooms break into song as you pass by. Yes, it's fungi for the whole family—especially if Daddy is tripping balls. You're on mushrooms; the mushrooms start talking to you. It's perfect.

Some of the magic of Villa Volta has been usurped by bigger, better, and higher budgeted rides. Universal Studios's Wizarding World of Harry Potter did indeed become the world's number-one attraction, but Villa Volta remains a favorite for many. Discovering the pleasurably consciousness-altering Villa Volta in the late 1990s provided a most psychedelic parallel to the life-changing adventure Boom Chicagoans found themselves on.

Horace Cohen: Efteling's typically the first big theme park Dutch kids go to. It's also the first place I ever took LSD—which was with Boom Chicago, actually.

Ruben van der Meer: You go with your school for a field trip. The first roller coaster Dutch children ever ride is at Efteling. It's the backdrop for our coming of age. As a juvenile delinquent, I both kissed a girl and smoked pot for the first time at Efteling.

Amber Ruffin: Boom Chicago actors like to get high and take mushrooms or E and go to Efteling. It's the most beautiful place I've ever been on earth. Or the mushrooms made me feel that way. Whatever, it was dope.

Rob AndristPlourde: When I first started going to Efteling, there was one conventional roller coaster, the Python, and it was a little underwhelming. Now Efteling has great, innovative roller coasters: Bird Roc, Flying Hollander, Joris and the Dragon, Baron 1898. But those weren't the kind of thrills that drew us to

Efteling. We have roller coasters in the US; we come to Efteling for the metaphysical fantasy shit you can't get anywhere else.

There's a moment in the Villa Volta where you think, *We're almost there. Phew, we made it!* And then the room flips around again in every direction, and you're like, *Oh fuck, what's happening? Where am I? Who am I?* And when the room turns totally upside down, this crazy music comes on: the Villa Volta theme. Hearing it, I know I'm in a magical place like nowhere else. This is not your brain on drugs; this is your brain on drugs *at Efteling.*

Andrew Moskos: Villa Volta represents the total Efteling experience: one part physical, one part mental. Moving the room and walls together, you feel it in your body, but not in a thrilling-scary way. It's more cool, spooky, and . . . confusing? It's hard to define: the sensation is uncanny—but that's the wizardry of Villa Volta, and the whole park, really.

Pep Rosenfeld: One of the best ways to compare the Netherlands with the rest of the world is looking at Efteling. Most amusement parks tear down trees, pour a layer of concrete, and build rides on top. Efteling did the opposite. It's not in a parking lot, but a forest; the surrounding woods aren't just part of the environment, but a major part of the theming. It's unlike any American amusement park.[22]

Greg Shapiro: Efteling's visionaries used their imagination practically: "We've got a forest, and that's pretty awesome already. Let's shove in an amusement park." Very Dutch thinking: no wasted space.

Pep Rosenfeld: At Disneyland Paris, there's no place to sit and

---

22 Well, except Dollywood, Dolly Parton's theme park in Tennessee. *That's* the Efteling of America.

chill without ordering food. Any grass is fenced off: you cross into it, and the disembodied voice of Mickey Mouse Big Brother is suddenly omnipresent: *"Huh huh huh! Hey there, pal! You weren't thinking of sitting there, were you? Grass is not for sitting. Grass is for looking at as you walk by on your way to purchase souvenirs! Huh huh!"* At Efteling, there's grass *everywhere*, and you're expected to sit on it. Often, the best part of Boom's Efteling excursions is just relaxing on the grass with shoes off and some cold beers—while being high as fuck. Turns out you can stare at the talking Hollebolle Gijs paper gobbler for a while before realizing you're staring at a garbage can. *Papier hier,* indeed.

Greg Shapiro: For the biggest ride at Efteling then, Droomvlucht ("Dreamflight"), you enter a suspended cable car, which rides along a track as you float into darkness, rising through the air.

Rob AndristPlourde: As you're greeted by grotesque, huge-eyed puppets from the 1970s and a different smell in every room. It's not a thrilling ride, but it's a treat for all your senses.

Greg Shapiro: I mean, when was the last time you were on a theme-park ride that sprayed odors in your face?

Rob AndristPlourde: Less magical: Monsieur Cannibale, a pretty racist spinning ride set in a boiling pot.

Pep Rosenfeld: *Pretty* racist? Monsieur Cannibale is *super* racist. Were African cannibals *ever* appropriate as a theme?

Ruben van der Meer: *[Singing the Monsieur Cannibale theme in a French accent]* "Monsieur Cannibale . . ." It's horribly graphic, featuring Africans with bones in their noses.

Andrew Moskos: The times finally caught up with Efteling. In 2022, RIP Monsieur Cannibale.

Pep Rosenfeld: But there's still the Carnival Festival ride and its quaint journey through global ethnic stereotypes. It's basically Disney's A Small World, except it's a smaller, even more racist world. Which, in 1955 or whatever, might've been a fine description of Holland.

Andrew Moskos: Early in our relationship, I told Saskia I was really into amusement parks. She said, "Well, Holland has this amusement park called the Efteling." I literally patted her on the head and said in the most patronizing, mansplaining way possible, "That's cute: a Dutch amusement park. Look, you Dutchies do *gezellig* cafés well—but leave amusement parks to the American experts." Guess what? I was wrong, and Saskia was right. See, honey, now it's in print.

One thing about Disneyland's design is it creates great views of what are called "weenies." Weenies are big things you see on the horizon, like the Disney Cinderella Castle or Space Mountain, that make you think, *I have to ride that, now!* At Efteling, there are no weenies except maybe the Pagode—which, like Villa Volta, is iconic. There are bigger and faster rides, but there's only one Pagode, in all its minimalist perfection.

Pep Rosenfeld: You always end with the Pagode. You never *start* with the Pagode.

Andrew Moskos: It's a slowly rotating disk hidden among the trees that soars into the air to give you great views of the park. As it ascends, the Pagode unfolds like a giant Pixar desk lamp.

Brendan Hunt: The Pagode is one of my favorite things in the world. The first time you see it rising out of the forest, it looks like a UFO. It's the simplest ride in the world: a metal disc which meditatively floats up and spins around—giving you the most sublime, panoramic vistas of everything you just experienced at Efteling. It's really about looking around and discovering things—a balloon ride crossed with *Close Encounters of the Third Kind*.

Greg Shapiro: We have this great tradition: no talking on the Pagode. Brendan always said, "This is something that must be experienced in silence." It's such a wonderful idea—flying above the trees for a most peaceful, contemplative experience. Since then, the Pagode has remained one of the few comedy-bit-free zones in Boom Chicago's canon.

After the Pagode one day, we were relaxing on the grass and it was my turn to get beers. But I was too messed up. I went into the bathroom to splash some water on my face. Bad plan. When I looked in the mirror, I started having an out-of-body experience—staring at my own face, asking myself, *Who's this stranger?* My eyes were now dark, deep, and sunken into my skull, my eyebrows heavy and thick: I realized everybody was too nice to tell me what I'd just discovered: I was grotesque. Suddenly every toilet-stall door opens, and out spills what looked like zombies from "Thriller." I thought, *Oh my God—I'm one of them!* I never managed to get the beer, and had to be rescued from the bathroom, where I remained transfixed by my own reflection.

Andrew Moskos: It's possible to overdo it at Efteling with the mushrooms. During one visit, we all rode the Panda Dream attraction. You're in a dark cave with a three-dimensional panda—that's pretty much it. So we all filed in, the lights went down, and the three-dimensional audiovisuals and surround-sound effects began. Suddenly, I heard murmuring. Walking toward the sound, I came upon Seth quietly repeating a mantra to himself: "Keep it together, Meyers . . . Keep it together, Meyers . . ."

Seth Meyers: And that's not a ride where people usually have any trouble keeping it together.

Pep Rosenfeld: When asking audiences for interesting locations during Boom shows, occasionally someone shouts out, "Efteling!" Casts usually begin playing a trippy, surrealist scene. This never works, because audiences don't recognize this from their own Efteling experience. For normal people, Efteling is a family amusement park—a place you only go as a kid, or with your kids.

Andrew Moskos: But for us, Efteling remains a wonderland to explore with adult friends—and the Villa Volta remains the central attraction. As we sit in Villa Volta, our bodies telling us that we're upside down, we're actually supporting the pinnacle of Dutch creativity and innovation. Viva Villa Volta! Viva Efteling! Without you, Boom Chicago wouldn't be the same. Imagineer that!

CHAPTER 5
1997

THE FIFTEENTH (AND LAST?)
ELFSTEDENTOCHT SKATING RACE:
RAPPING, CLUBBING, AND EUROPERVE

One of the most enjoyable unwritten Dutch traditions is that on the first sunny day of the year, everyone knows that the week has become that much less productive. How much less productive? Well, imagine how much work gets done by the flocks of Dutch cosmopolitans wearing white pants and sipping rosé for hours across every terrace in town. So we wonder, how can so many people just sit outside doing nothing for the entire afternoon? Is *everyone* a graphic designer?

The sudden eruption of sunny-day terrace boozing is nothing compared to what happens when the thermometer goes the other way, dipping down below zero. At first, everyone's complaining. But once it's been brutally, unbearably frigid for long enough, something else happens.

Elfstedentocht fever kicks in.

Elfstedentocht (elf-STAY-den-tocht) is a truly Dutch phenomenon where seventeen million people freak out over what, to the rest of the world, sounds like something nasty farmers do to amuse themselves, like cow-tipping or sheep-screwing. This isn't exactly wrong.

Around for as long as canals have been freezing over, the Elfstedentocht is Holland's long-distance endurance competition on ice, with some geography lessons thrown in. The idea behind this beloved tradition is, like many things in the Netherlands, both simple and totally fucking nuts. Elfstedentocht's foundational concept is basically this: when it gets cold enough to freeze water into ice thick enough to skate on, most of the population in the northern province of Friesland joins a contest to skate 120 miles through eleven towns linked by the frozen canals.

When the temperature goes below freezing, national conversation quickly turns into frenzied Elfstedentocht speculation: "Will it really happen?" And when Elfstedentocht's walrus-mustached ice master declares the ice officially six inches thick, the countdown begins: within forty-eight hours, the race will commence. Skaters take time off work. Energetic parents drag less enthusiastic children to the canals. Historic towns like Dokkum and Franeker prepare for their day in the (cold) sun, selling pea soup to shivering Dutch city tourists who quickly wish they had booked a real hotel in Leeuwarden instead of their authentically underwhelming B&B.

The Elfstedentocht ritual, alas, hasn't happened much in the last thirty years—pretty much since right-wing lunatics started denying global warming. For decades, Holland winters just haven't been cold enough. Hell will probably freeze over before the next Elfstedentocht blesses us.

The last Elfstedentocht to date—and perhaps forever—happened in 1997. That was also the year Boom Chicago started regularly "bringing the heat" to Amsterdam's winter comedy season. Coincidence?

1997, after all, was when Boom Chicago moved to Amsterdam full-time to perform shows all year round—scoring some of our most notable cast members in the process. Take Allison Silverman. After graduating from Yale University, Allison honed her craft at Chicago's prestigious iO, where she gained notoriety as a comedic badass. Years later, Allison would become an Emmy-winning television writer for some of the best, most relevant shows on TV: *The Daily Show with Jon Stewart*, *Late Night with Conan O'Brien*, *The Colbert Report*. 1997 was also when Boom Chicago brought two recent Northwestern University grads to Holland, Peter Grosz and Seth Meyers. BFFs since college, comedy bromancers Pete and Seth arrived at Boom as a package deal, and went on to do quite well, separately and together. Seth, Pete, and Allison became Boom's dynamic threesome—driving a cast that included newcomers Phill Arensberg, Gwendolyn Druyor, and Lisa Jolley.

After Boom, Pete would become a beloved writer/performer on *The Colbert Report*, as well as appearing in weird movies like *Stranger Than Fiction* and *The Weatherman* (late-period Nicholas Cage, say no more). In classic Boom fashion, Pete also created his own distinct sideline playing memorable political characters, including four seasons on HBO's award-winning *Veep* as cold-hearted nonrenewable-energy lobbyist Sidney Purcell. In the wake of America's Trump tragedy, Pete brilliantly embodied Vice President Mike Pence in the show he helped create, Comedy Central's *The President Show*.

Seth, meanwhile, also found his niche mining the absurdity of America's political climate. Cast as a *Saturday Night Live* writer/performer in 2001, Meyers would go on to become *SNL*'s head writer and anchor of its legendary newscast satire, "Weekend Update." In addition to Seth and Pep, Boom alumni Liz Cackowski, Heather Anne Campbell, Joe Kelly, and Jason Sudeikis would also go on to write or perform on *SNL*. In 2014, Seth began hosting the storied *Late Night* show, a role made legendary by creator David Letterman and subsequent hosts Conan O'Brien and Jimmy Fallon. Not bad, eh? And who would join Seth on his writing staff? Old college buddy/ex-Boom émigré Pete Grosz, of course, as well as Boom superheroine Amber Ruffin.

In '97, though, the Elfstedentocht was much more familiar to the Dutch than the steady stream of comedians unexpectedly trickling in from Midwestern USA. Back then, the Netherlands was busy not looking outward, but iceward (if such a word existed, that is). Once temps dropped below freezing, 1997 was all about the return of the Elfstedentocht—the nation intensely focused on sparsely populated Friesland. This is also something that has never happened since . . .

Andrew Moskos: Ah, Friesland. We know you're *so* different that you need your own flag—your accent *so* thick, it might as well be a different language. And . . . Sorry, we dozed off for a moment there, because everything you brag about is *so* dull.

Pep Rosenfeld: Amsterdammers may roll their eyes at Friesland—but the Force is strong with Boom Chicago and Friesland. Greg Shapiro actually became a spokesman for the tourist board of Friesland and performed a special show there.

Horace Cohen: The Elfstedentocht is basically an ice-skating race through different cities connected by canals. It doesn't get more Dutch than that.

Ruben van der Meer: Every winter, Elfstedentocht fever starts building—bubbling up from the event's eleven cities into the rest of the Dutch consciousness. Everybody always thinks *this* could be the year it happens again, if it only gets cold enough . . .

Pep Rosenfeld: Which it rarely does. Shit, Elfstedentocht has only happened fifteen times since 1909.

Carice van Houten: Elfstedentocht? Forget about it. I cannot even *stand* on fucking ice skates. I'm not exaggerating. I'm useless on ice skates, roller skates, skateboards—any kind of skates.

Pep Rosenfeld: You're pretty un-Dutch in that way.

Carice van Houten: I know—it's weird. I can imagine that it's probably really nice . . . No, it's terrifying.

Ruben van der Meer: I skated in the last Elfstedentocht, which was eleven years after the previous one. Now we've hit a record for the longest time between Elfstedentochten. We got close a couple of times, but it just didn't happen.

Rob AndristPlourde: No ice, no dice. People have been on the Elfstedentocht waiting list since January 1997. King Willem-Alexander, while still a prince, skipped the list: "Who let this guy jump the line? Oh, wait, it's Prince Willem . . ."

There's even a connection between Elfstedentocht and Dutch rave culture, which at the time was all about a fast-paced hardcore dance-music style called *gabber*. Typical *gabber* has a tempo around 190 beats per minute—i.e., too many beats per minute. It's a genre that not only requires drugs to listen/dance to, but specific ones. It sounds great on Red Bull and coke. No, not Coca-Cola . . .

Ruben van der Meer: I had a chart hit back then as the character Supergabber. I was like a Dutch Milli Vanilli—the face of a *gabber* group, Hakkûhbar. In our videos, I mimed to somebody else's voice. I can't sing, so this much older established musician sang on Hakkûhbar records, but I was the public frontman.

Rob AndristPlourde: Ruben nailed the classic *gabber* freak: shaved head, zipped-up windbreaker, jaw twitching away . . .

Horace Cohen: Supergabber was huge. Ruben got so famous in Holland as Supergabber, they made a doll of him.

Ruben van der Meer: I also performed on Hakkûhbar's club tours. And when the Elfstedentocht happened in 1997, it was the height of *gabber* and my fame as Supergabber.

The first actual night of the Elfstedentocht, Hakkûhbar booked a show at a bar called Flintstone's in one of the cities on the race's route. Usually, I'd wear a sweatsuit and matching Nike Air Max sneakers onstage as my Supergabber costume. For this occasion, however, I wore a necklace with the thing you get stamped for every Elfstedentocht city you reach during the race, and I also wore ice skates. Opening the show, I'd do a little bit about *klunen*, which is when the ice isn't thick enough so you stop and walk on land, messing up your race time. That bit played very well in Friesland.

Greg Shapiro: Let's return to Amsterdam. At first, Boom focused largely on tourists, and then the aim was to build the Dutch audience. By '97, our audiences had become basically half and half, which was great.

One sketch from then was based on Pep and Andrew going to a coffeeshop for the first time and smoking themselves into *Oh my God!* epiphanies. For the American tourist, it's like, "That's us, dude!"; Dutch people, though, were more, "It's *them*, not us." Maintaining that balance was essential to our appeal: making fun of the American point of view first was key. Ridiculing yourself always makes it easier to satirize everybody else. Boom Chicago still does that to this day.

Rob AndristPlourde: Whenever Boom brought in new actors, the first thing they were always told was, "Slow down." The Dutch may speak better English than the Chicago Cubs's starting lineup, but remember it's their *second* language. Rule number two: don't make jokes with heavy American references—think globally. This was back before the Internet, but it's still true even today.

Andrew Moskos: Actually, it was more like the dawn of the Internet. Our 1997 show was actually called *boomchicago.nl: The Internet and other Modern Frustrations.*

Peter Grosz: It really was the nascent days of the Internet. I actually got my first email address at Boom Chicago. In fact, I still use the same one today.

Ken Schaefle: Pete and Seth had come out of the Mee-Ow Show, a musical-comedy group that's about as close as Northwestern University got to something like Harvard's Hasty Pudding. It was a very competitive, talented group: Mee-Ow had already produced greats like Julia Louis-Dreyfus, Ana Gasteyer, and John Cameron Mitchell. Many of Boom Chicago's best came out of Mee-Ow: Pep, Josh Meyers, Liz Cackowski, Heather Anne Campbell. In fact, the first stage I ever built was for a Mee-Ow show.

Seth Meyers: After graduating Northwestern in 1996, Pete and I kicked around Chicago, just waiting tables and doing Improv Olympic stuff.

Peter Grosz: Seth and I had been super close since freshman year. After college, we were performing together in Chicago when we auditioned for Boom.

Seth Meyers: More than anything, we were aiming for a spot with Second City. We'd committed pretty strongly to making comedy our career, and in Chicago, Second City was what everyone hoped was their next step. But then Pete found Boom's audition notice in the *Chicago Reader*. Really, we did it as a lark.

Peter Grosz: We auditioned together for Pep and Andrew, and it went really well. I mean, we were twenty-three years old: it was the first audition I'd ever done that I'd actually felt good about. I remember saying to Seth, "I think there's a really good chance we might get this."

Pep Rosenfeld: Blown away by their joint audition, I pulled Pete aside and told him, "You guys really need to come to Amsterdam so you can finally get weaned off suckling the almighty teat of Second City."

Peter Grosz: But Boom was still pretty new. I knew a few people like Tami Sagher and Sue Gillan who'd returned to Chicago post-Boom. They had great Amsterdam stories, but it wasn't like Boom had this alumni network doing all these amazing things yet. And doing something professional in another country was uncharted territory. This was a big leap, and it made me nervous. But the allure of not waiting tables and actually getting paid to perform four shows a week with my best friend while living in Europe ultimately won out.

Seth Meyers: Neither of us had thought far enough ahead about what would happen if we actually got the job. I'd never been out of the country! I really did think it would just be an adventure.

Holly Walker: You have to be adventurous to uproot your life and move to a foreign country to do improv. Or really into weed. Or both.

Colton Dunn: I was like, *I have the opportunity to get paid to do short-form improv comedy—in a country where there's legal weed? Voilà!*

Greg Shapiro: Boom Chicago also started doing corporate shows in 1997. We'd tailor them to whatever team-bonding outings these companies did.

Andrew Moskos: We'd actually doubled the cast because we had so much corporate work.

Greg Shapiro: Corporate shows went on to become quite sophisticated, and part of Boom's bread and butter, but back then they were basically an insane proposition. We'd just take everything we had—mics, amps, speakers, PAs, backdrop, stage—somewhere random in nowheresville Holland, set up, do a show, break it down—and then drive as fast as possible back to civilization.

Pep Rosenfeld: Jen Burton used to say we were making the world laugh, one Dutch fishing village at a time.

Andrew Moskos: Kay Cannon, who'd later make films like *Pitch Perfect, Blockers,* and *Cinderella,* started running the corporate shows division.

Kay Cannon: It was, in hindsight, a crash course that trained me to be a director/showrunner. After auditioning, Andrew said I'd made the short list for the mainstage cast, though I'd have to wait six months to perform—but there was a new position, corporate show director, that started right away. I accepted the job because I thought, *I am going to live in fucking Europe? All by myself? Holy shit, yes!* The stakes felt very high, though. There was lots to learn, and I soaked everything up.

In the end, what truly helped me was taking a position I was too green for and *just doing it.* I had to manage lots of different personalities while also performing in corporate shows. Greg was a corporate show dream: he spoke Dutch, clients knew him, and he's so damn tall. Clients would always address him like he was the boss. Greg would then always introduce me as the director—he's crazy respectful like that. That year, we did over 185 corporate shows. Thankfully, I had Seth working with me as a corporate show writer to tailor scripts to our clients.

Brendan Hunt: Seth's work ethic was, and remains, inspiring. After we'd finish a show, the cast would all go out clubbing and partying until dawn. Seth would also come party with us—but first he'd spend a couple hours blasting out corporate scripts.

Andrew Moskos: Seth was a big part of writing Boom's tailored shows. He was just amazing at cranking them out. Even then, he brought incredible professionalism to it.

Seth Meyers: There's that thing about being a professional: it gets into your blood. You take what you do more seriously and value the work more when the people who hired you value you enough to pay you.

Saskia Maas: I was running the corporate show department, and Seth called me one day, panicking: he'd lost the briefing to base his jokes on. "Nothing you can do about that," I told him. "Just see what you can make up from memory." It turned out he remembered more than you would think about saline versus sodium-based solutions.

Seth Meyers: I'd basically landed in Amsterdam and immediately had to figure out how to do shows for the Dutch. Amsterdam was just a more global place than Chicago: I was hipping myself to this new world, this new culture, this new way of talking—and then finding a way to take that information and make comedy the same way I'd made comedy before.

Rob AndristPlourde: My favorite was Boom's Hawaii gig in 1997. Just when we needed some sunshine, the Netherlands hired Boom Chicago to go to Hawaii for a national conference of travel agents.

Andrew Moskos: It was a show to celebrate the best of Holland. So what did the Netherlands Board of Tourism and Conventions think would be typically Dutch—but also in English? Why, Boom Chicago! By then, we'd started getting a bunch of corporate shows, and the season was also going well in the theater. We were selling out weekends, so we added a second show on Saturday and a cheaper, more relaxed show called "Boom Chicago Late Night" on Fridays.

Pep Rosenfeld: Soon it was "Heineken Late Night." The fun of the show was that drinking was part of it. We gave out free beers for good suggestions.

Andrew Moskos: Another part of the magic was that actors would sit in the audience and drink when they weren't onstage. The "Late Night" shows were the opposite of corporate ones. If you said the things we came up with at "Late Night" during the office Christmas party, you'd definitely be fired. It was a dirtier, meaner outlet so we could be nicer during the week.

Greg Shapiro: "Late Night" was a creative lab where we all got to blow off steam and swear and drink. We thought, *We'll just do that one Friday and see what happens.* And "Late Night" has been going in one form or another for over two decades now.

Rob AndristPlourde: The best experiment in that creative lab was when we decided to explore our passion for hip-hop in the "Late Night" shows. Summer '97, you'd hear the Fugees and Wu-Tang Clan *everywhere*. It was a natural evolution to rap ourselves, as we were already huge fans of hip-hop.

Greg Shapiro: Rob, Pep, and I created "Yo! Here We Go" in 1997 for "Late Night." That was a big step, and a chance for us to flex some new muscles too.

Rob AndristPlourde: Greg, Pep, and I could all beatbox. One of us would take the mic, the others would make the beat. Someone would drop a melody, and we'd all freestyle. Then we were like, "What should we call this?" We were huge Tribe Called Quest fans, so Greg just flipped Tribe's *"Here we go, yo / What's the scenario?"* chorus, and it stuck.

Pep Rosenfeld: I definitely remember saying, "'Yo! Here We Go'? Really? Okay, we'll use it tonight—but we *have* to come up with a better name." That was over twenty-five years ago. But it didn't matter: we were rapping onstage. When Adam Yauch of the Beastie Boys died, it hit us pretty hard. That weekend when we did "Yo!," I told the audience, "When I was in school, I'd listen to MCA and the Beastie Boys and dream of being a rapper when I grew up. And now, once a week, I am."

Andrew Moskos: Part of the thing doing "Yo!" was that you invented your own rap character. Pep makes up new characters based on the news or whatever movie he just saw, but mostly everyone else sticks to their one character. Like, Ike was always "The I," which was just an angrier version of him in a hat and sunglasses. He was all about The I: *"Don't step to me 'cause I'm so fly / If you fuck with me, you're fucking with The I!"*

Pep Rosenfeld: You know, whenever I heard that I thought, *Yeah, you just told us you were The I. So of course if I fuck with you, The I is with whom I'm fucking. What's your point, sir?*

Rob AndristPlourde: One of Josh Meyers's rhymes as MC Fa-Shawn! I still remember years later: *"Yo, everyone, it's MC Fa-*

Shawn! / Bought a sectional sofa for my friends to crash on." That's a line direct from Amsterdam expat life.

Andrew Moskos: My favorite Seth Meyers character was MC Suburban Dad. He was a bit uncool, but shot off some great rhymes. Seth really knew how to build to an "out"—his last line would always get cheers. That's what happens when you put a writer up there. A very white writer. And that's MC Suburban Dad. Jordan was a writer too, and his rhymes were also really smart. But Jordan could pull off a B-boy: you believed he was a rapper. I didn't believe MC Suburban Dad was a real rapper.

Jordan Peele: My main rap persona was MC Nigga Please, who was an especially irreverent pimp-type character.

Pep Rosenfeld: Just think of all those reverent pimps—they get no respect in show business. Jordan had so many fun characters. He also did MC Forest Whitaker, well before Jordan did impressions of Forest Whitaker on *MADtv* and *Key & Peele*. As MC Forest Whitaker, Jordan famously rapped, *"I walk weird / I talk weird / My eye is Peter Falk weird."* That's one of the best rhymes *ever*, in the entire history of rhymes.

Jordan Peele: Hypothetically, if I were to assign Boom Chicago's top MCs with their equivalents in Wu-Tang Clan, it's accurate to say that Rob would be RZA, and Greg would be GZA. Brendan—aka MC Squared—is probably the Method Man of the crew; Josh—MC Fa-Shawn!—is Inspectah Deck. Maybe Ike is Ol' Dirty Bastard? In terms of those rankings, let's just say I'd consider myself perhaps Raekwon to Nicole's Ghostface.

Carice van Houten: I don't know why Ike comes to mind as Boom's best rapper. The idea of Ike rapping is just the funniest thing to me.

Pep Rosenfeld: I mean, you're correct in the second sentence, and incorrect in the first.

Kay Cannon: Best Boom rapper? Nicole Parker. Hands down. Don't tell Rob. *Doei!*

Rob AndristPlourde: The best rapper Boom ever had was indeed Nicole—or as she was known on the mic, Nickel Bag: *"I'm gonna spit some rhymes, I'm gonna bust a bit / If it ain't the Nickel Bag, it's counterfeit!"*

Andrew Moskos: Nicole's fans in the audience would jump in on *"It's counterfeit!"* She came out in this fake fur jacket and just owned the stage, and her rhymes were the best of anyone's. Nickel Bag was *gangsta.* Guys were intimidated by her because she had bigger balls than they did. In reality, Nicole was really sweet. She didn't drink. She didn't do drugs. She didn't swear. But when she was the Nickel Bag, she seemed to do all these things.

Rob AndristPlourde: Nicole to Nickel Bag was her version of Marshall Mathers becoming Eminem.

Nicole Parker: I remember spitting some of my dirtiest rhymes at this corporate event: *"I'm about to get my modem / And download his scrotum . . ."* This is the stuff my kid will never believe about their mother. When you go to a community like Boom, you want to create something original, that's all yours. Musical theater is my favorite thing in the world, but when I went to my first "Heineken Late Night" and the cast was rapping, I immediately was like, *Yeah, that'll be my jam.*

Andrew Moskos: Nicole could've had a full rap career. But she went on to musical theater on Broadway, starring in *Wicked* as the Wicked Witch of the West. Now, musical-theater nerds out there are saying, "Her character's actual name is Elphaba!" Pipe down, nerds.

Nicole was great in *Wicked*, selling out Broadway's biggest theater as its star. We were so proud. But as I watched her enthrall two thousand middle-aged white people as Elphaba, all I could think was, *This ain't the Nickel Bag. It's counterfeit!*

Heather Anne Campbell: I was MC Beverly Hills, this trashy Paris Hilton bitch in a fur coat who won't shut up about Hollywood. Learning to rap at Boom made auditions for improv shows like *Whose Line Is It Anyway?* so much easier. They'd ask, "Can you rap?" and I was like, "Yeah, I rapped every week for three years." That stuff is so in your tool belt by the time you leave Boom, everything else feels like training wheels.

Tarik Davis: When Colton Dunn told me I'd have to actually rap at Boom Chicago, I was like, *"Nooooooooo!"* I didn't believe him: I'd never come across rapping in what I'd considered "professional improv." I was very hesitant, but Colton was like, "You're just going to have to learn to rap, dude." It really took me awhile: rapping was the last mountain for me to overcome at Boom.

Rob AndristPlourde: We became mini rap celebs in Amsterdam. The highlight of my 1990s hip-hop career happened at Escape, one of Amsterdam's biggest clubs where DJ Marcello started the famous party Chemistry. He was spinning a special ten-hour set to celebrate twenty years being a DJ, and we were hired to provide intermission entertainment. We told him we were going to battle, and he loved that. On the night, Marcello scratched in a break and we busted into our routine and did fifteen minutes of straight improv rap. Wow.

Our musical experimentation wasn't just about hip-hop. Living in Amsterdam gave you new perspectives on pop culture. Learning to appreciate the Bloodhound Gang, for example, was also part of Boom's acclimation process. Bloodhound Gang was basically Limp Bizkit rap-rock, but fronted by a Pee-wee Herman impersonator. Something about that formula just clicked with the Dutch; in 1997, that group was Led Zeppelin–size huge in Amsterdam. Bloodhound Gang were from the US and had hit singles there, but they were just so incongruously massive here.

Ruben van der Meer: I don't remember the Bloodhound Gang.

Andrew Moskos: What? Dude! *[Sings] "You and me, baby, ain't nothin' but mammals / So let's do it like they do on the Discovery Channel . . ."* Music has always been so central to the Boom experience. We grew up hanging with punk rockers and Broadway musical vocalists, and I had a house/rap show on Northwestern's college radio station. When we got to Amsterdam, we went to clubs. You'd see it in the new cast members' transformation. Someone like Seth Meyers would've never liked house music in normal life, but because of Boom Chicago, Seth went to clubs and raves with the rest of us. After a year in Amsterdam, Seth was wearing silver Zara skinny jeans and going to crazy techno parties like everyone else.

Seth Meyers: I came straight from suburbia, so dance music completely missed me. But after enough time clubbing in Amsterdam, I acquired a real understanding of the joy of a beat dropping that I didn't have before.

Pep Rosenfeld: I'm not sure Seth ever got Euro enough for Euro-Perve, though.

Andrew Moskos: So around this time, we got booked to do a show at EuroPerve, an underground fetish party. I thought it would be funny to bring some lightheartedness into this dark, serious world, and EuroPerve's organizers agreed. But our show was horrible. We were doing a comedy show with mics and music, and we didn't get a sound check. When we started, the mics didn't work. Then the feedback started. It was humiliating, so we jumped to the end. For the finale, we'd rewritten our theater show's political musical number, "Don't Think," and called it "Think Kink." As I say it now, I have to admit: it was clearly a horrible idea. The whole thing was ridiculous, as it required a fetish crowd to pay attention to a comedy show in the middle of a sexy dance party.

Pep Rosenfeld: "Attention, perverts. Please enjoy the comedy stylings of Boom Chicago! Can someone please shout out the name of a style of literature? You there, stop groping each other." Truly awful.

Andrew Moskos: At least EuroPerve dressed us in these latex outfits. We looked great.

Pep Rosenfeld: After Greg finished Boom's show at the theater, he was going to join us at EuroPerve. He realized, though, that he didn't have an appropriate outfit. If you weren't wearing some kind of sexy, disturbing outfit, EuroPerve wouldn't let you in, so Greg came up with something on the fly.

We had a large plastic cactus next to the bar at Boom, so Greg started cutting out chunks of it. The big part he wore on his head like a helmet; then he fashioned a smaller cutout into a G-string, and added a cape. So off he went to EuroPerve, dressed as the new fetish superhero, Cactus Man. Apparently, however, EuroPerve's organizers were very disturbed by Greg's outfit. It freaked out the freaks. Greg really went all in: that's not show business, that's *show* business. I mean, would Greg have rocked an enormous cactus codpiece if he'd stayed in Chicago?

Andrew Moskos: Maybe. But in Amsterdam, everyone exhaled as part of the self-exploration the city forces you to make.

Ike Barinholtz: Clubbing is part of that self-exploration, and became a Boom Chicago tradition. It was social bonding, really. We were in our twenties, unleashed in Europe. We had to ask ourselves, *Do you want to be home all by yourself? Or would you rather be in the corner of a dance floor at six a.m.—completely out of your mind, sticking your face into bass cabinets surrounded by beautiful men and women with funny accents and all your best friends?* Andrew and Pep were pretty clear what their preference was.

Andrew Moskos: It's true. Do it. Try it. Grab it while you can, because who knows if you'll get another chance? That's what we told potential new performers when convincing them to come to Amsterdam. What have you got to lose? Skating on canals? *Yes, please!* Rapping onstage even though you're a suburban white improv comedian? *Ja hoor!* Going to fetish parties wearing a cactus codpiece? Why *niet?* To paraphrase Boom Chicago's advice to those attempting to take only half their Ecstasy tab, "Would you buy only half a plane ticket?"

Brendan Hunt: I can confirm this. After my first show at Boom, we went dancing to celebrate the new cast, and also because it was Seth and Jill's last show. We went around the corner to what I soon learned was the famous Amsterdam venue the Melkweg. At the club, someone offered me Ecstasy. I was like, "Um, I don't know. Maybe I'll take a half?" And then Andrew walks up and says, "Brendan, at Boom Chicago we take the whole pill." "All right, boss." Of course, Andrew's logic didn't actually make sense, but it was such a powerful charm. I'd never taken Ecstasy before that moment. I had a lot of room on the dance floor that night, and I took it. That would set the tone for the rest of my Amsterdam days.

Andrew Moskos: What it really comes down to is, in Amsterdam you've got to take the full ride. So if by some stroke of luck there's another Elfstedentocht in our lifetime, our advice is to do it.

Pep Rosenfeld: Well, unless it's *really* cold.

Seth Meyers: I was about to go home for Christmas, and I'd decided to not return for another season at Boom. Pete had already left early in October because he got cast by Second City.

Peter Grosz: Between getting hired by Boom and getting on a plane to Holland, I'd gotten an audition with Second City. Once I got to Amsterdam, I didn't really think about it. But some time later, Second City producer Kelly Leonard reached out to ask if I wanted to understudy. He needed me back in Chicago by October, before Second City's touring schedule heated up. When I told Pep, he was like, "That's cool. It's a good opportunity." I'd felt like I was just getting started: ultimately, it was nerve-racking to go to Boom—and then it was nerve-racking to leave and work my way up from the bottom at Second City. Seth and I had been such a tight unit: we were so close, we lived together, we loved each other so much. It was so great that we'd gotten to go through the Boom experience together—it bonded us even more. But once I got to Chicago, I had to stand on my own two feet a little bit, and that was good.

Seth Meyers: It was still in my head that joining Second City was what I wanted to do most in the world. That ambition—

combined with my best friend going back home to do just that—really reinforced that I was supposed to be back in Chicago. It had been a good run in Amsterdam, yet I started thinking I was ready to go. But Andrew's a salesman: ultimately, he just talked me into the idea that it was better to stay.

While thinking all this over, I went out really late one night with a bartender from Boom. I didn't know this bartender that well, but we all ended up at this strange apartment with his girl-friend and some of her friends. There was a turntable setup, and a bunch of weird plants everywhere—like, way too many ferns. There was just something romantic and weird about randomly hanging out with a guy whose name was something like Case, but spelled the wrong way, and girls with silent j's in their name. I vividly remember sitting there and thinking, *Well, this is so much more interesting than the bars in Chicago, where I'll see all the same people I've known forever all the time. So maybe I will stay awhile in this city full of young, beautiful people where everybody is interesting after all . . .*

CHAPTER 6
1998

GOLD MEDAL IN HANDBAG THROWING?
AMSTERDAM, THE WORLD'S GAYEST CITY,
HOSTS EUROPE'S FIRST-EVER GAY GAMES

A friend of ours—a prominent Dutch-Belgian professor of semiotics who's gay and married with a husband— was asked at an academic conference what he thought Hitler's impact on modern thought had been. After a moment of deep concentration, he leaned into his microphone and said, "The modern conflict is thus: of course I hate the Nazis—but I love the boots."

We like that story because our friend's gayness, and what that might mean about his love of stern-looking boots, is such a nonissue. That sums up Amsterdam's attitudes toward homosexuality and other totally normal proclivities that some Americans back home consider "alternative lifestyles." At Boom Chicago, we just call them "lifestyles."

Of course, we've had plenty of LGBTQIA+ at Boom Chicago: it's a *theater*, people! Add in some even more self-congratulatory Dutch tolerance and, jeez, the whole atmosphere is more provocatively decadent than Paul Verhoeven's early movies.[23] After a week or so in Amsterdam, actors coming to Boom discover what natives Ruben van der Meer, Horace Cohen, and

---

23 People, *Spetters*? Wow. I mean, that movie is like a Dutch version of *Kids*, or a pansexual small-town psychodrama version of *Spring Breakers* set against the Dutch motorcross minor leagues in the early 1980s? Wow.

Boom's queen bee Saskia Maas grew up knowing: who you sleep with is no big deal—be it men, women, or a large chunk of wood with a prominent glory hole known as a "Dutch wife," invented by Dutch merchants out of desperation after too many sexless months at sea. (Google "Dutch wife." We dare you.) Whatever you're into, in Amsterdam you can find people who are into that too, without shame.

Theater people generally prove more open-minded about such things. (Well, until #MeToo blew that myth apart, but we digress.) Basically, if you wanna get your freak on, join a theater. But if you wanna really find out what your inner freak is into, join a theater *in Amsterdam* and hang out for a couple of years. We've seen many émigrés embrace their true sexuality while living in Holland. Our favorite story, though, was when a Boom actor experimented a bit—only to discover his true self was exactly what he'd originally thought.

This dude, whom we'll call Jerry, is a great guy. Super funny. Very intellectual, in a most thoughtful way. Jerry *really thought* about things. A lot. And one idea that he'd gotten into his head was: *What if I'm gay? What if I've been lying to myself and not enjoying life to its fullest because I've been denying my true desires?* Knowing Jerry, these thoughts spawned from intellectual curiosity, not any discernible fire in his loins. It was as if Data from *Star Trek* wondered if he was gay. (Data was, after all, fully functional.)

So one night, Jerry goes off all by himself to a gay bar. Gay bars in the States can get pretty wild, but everything in Amsterdam is extra-super-double over the top—like the bar Jerry found himself in, nervously squinting to see what randy cocks were on offer. There was not much in the way of lighting. This was, after all, a very famous local gay bar, complete with darkrooms and glory holes. The walls were covered with prints by Tom of Finland, the iconic artist whose images influenced gay masculinity. The clientele, many in buttless leather chaps, matched the decor.

Ah, darkrooms . . . Our American actors used to be surprised during shows when Dutch people would shout out "Darkroom!" as a suggestion for a scene setting. In the States, a darkroom is where predigital photographers would develop celluloid film into photos via chemical processes. But in the Netherlands, a darkroom is where people go for anonymous, temporary sex. Uh, at least that's what we've been told.

Back to Jerry. Marching into the darkroom, he starts an anonymous, temporary sexual relationship with a male stranger. First the stranger fellates Jerry, and then it's Jerry's turn to return the favor. As Jerry put it so memorably, "The worst time to realize you're not gay is when there's a strange man's dick in your mouth." But at least that strange man's dick is in your mouth in Amsterdam—that's the moral of the story. If you gotta go there, do it here, where no one gives a fuck who you fuck. This was clear all the way back in 1995 in the corporate show where we accidentally outed the CEO of the conservative membership organization that hired us. Oops! It went a little something like this:

Andrew: For our final scene, we'd like to interview someone you all know. He's the head of the company that invited everyone here today and made this day possible. Let's bring up Joost! How are you?

CEO: Nervous.

Andrew: Give Joost a big round of applause to make him feel comfortable! We want to do a scene about you, so we have some questions. What do you like best about this organization?

CEO: I like the people I work with best.

Andrew: Good answer, Joost! What's something you don't like about your job?

CEO: The parking. [Joost gets cheers.]

Andrew: Okay! So, Joost, are you in a relationship?

CEO: Yes, I am.

Andrew: What's her name?

CEO: Uh . . . Peter.

All art really is political—even a corporate gig in Eindhoven. Of course, no one was super shocked, and Joost ended up being totally cool about it. More recently, Boom cast members Stacey Smith, Katie Nixon, and Terrance Lamont Jr. wrote the ironic soulful anthem "White Man's Metaverse" for our show "Meta Luck Next Time," where they imagined the future from a female, lesbian, and Black perspective. One of our most beloved Boom bits dealing with sexuality, though, was written by Boom cast member E.R. Fightmaster (currently starring on *Grey's Anatomy* as the show's first nonbinary major character). E.R. has always been out and proud, wearing their queerness like the rock star they are. E.R. wrote a great song about how dudes always want to talk to them after the show, and invariably they introduce E.R. to their girlfriends . . . and that doesn't often end well for said dudes.

Another cast member, Tarik Davis, wrote a memorable sketch dealing with sexuality and homophobia from a religious point of view. (Just for the record, Tarik's not gay, though he'd still be a swell guy if he was.) Tarik's sketch was perfect for the show it appeared in, "Bite the Bullet." Religion and terrorism were its big themes: Heather Anne Campbell wrote a great sketch about a conservative American FBI interrogator accidently finding common ground with a Muslim terrorist over their shared feelings about women's role in society and gay rights. "Bite the Bullet" topically addressed the "maybe there's been too much tolerance" backlash after Dutch filmmaker and political agitator Theo van Gogh was killed on an Amsterdam street—payback for his public anti-Muslim provocations. Tarik's piece, erm, *nailed* the provocative tensions of this moment perfectly and hilariously.

From "Bite the Bullet," 2005, by Tarik Davis

Dad: I came all the way over here. This better be good!

Son: Dad . . . I think I'm gay.

Dad: You can't be gay. You're a Christian.

Son: But can't I love guys and God?

Dad: Son, I think you ought to consult your bracelet and ask WWJD? [Exits stage left.]

Suzi: [Stage right] In recent years, a born-again Christian mother in the US created a bracelet that said, WWJD. It stands for What Would Jesus Do?—implying that Christians should ask themselves that question whenever faced with big decisions. Now over 4.5 million kids in America wear these bracelets. And the Christian clothing industry makes over three billion dollars a year.

Son: What would Jesus do?

[Choir music plays. Jesus enters through center arch.]

Son: Jesus!

Jesus: Hey, baby. So you're gay, huh?

Son: Yeah.

Jesus: That's cool.

Son: That's cool? The Bible says it's wrong.

Jesus: The Bible? Man, I'm only in half that thing. Besides, at least four or five of my apostles were gay. C'mon, they were guys who wore dresses and left their wives to go camping with twelve other guys. One time while bathing, Judas tried to stab me in the back . . . And I'm not talking with a knife.

Son: Wow. So, Jesus, in regards to being gay—if you were me, what would you do?

Jesus: Well, I'd do like I did when I was in a cave. Wait three days, then come out.

In Amsterdam, one can talk openly about religion and homo-sexuality—well, unless you're Theo van Gogh. The city prides itself on its longstanding tolerance for those who are "other": other countries, other sexual lifestyles, other religions. That's why in 1998, the city proudly hosted the first international Gay Games—the largest LGBT+ sporting event in the world, taking place every four years, now with thirteen thousand participants.

In the beginning, the Gay Games served as an Olympic torch for tolerance. For a few weeks, gay culture moved out of dark-rooms and into the Olympic stadium. It was even on TV, show-ing gay people doing something else besides sex and partying.

This was the front line: Amsterdam was the first location outside North America to host the Gay Games, and the whole city embraced it. The Netherlands would also become the first country in the world to legalize gay marriage, years before it was recognized in the US—more proof that Holland leads the United States in almost every way . . .

Michael Diederich: Just before the Gay Games started, it was announced that Holland would be the first country in the world to allow gay marriage. We were super excited. Making it into a major event, Amsterdam's five-star Krasnapolsky Hotel was turned into a huge wedding location complete with hair, makeup, and dresses (mostly worn by men). And I was asked to officiate! Over nearly five hours one evening, I "married" more than 450 couples. It wasn't truly official, but the tears in the eyes of many participants made it real for me. I couldn't have been more proud.

Heather Anne Campbell: When I came to Boom, gay marriage still wasn't legal yet in America, and there were no lesbian bars in Los Angeles. It felt liberating moving to Amsterdam where there actually *were* lesbian bars and nobody gave a shit if you were gay. The Dutch truly didn't care: after an initial "Oh wow—this is nice!" impression, in the Netherlands one's sexuality just becomes invisible and you stop thinking about it. After that, going back to America felt even more repressive. Everyone was still up in each other's business about what people do in the privacy of their own homes. It's one of the worst facets of American identity. I mean, California voted to make gay marriage *illegal* in 2008. I'd returned from a place where nobody cares if you hold hands with a girl on the street to *that*.

Ruben van der Meer: When the Gay Games came to Amsterdam, these two Dutch comics, Theo and Thea, did a genius sketch about it on their TV show. It was a show for children, but so subversive adults watched it too. Theo and Thea's sketch featured them as Gay Games's organizers planning the event's premier competition: handbag throwing. It was so funny, especially because Theo and Thea are gay in real life. If two heterosexuals would have done this, it might've been less cool.

Andrew Moskos: One interesting thing was seeing gay athletes from other countries where homosexuality was not as accepted acclimating to Amsterdam. They couldn't believe that you could just walk down any street here as a couple, not just in gay neighborhoods. I remember one athlete from Eastern Europe saying he'd never kissed his boyfriend in a restaurant before, but he did in Amsterdam. To him, it was like walking on the moon.

Greg Shapiro: There's always been a strong gay culture in Amsterdam—not just gay bars and clubs, but gay film festivals, academic conferences . . . There's also the Homomonument, a public tax-supported monument paying tribute to those persecuted in the LBGTQIA+ community.

Andrew Moskos: Not a lot of countries put their tax revenues where their mouth is when it comes to gay rights and equality. Amsterdam was also one of the first cities to market its gayness to tourists around the world: *This is a gay-friendly city. You're perfectly welcome here, and you won't get arrested or beat up.*

Horace Cohen: Business is business: money isn't gay or straight. Ruben and I came to understand this while growing up in the Jordaan neighborhood next to the Red Light District on the Singel.

Ruben van der Meer: When I was in kindergarten, I'd go over to the Red Light District and look at sex shops. Seeing prostitutes standing around in lingerie, I'd go talk to them. After summer vacation, my mother walked me to school for the first day of first grade. All the prostitutes waved to me, yelling, "Hey, Ruben, how are you?" My mother asked me, "How do these women know your name?" "Oh, I fetch them cigarettes and magazines and they give me money to buy candy," I told her.

Andrew Moskos: Amsterdam is a sex-positive city, period. As someone once said, it's a great city for homosexuals, but it's really just great for *sexuals*.

Horace Cohen: Growing up, we'd see this guy skating around the city, always Rollerblading everywhere in his thong bikini, leather jacket, and really tanned legs.

Rob AndristPlourde: And his name was Greg Shapiro.

Andrew Moskos: *[Laughs.]*

Rob AndristPlourde: I also remember the G-string rope guy—an older gentleman who'd do amateur acrobatics on the Leidseplein square in his gold-lamé G-string, which even then had seen better days.

Andrew Moskos: He was actually a teacher in Haarlem who taught math to elementary school kids. Can you believe that? In America, a teacher could not swing around in a shiny-gold G-string in the town square.

Greg Shapiro: I was pleasantly surprised to learn that, in many ways, Holland was more civilized and advanced than what I was used to in the States. I call this phenomenon "culture shock therapy," where you're forced to realize that this European lifestyle is just better in so many ways than what you grew up with.

Saskia Maas: 1998, meanwhile, proved to be a big year for Boom Chicago. Until then, we only played in the summer—but as our Dutch audience was growing, we wanted to start playing in the real theater season.

Andrew Moskos: The guy we'd been renting from on the Lijnbaansgracht was happy we filled his space and sold lots of Grolsch beer during summer, but he had his own dinner-theater concept for older people with singers and classical music during the regular season. He kicked us out, and then his dream project closed two months later.

Luckily, the reps from Heineken were big Boom fans and regular customers. One night they literally said, "Hey, we love the show, but you're serving the wrong beer." We were like, "Funny you say that, because we need a new theater." They had this old disco around the corner that was available. It was a perfect space, with a bar in the front and a theater area in the back—and right on the Leidseplein, Amsterdam's biggest square. It was bigger than our other venues too, with capacity for 270 customers.

Up to then, it was known as the Cash Disco—a classless joint whose business relied on unsuspecting tourists from less cool places outside Amsterdam. The owner went bankrupt when he opened up a jazz-club steakhouse in then-sleepy Amsterdam North. This project failed massively, killing his entire empire. Today, of course, the north is a funky hotspot. Luckily for us, he was twenty years ahead of his time.

Pep Rosenfeld: When we visited the Cash, it was weird: the place had clearly been abandoned abruptly. There were empty glasses on the tables, cigarette butts in the ashtrays. But the Cash Disco's demise was especially bad news for the fish floating dead in the aquarium.

Andrew Moskos: Sure, the Cash needed lots of work, and the filthy crap in there would fill many dumpsters, but we saw a future there. Unfortunately, we were Americans in our twenties with zero capital. Why would Heineken take a chance on us? Big chains with deeper pockets and proven track records like TGI Fridays and Planet Hollywood were eyeing the same space. Planet Hollywood especially seemed a better bet than Boom Chicago—a Hard Rock Cafe–style restaurant decorated with movie memorabilia, with Arnold Schwarzenegger, Sylvester Stallone, and Bruce Willis as celebrity investor-ambassadors who'd gladhand at openings. The franchise promised Hollywood glamour—but there was no glamour, no atmosphere, and zero interest from locals. Looking back, it was a ridiculous concept: overpriced American food made in a production kitchen from frozen ingredients, served in front of movie-prop replicas? *Gross.* Still, Planet Hollywood had opened in every serious city, and now they wanted one in Amsterdam.

Regardless, we went to Heineken HQ to make Boom Chicago's case. In our presentation to Heineken's operations team, we explained that Boom Chicago was actually the safe choice. Not only did we have youthful creativity, drive, and new ideas, we planned to be in Amsterdam longer than Planet Hollywood ever would. The corporate types bought our line, and went with us to the bank to guarantee our loan.

Pep Rosenfeld: For the record, Boom Chicago *did* outlast Planet Hollywood. They opened a year later across from the famous Tuschinski cinema, then closed after three years. Meanwhile, still in our twenties, we were now working with the most iconic Dutch brand in the world and moving Boom to the Leidseplein—the busiest nightlife area in the Netherlands.

Greg Shapiro: For the last show in the old Lijnbaansgracht space, Andrew got onstage to address the audience: "Ladies and gentlemen, this is our last show here. So, do you want to be part of Boom Chicago history? Okay, fantastic! Stand up, grab a chair or a table or two, and let's walk them across the square to our new theater." Andrew convinced a paying audience to move all the tables and chairs to Boom's new space. It was hilarious.

Pep Rosenfeld: Andrew's ability to convince anyone to do anything is the secret sauce behind Boom's success. It was like watching Tom Sawyer getting his friends to pay him to paint the fence. Actually, I'm pretty sure Andrew could convince Tom Sawyer to paint *his* fence.

Saskia Maas: We did a few weeks of extra shows in the Cash to meet demand. We owned the fact that the space was a work in progress. We put up a sign saying, *If it looks like an exposed electrical wire, don't touch it, because it probably is.* Then we closed to build the Cash space into a proper theater—insane, unfamiliar territory.

Holly Walker: Boom's new Leidseplein theater had a magnificent location—straight-up Gucci. There were outdoor cafés, the Melkweg and Paradiso at arm's length, the International Theater Amsterdam, shopping, a jazz club, a casino . . . and Boom Chicago right in the heart of it. It was exciting. I recall slapping black paint on the walls with Ken *minutes* before the grand opening.

Saskia Maas: For the first time, we had to hire full-time, year-round people. Not just actors—bar and restaurant people too.

Pep Rosenfeld: Dutch people back then didn't understand service. Waiters were mean and inattentive. A bartender would slowly empty the dishwasher as you watched instead of getting your beer. It was actually hard to find people who enjoyed serving customers.

Seth Meyers: The Dutch made fun of American service as fake friendly, but I'll take fake American service over Dutch service where your waiter will let you know how bad a day they're having.

Andrew Moskos: It's so much better now. People travel more and know what good service is. Customers have gotten more demanding, and business owners got smarter too. But then, cafés were literally full of people with empty glasses trying to flag down waiters who just couldn't, or wouldn't, hustle. If you challenged waiters about this practice, they'd always snap back that they were understaffed—as if that was your fault, not their manager's fault. What was funniest to us was that restaurant/bar owners had this strange attitude that attentive service was sort of inhumane and somehow not *gezellig*. But there's nothing cozy about not getting the drink you ordered an hour earlier and having to stop your conversation with your friends to flag down a grumpy and harried server.

Pep Rosenfeld: Dutch waiters would straight-up ignore you in restaurants. They would literally pretend not to see you. They thought that was "keeping it real": *If I serve you too much, I am demeaning myself.* If you go to someone's house and your drink is empty, the host always pours you another glass of wine—because, of course, that's hospitable. But somehow, in Dutch bars in those days, no one thought that bars or restaurants were supposed to be hospitable. It was like the cliché of French service, without the French cuisine.

Saskia Maas: This made it especially challenging to hire the right people. We could find order takers, drink deliverers, check bringers, sure—but people who cared for the guest's experience were hard to find. Furthermore, you have to think very carefully before hiring anyone, since by law it's so hard to fire them in Holland. Plus, everyone hires one *less* person than they actually need just to be safe, so they don't have one extra person they don't need. Employees don't always realize the downside of contracts that are sometimes *too* strong.

Ruben van der Meer: Before we move on, let's return for a bit to the old Cash Disco.

Andrew Moskos: First off, as it was called the Cash, the design theme was money. It was like the worst of America: next to the big Statue of Liberty was a painting of a huge thousand-dollar bill. It aspired to be the kind of place where *Scarface*'s Tony Montana would go, but without the money, women, or drugs. Once we got in, the first order of business was to gut the building. Ken Schaefle led a team with a goal he wrote on the wall: *Disco out. Theater in.* It was a three-month demolition project. We took the whole space down to the studs, removing every bit of wiring, tubes, and plumbing. We tore out stairwells, and yanked the balcony down too. We buried the fish.

Peter Grosz: When I left, it was the end of an era for Boom Chicago and the beginning of a new one. 1998 was the start of a huge jump for Boom. The cast was becoming bigger and more inclusive, with more performers of color and more women. People started sticking around Amsterdam longer too, getting better as performers and finding their own style. There were talented people who'd come before, sure—but this was the moment when the Boom cast started filling up with people who'd go on to do big stuff in their future careers.

Rob AndristPlourde: When we opened a few months later, our first shows were "Think Quick" and "Everything's Going to Be All Right—and Other Lies." The cast continued to expand with talents like Holly Walker and Josh Meyers, Seth's brilliantly funny (and much more Euro) younger brother. Joining them were director Sue Peale, musician Jon Schickedanz, Jethro Nolen, and Kristy Entwistle (later Nolen). Josie was promoted to artistic director, and that was also the first year John Stoops and Jill Benjamin were hired for the cast.

Josie O'Reilly: Jill Benjamin made people *scream* with laughter. She was unique, and just so bold in her work with Seth.

Rob AndristPlourde: John and Jill invented a game called Krayons—the most unpredictable of all "Heineken Late Night" games. The device was an excuse to elicit horrible stories from this unhappy, toxic married couple, Tony and Jackie Krayon. Tony and Jackie always started the game as happily married; by the end, they'd be screaming at each other and berating the audience for their "bad" suggestions. They would become really mean, then calm each other down—and then get even more mean to each other and the audience.

Greg Shapiro: It was like the Boom Chicago version of *Who's Afraid of Virginia Woolf?*

Rob AndristPlourde: Seth Meyers took over the role as Tony Krayon and really made it his own. He and Jill had magical chemistry. The sketch only didn't work once, when we took it to the Edinburgh Festival. Edinburgh had this ugly late-night show called "Late'n'Live," which attracted an audience that was notorious for brutal heckling. We thought, *Krayons will be mean enough for this mean audience. They will shout at the crowd, and they will love it.*

Andrew Moskos: But by three a.m., the "Late'n'Live" audience was like, *What is this happy, friendly American shite?* If the bit had been able to go all the way, it would've been perfect, but it requires a bit of patience to get to its full blaze of anger and bile. Seth and Jill were supposed to be up there for fifteen minutes, but they only lasted two. Seth said that was the one time where he was onstage and realized, *Shit, I can't smile my way out of this one.*

Pep Rosenfeld: I always wondered if their marriage failed because Tony Krayon was secretly gay.

Rob AndristPlourde: In the real world, Michael Diederich was our first out gay cast member.

Michael Diederich: For years, I was the only gay guy at Boom. I actually found out about Jerry's darkroom experience immediately. I'd just arrived at that gay club when someone I knew came out and said, "I didn't know Jerry was gay." I knew about his gay experiment before he'd unlocked his bike.

Heather Anne Campbell: When I got to Boom, Tim Sniffen, Suzi, and I were like the gay people in the cast representing gay people in the sketches. I was totally out to everybody there, but I still wasn't, like, out on the Internet yet.

Suzi Barrett: I never dated a Dutch person during my time at Boom, but there was lots of romance between bar staff and players. I fell for an Australian girl who was Boom's waitstaff manager. We were in love, and ended up moving back to America together.

Brendan Hunt: Amsterdam is where you discover who you really are, and then you're accepted and supported for being that person.

Andrew Moskos: Indoctrinating the Euro-ness into unsuspecting young American actors is one of the best things Boom does. You might find out you're the kind of guy who's maybe not gay, but still likes to wear vintage lavender pants with puffy pink shirts bought from Zipper on the Nieuwe Hoogstraat. Take Josh Meyers. Josh was maybe always going to be an early adopter of, say, orange skinny jeans. But Seth Meyers wouldn't have ever worn tighter trousers if he hadn't become an Amsterdam local.

Pep Rosenfeld: Seth did get more Euro at Boom. I mean, everyone shifts at least one notch over. Maybe Pittsburgh Steelers football fan Seth learned to swing a little left here, which helped turn him into, you know . . . Seth Meyers.

Rob AndristPlourde: That transformation was helped along by our shows at the Edinburgh Festival Fringe, which really gave us an international profile. 1998 was the first year Boom went to the Fringe, and we just *killed*. We really laid waste to it. It was amazing.

The Fringe is huge, with about a thousand shows every day spread across any room that could be turned into a theater venue. There is no creative committee selecting the best shows, or guaranteeing money for performers. You just find a venue, pay for a listing in the guide, and voilà—you're in the festival. The pessimist's view is that most Fringe shows are bad; the optimist's view is you never know what gem you're going to find. And then word of mouth spreads about said gems, and you have conversations like this in a pub: "I saw this great show called "Are You Dan Gorman?" This comedian Dan Gorman went around the world to talk to other guys named Dan Gorman, and they were all weird. It's on daily at two p.m. above a pet store."

That first year, the city's premier critic, the *Scotsman*'s Kate Copstick, gave Boom's show five stars. Our reputation, combined.with active street promotions, meant that the show even turned a profit—something nearly unheard of at the Fringe. We were inspired by the creativity all around us. Andrew saw an Edinburgh show by Simon Munnery, an alternative comedian who was political and surreal in his freeform approach. Unusually, Simon used video screens while triggering images of himself in the show. Around the same time, the high-tech Blue Man Group opened its show. Theirs wasn't a comedy show per se, but it used multimedia to make funny points about technology, fame, art, and more. Blue Man Group's energetic finale with club lights and strips and strips of unrolling paper to the tune of "I Feel Love" was a religion-less religious experience. Andrew wanted to bring that energy to Boom.

Andrew Moskos: Live comedy, until then, was still a low-tech operation. In London, the Comedy Store Players played in an unglamorous basement with low ceilings. Our inspiration, Second City, had a dumpy sound system, an old-time piano player to set the mood, and a set that consisted solely of chairs placed around the stage.

Rob AndristPlourde: Andrew was excited and inspired to use technology in the show. Boom Chicago already had a technical whiz in Ken Schaefle, who could bring this new thinking to life. With Steven Svymbersky, a second technician, they fitted the theater with large screens, as well as the ability to pull images and video from the Internet and edit them in real time. On the rig, they added club lighting, smoke machines, and a water-cooled laser.

Josie O'Reilly: Tech was always what differentiated Boom's shows from so many other crappy improv shows around the world.

Ruben van der Meer: Boom brought multimedia into comedy in such a fresh way. I tried to explain to the *De Lama's* technicians that I wanted to do something similar, but they didn't get it. They could never do it like Boom with video, sound, music intros, digital backdrops, green screen effects . . . That was really amazing.

Horace Cohen: Steven became a real artist in the tech space. They called him "The Wizard."

Rob AndristPlourde: What Ken and Steven did was so crucial. They made the shows look great, and it was they who timed the ends of improv scenes. They actually determined the pacing for the show.

Brendan Hunt: The improv games we'd do in Boom shows had a rhythm and wavelength that the technicians had to be in on—something that Boom was very sophisticated with. These techs didn't just have a lighting board where they brought up faders on sound cues: they were improvising right along with the actors. It's an art to get stuff up on screen in seconds to anticipate and accentuate punch lines we were making up on the spot.

Ruben van der Meer: The technicians had to be comedians themselves to know when those moments happened.

Rob AndristPlourde: One of the best scenes I ever saw involved Steven versus Josh Meyers. We had a game where the cast froze, and whoever froze last had to perform solo to continue the scene, with a song improvised on the spot. One night, the suggestion for that particular scene was "bad technicians." The scene became about rivalry between the actors and the tech team. Josh started to sing, *"Oh, tech, I don't need you . . ."* So Steven took his mic out of the mix. And then Josh sang, *"But I can sing louder . . ."* So Steven pumped up the music to drown him out.

And then Josh goes, *"But I can still be onstage."* So Steven cut off the lights. It was a brilliant tennis match.

Brendan Hunt: As soon as something interesting and cool became vaguely technically accessible, Steven and Ken and Boom incorporated it—video editing, the Internet, digital libraries of music and sound effects, using Macs as controllers . . . Andrew always pushed for the latest state-of-the-art tech. He always wants Boom to be as high-tech as possible because that's what he likes himself.

Pep Rosenfeld: The coolest use of our amazing technical bells and whistles was for internal stuff. Don't get me wrong—the way we use it in shows is fantastic. But Steven's *Jesus Christ Superstar?* That's why lasers, lights, and smoke machines were created.

Jason Sudeikis: Somewhere, somehow it came up that mine and Jordan's favorite musical was *Jesus Christ Superstar*. Steven Svymbersky was like, "Me too! I love that thing so much." He'd listened to *Jesus Christ Superstar* with headphones every Easter for years—but now that he had this theater, Steven did a *Jesus Christ Superstar* light show once a year, only for himself. He'd get baked and play the soundtrack as loud as he could in that theater, which had a remarkable sound system. Then he'd use all the tricks and the lights and lasers and smoke.

I was like, "That sounds amazing!" So Steven says, "Hey, I want to give you a Christmas gift." So Brendan, Jordan, Svymbersky, and I met up at Boom at eleven a.m. on December 24. Brendan and I took mushrooms, while Jordan smoked a giant joint all by himself in, like, two puffs. And then it starts: *"Down, down, down, down, down . . ."* Steven knew that musical probably as well as Andrew Lloyd Webber, and he knew that light board better than anybody else.

The show Steven put on that day blew all of our minds. Like, each light would have a *personality*. *That* light was Jesus . . . There was this smoke . . . I mean, we were all going through something together, with lots of tears and smiling. During "Everything's All Right," I looked over to Jordan. He and I had this catchphrase: we'd say, "Boy, a lot of stuff going on out there, huh?" So, I leaned over to Jordan and said it. He just nodded, looked at me, and said, "Dude, I just quit smoking. Right this second, I quit smoking cigarettes." And I believe that literally for the rest of his Boom journey, Jordan stopped smoking. He quit because everything was made all right from that experience.

It was a profound gift that Steven gave us that day, and I look back on it fondly. And every time I'm brought back to that moment, I smile knowing we only could have experienced it because of the opportunity that Boom Chicago afforded each one of the four of us by hiring and trusting us with their incredibly odd idea. I'm so proud to have benefited from it, and hopefully in some way they benefited from me.

Steven Svymbersky: You're welcome, Jason. I'm just glad we had video then. In 1999, we added screens. Jamie Wright was a bartender at Boom, but he had a background in video. We brought him up to the tech bridge and he'd operate cameras and edit in real time. Jamie became our first video director. No one was doing much of that at the time: it felt innovative, and I learned a lot from him.

Andrew Moskos: Things that were amazing back then have become normal. Boom's groundbreaking tech is a part of many comedy shows now. It was similar to how social trends played out. Where Amsterdam was once a leader in the gay scene, now most big cities have a vibrant gay scene too. Even Warsaw has a gay pride parade these days.[24] Every city has sort

---

24 But Amsterdam's is still special. In the 2022 gay pride boat parade, the police

of come 70 percent as far as Amsterdam's tolerance was in the '90s.

While less gay cities have gotten gayer, gayer cities like Amsterdam have gotten less gay. The Internet and apps took away some of the gay social scene. Today you don't need to go to bars to get laid: you can just swipe right on Grindr. In the meantime, gay culture merged with straight culture. Gay people go to every bar, club, and restaurant, not just gay clubs, bars, and restaurants. Young people are more fluid—pretty much everything is mixed now, so there's less need for those celebratory safe havens which Amsterdam had first in the world.

Perhaps it's a testament to how far we've come that the gay scene is less fabulous and more *gewoon* ("ordinary") today. The current danger is that freedom and tolerance could actually lead to tolerating intolerance. There's anti-gay feeling growing that seems to have gotten stronger, even in supposedly tolerant Netherlands. Even Amsterdam has its backsliding moments, and it's not just directed at gay people. Some hurl anti-gay slurs at adversaries regardless if they're gay or not. What's the right response for a straight person? Saying, "No, I'm not gay" gives credence to a world where such insults are fair if the recipient *were* gay.

Pep Rosenfeld: I'm a big believer in, "I see where this is going, and I'm flattered. But no thank you, I'm a married man."

Andrew Moskos: Oooh, not bad. I have the best one, though. One day, in a familiar taxi-versus-bike disagreement, a driver speaking broken English called me a "fagger." I slapped him across the face and growled, "The word is *faggot*." When the driver bounded out of his car, he accidentally put the taxi in reverse—and then backed into a scooter, knocking it down. The

---

had their own boat—and as their boat filled with dancing cops floated past on the canal, the LGBTQ-heavy crowd of thousands cheered them. And no, not because they thought it was a surprise appearance by the Village People . . .

scooter driver was bigger, muscular, and angrier than me—and perhaps gay. That situation replaced my beef, and I biked away victoriously. I felt like I'd won a gold medal for homophobic taxi-driver slapping. If only that had been a sport at the '98 Gay Games . . .

Pep Rosenfeld: Really, Andrew—you gotta work on your hand-bag throwing.

CHAPTER 7
1999

SO RUUD: THE YEAR THE DUTCH INVENTED REALITY TV (PLUS FUNNY STORIES ABOUT IKE BARINHOLTZ)

I f you haven't noticed yet, an obvious subtheme (to us, anyway) of the Boom Chicago origin story is that we discovered that the Dutch were consistently a decade or more ahead of their American counterparts in many key areas of globalization and contemporary progress:

Stock market? *Check.*

Outlawing slavery? *Check.*

Sensible drug policy? *Check.*

Gay marriage? *Check.*

Bike infrastructure? *Check*

Euthanasia laws? *Check.*

Reality television? *Check.*

Reality television, you say? Why, reality television seems as innately, trashily American as, you know, *Jersey Shore* or *Keeping Up with the Kardashians.* The feudin' families and cheatin' husbands getting lunged at by wives, mistresses, and secret baby mamas on the infamous *Jerry Springer Show* seemed as born in the USA as Bruce Springsteen's ass in front of an American flag—a precursor to the 2000s' reality-TV future schlock.

Well, Jerry Springer *was* American, but his was still a standard-format talk show. There was a titular host. There were guests. And boy, did they talk. Sure, Springer's guests sometimes descended into physical violence, but that was why they had Steve the bouncer. Jerry ran the show: he asked the questions, gave his opinions, and ended the show with his final thoughts. It was captivating and shocking for its time. Jerry Springer had become a lightning rod for many issues swirling around in 1999—signaling a serious decline in Western civilization at the dawn of the millennium. Not for nothing did Boom Chicago title that year's main show "Two Thousand Years Down the Drain: From Jesus Christ to Jerry Springer."

But the topics and "reality" of Jerry Springer were nothing compared to the moment ushered in by the 1999 debut of the most influential reality-TV phenomenon of all time, *Big Brother*. And although many infamous international reality-TV formats would bubble up over the following decades, as with so many things, the Dutch got there first. *Big Brother* would go on to be a ratings blockbuster all over the world—but it was first conceived by Dutch TV powerhouse Endemol. In the Netherlands, *Big Brother* aired on the commercial network groovily named Veronica. For the record, we think more TV networks should have names like Veronica, Esmerelda, Shakira, etc., but that's a subject for Boom Chicago's next book, *She's a She: Ships, TV Networks, and Old-School Hurricanes*.

Big Brother removed the host and just left the degenerates. Soon enough, this template would define a whole new television genre. The concept of *Big Brother* was both simple and futuristic: stick a bunch of eccentric personalities together in a mansion, don't let them leave, film all of it, and then give the last man/woman standing 250,000 guilders. (Yes, guilders: back then, a quarter of a million guilders was about equivalent to 150,000 euros, or approximately $154,000 today.) In a nod to the millennial Internet era dawning, *Big Brother* proved one of the first pop-culture mainstays outside of porn to exploit the web's ability to stream surveillance video 24/7 to an increasingly computer-bound public.

From George Orwell's *1984*, *Big Brother* borrowed both its title and concept of an omnipotent all-seeing eye invading the populace's privacy—so much so, the Orwell estate sued Veronica (and won a still-undisclosed major settlement). To be fair, *Big Brother* borrowed more from Aldous Huxley's *Brave New World*. The chatty, back-stabbing inhabitants of the *Big Brother* house were psyched about the cameras' presence. This was less "The Party wants me to believe 2+2=5" and more "Me minus these other assholes=250,000 guilders. Let's party!" And after *Big Brother*'s first-season finale in which contestant Bart defeated rival contestant Ruud, we were introduced to another unfortunate new concept: the reality television star.

While *Jerry Springer's* reality made for lurid, revolting, oddly compelling television, it was over in forty-five minutes plus commercial breaks. But after TV viewers spent a season with the formerly nobody cast of *Big Brother* twenty-four hours a day, the contestants really did become famous in Holland. First-season winner Bart Spring in 't Veld (try saying that three times) couldn't handle his newfound fame, resulting in numerous breakdowns during his post–*Big Brother* existence. "*Big Brother* stole my life," became Bart's stock refrain. The show's obnoxious runner-up, the aptly named Ruud, continued his *Big Brother* persona in real life (or was it vice versa?). Ruud partied incessantly in public—behaving badly in the Leidseplein's tackiest celebrity-worshiping temples to the delight of *Privé* magazine readers across the Netherlands.

After *Big Brother* opened the reality-TV Pandora's box, we've been forced to live through a couple decades of absolute shit reality television posing as actual culture. And once again . . . the Netherlands was there first. *American Idol*? Had it in Holland as *Idols*. *The Voice*, meanwhile, was developed from *The Voice of Holland,* a staple of Dutch TV before Gwen Stefani ever sat in one of those spinning black-and-red thrones. We have the Netherlands to blame for all that crap. Uh, *bedankt?*

Ike Barinholtz: You didn't have to speak Dutch to see that *Big Brother* and the new reality shows were much bigger in Holland and Europe at first, before they caught on everywhere else.

Joe Canale: Ruud was the star of *Big Brother* in Holland. He never wore a shirt and was a party dude; basically, he was a lot like a Dutch Ike Barinholtz. I might add Dutch public-access television is the weirdest fucking shit I've ever seen. I once saw a show there featuring a guy hitting a stuffed bird against glass for ten minutes. That was the whole concept: smacking a dead bird up against glass. That's more than a little bit weird, okay?

Brendan Hunt: I didn't really watch Dutch TV at all because I didn't learn the language that first year. Andrew would just come in and explain what these new shows *Big Brother* and *Survivor* were about, and then say, "Okay, let's make a sketch about them."

Greg Shapiro: Boom tapped into the zeitgeist bubbling around us. *Big Brother*'s first season coincided with the show we were doing at the time, "Two Thousand Years Down the Drain: From Jesus Christ to Jerry Springer." We had a bit in it where Jesus and Mary appeared as guests on *The Jerry Springer Show*. It was like, "This is not your real son, Mary. Get the hell out of here, you slut!" Then security would violently eject Mary from the stage.

Andrew Moskos: At the time, Jerry Springer was the apostle of this new, violently divisive reality television. That was a deep realization for me at the time: it wasn't a coincidence that all this had been marinating while the *Big Brother* phenomenon exploded around us. *Big Brother* was truly symbolic of that era: the whole theme of everything that year was, *You've given up* *your privacy to cameras and the Internet.* In today's world, it would feel utterly normal, but back then we were just getting used to having cameras everywhere.

A couple funny things in the show spoke to this. We hid a camera behind a two-way mirror where people stood in line for the show. Assuming it was a normal one-way mirror, audience members absent-mindedly played with their teeth and picked their noses while we recorded the whole thing. We'd then quickly edit it together and reveal it during the show. It was so funny—people hadn't seen anything like that before.

We also had a scene where Josh Meyers would go onto the Leidseplein square and pretend to be a busker, singing songs with acoustic guitars. As people gathered around, the actors would improvise with people in the crowd who didn't know that all the while an audience in a nearby theater was watching their every move, laughing away.

Pep Rosenfeld: Before the show, we'd videotape two audience members talking in a booth. Then we'd play it back on video screens—but with us having redubbed their dialogue with our own. Solid bit.

Ike Barinholtz: What's great was that partying was part of our job description. At Boom Chicago, you're not just encouraged but *contractually obliged* to hang out at the bar and drink with audience members after shows. That's so Andrew. Those guys are so smart. I didn't think anything of it when they told me that, but once I started doing it, I understood how important that little twist was.

Seth Meyers: Let me make something very clear: even if he wasn't contractually obligated to do so, Ike still would have been at the bar.

Ike Barinholtz: It was so great mingling with audiences at Boom because we'd get the opposite reactions we'd get in Chicago. If you do a bad show in America, people are like, "Yeah, it was great." But those honest Dutch people . . . Dude, sometimes they'd be like, "I didn't enjoy the show tonight. There were a couple of good moments, and the Black man was very funny. But when you sang a song at the end, it was not successful." Their honesty made you want to do better.

Holly Walker: Dutch honesty *is* shocking. A Dutch woman who worked at Boom once bluntly asked me, "How old are you?" I said, "Thirty-two." She responded, "Shouldn't you have babies by now?" *Ha!* A Dutch man, whom I consider a good friend, said to me at Boom's twenty-fifth-anniversary celebration, "You looked better the last time I saw you. Are you unemployed?" *Hahahaha!* They're truly not being rude—that's just how they are.

Ike Barinholtz: I had such a great support system with Josh, Brendan, and everyone. And then, halfway through the year, we got reinforcements with the arrival of Liz Cackowski, who was amazing. Right away she became one of our besties, and was so great onstage.

Josie O'Reilly: Liz Cackowski, Brendan Hunt, and Josh Meyers were the most reliable, consistent performers. They could do any scene, always hit the mark, and got better at everything the longer they stayed.

Ike Barinholtz: Playing with them changed me so much as a performer, especially those first weeks where I was not good. They were really nurturing, and that turned me into who I am. I grew up thinking I wanted to be a politician. But when I got to college, I just started like, I don't know . . . doing drugs, watching movies all day—all the things that prepare you for a beautiful life.

Jordan Peele: Man, you're preaching to the choir here.

Ike Barinholtz: We were all very young when we were first in Amsterdam, so we were just *unbreakable*. We could do a show, go out to a club, do some pure MDMA, dance for six hours, go watch a movie at someone's apartment, fall asleep, and then go do another show. We just got right back up and did it again. So I love Boom Chicago. I love Brendan Hunt. They saved me, in their way. And while Seth was technically no longer at Boom, he wasn't yet at *SNL*, and hadn't totally cut the cord. We were actually there just in time to catch Seth and Jill's last night performing as members of the cast, which was both so inspiring and humbling. We were basically replacing them, and we had our work cut out for us.

Joe Canale: Seth was doing "Pick Ups & Hiccups" at the time. It was like a dating show, where Seth and Jill went through all these hilarious dating scenarios. "Pick Ups & Hiccups" is really what pushed Seth into other, bigger things.

Seth Meyers: "Pick Ups & Hiccups" with Jill Benjamin was the last thing I did at Boom, at the very beginning of '99. I love it: it's classic to me.

Kay Cannon: I wanted to own the stage the way Jill Benjamin did. Getting hired by Boom was why I had to get my first passport! Arriving in Amsterdam, I remember being incredibly nervous, jet-lagged, and thinking that everyone was so tall and beautiful. Then I walked into the Boom theater on the Leidseplein, got a huge hug from Ike, met the rest of the cast, and my nerves calmed.

Rob AndristPlourde: Around this time, Boom did a bit in the show where we recreated the *Big Brother* house onstage and had the audience vote us off.

Andrew Moskos: 1999 really ended up being not just the moment Kay arrived, Ike found himself, and Seth finally left the building—it was also year zero for reality television as we think of it today. *Big Brother* spawned all of what was to come next in this realm. *The Voice of Holland* would be made into a series of successful spin-offs around the world. This was now a global phenomenon. Everyone watched their country's version of *The Voice*, which made it easy to make fun of.

Rob AndristPlourde: Our riff on *Big Brother* proved to be comedy heaven. What made it great was all these Boom alphas in the cast flexing onstage and letting their competitive streaks come out. Ike and Josh could get pretty physical; add in the arrival of Jason Sudeikis later that year, and they'd freak out the audience in their masculine quest to get the most laughs. I just remember whenever Jason Sudeikis would play in the *Big Brother* house, competing against his charisma and charm was futile.

Greg Shapiro: Sudeikis's *Big Brother* bits were amazing. Toward the end of '99, Jason had been coming out a lot to be with his fiancée, Kay Cannon. He wasn't a cast member yet, but it was destiny.

Jason Sudeikis: Going to Boom couldn't have come at a better time for me personally. Kay and I were getting back together, so I quit Second City's touring company and moved to Amsterdam. It was nice getting a new perspective from a distance on my Chicago comedy experience, but still rooted in that type of work. So that and love is what got me there. I think I'd maybe smoked pot no more than ten times prior to joining Boom—the majority of which was on an earlier trip to Amsterdam to visit Kay. Getting to know the city from a place of empathy versus just being a fucking tourist was life-changing on a cellular level. The other thing is that Andrew taught me how to play pinball for real. We'd play *Medieval Madness*, which is still my favorite pinball machine. That's a direct connection to Andrew's gift at sharing his enthusiasm with other people.

Rob AndristPlourde: That Jason became a movie star made total sense. We saw that in action. He was always the audience favorite: he'd just smile, wink, and win them over every time. And he had the balls on him: from jump, Jason's attitude was, *I'm going to be on* SNL, *and then I'm going to make movies*. There was no plan B.

Ike Barinholtz: Jerry Springer was one of my early impressions that I did onstage at Boom Chicago.

Rob AndristPlourde: Ike is one of the smartest people I know, but not so bright sometimes. One Saturday afternoon, the sun was weirdly out, but Ike didn't use any sunscreen and got burned so badly.

Ike Barinholtz: I had a big crush on a Dutch woman who worked at the Boom bar. She'd invited me to go to the beach in the Lowlands with her and her friend, and the three of us took an early train there.

Joe Canale: To call it a "beach" is rather strong. It's more like a landfill with water or something. The fact that it was a topless beach was way too much for Ike to handle.

Ike Barinholtz: When we got to the beach, right away, the women took their tops off. As an American, I just wasn't used to that. I was so distracted: it just didn't happen in the US that a girl you're crushing on suddenly takes her top off! We were drinking, tits were everywhere, and I was trying to be, like, really cool and stuff—and just totally forgot to put on sunscreen.

We laid out there on the beach for hours until I had to get back for the Saturday-night shows at Boom. On the train, I remember thinking, *God, it's so hot in here* . . . I got back to my apartment, took a quick shower, looked in the mirror, and was like, *Holy fuck!* My whole body—face, arms, thighs—was bright crimson. By the time I get into costume as Jerry Springer for the first show, I was fucking beet red. The audience started laughing the minute I walked onstage: they thought my over-the-top redness was my Jerry Springer makeup. Meanwhile, I had sun poisoning and was feeling worse and worse.

Rob AndristPlourde: When Ike got to the theater, he already looked like a lobster. After the first show, he was in terrible agony. He was backstage between sets just burning up. Desperate, Ike asked the kitchen workers, "Guys, do you have anything that could help?" The cook said, "Put this yogurt all over your body."

Joe Canale: Because he'd gone to the beach in just a Speedo, Ike was top-to-bottom crispy. He was standing there, arms extended like Christ, screaming and crying as his body was rubbed all over with Holland's finest yogurt.

Rob AndristPlourde: Ike had his back toward the door when an audience member accidentally walked into the backstage area.

Ike Barinholtz: People were constantly coming into the cast's dressing room, thinking it was the bathroom. So when this lady opened the door, I'd literally just taken my pants down and reached into a bowl of yogurt. I was looking her directly in the eye as I started rubbing yogurt all over my charred flesh.

Rob AndristPlourde: All this audience member sees is Ike with one hand on his crotch, the other in a vat of yogurt, yelling, "Oh God, this feels so good!" The door quickly shut, and that's the end of the story.

Pep Rosenfeld: She must've thought she had wandered into the most bizarre reality show she had never heard of, and Ike was the star. The overcooked, yogurt-covered star.

Andrew Moskos: In addition to Ike slathered with yogurt, there were new "stars" and new TV formats to mine for fodder. Now we're trapped on an island; now we're competing in a kitchen on a cooking show; now we're trying out contestants to become the new cast member of *De Lama's*. Naturally, all of this proved topical improv gold to the cast and audiences of Boom Chicago. Voting for things on TV was now part of our culture. Game shows like *The Weakest Link* had a voting component, making the show's harsh host, Anne Robinson, an international star with her trademark line, "You are the weakest link. Goodbye." Two years later, Boom Chicago's version of *The Weakest Link* featured a dumb President Bush trying to join the European Union.

While new TV formats and celebrities were blowing up, so was Boom Chicago. Our once-nascent comedy collective was now six years young in its adopted hometown, and attracting some of its strongest cast members—ones who would go on to reshape popular culture in their own images. Pep was about to begin his short-but-illustrious tour of duty as a *Saturday Night Live* writer. This is also when Seth would move to the US, still writing Boom Chicago corporate scripts by day to pay the bills. This trajectory would lead Seth to become head writer of *SNL* and then the host of his own talk show. All was not lost, however. Josh stayed on to maintain the prestige of the Meyers family name on the Amsterdam improv comedy circuit.

Pep Rosenfeld: To fill these unfillable voids in the cast, a new crew of players would join the OGs. Dave Asher, Ike Barinholtz, Liz Cackowski, Joe Canale, Juliet Curry, and Brendan Hunt had arrived to give Boom a jolt of youthful ambition, rock star decadence, and massive talent. Music Director Gerbrand van Kolck provided the beats. It was all up from there! At this point, I was pretty much out of the picture at Boom. I'd moved to New York, as I'd been hired on the writing staff at *SNL*.

Greg Shapiro: When we all came out to Amsterdam, Pep's attitude was, "Yeah, let's do another summer, and another summer, and another summer, and another summer—and we'll see how far this goes." But he also wanted to see through his own ambitions as a solo performer. Pep ended up in LA doing a showcase of his solo show "Rosenfeld for Dictator!," which Rachel Dratch saw. Pep knew Rachel from Second City: she was already on *SNL* at that point, so she got him a meeting. That led to Pep getting hired to write for "Weekend Update" during *SNL*'s 1999 dream season.

Rob AndristPlourde: To send Pep off to *SNL*, we had a going-away party. During a "Late Night" show, we set up a guessing game where Pep had to leave the room. When he was gone, Andrew got on the microphone: "Hi, everybody. We're not going to play this game. Essentially, the evening's entertainment is over, but we want you guys to stick around to celebrate our friend Pep. What we'd like you guys to do is come up to the balcony and be very quiet. Don't say a word until he walks into the room."

Pep came back into the room to play the game, but it was empty and silent. He was like, *What's going on?* The moment he walked underneath the balcony, confetti and balloons fell on his head, and all 150 people in the audience yelled, "Everybody loves Pep!"

Greg Shapiro: The irony was that Pep was let go from *SNL* after one season—and then got nominated for an Emmy for his work. The anchors for "Weekend Update" at that point were Tina Fey and Jimmy Fallon. Tina Fey was a great writer of her own jokes, so Pep's job became writing for Jimmy Fallon's voice. However, Jimmy Fallon already had his own guy, so this was not a recipe for success. Pep got a lot of, "Can you dumb it down?" That's just not what he's on about in his comedy. It was tough to have him gone, but we compensated somewhat with a great cast.

Andrew Moskos: Pep getting the *SNL* gig was the beginning of when people started to blow up from their involvement with Boom Chicago. The talent from Boom's class of '99 was stagger-ing. Ike would go on to become a comedic force in movies and TV like *MADtv, Blockers, Suicide Squad, Bad Neighbors,* and *The Mindy Project.* Brendan Hunt, meanwhile, arrived as an as-piring theater-kid improv comedian from Chicago at the crux of an identity crisis; he'd leave five years later as the poster boy for Boom Chicago's transformative powers—indeed, the genesis of Brendan and Jason's later success with *Ted Lasso* would be un-knowingly planted during this time. And Michael Diederich—an American who had been resident in Amsterdam long before Pep and I went native—had a star moment on television as a contes-tant on, yes, *The Weakest Link.*

Michael Diederich: For years, I was the only Boomer who spoke fluent Dutch. Pushing myself, I decided to try out for the Dutch version of *The Weakest Link*—and got on the show.

Being an entertainer, I made sure the other contestants were having a good time when the camera wasn't rolling. This worked out to my advantage: out of the nine rounds, I was literally the weakest link for five or six of them, but wasn't getting voted off. It came as a great surprise to me (and everyone else) when I made it to the final round to play for the big money. Unfortunately, I screwed up a question about musical theater, of all things. I lost, figuring my game-show career was over.

But then a month later, the producers of the show called me to do a special episode with the funniest losers from the season. For the first time in my life, I was glad to be a loser. I entertained just like the first time around: once again, even though I was often the weakest link, I made it to the finale. Second time around, the gods smiled on me. Not only did I get a question right about megalomania, but my opponent missed an easy one. I went home with 1,280 euros as the winning loser!

Pep Rosenfeld: Michael was not the only small-f famous Boomer around town. Cast members were now becoming local Amsterdam celebrities. We were no Ruud, but still . . .

Andrew Moskos: Sometimes they would be recognized by club bouncers, who might say with typical Dutch honesty, "Hey, are you guys from Boom Chicago? Come right in! . . . By the way, I do not think your show is funny." Indeed, as we found ourselves collectively sliding into a new millennium, the golden age of Boom Chicago was now truly underway.

Liz Cackowski: Looking back at who I was performing with in my first year, it's incredible—Jordan, Ike, Brendan, Josh . . . Seth had left, but would still come back to help direct the show and see Josh. It was just wonderful: every day was just about hanging with this crew at Vondelpark, biking around everywhere, going out on the boat, seeing movies, and then doing a show. My cohort was like a sports team—a very nerdy sports team. You wanted to be at the same level as the other people you're playing with onstage, but it didn't feel competitive. We were all working very hard to bring each other up.

Kay Cannon: At Boom, there's all the stories of partying, drugs, and trips to Efteling on 'shrooms—but the secret is that everyone actually works really hard. You rarely sat idle. I treated my Boom experience like graduate school. If I wasn't in a show, I was watching a show. I was staying after to hear the notes the director gave to the performers. I observed when I wasn't great. You were given second chances at Boom; I was acutely aware that this was a place where one could fuck up and still be supported. Between constant performing, rehearsals, writing (and early on, promoting), it was all about pushing yourself and the show to something bigger, something greater. That you also had memories that last a lifetime? That's the value of Boom.

Brendan Hunt: When I got to Amsterdam, I thought I was going to stay for maybe a year. I discovered, though, this whole new world offered me great awareness of myself. Pounds of guilt, baggage, and self-judgment that I carried around all day, every day . . . just wasn't there anymore. Suddenly, I was in this place that had no judgment at all about me. It was mind-blowing. I didn't even realize the power of it all until I'd been inside it for years . . .

CHAPTER 8
2000

AMSTERDAM'S TAXI WAR: CABBIES, COPS, AND CRIMINAL CYCLISTS COLLIDE

As much as Dutch culture has contributed to the world, progress in the Netherlands in some key areas had ground to a halt well before Boom Chicago arrived. There were many things crucial to everyday existence that had topped out at a comfortably Dutch level of mediocrity—like taxis. During the pre-Uber era, the Netherlands had the best *and* worst taxi system simultaneously. Change seemed unlikely, until the whole conundrum reached a breaking point that threatened to tear apart the country.

The upside was that taxis were driven by professionals who had nice cars, spoke both Dutch and English, and never cheated you. They were the highest-status blue-collar workers in the city. They kept their cars clean, and made a good living. Many drivers wore designer suits on the job. Their labor was not physical, and they all drove nice Mercedes. For these working-class white males who wore gold chains outside their clothes, life was pretty good.

There were other benefits as well. An Amsterdam quirk was the practice of having cabs congregate at taxi stands, each of which had a phone. When you wanted a cab, you called your local taxi stand. The driver at the front of the line would answer the phone and take down your address. Three minutes later, the same guy you spoke to would pull up in his Mercedes. Pretty good system. But it wasn't cheap. Average fares seemed to be about the same as in other cities, but here you were only going a few miles. In New York, the fare from Manhattan to JFK Airport was about the same as the fare from central Amsterdam to Schiphol Airport—but the ride was half as long.

Taxi drivers knew they were in demand. They drove fast down tram tracks like they owned the streets. Takeout food, even wrapped well and sealed, was not allowed in taxis. If you tried to bring a large box with you, the driver would immediately inform you that his cab "is not a moving van" and speed off. Rear windows would always be locked: if you wanted fresh air, you had to ask permission from the Great Master of the Taxi. If you were respectful enough (and not already on the freeway), the Great Master would allow the window to be lowered. You're welcome.

TCA, the taxi drivers' confederacy, was basically a mafia, and TCA head Dick Grijpink was its godfather. At the time, he was only their *suspected* criminal mastermind: later, Grijpink was convicted for tax and drug crimes. But back in 2000, from a legal perspective, like many taxi drivers then, he was just an asshole.

Worse, there just weren't enough cars on the road, inevitably creating an ugly sellers' market. With only sixteen thousand taxis in circulation, drivers called the shots. We needed them more than they needed us. There was always another customer, but thanks to a limited number of taxi medallions—expensive, hard-to-get licenses required to legally drive taxis—it often proved unreasonably hard to get rides.

The situation went to the drivers' heads. They preferred to work during the day, when businesspeople were (usually) less drunk and unruly than party people spilling out of Amsterdam's bars and nightclubs at night. On Saturday nights, passengers waited in long lines for cabs, the endlessly ringing taxi-stand phone remaining unanswered. And getting a cab on New Year's Eve? *Fuggedaboutit.* As the taxi drivers would explain, "New Year's Eve is a time to be at home with your family."

As internationalism ushered in improvements in sandwiches, coffee, service, shopping hours, and connectivity, taxis, too, would be forced to change with the times. On January 1, 2000, the Dutch government opened up the taxi market in one fell swoop. It was a pretty hard-core move, overnight changing the Netherlands from one of the world's most protected taxi markets into one of the most unregulated. Taxi medallions, which that December 31 had a value of 100,000 guilders ($45,000 today), instantly became worthless the next day. Anyone could now get a taxi license, the goal being improved service with lower prices for customers.

That didn't happen. Instead, Amsterdam got a taxi war.

TCA and its drivers, it turned out, didn't welcome passengers' new options. For years, their Hugo Boss suits and Mercedes C-Class sedans told the world, *See? We're just like the fancy businesspeople we take to the RAI Convention Center.* But once the taxi war began, it turned out that drivers had less in common with their passengers than they'd imagined. Baseball bats now appeared in taxi trunks, with the hotheads among them physically intimidating drivers from the TCA's new competitor, Taxi Direct. Sometimes they attacked Taxi Direct's understandably freaked-out passengers too.

Can you imagine? You're in town for a tech conference, you get into a cab—and out of nowhere, you're stopped by a bunch of thugs in suits wielding baseball bats? It was like a straight-to-video Chechen crime drama crossed with *The Warriors*. In the three years after the taxi market opened up, the number of cabs shot up by 50 percent. In the few years after that, those numbers would double again. But these taxi drivers were very unorganized: many of them seemed less prepared and professional than their TCA predecessors.

Sure, *onze eigen* TCA was full of arrogant thugs, but they were *honest and knowledgeable* arrogant thugs. Some of these new drivers, meanwhile, were downright crooked. Scammer drivers from all over the region came to Amsterdam to rip off unsuspecting passengers. All you needed was a taxi light on your roof, and you were in business. Many supposed taxi drivers were actually mobile drug dealers, but driving cars they could now write off as a business expense. What followed was twelve years of transportation chaos, all mined for comedy gold . . .

Ruben van der Meer: Complaining during the taxi wars was like talking about the weather—an art in itself.

Rob AndristPlourde: The distinct thing about Boom is the topicality of the humor. All the jokes are about conflict or comfort within your environment. Naturally, just from living in Amsterdam, taxi bits would make it into the show. We had a sketch about a taxi-driving lesson. In it, you went to a special school where you were taught how to drive carelessly and aggressively in the classic Amsterdam taxi-driver style. The lesson climaxes with the instructor stating, "If by this point your passengers won't cooperate, you're going to have to shoot them."

Brendan Hunt: This wasn't as much of an exaggeration as you might think. At the dawn of the millennium, Amsterdam was in the middle of a civil war: it was the taxi drivers versus . . .

Pep Rosenfeld: Andrew Moskos.

Horace Cohen: And pretty much everyone else in the city. They blocked off the Marnixstraat one night: a hundred cabs just popped out of nowhere and parked in the middle of the street.

Ike Barinholtz: TCA was a bunch of thugs. I actually got into a fight with a driver during the taxi war. This guy refused to do some mundane taxi things, and was such an asshole; I actually punched him, he was so horrible. Another time, I was with Jordan Peele when I got into another disagreement with a driver about opening a window. The driver stops in the middle of the road, at which point he and I are shouting at each other. I look at Jordan—normally the calmest, nicest guy—and he's also furious. I can't think of any other time I've seen Jordan so mad he wanted to fight. That's how big a jerk this driver was.

Pep Rosenfeld: In the year 2000, the taxi drivers' anthem was definitely "Sandstorm" by Darude. Drivers were especially concerned about their ability to maintain a healthy budget for the bad techno CDs required to be played at top volume during every trip.

Andrew Moskos: For years, I was convinced there was a special radio station for taxi drivers that just played the bad techno you only hear in Dutch cabs. And then all of a sudden, when the laws changed, that was the day the music died for Amsterdam taxi drivers. See what I did there?

Brendan Hunt: Thinking about taxis in relation to Amsterdam, I always return to Andrew and his ongoing personal war with taxi drivers.

Ike Barinholtz: I was pissed off about the taxi wars, but Andrew was *obsessed* with it. He was very wrapped up in the taxi situation for many years, and always wanted to do sketches about it—he would've done a full taxi wars show if he could've gotten away with it. I was like, *Um, it's interesting, sure, but . . .*

Rob AndristPlourde: In one sketch, I played an old TCA driver complaining to a passenger about the new guys taking over the business: "Fuck Taxi Direct, they take our money. They're fucking cockroaches!" For the punch line, the passenger gets out of the car and says to the audience, "I'm from Taxi Direct, and I just took a shit in that guy's cab."

Ken Schaefle: By 2000, Boom Chicago was at its peak. Our shows were as good as anything on the Second City mainstage at that point.

Greg Shapiro: Our show "Live at the Leidseplein: Your Privacy Is Our Business" had an incredible cast—in retrospect, it's hard to believe the talent in that show: Boom lifers like Andrew, Rob, and me, plus Holly Walker, Liz Cackowski, Josh Meyers, Juliet Curry, Dave Asher, and Brendan as holdovers. Then there were new cast members who brought in this cool new energy: Jennifer Bills, Dave Buckman, Bumper Carroll, and director Dave Razowsky. Kay Cannon got bumped up from corporate to mainstage too.

Liz Cackowski: With that show, we were writing something that was of the moment, taking what was happening right then and using it. Andrew had the idea of having cameras onstage, which was very exciting. Of course, now having cameras everywhere is normal, but at that time it felt new. That influenced my brand of comedy: finding truth in what's happening now and how humans react to it. There was such great creative energy then, and we were all really lit up by it. I was so psyched to go to rehearsals. That group really brought their brains together to create this new cool thing.

Greg Shapiro: "Your Privacy Is Our Business" would also be Jason Sudeikis's first show performing with Boom Chicago.

Steven Svymbersky: Everyone knew Jason from Second City, and you saw his experience onstage immediately. Eventually, he and Kay went back to the States together, although Kay kept writing for the corporate shows.

Andrew Moskos: Some people needed time to learn the Boom Chicago gig, but it was clear from Jason's work in "Your Privacy Is Our Business" he'd nailed it immediately. He could engage an audience and lead a scene from day one. It was no surprise to us that he became someone who could open movies and make *Ted Lasso* a global phenomenon.

Ike Barinholtz: I'd known Kay and Jason before I came to Boom. We'd performed together in this famous group in Chicago, J.T.S. Brown, that we helped create along with people like Pete Grosz. I worked with Kay so much at Boom, we became really close friends. And Jason was amazing. By that time, he was already one of the best guys in Chicago: when he came to Boom, he was just *so* funny. He did a sketch with Jordan where he had Jordan saying phrases that he would never say. I can remember one of Jordan's was, "I'm done with water," to which Jason responded, "I'm *not* done with water." That cast was popping, man.

Brendan Hunt: What was *not* popping was Andrew always trying to bring the taxi situation into the show. There are two stories that I think are not only revealing about Holland, but also about Andrew. I wasn't there for either, though they are the stuff of legend—long been shared, like *Beowulf* style.

   During Boom's early days, Andrew was biking down some busy street when a cabdriver cut him off. From the bike lane, Andrew maybe hits the car with his hand or something. This cabbie gets out, shoves him, calls him a foreigner tourist, and then drives away. Andrew wrote down the driver's license plate. The next day, Andrew goes to the police station. He hands the driver's information over to the desk sergeant who—in a way that manages to be both helpful and patronizing—starts doing some research. The sergeant dials a number on his phone, and then starts speaking urgently in Dutch. Andrew notices that whatever the cop is hearing is convincing him that Andrew was in the right, and the driver was in the wrong. After some back and forth, the desk sergeant removes the phone from his ear, covers the receiver, turns to Andrew, and says, "The driver would like to apologize."

Andrew Moskos: I was like, "He wants to do *what?*" And the officer says, "Look, you can press charges, but it will take a lot of time, and the penalty is not so severe. Or he can say he's sorry."

Brendan Hunt: Andrew accepted the driver's apology, albeit a bit reluctantly . . .

Andrew Moskos: I left the police feeling that, given the situation, this was the exact right amount of justice. Sometimes the right punishment is no punishment. An apology—even one that's a bit reluctant—was the best I could hope for. It's a big city; no one goes to jail for being a douche. But what if that douche says he's sorry? It makes it a little better, these tiny victories.

Brendan Hunt: The other story is from around 2008 or 2009. Coming back from a corporate show with young Becky Nelson, Boom's new video person, Andrew had some typical Andrew argument with a cabdriver about what route to take, how he was being ripped off . . .

Andrew Moskos: I was being ripped off! After the taxi market liberalized, there were too many taxis on the street.

Rob AndristPlourde: Here he goes . . .

Andrew Moskos: This resulted in too-long lines at the Leidse-plein cabstand. Any driver who got me would be mad they'd waited in line for an hour to get my crappy eight-euro fare. But that's the game: sometimes you get an airport fare, and sometimes you get me. They'd curse me and illegally refuse my ride. A tourist might get out, but I knew I had a right to be taken home, and didn't want this guy to be rewarded for refusing a fare. Besides, what other driver is going to take a fare who was kicked out of a cab? I had to get home—what could I do? My answer: get a cab from the end of the line. He'd sneak in a quick eight euros before returning to the line for a longer fare. Win-win.

One day, facing a long line at the taxi stand, I got into a car at the back of the line with Becky Nelson; I took the passenger seat, and she got in the back. I tell the driver our destination, and he goes, "Oh no—too close." I'm like, "You've just joined the line and haven't waited for a minute. Just take me home and you'll be back in line in ten minutes." He was like, "Get another cab, tourist!" So I responded (correctly), "Nope. I'm in your cab, and you have to take me. It's the law."

The driver starts cursing me out. Getting aggressive, he pulls up the emergency brake. As it's just starting to rain, he gets out of the car—storming around the front to open my door and drag me out.

Brendan Hunt: As the cabdriver readies to eject Andrew and fight him on the street, Andrew calmly locks his door.

Andrew Moskos: Now he can't open my door—at which point I reach over and lock the driver's-side door too. He goes to the driver's side and yanks the door handle, but it doesn't open. Now getting doused by rain, the driver has this Yosemite Sam moment when he realizes he's not only locked out of his own car—the keys are still in the ignition. He's banging on the window, telling me to get out of his car *right now*. But if he's Yosemite Sam, I'm Bugs Bunny. "First of all," I say in my most reasonable voice, "calm down." Obviously, the most annoying thing you can say to any furious person is to calm down.

Brendan Hunt: Poor Becky must've been in the backseat like, *Who are these crazy fucks?* Meanwhile, slowly, the cabdriver realizes he's been beat.

Andrew Moskos: In defeat, he calmed down a bit, so I opened the locks. Becky and I quickly got out. Luckily, there was a policeman at the taxi stand. I calmly walked over and said to the cop, "This driver refused to take me to my destination." And the cop wrote him a ticket. It was my best taxi conflict ever because I was 100 percent right, and the rogue driver was appropriately punished.

So now the taxi market was flooded with thugs and mobile drug dealers, but both national and local governments were unable to improve the situation. Nothing worked. The scams and intimidating behavior continued. Meters were now frequently "broken," and anyone who spoke English going to Schiphol was guaranteed a route that went through the IJtunnel. To put it mildly, this was not the fastest route.

Things improved in 2012, when Uber arrived in the Netherlands: the rideshare revolution fixed everything. Uber was so successful, at first it confused the government. You need a meter, civil servants demanded—ignoring that Uber's software *was* a meter, one that made it almost impossible to rip off passengers. Keep a paper log, they insisted—despite the traceable records Uber rides created automatically. In Amsterdam, Uber lowered prices by 50 percent, eliminated cheating drivers, and provided much better service. Sure, sometimes you paid more with surge pricing, but it used to *always* be surge pricing. And by rating passengers, they raised the quality of passengers as well. Drivers and riders were no longer invisible, so everyone behaved better. In olden days, a driver would describe a robber as, say, "Six feet tall, dark hair, in his twenties." Now he could point to his phone and say, *"This* dude." And of course with no cash required in an Uber transaction, there were also fewer robberies. Did people mind that white Dutch career drivers were replaced by younger people from immigrant backgrounds? Only old drivers who'd lost their monopoly.

The most important way people get around Amsterdam is, of course, by bike. Getting around the city by bike was one of the first lessons new Boom actors learned. If you could get used to making split-second decisions in which life or death was decided by a centimeter or two, you could probably handle drunks in the theater on a Saturday night. If there's one thing Dutch people could learn from Boom Chicago, it's the proper terminology describing when your date sits on the rack over the back tire. The Dutch call it *achterop zitten*. (Yawn . . .) At Boom Chicago, however, we "sweetheart" each other. As in, "I left my bike at Boom. Can you sweetheart me there?"

Nicole Parker: I got goddamn good at sweethearting. I once sweethearted Colton for the entire forty-five-minute journey back to our place in Osdorp. It was way outside of town, I was wearing chunky-ass heels, it was one in the morning, and both of us were totally drunk from an Oscar party we just left. I don't know how we survived. We just laughed the entire time.

Brendan Hunt: Amsterdam is a biking city, period. And you're never judged by your bike. If your seventy-year-old piece of garbage still works, knock yourself out. In fact, if you have too nice of a bike, it will inevitably disappear. I was given the nicest bike of my entire life as a gift from Boom for my five-year tenure: "Congratulations, Brendan, Boom Chicago loves you, *heeeeere's* your new bicycle!" This was at a big Boom "Christmas in July" party: I was biking it around the Leidseplein theater because all the chairs had been removed to make a dance floor. I was happy as a child with this new fancy bike—and then it was stolen that night. The next morning, I bought a beater for twenty euros.

Andrew Moskos: Most bikes then were purchased from junkies. Near Amsterdam University's law school buildings, there was the "junkie bridge," where a fistful of guilders and a high tolerance for foul odors could get a used bike for cheap. These days, the bridge is cleaned up and we buy our bikes legally—ah, middle age—but back then, buying a bike was an adventure.

Michael Diederich: A friend I was staying with said buying from a junkie was a horrible idea. "The junkies steal the bikes, sell them for drugs, and then the cycle begins anew." But you could get a bike from a junkie for just ten guilders; legit used bikes cost at least a hundred. To me, it was a no-brainer.

A friend went with me to the bike bridge, even though she disapproved of the practice. We arrived in time to see a bike being sold to a couple of tourists. After money was exchanged and the junkie salesman scurried into the night, my friend ran toward the tourists, screaming, "Stop, that's my bike!" When they said they'd just bought it, she suggested we all go to the police station and let the cops settle it. The tourists didn't like where this was going, so they surrendered the bike, then quickly went off. My friend then presented my first bike to me, proud that I hadn't paid a junkie for it. Apparently, stealing a bike from tourists was okay, but buying one from a heroin addict was not.

Andrew Moskos: No one at Boom ever got in real trouble for buying a stolen bike. But Pete Grosz came closest when he became the most famous stolen-bike buyer in Amsterdam. We'll let him tell the story himself.

Peter Grosz: A few months into my time at Boom, my girlfriend from Chicago, Angel Innocent, came to visit me. Of course, that wasn't her name, but I've changed it here so as not to besmirch her character—ultimately, to protect her from any legal ramifications that might come from her being an accessory after the fact to the crime I committed for her in the name of love.

When Angel arrived in Amsterdam on a lovely June day, I explained to her that we had a week of quaint, bicycle-bound romantic exploration of the picturesque city ahead of us. But first we needed to pop over to the rusted-out bridge where junkies sold stolen bikes for heroin money. Angel—ever the angel, bless her soul—didn't balk at this suggestion, and we were off.

We arrived bright and early to see the usual assortment of strung-out, scraggly Dutchmen milling around, all pushing hot bikes they'd stolen just moments before. It was like walking into a bakery at sunrise and smelling fresh croissants—only the croissants were contraband bikes, and the smell was piss. I was understandably nervous: at twenty-three, I'd never purchased stolen merchandise before, and since Boom had loaned me a bike upon arrival, I hadn't even broken my buying-a-stolen-bike-from-a-junkie cherry yet.

Angel and I cautiously sauntered up to the least intimidating guy and asked him, "How much?" "Twenty guilders," he calmly answered. Checking my wallet, I quickly realized I had not come prepared for a wide range of stolen bicycle prices. I had only a ten-guilder note and a fifty-guilder note, a fact that I decided to share with our salesman; I assumed he'd take the ten guilders, happy with the 1,000 percent markup he was getting on his stolen merchandise, and that would be that. Instead, he brusquely repeated, "Twenty guilders." I asked, "Do you have change for a fifty?" He looked at me like I'd asked him if he also sold motorcycles. "*Nee,*" he said dryly. After three months in Amsterdam, I'd learned that this meant "No"—but rather than walk away and find someone else, or simply offer him ten guilders again, I just said, "Okay," and handed him my fifty-guilder note. He looked at me again—this time like I was an idiot—took my bill, and handed me the bike.

As we walked away, I knew that, from a financial perspective, I had failed miserably—but from a good-boyfriend perspective, I'd nailed it. I had courageously brought Angel into this den of thieves and secured her a bicycle without getting her killed. However, as we started biking away, Angel discovered something unexpected. Or, put another way, something totally expected: the bike sucked. It wobbled, it squeaked, the handlebars weren't affixed properly. It was a total lemon. My pride quickly turned to shame. I had been duped—even more than I was aware of. Angel wanted to just ride it anyway (again, what an angel), but I was indignant and determined: we were going back and getting a new bike.

We marched back to the bridge to find our junkie already in possession of another bike. (For a listless junkie, this guy worked very fast.) I sternly strode up to him to give him a piece of my mind. *Unacceptable!* I screamed in my head; in reality, I mumbled, "Hey, man, can we, like, get a different bike?" In what was kind of becoming "our thing," he flashed me another stupefied look and said, "What?" "It's no good," I said. "We want a different one. What about that one?" I pointed to his new bike. Again, he hit me with another, *"Nee."* Now we were at an impasse.

I'll admit I panicked here. My "good boyfriend" status was vanishing, my tough-guy-who-can-handle-the-streets veneer was fading, and my non-moron-who-can-competently-negotiate-the-purchase-of-a-stolen-bike-from-a-desperate-junkie cred was already long gone. Improvising, I asked, "Can we have that bike if I give you this bike and ten more guilders?" No longer surprised at the monumentally stupid things coming out of my mouth, our junkie just shrugged and said, "Sure." I gave him the shitty bike and ten guilders, and he gave me a slightly less shitty bike and my dignity tied up in a little bag. We walked away, and I calculated the sum total of what had just gone down: I had spent sixty guilders, three times as much as he wanted. In today's euros, adjusted for inflation, it would roughly be the equivalent of:

THE WORST EXAMPLE OF BARGAINING EVER!

We spent the day traversing the city—eating, drinking, smoking, and generally just being in love in Amsterdam. It was awesome. The following morning, I showed up at the theater and our bartender greeted me, asking, "So, did you see your photo in *Het Parool*?" I hadn't, of course, since I never read Dutch newspapers; I couldn't imagine what I'd be in there for. I assumed it had to be something about Boom since I hadn't done anything of note in Amsterdam yet.

When he showed me the paper, I realized I, in fact, *had* done something worth documenting: I had purchased a stolen bicycle from a junkie the day before, and now everyone in Amsterdam could read about it. One of the dumbest things I'd done at that point in my young life had been captured in three surveillance-style black-and-white photographs taking up the entire front page.

The first photo was of Angel and me talking to the junkie; the second image was of me handing him money; and the third was of me throwing my leg over the bike and riding away. Our faces were minimally blurred out to protect our identities, but anyone who knew me could clearly tell who it was. It certainly didn't fool our bartender. The paper was apparently doing a big exposé on the stolen-bike traffic at the bridge, so they'd set up a photographer across the street to take pictures. I'd been snared in a sting! These weren't just photographs, they were evidence of my guilt. I was embarrassed at first, and then worried about my legal status as a foreign worker in the country. But in the end, I laughed it all off, realizing that even if I got kicked out of the country, no one would ever know the true level of stupidity I'd displayed that day.

I've been back to Amsterdam many times since, and have always legally rented a bicycle. I can't bring myself to head down to that bridge again.

Seth Meyers: You can't believe how comic-bookish it was with those three photos: man handing money to a junkie, junkie handing bike to man, man biking off, junkie going to buy drugs with new money. And it was so obviously Pete as well. It was wonderful.

Andrew Moskos: Despite some tragic interactions with junkie capitalists, it's great to live in a city where none of our transportation stories involve our own cars. It's probably why there haven't been drunk-driving or auto-accident stories in Boom Chicago's history. When one of our actors actually made the front page of the paper for an actual crime he committed, it was only for buying a stolen bike.

It's also great that we've moved past the early 2000s' taxi chaos. If they ever want to make an English-language movie about the Amsterdam taxi wars, Jason Sudeikis would be a perfect star. He could play the sympathetic lead taxi driver, beset by economic forces beyond his control. In that movie, he would *have to* fight Ike. Ike would play my character, the heroic passenger who tries to protect fellow travelers—and ultimately, all of society—from getting ripped off.

Nicole Parker: When he was at Boom, Jason's bit would always be to get into a taxi and say, "Take me to the Statue of Liberty," or, "I'd like to go to the Eiffel Tower, please."

Greg Shapiro: Another big topic that year was the never-ending election between George W. Bush and Al Gore.

Andrew Moskos: Oh, that little thing. As the months dragged on, the Dutch were dumbfounded: "How is it that you still don't have a president yet?" Trying to explain the logic-defying vagaries of the American electoral system to the one-citizen, one-vote Netherlanders was a challenge, to say the least.

Josie O'Reilly: It wasn't enough to just be funny at Boom. These were young Americans seeking to be more aware of their place in the world. You had to have a take on what it was to be American.

Andrew Moskos: Like Rob said earlier, topicality was the foundation for Boom's content. We were raised on "Weekend Update" our entire lives as the comedy ideal—well, that and Monty Python. And with Pep having done his stint at *SNL*, he'd actually written for "Weekend Update" by this point. So it made total sense that, during this American election riveting the world, Boom Chicago should step up our broadcast presence as news commentators in a big way. So Greg, of course, became the resident Jon Stewart of Holland, basically.

Greg Shapiro: 2000 was when *Boom Chicago News* first appeared on TV. We had a show on Dutch Comedy Central for a while when the 2000 election seemed like it was never going away.

Pep Rosenfeld: The full title of the show was actually *Comedy Central News: Because Dutch News Is News, Too!*

Greg Shapiro: A big *CCN* story was when Benazir Bhutto got assassinated. Rob played Pervez Musharraf and Jen Burton was Benazir Bhutto. That was lit!

Colton Dunn: I remember the first sketch I wrote that made it into a show was one of the more political ones. We'd brought these business cards soaked in liquid acid to a touring show in Singapore. We took the LSD there and it was amazing. I then went into the business center at the hotel and wrote a sketch called "Holy Road Trip": it imagined Moses, Muhammad, and Jesus all driving together in an '80s road-trip movie. That sketch got into the mainstage show, and then was in the "Best of Boom" shows for a while. Andrew said some people did send them letters suggesting maybe they shouldn't have Muhammad as a character in the scene. This was *way* before *Charlie Hebdo*.

Brendan Hunt: "Live at the Leidseplein: Your Privacy Is Our Business" was very political too.

Andrew Moskos: Surveillance and privacy were really on people's minds at that point. It seems quaint now: it was only the Republicans manipulating the voting results—they didn't have help from the Russians at that point.

Brendan Hunt: Going into 2000 was cool just because of the excitement about the millennium. But that vibe in Holland, and probably everywhere, was slightly muted because of Y2K bug concerns. It was like, "Gosh, guys—I hope we're going to be okay!"

Ike Barinholtz: The comedy was evolving with the audience. Before I left, Boom Chicago's audience was 50 percent Dutch; by the time I left, it was almost 70 percent Dutch.

Steven Svymbersky: Each night, as the show was winding down to the end, Jordan and I would take a break and sneak off for a little mini hit, and then get back to finish the show.

Jordan Peele: I would smoke weed and perform on the regular. I don't know about anyone else, but I definitely could play stoned—and I did. It was great: it works for some people, and it worked for me, and I was free.

Ruben van der Meer: Look, let me be honest: there's only one person on this planet who can improvise perfectly—really, even better than perfectly—when he's totally high. And that's Jordan Peele.

Ike Barinholtz: I think this is probably where we note for the record that Pep is definitely the drunkest person I've ever seen attempt to actually perform on a stage. Pep was always unbeatable in that arena.

Jordan Peele: Pep's line was always, "Jordan is the tightest person onstage, and the loosest person offstage." You're just trying not to get *too* wasted. That's part of the fun: smoking weed just made me feel good, but especially in Amsterdam. The freedom of smoking weed in a place where it's legal or tolerated has a profound effect on the experience.

Brendan Hunt: What was great about the freedom of Amsterdam and going out then was the fucking camaraderie of it. We would often go dancing straight from a show—biking together in a pack to Club Vegas. When I think of idealized nights out in Amsterdam, Club Vegas is really what I come back to. Club Vegas was a '70s party night held in the bar at the Winston Hotel in the Red Light District, which everyone from Boom attended religiously. Club Vegas's dance floor would be filled with Boom Chicago cast members in costumes and '70s loungewear.

Some guys who hung out at Club Vegas had then started their own party at the Winston called "Ex Pornstar," which was like the trashier, porn-ier cousin of Club Vegas. The vibe basically made you feel like a character in *Boogie Nights*. Around this time, Viagra had just come out—sex stores in Amsterdam actually had a barely legal hustle selling Viagra semi–under the counter. At this point, the public didn't really know much about this incredible new miracle drug or understand how it worked. As such, at one Ex Pornstar party I promised the hosts that I'd take Viagra the whole night to demonstrate this medical advance to the crowd: "And then at the end of the night, I will dance onstage with this massive boner that's not going to ever go away. Oh, and I'll wear a bridal gown."

It didn't totally work out like that, alas. First of all, you've got to do this bit while people still care; I'd saved it until two o'clock in the morning, when hardly anybody was left in the club. That night, I learned two things. One is I have a thyroid condition, and it's tougher for Viagra to work with thyroid conditions. And second, something has to be, uh, *happening* for Viagra to work. I was standing onstage with a microphone in a bridal gown, in an increasingly cold room, attempting a boner and failing. Backstage, my then-girlfriend served as fluffer to get the boner started—that didn't last either. I still danced my heart out in that bridal gown, that's for sure.

Ike Barinholtz: I can't even imagine what would've happened if there'd been actual easy access to video while I was at Boom Chicago; I'm pretty sure we'd all still be in jail. Case in point: the Casa Rosso . . . Other than Club Vegas, we didn't go out in the Red Light District a lot. But when we did go, we'd always end up at the Casa Rosso, which is this big gaudy sex show where the fucking onstage is real.

Seth Meyers: I think I really only went into the Casa Rosso for about ten minutes in all the time I was living in Amsterdam. Thank God.

Joe Canale: Casa Rosso was notorious in Amsterdam, and not only for its live sex shows. There were rumors that it had been funded with ransom money from the mafia kidnapping of Dutch beer-company heir Freddy Heineken!

Ike Barinholtz: The Casa Rosso is actually a big mainstream tourist attraction, always packed with tour groups because it's so Amsterdam. All these old English biddies go there fresh off the tour bus like, "Be a dear and please take a picture of me next to an actual dick that I can show my friends back home for a laugh."

Joe Canale: We went to Casa Rosso a few times, always in big groups. It was kind of an unofficial initiation tradition. This one time I remember most vividly . . .

Ike Barinholtz: I was there too. It's not something one forgets easily.

Pep Rosenfeld: It's the one time everyone remembers the most. The Casa Rosso incident is a very famous chapter in Boom Chicago history that gets passed down like folklore from generation to generation as a cautionary tale.

Andrew Moskos: Just last year, a friend of ours was discussing Amsterdam with the driver in a shared Uber in Los Angeles. The other passenger in the backseat, a young millennial woman, yells out, "Ohmygod, I just got back from Amsterdam! I was a cast member at Boom Chicago for two years." Our friend turns to her—someone he'd never met—and asks, "So, do you know the famous story of . . ." And she says, "The Casa Rosso? Of course."

Ike Barinholtz: I think Brendan one night invited Boom's latest hire, a woman in her twenties who'd recently joined the behind-the-scenes team. She was like, "What's Casa Rosso?" So we explained it to her: "It's a totally ridiculous live-sex show—not an orgy so much as cheesy tourist entertainment." And she was like, "Oh, okay, I'll go." At least five other women were in our crew too.

Joe Canale: She seemed really nice and cool, though we didn't know her very well. But we'd all gone many times before to Casa Rosso, so we knew the show's whole routine.

Ike Barinholtz: They have these different cheesy scenarios. One has a *Matrix* motif, for example. Another aspires to "classy" James Bond vibes: As the 007 theme plays in the background, this guy vaguely resembling George Lazenby comes out. He'd suck some girl's nipples for five minutes, and then they'd have sex while people were mingling at the bar. But the centerpiece at Casa Rosso was always Batman.

Joe Canale: For the main event, a large gentleman of Afro-Carribean descent comes out onstage to a Prince song dressed in full Batman costume—mask and everything—except he's naked from the waist down, and has an enormous penis.

Ike Barinholtz: Batman's cock was basically the size of a small Midwestern city. It was the Terre Haute, Indiana, of dicks.

Joe Canale: Once he's made his grand entrance, Batman calls for a female audience member to join him onstage.

Ike Barinholtz: It's what we call a "schmo game" in improv comedy: we'll grab a schmo from the audience and put them in the bit. At Casa Rosso, usually it's some drunk tourist whom Batman tries to get to take their shirt off. They're always like, "Hell no!" in whatever language they speak.

Joe Canale: The willing victim typically gets embarrassed for a few minutes as Batman tries to convince her to have sex with him in front of the crowd. She reacts with mock outrage, everybody laughs, and she goes back to her seat. And after that hilariously awkward moment to break the ice, the real show begins: a woman comes out from backstage, has sex with the majestically endowed Batman, and then it's over before you know it. That had consistently been my experience with Casa Rosso up to then. But when we went out this one particular time, Batman chose his partner for the two-hander that started the show from our group; actually, she volunteered. Batman came over, clearly drawn to her; after he finished his spiel, she looked around laughing and said, "Okay, I'll do it."

Joe Canale: So our new friend gets onstage during Batman's intro bit before the main event—and before we know it . . .

Ike Barinholtz: She'd stripped down to her bra and panties and started going down on Batman!

Joe Canale: I've blocked as much of that memory as I could. It was like, "Ha ha," when she got onstage at first. But we weren't expecting *that*.

Ike Barinholtz: I'd been to Casa Rosso a few times, and I'd never seen anyone from the audience actually touch Batman— let alone blow him. I think maybe one time a female audience member started to take her shirt off, and her friends were like, "No way, stop!"

Joe Canale: This was a most unexpected development—so when Batman signaled for a condom so he could start banging our new friend, we all started screaming at her to get off the stage. It became uncomfortable, that's for sure, seeing our new coworker like this.

Pep Rosenfeld: Certainly, this was a different era in terms of human resources.

Joe Canale: Yes. Your first day on the job, your coworkers take you to a live sex show where you volunteer to get fucked onstage. I mean, that sounds urban legend-y, but I was there and it did happen. As she took her clothes off, she looked at us and mouthed, *Should I fuck Batman?* And we were like, "No! No!

No!" But of course the rest of the crowd was freaking out and screaming, "Yeah! Do it!"

Ike Barinholtz: We started looking at each other, like, *Hmmm, what's going on here, exactly? This isn't how the show goes.* And then we were like, "Whoa! She's going for it!" When she started giving Batman a blowjob, everyone went into a panic. This was one of the craziest things I'd ever seen in my life; I still can't un-see it now. It was like that inevitable scene in a Spike Lee movie where the camera floats on a dolly—an out-of-body experience. And it got crazier.

After she'd blown Batman for a while, suddenly she turned around and bent over. As she pulled her panties down, she looked at us one more time with this expression like, *Can I have sex now?* We all ran up onstage and said, "Okay, got to go!" She got her clothes back on and we ran out of there. It was insane. That was the last time we went to Casa Rosso. After the whole thing, she was still super chill and nice as we got to know her. She actually ended up working at Boom for a while.

Andrew Moskos: She was a total feminist, with fascinating ideas about personal sexual liberty—and definitely the first person I ever saw reading *The Ethical Slut.* That night, she made us sea-soned Amsterdammers feel like fucking prudes.

Brendan Hunt: By the end of my first year at Boom, the figuring-out bit was over, and the finding-your-place part really kicked in. I was growing in ways I never had before—making year three just really fun. Well, except for that whole 9/11 thing.

CHAPTER 9
2001

IT'S NOT FUNNY HAVING "BOOM" IN YOUR NAME DURING 9/11

I n the United States, 2001 started out pretty simply. The 2000 presidential election was marked by hilarious antics. The voting took the usual day, and was over quickly—I mean, how long can it take for less than half of the eligible population to vote? But the vote counting was *not* over quickly. First it was Gore. Then it was too close to call. Then there was a recount in Florida. Then the Supreme Court stopped the recount. For more than a month after Election Day, the thing was undecided. It felt almost like a Dutch election.

But in January, George W. Bush became president, and the whole comedy world could take it easy for a while: the shit just wrote itself every time Dubya opened his mouth. Bush was perfectly easy to make fun of: cocky and dumb enough to confirm European stereotypes about Americans, while simultaneously giving American comedians someone to publicly distance themselves from. Bush 2.0 made it easy to be an expat.

Then, quite suddenly, everything changed when planes smashed into the World Trade Center in New York and the Pentagon in Washington, DC, on September 11. Besides the obvious shock of so many people being killed in the first attack on American soil since 1941, experiencing 9/11 in real time—especially as Americans living abroad—was surreal. No one knew what to do, or what was right. People predicted 9/11 would be the death of irony, and the end of comedy. We were suddenly in a "War on Terror," whatever that was. And as George Bush catapulted from village idiot to wartime president, no one wanted to see him as dumb anymore because, you know, it's not super comforting to have an idiot running this War on Terror thing. So people kept it to themselves for a bit. Bush said everyone had to be either for us or against us (though we're pretty sure he actually said, "Fer us or agin' us"). So the whole world rallied around Bush. We all know how well that turned out.

Andrew Moskos: On September 11, there was the question if Boom wanted to do a show that night. I was like, absolutely yes. About seventy people canceled their reservations, but another seventy bought tickets that night. We ended up sold out: after spending hours at home glued to CNN, a lot of people wanted to be out that night.

The next night, September 12, I was asked to be on a round-table discussion show on Amsterdam TV station AT5. I was on a panel with Amsterdam mayor Job Cohen and some other interesting types trying to put the attacks into perspective. I remember thinking, *What the hell do I know about what September 11 means on September 12?* But I did my best to give my take—in Dutch, no less—on what should happen next. I forgot exactly what I said. Really, I was still in a daze.

In 2011, on the tenth anniversary of 9/11, AT5 came back to me for a quote. They played me something I'd said in 2001, and I was surprised to hear that it was pretty spot-on. On TV that day, I said that I was worried that George Bush would "begin an unending war on terror that would be just as successful as the War on Drugs." I actually used the phrase "war on terror" before George Bush ever did! Maybe he watched AT5 the way Trump watches *Fox and Friends*? Three years after 9/11, we wrote the following scene for our 2004 election show:

From "Mr. America Contest," 2004

Patient Pep is in a coma in a hospital bed. Doctor Greg is at his bedside.

Pep: [Waking] Where am I?

Greg: Mr Rosenfeld! You're in a hospital here in New York . . . Brace yourself: you've been in a coma since August 2001.

Pep: A coma? What? I don't understand . . . One minute I'm seeing Shrek, *and the next thing I know I wake up here? How long have I been out?*

Greg: Three years. It's 2004. What's the last thing you remember?

Pep: Princess Fiona was actually an ogre!

Greg: Before Shrek.

Pep: Oh. Well, let's see . . . The president is George Bush. He's really dumb, but that's okay because he's on vacation a lot and there's really nothing important going on in the world. That still pretty much the story?

Greg: Look. I don't know how to say this, so I'll just say it. There was an unbelievable terrorist attack on American soil.

Pep: OH MY GOD!

Greg: We're in the middle of a worldwide War on Terror.

Pep: OH MY GOD! And George Bush is running the war?

Greg: Yes.

Pep: OH MY GOD!

Greg: Yes.

Pep: Wow. Who did it? Who attacked us? Was it Saddam Hussein?

Greg: No. It was Osama bin Laden.

Pep: Of course! So what did we do to get Osama bin Laden?

Greg: We invaded Iraq.

Pep: To get Osama?

Greg: To get Saddam.

Pep: But I don't . . .

Greg: No one understands.

Pep: Who's running for president?

Greg: John Kerry.

Pep: The senator from Massachusetts—he's a war hero!

Greg: Not anymore. Bush says he was a Swift Boat coward.

Pep: But . . . isn't Bush a draft dodger?

Greg: Not anymore. Now he's a "war president."

Pep: Wow. I'll need cash. I better sell all my stock in Enron.

Greg: Enron? I'm afraid Enron didn't make it.

Pep: This is terrible. I better talk to my accountant at Arthur Andersen.

Greg: Sorry. Arthur Andersen didn't make it either.

Pep: Look, Doc—can I get out of this hospital? I'm anxious to get back to my job. This is still New York, and I still work downtown.

Greg: [Nervous] Uh . . . where downtown?

Pep: Starbucks.

Greg: They're doing great! Which Starbucks is it?

Pep: The one in the World Trade Center.

Greg: Sorry . . .

Andrew Moskos: 9/11 was quite a thing for us. As American comedians, we wanted to criticize things that we thought were going wrong without being assholes—but it was hard to make jokes about a subject that felt, for a while, to be beyond the reach of humor. And not just at Boom.

Greg Shapiro: The first show that Seth worked on at *SNL* was in fact the first one that came after 9/11, if you can imagine. That must've been rough.

Pep Rosenfeld: 9/11 happened right after my time at *SNL* ended. I'd actually been back in Amsterdam for a project we were doing at Boom, and was heading back to the States because all of us *SNL* writers that year had received nominations for Emmy Awards. The ceremony was in Los Angeles. On my way to LA, however, I thought I'd stop first in New York for a few days. So I flew out from Amsterdam and landed in JFK on September 10. Great timing. I was staying at Seth's place, which was my old place, and went to sleep jet-lagged as hell. When I woke up on September 11, Seth had already gone to work.

Seth Meyers: On the morning of 9/11, I was hearing all these sirens as I was going uptown, and I thought, *Oh, that's just how New York sounds.* When I got to *SNL*, there was no Internet, and I realized something was going on.

Pep Rosenfeld: First thing I did was log onto CompServe—hey, it was 2001—to check my email. I logged in after the first plane had hit the World Trade Center, and the home page headline was something like, "Plane Hits World Trade Center, Building on Fire." Now, I saw that and couldn't even imagine what was actually happening. In my brain, it was maybe a crop duster or small private plane piloted by someone who'd lost control or was drunk and crashed into the building by accident. So I wrote a snarky note to Seth, like, *Hey, if you're near the Twin Towers, be careful—there's a fire and you might get burned.* Of course, I had no idea what was really going on. So I took a shower, got dressed, and went outside. I saw the building's superintendent, who didn't speak English particularly well. He pointed downtown and said, "Look, the buildings are fall down." And I'm thinking, *I don't know what you are trying to say, funny foreign man.* But when I looked over, the Twin Towers were no longer in the skyline. They'd already fallen between the time I'd gotten out of bed and finished my shower.

That evening, I had dinner in Midtown Manhattan with Seth and another Boom alum, Allison Silverman. Afterward, Seth and I walked back downtown. When we got to 14th Street, the police stopped us: "You've got to show us some ID proving you live here." And I said, "Funny story: I used to live here, but don't anymore, so I don't have any ID. And my friend Seth here just moved to New York a month ago, so he doesn't have an ID that shows where he lives either, which is also where I used to live." The cop just stared at us and said, "Fellas, you know what happened here today, right? I can't let anyone through."

It was a real symbolic moment of New York dealing with 9/11 on 9/11. On the one hand, no one knew what was happening or why, or if it was going to happen again. The streets were weirdly empty of normal traffic, as the only cars being allowed downtown were emergency vehicles. And creepily, they kept coming and coming. So the policeman had every reason to keep us from crossing the street. But he also realized that we were all in this together. And after a long, awful day, we just wanted to get home. So he let us through.

Seth Meyers: You know, 9/11 sped up how quickly I felt like a real New Yorker. Just from sharing with fellow New Yorkers in something like that, and then seeing how quickly the city recovered and being a part of all that too, I just realized, *Oh, this* is *where I want to be.*

Pep Rosenfeld: That whole week, from when 9/11 happened until I was able to leave New York, I thought, *What am I doing here? Should I drive to Chicago?* And the entire time, I wanted to do something, like, *What can I do to help?* It turns out that, in times of national crisis and mourning, no one's asking for jokes. Nobody's saying, "Help! Is there a comedian in the house?"

Nicole Parker: Boom Chicago was the first American comedy show to really deal with 9/11. Certainly *SNL* wasn't going to, and it didn't seem like Second City material, either. But every time we asked for suggestions from Boom's audience, they'd always yell out, "Osama bin Laden!" It got to be like, "My God, we have to address this."

Andrew Moskos: It took awhile for 9/11 jokes to be accepted. Ten years later, though, we did a show about it called "9/11 Forever."

Pep Rosenfeld: "9/11 Forever" was Greg, Mike OT (aka Michael Orton-Toliver), and me, with Andrew directing. We wanted to do a show that looked at how 9/11 affected people at the time and, more interestingly, what had happened since. We felt like America had taken national unity and used it to take scary steps toward authoritarianism and angry jingoism. I'd never heard anyone call the USA "homeland" before. It sounds a little too much like *vaderland* to me. And then our government took international unity and used it to push this neoconservative agenda of regime change in Iraq. The four of us wanted to say all that *and* be funny at the same time.

Andrew Moskos: We got two reviews that, put together, really summed it up. One critic raved: "Finally, someone is addressing the issues and causes and results of 9/11." Another had the opposite attitude: "How *dare* Boom Chicago do a *comedy* show about 9/11?" I was happy we got both perspectives. You know you've struck a nerve when you're both praised and criticized for saying something. And ultimately, isn't that comedy's job?

Pep Rosenfeld: For a while, it felt like comedians couldn't do their job. Bill Maher lost his show, *Politically Incorrect*, after he said something like, "Say what you want about suicide bombers, but they're not cowards. Dropping bombs from a mile up; that's cowardice." This was not, uh, received well.

Andrew Moskos: You couldn't even *say* 9/11, especially right after it all happened. People would literally say, "The tragic events of September 11" all the time. Being the American voice in Amsterdam, and also for ourselves personally, we had to deal with it; it had really affected all of us. So especially on the day, the questions for us as comedians were: What do we say? What do we do?

Brendan Hunt: On the day itself, I walked in the door of my apartment and saw one of my roommates watching CNN, which was weird because he had a day job. Then he said from the couch, "Something's happening in New York." As I sat down on the couch next to him, I could see that one tower had already been hit. CNN was sort of trying to make sense of it in a very calm and responsible way.

Jordan Peele: I was at the theater, and Steven Svymbersky got on the mic and said, "Hold on—something bad is happening." On his computer, he'd pulled up the image of the Twin Towers after they had been hit by the second plane, and put it on the theater's screen for us to see.

Brendan Hunt: When the second building got hit, it was like, "What the fuck is going on?" We just sat watching the whole thing happen in real time, right before our eyes. We didn't move, we didn't talk. Suddenly, this big cloud of smoke filled the screen, and my roommate said, "That building is gone." Seeing that, I turned to him and said, "I think I've got to go be with Americans right now."

Jordan Peele: You know, life just stopped—it slowed down to a halt at that moment. My mother and the rest of my family were in New York, so I was trying to call her over and over. Having grown up in New York City, it was horrific—just terrifying. Obviously, anybody who was on the island of Manhattan that day was close to the incident: Everyone I've talked to who was there that day still has a kind of PTSD about it.

I myself had a weird feeling that was very different from anything I'd felt up to that point. I didn't know if anyone I knew was going to die, and I needed to make sure they were safe. I just remember going back to my place and finally getting in touch with my mom. When I reached her, she was at her place on the Upper West Side. I broke down when she said she was okay. God, it was so fucked up.

Brendan Hunt: I went over to Boom, where there was a great debate going on about whether to do the show. A lot of folks felt like we *had* to do it, but I was unable to get on the gung-ho-enthusiasm train. Finally, everyone had agreed that the show would go on as planned. I was not in the cast that night, so I was like, "More power to you guys, but I don't think I can do it."

Andrew Moskos: I definitely wanted to do a show that night. People wanted to come together after such a tragic event. Greg opened the show with a mock newscast. His opening joke dealt with the world's desire to think about anything except explosions: "Our top story tonight: Boom Chicago changes its name to 'Hello, Chicago.'"

Brendan Hunt: The audience was really with the cast that night.

I recall Joe Kelly being really moved by the end of it. He later told me it was one of his favorite memories at Boom Chicago.

On September 12, the promoters at Club Vegas were throwing a new party night at this huge megaclub Panama, just east of Centraal Station. There was some debate among the cast whether we should still go. I lobbied for yes. I felt we had to support our Club Vegas friends, so we went. It turned out that the only people who showed up that night were fifteen close American friends of the organizers.

We had this whole dance club to ourselves, and it turned out to be a great evening. After all the tension and angst built up during the previous twenty-four hours, dancing with our Club Vegas fans became a great sort of mini catharsis. We'd felt all this helplessness, so we shook it off on the dance floor.

Pep Rosenfeld: Even us—a bunch of hyper-cynical, self-critical Americans—were dropping the self-awareness for a few days. We didn't need anyone talking shit about America while there was still smoke in the air at Ground Zero. Greg told me that just a few days after 9/11, he was doing a show and a Dutch guy came up to him afterward and said, "'You're American? Let me buy you a drink." Greg thanks the guy, and as he's lifting the beer to his lips, the Dutch dude says, "You know 9/11 was America's fault, right?"

Andrew Moskos: Oh, that winning Dutch honesty. Greg downed his beer and walked away. I'm pretty sure he was thinking, *I don't give a fuck that you just bought me a beer. You can shut up now, you horse-toothed motherfucker!* So yeah, Dutch and American responses were pretty different. And the Americans wanted to be together.

Dave Buckman: It's true. Random Americans started showing up to the theater over the next couple of days—dazed and scared, just wanting to be with other Americans. It was actually very moving to see this community of strangers come together under Boom Chicago's roof. After a few days, Andrew wanted something in the show that had our take on 9/11.

Andrew Moskos: I knew we had to somehow tackle the topic in the show. People were coming to see it—American *and* Dutch—and we had to have an opinion about what had happened. We had to say something about it.

Dave Buckman: During those days, we'd smoke weed and watch CNN, just shaking our heads. One question that was percolating that whole time was, "What's the Taliban?" The world had a lot of open questions about these people, who we all assumed had done it before bin Laden's name surfaced. But who were the Taliban—these weird guys in robes and sandals who lived in caves and took down skyscrapers?

So when Jordan and I would see clips of the Taliban on TV, we just started doing voices for them with the sound turned down—making fun of them, but also trying to make them real people too. Eventually, we fell into these Cheech and Chong stoner characters. So for the news segment of the Boom show that night, we dressed up as Taliban and took questions from the audience: whatever questions were needed to be asked of the Taliban, these stoner terrorists answered. It was cathartic to laugh at something that in reality was so frightening and raw.

Andrew Moskos: I'm not sure Taliban Cheech and Chong was what I had in mind as Boom Chicago's take on 9/11—but yes, it was just what the audience needed. Meanwhile, we started to notice a change in people's attitudes toward America and Americans. Europe was largely pro-America during Clinton's presidency—which turned into anti-Americanism almost immediately with the corrupt election of George W. Bush. As you can imagine, Dutch opinion of Bush went even further downhill from there with the Iraq War.

Dave Buckman: A few days later, the first episode of *SNL* that Seth worked on aired.

Nicole Parker: We all got together in the theater to watch Seth's *SNL* debut. It was so exciting.

Dave Buckman: It would prove to be one of the most beloved and watched in the history of the show. I think in a way, that particular episode made it okay for our fellow Americans to laugh again too.

Greg Shapiro: For years after 9/11, everyone talked about the Taliban and Osama bin Laden. Before 9/11, most people hadn't even heard those names before. Most people, that is, with the weird exception of Dutch B-movie director Dick Maas. One of his movies contained a very strange premonition about 9/11. Remember Maas's movie *Down*? No? I don't blame you. *Down*—Maas's shoddy English-language remake of his 1983 horror classic *De Lift*—came out on September 6, 2001, eerily presaging many details that would become reality five days later. *Down* was about people trapped in an elevator in a New York City office building who think they're under terrorist attack—when in fact they're being hunted by a haunted elevator. In this movie, there are lines like, "We're going to blow up the terrorists with Stinger missiles—take that, Osama!" Somehow, Holland's premier horror-schlock director knew about Osama bin Laden before George Bush had ever heard of him—admittedly, a low bar.

Pep Rosenfeld: Andrew was watching *Down* in an Amsterdam cinema on September 11, and when he arrived home after watching a fake New York tower on fake fire, he turned on CNN and saw *real* New York towers on *real* fire after being attacked by *real* terrorists.

Andrew Moskos: It was one part surreal and four parts awful. And because they shot the film in Amsterdam, many Boom actors were in *Down* alongside its star, Naomi Watts. We were pretty excited, but the movie was almost immediately pulled from theaters. In the fall of 2001, no one wanted to see a movie about a New York skyscraper disaster—especially not a terrible movie about one. The world never got to see Greg Shapiro as a computer expert named Chip. Get it? Hey, I said it was terrible.

Rob AndristPlourde: Weirdly, 9/11 happened in the middle of Boom Chicago's second real golden age.

Brendan Hunt: We had an incredible cast that year. Greg, Rob, Josh, Holly, and I were still in the cast, but that was the first year for Jordan Peele, Nicole Parker, Lauren Dowden, Joe Kelly, and Becky Drysdale. In hindsight, that's a pretty astonishing crew to come together in Amsterdam at the same time.

Josh Meyers: When I was onstage with this group, I could really *feel* how good the cast was. No matter which five people you had on a given night, the show was going to be great.

Josie O'Reilly: Holly Walker was gold with an audience. She rocked that theater and the credit and style was all her own.

Kay Cannon: Holly Walker was a standout: crazy funny, beautiful, a force onstage, and with the widest, warmest smile I had ever seen. Audiences *lurrrrved* her. And Jordan stood out too—and not only because he is *ridic* talented. For me, it was his thoughtfulness and approach to the work. The moment I remembered thinking, *This guy is a leader*, was when Boom brought over an incredibly well-respected improviser from New York to do a workshop with the cast. This incredibly well-respected improviser then vocally shared with us his utter disdain for what we were doing at Boom: he hated games and short-form improv, and didn't hold back from telling us so. In my mind, I thought, *Why are you here? How are you inspiring or teaching us like this? What a bummer.* But Jordan actually said it: this twenty-two-year-old kid spoke up and, in a respectful but poignant way, told the elder improviser that how he was treating us, and the message he was sending, was horseshit. What a lesson we all learned that day.

Jordan Peele: I was so glad to be there. Even then I knew the most valuable thing in comedy was experience: you need to get your reps. Learning to be an improviser is so frustrating. In Chicago, I was doing everything I could to compete for maybe a couple hours of stage time per week. You do a show, and maybe it doesn't go well. Then you have to stew on that for two weeks until your next show. Only then can you try to dig out and restore both your professional reputation and self-esteem.

Seth Meyers: I have to say, the aspect of Boom Chicago where you're really working on your craft and being onstage for five or six days a week, not to mention doing corporate shows—it's undervalued, or it was by me. I didn't anticipate how huge the benefits would be—but I'm not surprised Jordan did. He's a very pragmatic person.

Brendan Hunt: I worked with Jordan a lot when we made 2001's new show, "Europe: We've Created a Monster." At that time, the euro was still a year away, and our poster was Frankenstein made up of European countries.

Pep Rosenfeld: Chicago comedy legend Ron West directed the show, which was about all that could go wrong with the European Union. It foresaw the potential problems of the euro, picking a national anthem, letting too many countries in, and mad cow disease, to name just a few.

Jordan Peele: One of my favorite characters in "Europe: We've Created a Monster" was Uta, a Danish supermodel who hosted the Eurovision Song Contest. I watched the competition that year for the first time. It was crazy: Denmark hosted that year, and there was this Danish supermodel on the show, and every time she tried to speak English, she had this crazy accent that made everything come out like a Speak & Spell. I based Uta on her.

Ruben van der Meer: I don't think I laughed more at anything than when Uta tried to say the word "because."

Jordan Peele: "Because" was in all her sentences. Like, "Yes! *Because!*"

Pep Rosenfeld: But when Uta said it, "because" sounded more like "be cows" or "be kaas" or "Bah! Kiss!"

Andrew Moskos: Uta's Euro accent was a wonderful moving target. In just two syllables, Jordan-as-Uta basically managed to linguistically represent the entire EU at once.

Jordan Peele: The whole bit was that Uta was an adorable Danish supermodel who'd learned English just in time to host the Eurovision Song Contest along with Brendan's character, Michael Shmichael. I put on a blond wig and a boa, and Uta was born. We did this simple improv game: whenever Michael Shmichael said something, Uta clearly misunderstood whatever he was trying to communicate. Regardless, she would respond with all the confidence and charm in the world—trying to hang with the conversation that was being broadcast on live TV to a global audience of millions.

From the moment we got onstage, it was clear the audience was magnetized by the dynamic between these two characters. I think they recognized something in the type I was mocking, but at the same time, there was also something universal there. It worked, and infinite variations seemed possible, so Uta became a cornerstone of the show for a long time. Uta was actually the first woman character I'd ever attempted.

Andrew Moskos: And Jordan would go on to play his fair share of convincing women later on *Key & Peele*.

Heather Anne Campbell: I might point out here that, when actors were improvising onstage at Boom Chicago, we could play any gender, any age—whereas at Groundlings, that's not allowed: if you're a woman, you can't play a man in a scene, and vice versa. They'd be like, "The scene is off—you can't do that." At Boom, thankfully there were no such rules; it was total freedom of expression. It's a strange thing to restrict. When done right, sometimes there's nothing funnier than playing a gender other than the one you identify with.

Jordan Peele: With Uta, I tried to do it legit: I wasn't trying to be a guy being a woman, but a *woman*. I wanted to be pretty; I wanted to be perceived as hot. I really submerged myself into this character with a stake in my own manhood, and the audience could feel that I'd committed to this. If you believe in what you're doing as a performer, your audience will follow you: they sort of suspend their disbelief and go with it.

One of the best moments in my entire career was playing Uta at the Edinburgh Festival Fringe. We were in this big space, and everyone in the crowd was well versed in the Eurovision phenomenon, so they were on board. We came out to introduce the second song—and all of a sudden the lights in the theater cut out.

Suddenly, three hundred people were trapped in a completely dark room, captive with us onstage. Thankfully, for some reason our microphones were still working. As we waited for the lights to come back on, we stayed in character, and Uta became sort of scared. Because it was happening in the moment, the audience knew what was happening onstage wasn't scripted but clearly improvised. This created even more titillation: the audience actually felt what was happening as it happened. We'd received this huge glorious gift by having to cope with the awkwardness of this real-life glitch.

We were in total darkness for twelve minutes, trying to figure out what was going on. It was the most magnetic, electric twelve minutes onstage I've ever had. Afterward, Brendan and I and everybody looked at each other and just went, "Wow!" That was just such a cool moment that will never happen again.

Andrew Moskos: Uta also came in handy when we ran into trouble with another piece in the "Monster" show, the *Weakest Link* sketch.

Dave Buckman: The *Weakest Link* game show scene gave George Bush a lot of punch lines—but within a week after 9/11, we noticed that no one was laughing at it anymore. People had reframed Bush as a hero, and no one wanted to laugh at him. We rewrote the scene with Uta in the Bush slot and gave the better Bush jokes to a Polish character. It worked.

Andrew Moskos: What a time! We had a great crew of people in the theater, and that enabled us to deal with the cataclysmic changes of the real world. We also had some big departures that year, though accompanied by big arrivals.

Ike Barinholtz: 2001 was actually my last year in the Boom Chicago cast. It was a really fun way to go out, leaving that cast there, taking care of business. Boom was in great hands, creative-wise. I'd say the cast that year included the two best performers from Boom Chicago ever, Brendan Hunt and Nicole Parker. They were built for the part. Nicole may actually be Boom's number one. She's this thoroughbred of a performer. And it goes without saying that I was amazed by Jordan too.

Pep Rosenfeld: It's always sad when people leave, but it's also exciting. We thrive when new young people arrive in Amsterdam hot to make their mark on our stage. And we want our cast to get great, and then leave to get more prestigious jobs.

Seth Meyers: I was lucky to have a two-year break between leaving Boom and going to *SNL*. I remember talking to Pep a lot the first year after I left about how much I missed being at Boom, and being in Amsterdam. Since Pep had gone through all that already, talking to him helped with my expectations of what I wanted to be doing, and where I'd end up.

A key part of the appeal of doing *SNL* was to be part of a *thing* again. The thing I'd missed most about leaving Boom was being a part of a group of people working together. Doing auditions in LA had been a lot lonelier than Boom had been, and that's what *SNL* became for me.

Josh Meyers: I didn't actually think about leaving until Seth got on *SNL*. At Boom, we weren't trying to get famous; we were just trying to do comedy. People weren't thinking about being in movies or TV. I certainly never thought, *After this, I'll go to Hollywood!* I'd thought seriously about staying in Holland; I considered never moving back to the US. I was actually getting my Dutch-language skills up, and had even been in a couple minor Dutch movies. I was young and happy in Amsterdam, having fun and succeeding in what I was doing at Boom.

Pep Rosenfeld: And then Seth arrived at *SNL* just in time to do his first show the week after 9/11. Great timing, right?

Andrew Moskos: But in some ways, it *was* great timing. 9/11 was literally unbelievable. It was one of those rare moments when you're not just watching the world change in front of you, you actually feel the changes as they happen. At first, you don't know what to do. You feel paralyzed. But then you just get on with it and do your job. Our job is comedy. We help people deal with hard situations. At our best, we try to help make sense of what doesn't seem to make any sense. At worst, well, even a dick joke that makes you laugh can distract from tragedy for a little while.

Pep Rosenfeld: And somewhere in the middle is the Cheech and Chong Taliban . . .

CHAPTER 10
2002

THE ROYAL WEDDING—NO, NOT THAT ONE: THE NETHERLANDS HAS KINGS AND QUEENS TOO . . .

O kay, when the world thinks of kings and queens, let's face it, England gets the hype—and hey, Brit royalty ain't dull. There's the fascinating duality between Prince William and the No-Longer-Prince Harry, Markle vs. Middleton. Prince Andrew and his disgraceful association with Jeffrey Epstein, King Charles's succession blues as he rises from the middle, and the endless lamenting of Queen Elizabeth's passing—all mostly by those people who still actually buy trashy gossip magazines in grocery checkout lines. With that cast of colorful characters, there's a reason why a hundred Princess Diana biopics exist and Netflix did its own royals show with *The Crown*.[25]

Indeed, the UK so dominates the royalty space, the residents of Buckingham Palace completely overshadow the continuing existence of the admittedly less flashy and sordid (and hence, very Dutch) Royal House of the Netherlands. Landing somewhere between beloved and tolerated (again, very Dutch), Holland's constitutional monarchy may seem somewhat out of place in modern times. The kingdom's ongoing role in Dutch society—and how *Nederlanders* feel about supporting *onze ei-*

---

25 Full disclosure: one of Boom's founders fell asleep just thinking about the last paragraph. He can hardly contain his disinterest in the British royal family.

gen royal family—was made abundantly clear, however, in the 2002 union of heir apparent Prince of Orange Willem-Alexander and Princess Máxima.

Barely a blip in the international media, the first Dutch royal wedding of the aughts proved a major obsession in the Netherlands—as did Queen Beatrix's abdication of the throne in 2013 on the totally gonzo Dutch holiday formerly known as Queen's Day. This was a seismic event: not only did the end of Beatrix's three-decade-plus reign instantly turn Willem and Máxima into Holland's new king and queen—this power move also inadvertently turned Queen's Day into King's Day, causing Dutch citizens to go, "What are you doing for Queen's Day—I mean, King's Day," for years. Yes, change is slow in the Netherlands, but when it happens, there's no going back. King's Day it was.

Many expat Boom stars happened to be around for the Dutch royal wedding—especially as its ensuing parade conveniently ended in the Leidseplein near Boom Chicago's theater. But Boom cast members also never wanted to miss celebrating Queen's Day. An absolutely riotous annual event, Queen's Day has basically become a national excuse to fuck off work, wear orange, sit outside in the warm(er) spring weather, and get really, really wasted (all of which organically turned it into an ongoing Boom Chicago tradition).

2002 also proved a most auspicious moment for the succession of comedy royalty. That year, Boom Chicago did its first stateside performances in what became known as the Comedy Swap. Boom Chicago's cast traveled to Chicago's iconic improv institution Second City to perform for a week on its famed mainstage; likewise, Second City sent their troupe to Amsterdam to do its thing in Boom's Leidseplein theater.

Second City's status as the ruling kingdom of improvisation was never in question, but revolutionary upstarts Boom Chicago did show them some new moves during the historic cross-continental residency. Most significantly, Jordan Peele met Keegan-Michael Key for the first time at the Comedy Swap—setting the stage for their creation of the absurdly groundbreaking (and groundbreakingly absurd) *Key & Peele* show.

Steven Svymbersky: There are few kings and queens left in the world, and I'll admit it, the royal wedding was exciting. I still have my Willem-Alexander memorial spoon that I got from Albert Heijn. It's one of the few souvenirs I took when I left Amsterdam.

Michael Diederich: Having arrived in Holland in 1993, I was already enamored with the royal family.

Andrew Moskos: Pep actually met Holland's beloved Queen Máxima once, and not at her wedding, alas. Remember when TED Talks were getting big? I mean, like long before you'd be at a cocktail party saying, "Did you see that TED Talk that so-and-so thought leader gave about blah blah blah?" and everyone would nod knowingly? Or before it was a thing you'd make fun of in your comedy show (as Boom Chicago did in 2002)?

This happened around the time TEDx Talks started spreading from real cities like Amsterdam to so-so cities like the Hague. This is when Pep got involved with the Dutch TED folks, naturally. In 2008, he hosted the simulcast of TEDxAmsterdam at Boom Chicago. Two years later, he hosted it for real at the prestigious Stadsschouwburg of Amsterdam. Then in 2011, he gave a talk himself at TEDxAmsterdam called, "Fight, Flight, or Make Your Enemy Laugh: The Power of Comedy."

Saskia Maas: Then in 2012, Pep was asked to host TEDxBinnenhof in the Hague, with a government theme. (See "spreading to so-so cities like the Hague" above.)

Andrew Moskos: It was actually a pretty cool setup. The event took place in the historic Ridderzaal. It was a short program (well, short for TED, anyway) featuring ten seven-minute talks given by cool innovators from the Netherlands: Claire Boonstra, Rob Baan, Daan Roosegaarde . . . Seemingly all the Dutch tech cognoscenti with double vowels in their names were on the bill. Everyone brought something cool too. Daan had a model on-stage wearing an "intimacy dress," which was like an old-school mood ring in dress form. And instead of just changing color, when the model got excited, the garment would change color *and* become a little see-through (which got the audience a little excited).

The highlight for many, though, was the attendance of the crown prince and princess, Willem-Alexander and Máxima. In 2012, they weren't king and queen yet; still, having them at your event was a pretty big deal. Such a big deal that royal handlers were more than a little wary having a comedian from Boom Chicago introduce them. Boy oh boy, did they go over the formal (but not all that difficult) way Pep was instructed to name-check Dutch royalty: "Their Royal Highnesses, the Prince of Orange and Princess Máxima of the Netherlands . . ." Easy. Pep introduced them just as he was told: "When their Royal Highnesses come in, please greet them with your applause—not by filming it on your phone. This isn't *RTL Boulevard*."[26] Or, "Welcome, our Royal Highnesses: it must be a nice change to be somewhere where you can be sure that absolutely no one has come to hear what you have to say."

Okay, there were a *few* zings. No one said it had to be zing-free.

Pep Rosenfeld: Afterward, I did get to meet Máxima, Her Royal Highness (then) Princess Máxima of the Netherlands. Chatting a bit, I asked her whose Dutch she thought was worse: hers or mine. She answered in perfect, if charmingly Argentinian-

---

26 *RTL Boulevard* is basically the Dutch *Entertainment Tonight*.

accented, Dutch, and . . . I couldn't follow her answer. So, mine was clearly worse. Or she was doing an awesome bit where she spoke Dutch-sounding gibberish to make me think my Dutch was worse. Which I totally hope she was doing.

Andrew Moskos: I later met the king at the sixtieth anniversary of the Amsterdam American Chamber of Commerce in 2022. I was interviewing the heads of Google and Albert Heijn, but also introducing the king, so I needed three jokes for when he sat down.

Pep Rosenfeld: I pitched, "Thanks for taking time, Your Highness, out of your busy schedule. I mean, I assume it's busy. Because I have no idea what you actually do."

Andrew Moskos: That was a bit harder-hitting than I was looking for. I needed something funny enough, but that didn't make the paper the next day. So I went with, "Welcome! As an American, we don't have a royal family. The closest thing we have is the Kardashians." Looking right at King Willem seated in the front row twelve feet away, I continued: "And the closest I have ever been to royalty is the Dutch expression *The client is king*. But I have lived here for a long time, and that is not true. In fact, I think that expression is disrespectful to the king." King Willem and the audience laughed hard. Mission accomplished.

Later at the reception, I went over to the head table where I was unfortunately not sitting. "Andrew, you have a great take on the Netherlands," King Willem said, thrusting out his hand. After thanking him, I inquired if it was inappropriate to ask for a photo. "*Everyone* has been asking me that today," my new pal Willem groaned with a suddenly serious expression. "I said no to everyone." Then he smiled. "But for you, yes!"

Pep Rosenfeld: Now, I don't remember their wedding itself. I'm not such a big royal family guy. But I bet it was romantic. I mean, you know, romantic-ish. Not quite over-the-top-American-wedding romantic. Dutch-wedding romantic.

The core of a Dutch wedding is different. For an American bride, this is the most wonderful, important day in her life. She's waited all her life for that fateful day when she'd walk down the aisle, to be given away by her father—which, when you think about it, is a little creepy. For Dutch folks, weddings are the day when, in front of the world, you look your partner in the eyes—and sign a legal contract. A Dutch wedding is a public contract signing. Sexy, I know . . .

At American weddings, there's a best man. He's the guy who's got your back, as in: "Buddy, I know you . . . I love you . . . I'd do anything for you . . . I'm your *best man*." But there's no best man at a Dutch wedding. Instead, there's a witness. The witness is the guy who looks at you, looks at the bride, looks at the *contract*, and then says, "Buddy, everything here appears to be in order. Sign away."

Meanwhile, this formal phrase is reserved solely for weddings: "I do." We *only* say that at weddings. Like, if my buddy asks me if I want to see the new Steven Spielberg movie and I say, "I do," the rules specify that we're legally married from that point on.

But you don't say "I do" at a Dutch wedding: you say *ja* ("ya"). Yes, the word "yes" (especially in Germanic languages, jus' sayin') is clearly the most clinical, unromantic way to answer a romantic question. It sounds like you're agreeing to do a chore. Will you take out the trash? *Ja*. Will you do the laundry? *Ja*. Will you spend the rest of your life with me? *Ja*.

Andrew Moskos: There's this Dutch thing where it's free to get married on Mondays. This was supposed to be so that poor people could get married too—but Dutch people being Dutch, now there's a nine-month wait to get married on a Monday. I suppose twenty years from now, they'll want to look back on the most romantic day of their life and think, *Such good value!*

Pep Rosenfeld: Even Dutch dates aren't romantic. Dutch people don't date: instead, you have an *afspraak*, or "appointment." How sad is that? You use the same word for a business appointment and a chance to get laid. *Ah, let me put that in Google Calendar . . .*

See, when Americans ask each other on a date, it's a big deal. We get nervous. We get sweaty. It's a *thing*. Now, I've never been a Dutch guy asking someone on a date, but I assume it's super practical—like, "Marijke, I have an opening in my agenda this weekend, and I would like to fit you in. I will meet you at eight o'clock. We will eat dinner and, contrary to stereotype, I will pay for the meal. Then we will have a drink at your apartment, and take off our clothes. If you like, I can put my penis inside you and move it back and forth."

And with any luck, the answer will be *ja*. We can only assume that's what Willem-Alexander said to Máxima before their first date. Only back then, she probably responded, "*Sí.*"

Ruben van der Meer: For some Dutch people, the royal wedding was an important event. Willem didn't actually do anything on this day. The old queen said, "I ring this bell and wear these gloves, and now you are king of the Netherlands!" And then the royal bride and groom came out on the balcony to address the people who were waiting below. Willem did his king thing, which is waving. The Dutch royal family is very big on waving. Willem was now the new royal waver.

Rob AndristPlourde: As the official parade that followed Willem's coronation wound through Amsterdam, with crowds lining the streets, someone threw a cake at the carriage carrying the royals. Willem just took it stride: he knew it was cooler to not be fazed, which seemed very Dutch.

Andrew Moskos: You know if that happened to King Charles, he would've thrown a hissy fit like a little bitch!

Steven Svymbersky: A big thing was all the controversy surrounding the new queen's background—chatter about her father being a former Argentinian dictator/mobster–type accused of secretly having people murdered. Ultimately, after much *polder*, Dutch people concluded, "Well, Máxima is not her father."

Michael Diederich: I had a brush with Dutch royalty once. One Tuesday, I'd finished an afternoon workshop in Leiden. It was near a bowling alley, and I had time to burn, so I was like, "Let's bowl!" I didn't notice the black cars with tinted glass in front, or the security guys subtly standing around. Asking for bowling shoes and a lane, I was told I could have lane ten because the other lanes were bought out by a private party. Looking around, I noticed all the lanes were empty . . . except one. And there she was: Máxima. In full-on mom clothes. Surrounded by a bunch of giggling girlfriends. *Bowling*. The shine came off the royal family that day.

Steven Svymbersky: People do complain about how much it costs the public to support the royals. So the Dutch use the king for business promotion. He's the global ambassador for Holland, and that's the benefit in maintaining the royal line. It's a very practical Dutch thing: to make it worth having a king, he has to earn his money back by going around the world and promoting the country.

Ruben van der Meer: I do celebrate King's Day, but it's a strange celebration. We could do the whole thing without royalty being involved. It's really about welcoming the new spring season.

Andrew Moskos: In other words, a pagan bacchanalia teeming with thousands of people getting wasted and wearing orange? That's really what it is. Actually, you know what's becoming a sort of new King's Day? The day of the Pride Parade. First of all, it's a huge boat parade. Everyone dresses sexy, slutty, kinky, and recently even straight-ish guys are exploring their lingerie fetish in public. So instead of the day's theme built around orange and royalty, it's about sexy tolerance and living your own life—sort of Brendan Hunt Day.

Jordan Peele: When it was still Queen's Day, it was the best. It's a total challenge of endurance that brings out the merry prankster in everybody. It really does feel like you're seeing everyone's alter ego.

Steven Svymbersky: Queen's Day is about walking around with friends, drinking a lot, and getting really, really high. I mean you are *definitely* going to be high on Queen's Day.

Brendan Hunt: Queen's Day was basically the Fourth of July times Mardi Gras, minus assholes. It's really one of the greatest things about Holland. I remember the first year I got to spend Queen's Day at my house with my mix of Dutch and Boom friends. We were having a great time; there was a lot of laughing, but some people were, shall we say, becoming *overserved*. By the end of night, Kay Cannon had completely passed out.

No one knew how to get her home. We were actually out on the street at this point, dragging Kay around like *Weekend at Bernie's*. There was no way to catch a cab on Queen's Day, and the trams weren't running. Then one of our actors runs around the corner, yelling, "Guys, I've got a solution!" She'd found an errant shopping cart among the Queen's Day rubble, so we dumped Kay in it and carted her unconscious self to her apartment. Now she's a fancy movie director.

Andrew Moskos: It could have been a scene out of *Blockers*.

Kay Cannon: Yes, I *was* dropped off in front of my apartment in a shopping cart. I'm still high from Queen's Day 2000. I'm a drug loser, although I *have* done mushrooms—only twice, and only in Amsterdam. Best days of my life.

Brendan Hunt: Queen's Day was nuts. Walking to the Dam from the Leidseplein, you'd come across these little parties everywhere. There's no official Queen's Day party: they're all over the place, which is what's so great about it. When we got to Dam Square, it was packed; it normally took twenty seconds to cross the square, but we couldn't move. We found ourselves stuck in a Radio 538 party: as we arrived, "Paradise by the Dashboard Light" was playing. The area was so full, it took us the entire length of that song to make our way through the crowd—every single person there was dancing their faces off and singing every word by heart, at the top of their lungs.

For the entire *"Let me sleep on it / Will you love me forever?"* part, the women sang the words, then the rest of the crowd responded, *"Let me sleep on it / Baby, baby, let me sleep on it."* Everyone was into this so hard that Josh Meyers, Joe Canale, and I were forced to traverse a cautious line as if we were living out one of the more dangerous parts of *Jumanji*.[27] Fireworks and explosions were going off all around us too. It was exhilarating. It was also the first time I even realized how much American pop culture means in Holland. Mostly, though, that experience reflected the degree to which people are like, "It's Queen's Day, let's go all out!"

Jordan Peele: Pretty much every holiday is an excuse to party

---

27 Pep Rosenfeld: Wait, of all the adventure movies ever made with traps to avoid, you chose *Jumanji*?

in Amsterdam. That's true everywhere, but Amsterdam is more extreme.

Brendan Hunt: In other cities, New Year's Eve is the biggest party of the year. In Amsterdam, it's just preparation for Queen's Day. It's *Apocalypse Now*[28] with champagne and weed.

Ken Schaefle: I think the Merry Pranksters would be proud of our parties. We threw incredible parties—foam parties, ball parties, a roller rink inside the theater, multiple Jell-O wrestling events, hot tubs, smoke machines, disco balls . . . There was also a house band: I was the bass player, and Jordan was an occasional backup vocalist. Naturally, Brendan was lead vocalist.

Brendan Hunt: Every New Year's, we'd get on the roof at the Leidseplein theater and watch the explosions going off for hundreds of miles in every direction. It was total shock and awe. And no one had, say, filled out the necessary legal forms to handle this massive ordnance. Nope, no one was in charge. On the street, people just blew shit up like twenty feet from where you were standing on the sidewalk. You just trust it's all going to be okay.

Jordan Peele: On New Year's, everywhere you look around you, full 360 degrees, fireworks are constantly going off. It's this sort of beautiful, surreal experience—like *Apocalypse Now* with champagne and weed.[29]

Andrew Moskos: If Willem-Alexander and Máxima would ever join us on the roof one New Year's Eve at Boom Chicago, let's hope that Pep would be on hand to address them correctly and ask them the right question: "His and Her Majesty, the King and Queen of the Netherlands . . . would you like some champagne?"

---

28 Pep Rosenfeld: Now, *that's* an appropriate movie reference.
29 Yes, they both said this independently.

Pep Rosenfeld: "Or weed?"

Andrew Moskos: Other great things happened in 2002, many at Boom Chicago. Pep returned from his stint on *SNL*. Jordan Peele, Joe Kelly (future writer on *How I Met Your Mother* and future cocreator of *Ted Lasso*), and Colton Dunn (later to star on *Superstore* and *Parks and Rec*, as well as write and produce for *Key & Peele*) were killing it in the cast.

Colton Dunn: I had moved to Manhattan from Minneapolis. I was just trying to make it in New York—tutoring, working at video stores, trying to get onstage at Upright Citizens Brigade, and doing college tours for this Second City–type place, Chicago City Limits. I'd started acting in these little comedy sketches on *Late Night with Conan O'Brien*—playing random characters like a security guard or a member of a boy band. Somebody told me about this audition for a short-form improv show—something I'd done a lot of. I didn't know where Holland was, exactly. I may have thought it was one of the Scandinavian countries.

When I got to Amsterdam, I realized I was joining Boom Chicago at a very successful moment. I remember seeing Boom Chicago ads in the trams. Those ads were everywhere. If that cast was a rock band, then we were Led Zeppelin. I remember seeing Jordan and Brendan onstage, thinking, *All these people are going to do their thing in a big way someday.*

Andrew Moskos: 2002 was also the year Boom brought some fresh ideas from our European perch back to the US comedy scene. We did a cast and show swap with the famous Second City, our original inspiration in Chicago to go on this journey. We had been going to Second City with our parents since we were barely old enough to stay up that late, so it was a big deal to play there. An even bigger deal was the fact that the Comedy

Swap was the first time a visiting troupe had ever performed on the Second City mainstage. It was also the first time a visiting show had played on Boom Chicago's stage in Amsterdam—but they had almost fifty years of history to our nine.

Pep Rosenfeld: We returned to our hometown as prodigal improvisers with our show "Rock Stars"—bringing a cast of comedic rock stars with us: Jordan, Colton, Brendan, Nicole Parker, Rachel Miller, and Dave Asher. Back at Boom, meanwhile, Randall Harr, Kristi Casey, and Dani Sher welcomed their Second City counterparts to Amsterdam.

Andrew Moskos: Every seat for the week sold out, and we got great reviews from Chicago's top local critics. The *Chicago Tribune*'s Chris Jones (now its chief theater critic) was especially impressed with our show and style, and continued to report on our alumni in the intervening years. One thing that immediately stood out about Boom Chicago in Chicago, though, was our production values. Second City's, in comparison, proved comparatively quaint. They had a piano player, no microphones, and no pizzazz. That had been standard Second City style for decades; no one had ever complained. Then we got there and were like . . . *shikka, shikka, shik!*

Pep Rosenfeld: Ah yes, *shikka, shikka, shik.* The internationally understood phonetic sound of a turntable-scratched intro.

Andrew Moskos: Today, improv comedians rap all the time. Back then, however, they decidedly didn't. We started our show with our showstopper "Yo! Here We Go." We interviewed three people in the audience and then rapped about them—sometimes dirty. Jordan opened, and we rotated the second position among the cast. Nicole Parker provided the death-blow lyrical finale as the one and only Nickel Bag.

Nope, Boom Chicago aggressively did *not* have a piano on-stage. When Boom's musical director David Schmoll unloaded his gear, it was like when Bruno arrived at the *Fame* school.[30] We'd deployed our three genius technicians—Ken, Jan, and Jamie—who'd brought screens, beamers, video, and concert-level sound. Second City was like, "Oh shit—what we do feels so *small* in comparison." Then they went out and bought that stuff themselves, adopting a hipper approach that continues to this day. Even with Second City's half century of experience, Boom Chicago opened their eyes. That made us very proud.

Peter Grosz: I believe Andrew's wrong in asserting that he and Boom Chicago solely brought technological innovation to comedy in general, and Second City in particular. Okay, sure, Boom *was* just a little further ahead in terms of using new tech in shows, and did have a really cool thing going using recorded music, sampling, and serious sound systems to make music a bigger part of the onstage spectacle. And yes, Second City's style at the time was far more reserved, very *We're too cool to show too much enthusiasm.* That eventually went away—but that was also influenced by Second City's Detroit company, too, who also used amped-up sound to make their shows feel more like a pop-music performance. Really, all that stuff happened from a combination of what Boom Chicago and the Detroit folks were doing, along with technology just advancing as it did in the 2000s. So, ultimately, I'll give Andrew and Boom one-third of the credit for comedy's technological revolution of the early aughts.

Andrew Moskos: I can agree it wasn't solely us—but Second City producer Kelly Leonard did tell me that Boom really showed up Second City technically, and forced them to up their game. So there, Groszie!

---

30 This extra-old-school reference was made so Schmoll, the oldest man in the Boom Chicago family, will also get it.

Pete Grosz: Credit aside, Boom's Comedy Swap with Second City turned out super cool. I was in the Second City cast with Keegan then, and it was great hanging out with Jordan that night. I was basically the Second City ambassador to Boom Chicago: doing sets with them was very fun for me because I knew and loved all those people. And Boom's cast did awesome—they killed. Brendan and Jordan's Eurovision bit remains one of the funniest damn things I've ever seen. Brendan played Jordan's straight man perfectly—he's very much the straight man on *Ted Lasso* now, but that wasn't something you'd say about him often then.

Colton Dunn: I stayed back in Amsterdam during the Comedy Swap. Audiences mostly didn't know what Second City was, but their shows did well. Their vibe was a little slower, and there was a piano, and absolutely no visuals. For audiences used to seeing Boom shows, they were probably left a little more like, *Oh, that was funny*, as opposed to, *Oh my God—that bit that blew my mind! How do they come up with rhymes on the spot when rapping?*

I did become a Second City performer briefly, however. I had to fill in for the Black guy in their cast, who had to go back to Chicago to deal with some emergency. So I learned his parts and did the show; I vaguely remember it being about *Lord of the Rings*. It was just super fun to tick off that box so I could say I played onstage with Second City.

Jordan Peele: Since this was soon after 9/11, traveling to Chicago for the Comedy Swap meant lots of extra security at the airport. They certainly asked a lot more questions.

Greg Shapiro: Everybody had one check-in bag with clothes, and an extra check-in bag carrying pieces of tech gear for the show: video boards, mixers, beam splitters . . .

Pep Rosenfeld: The technicians were super clear: "You *will* be asked what's in your bag, so you have to know what everything is, and what it does. So this is a beam splitter . . ."

Greg Shapiro: After checking in, Jordan Peele gave us his classic technique for sleeping on planes: smoking strong-ass weed beforehand. He claimed to have stuff that was guaranteed to knock you out.

Pep Rosenfeld: So we went outside to Schiphol's smoking section and passed around Jordan's allegedly narcolepsy-inducing joint. I found it had the opposite effect. I got . . . super high. Too high. Like, super-paranoid too high.

Greg Shapiro: Right in time for security check. Being after 9/11, they had interrogation stations set up even before you reached security.

Pep Rosenfeld: There was now security before the security. Of course, the first thing they ask is, "Did you pack your bags yourself?" And for the first time in my life, my super-high paranoid brain realizes the answer is actually . . . no. One bag was actually packed, in fact by a tech who was Boom's resident anticapitalist conspiracy theorist, and just happened to be reading *The Anarchist Cookbook* at the time. So I was sweating bullets, but somehow managed to say yes at the correct moment. Turns out that's not such an effective question for catching people. I mean, I was high AF, totally lied, and passed.

Jordan Peele: Paranoid vibes weren't just at the airport. There was also a heavy vibe in the theater then too. Our Cheech and Chong Taliban sketch kind of freaked people out.

Pep Rosenfeld: We typically offended Americans more than Dutch people, but that's just because the Dutch are harder to offend. In 2003, a letter appeared in the *New York Times* responding to a piece about us. Greg and I were doing "Yankee Go Home," and there was some critical stuff about America in there, as Bush had just kicked off the Iraq War. A military guy stationed in Texas wrote this polite-but-angry letter: *I hate your easy, anti-American show. What about the Dutch soldiers' role at Srebrenica? Do you mention that onstage? I doubt it.* I wrote him back and said, *Of course we mention Srebrenica—and I proudly get booed by the Dutch every night when I do. We're not anti-American, we're anti-hypocrisy.*

Andrew Moskos: And capitalist enough to be pro–making money. I loved this part of the *New York Times* article: "'Americans making fun of themselves, I'm telling you, it sells like hot cakes,' said Greg Shapiro, a tall, angular American who cowrote Boom Chicago's sellout show, 'Yankee Go Home! Americans and Why You Love to Hate Us.'"

Pep Rosenfeld: "Yankee Go Home" had a pretty good ending. Greg played a Dutch person, Jan (sounds like "yaan"—"yawn" minus the "w"), trying to turn my character Kees (pronounced "case") into a Dutch person. In the bit, we explained the origin of the word "Yankee." Greg pointed out that it stemmed from an insult leveled at the Dutch that combined the English pronunciation of those two traditional *Nederlander* names: Jan + Kees = Yankees. So Dutch people in the Bush era might say to us, "Yankee go home," but we were in the Netherlands, so we were already home.

Andrew Moskos: Can you imagine an era when you needed anti-Dutch insults? Some people try to force "Cloggie," but that's not really a thing.

Pep Rosenfeld: Nobody hates the Dutch anymore,[31] but they sure can be a tough audience. They don't give you much: you have to win them over. Boom Chicago taught our actors that if you can win over Dutch people, you'll win over audiences at your next job too.

Kay Cannon: Folks returning from their year abroad with Boom exuded just unwavering confidence onstage. By the time you leave Boom, you've experienced a lot: hecklers, language barriers, cultural differences. But most importantly, you had plenty of stage time to gain the experience needed to warrant such confidence.

Literally, the very next day after I returned to Chicago from Boom, I successfully auditioned for Second City. Hired as an understudy, I quickly moved to the Second City mainstage touring company in Las Vegas. I was working and living with Jason and Joe Kelly, and Holly Walker was in that cast too. Getting our finger on the pulse of Vegas audiences was tricky, requiring lots of trial and error. We were successful, though, because most of that cast had Boom experience. The jump-in "Yes, and . . ." attitude that Andrew, Pep, Ken, and Saskia had starting Boom really stuck with me, and shows up in all the work I do. I was crazy green when I got hired on the writing staff of *30 Rock*—but like at Boom, having Andrew's voice in your head going, *Don't start small! You can do it!* makes you really feel like you can accomplish anything.

Ike Barinholtz: There is zero chance I would've ever gotten hired on *MADtv* had I not been in Boom Chicago. The first time I walked onto the *MADtv* set, I couldn't have been more ready and confident. By then, I'd already opened for thousands at Lowlands with Boom Chicago. Whether playing for 250 or

---

31 Except the Belgians. Always the Belgians . . .

2,500, Boom gives you the confidence to stand in front of a crowd and get them psyched up. There's a bit of game-show host in my presentational style, and I really learned that at Boom.

Peter Grosz: When I came back to Chicago to do Second City, I definitely felt prepared. I quickly realized nobody there knew how to stand in front of an audience and really welcome them to the show. If you went to, say, Improv Olympic, most improvisers onstage then would just mumble when it was their turn to talk in a scene. Specifically, people didn't know how to take personal responsibility for the show. That wasn't taught at Second City— you learned that at Boom Chicago.

Jordan Peele: By the end of my first year at Boom, I felt like, *I'm really* the dude *out here, I'm kicking ass!* It was a great feeling. Then all of a sudden, Pep was there, which was new and exciting. The first time we met, I said to Pep, "Hey, welcome, it's great to see a new face here." And he goes, "I was going to say the same to you."

At that moment, I was totally humbled. I realized, *Oh, yes— there's a history here: I just welcomed not a new cast member, but one of the founders of Boom Chicago.* I understood why Pep came back, though. It was cooler to be his own boss in Amsterdam than working for the man on *SNL*. It's hard to do someone else's thing when you've already built your own.

Seth Meyers: The most important aspect of Boom Chicago was that you worked for self-starters, which is what Andrew, Saskia, and Pep are. They basically created their own part of the landscape, which didn't actually exist before. Outside of the comedy, the most inspirational part of Boom was the business and professional aspect—just the entrepreneurial pioneer spirit these people had. That provided another layer of self-selection that made Boom unique.

I think when you look at the many of us who left Boom and did other things, what we all shared was that we never wanted to be in a situation again where we were sort of just waiting for the right thing to come up. That's the part of working for Boom that I appreciated most.

CHAPTER 11
2003

THE *POLDERBAAN* RUNWAY OPENS AT SCHIPHOL AIRPORT: DON'T BRING WEED TO THE US EMBASSY

Travel plays a huge role in Boom Chicago. We fly actors over from Chicago, New York, LA, and London. We take planes to perform all over the world, use trains to do shows all over Europe, and ride Ubers to shows all over Amsterdam. So when Schiphol Airport added a runway in 2003, it was good news for Boom Chicago.

Sort of.

See, the *polderbaan* is a part of Schiphol the same way, say, Cambridge is a part of Boston. You're near, maybe even adjacent, to that place you say you're part of. But Jesus, in reality you're pretty far away. Taxiing from the *polderbaan* to the airport takes a long-ass time—like "answer all the emails and messages you missed during the long flight" long. "Finish that Netflix movie you started way too late in the flight" long. "Am I allowed to use the toilet while the plane is taxiing?" long.

On the upside, it's named after the *polder*—which, as any student of Dutch history (or the 1993 chapter of this book) can tell you, is the part of the Netherlands that was reclaimed from the sea in classic Dutch style. Other runways at Schiphol are nonironically named after the neighborhoods and towns residing under their flight paths. The strangest is Kaag, a town of 450 that inspired the *Kaagbaan*, an eight-letter word where half of the letters are a's and one is a spit-making "g" sound: *Kaaggggbaan* . . .

The *polder* is a testament to the can-do ability of Dutch people to solve big problems. If you ask us, Schiphol's other runways should also be named in tribute to big Dutch things like pancakes, ovens, and WeTransfer.[32] Like any big Dutch project, opening the *polderbaan* took longer to plan than to execute. Built in just nine months, the project required years of discussion, meetings, and debate. What about environmental standards? And noise pollution? And residents? And existing regulations? And regulations that would need to be created for this tiny patch of new runway?

There was plenty to discuss, but in the end, agreement was reached and the *polderbaan* was planned, built, and opened. We liked the symbolism of our flights taking off from a runway whose construction took so many meetings and compromises just to set more meetings about compromises—and whose name comes from the word most associated with the Dutch art of compromise. More often than not, we're flying somewhere where we'll use comedy to explain how Dutch businesses use compromise.

This is the gist of our love-hate relationship with Dutch bureaucracy. On the one hand, planning and compromise create projects that make things better—like a new runway. On the other hand, the process takes forever, inevitably becoming frustrating and ridiculous. And on yet another hand (a third hand?), we get to write jokes about the bureaucracy, and then charge the members of that very bureaucracy to make fun of them to their face.

Suzi Barrett: For a while, I was the head corporate scriptwriter at Boom. In 80 percent of the scripts, I'd write at least one joke like, "We need to have a meeting, but first, we need to have a meeting about the meeting. And only then can we have the meet-

---

32 Yet another thing you use every day that you didn't know was Dutch . . .

ing to discuss what the meeting about the meeting will really be about . . ." Those were guaranteed home runs.[33]

Ruben van der Meer: Meetings about meetings, the Dutch way of compromise: I'm definitely into that. It's easy to make fun of, but it works. Dutch tolerance is all about compromise. For example, we've always had problems with squatters in Amsterdam. Squatters will get into a house and say, "This space has been left vacant, so now it's ours." And the Dutch response is, "We have to respect everybody's rights here. It's not okay for you to squat, but you can stay until the owner says you have to get out. And the owner can't just leave it empty, either. He actually has to do something with the place and have someone live there, or he'll lose the property." So all parties have to compromise.

This is basically what the Dutch did in Manhattan, which, as we know, was first called New Amsterdam. The Dutch had the whole of New York, but then someone came up and said, "Hey, there are a bunch of English guys up north—should we kick them out?" And the leader of New Amsterdam said, "No. Instead, let's approach them and say, 'We're not going to kick you out. You can live here for now, but when we need this land, you have to go. And would you like to buy some bread and cheese?'"

Greg Shapiro: Tobacco is the new threshold challenging Dutch tolerance. You used to be able to go to a coffeeshop and buy a spliff and smoke it. Today, it's more like, "Whoa, there, buddy—there are new rules."

Andrew Moskos: They wanted to stop all smoking in bars, restaurants, and clubs, which was a good idea. But what about coffeeshops? It would seem weird to have smoking restrictions in an establishment which is there to sell weed. How do you

---

33 See the 2011 chapter about baseball terms being okay for use in the Netherlands.

make an exception? Ironically, weed wasn't covered in new anti-smoking laws; *tobacco* provided the legal problems. The *polder* compromise was that you could smoke weed in coffeeshops, but not mixed with tobacco in a spliff. For anything involving tobacco, there was a special smoking room which the coffeeshop would have to provide. Many places, like Rookies—the very coffeeshop where the idea of Boom Chicago was hatched—turned their entire seating area into a smoking lounge in response. But if you wanted to smoke at the bar, then please: cannabis only. Now *that's* a compromise!

Pep Rosenfeld: If you really want to see Dutch compromise meet American law and order, bring some weed on your next trip to the US Consulate in Amsterdam. Yes, it's a little bit of America right in the Netherlands. But sometimes the Dutchness rubs off.

Rob AndristPlourde: I almost got busted for smuggling weed into the US Consulate. The consulate is considered American soil, so if you're caught with anything there, you're an instant international drug criminal.

One day my family went to the consulate to get our passports renewed. The entrance is a tall iron gate, where security guards with gun, metal detectors, and clipboards keep watch. First, the guard asks my wife and my daughter to approach with their arms out, after removing their coats and jewelry for inspection. After a cursory shakedown, they're let through. Suddenly, bells start going off in my head: *Oh shit, my pipe is in my jacket that's about to be searched by this guy.* I had no good options. If I tell him that I have weed, I'm screwed; if I don't, and he finds it anyway—well, my daughter won't get her passport, can't travel to America, and I'll go to jail. I decide to take the risk: Taking a deep breath, I step up and hand over my passport. The guard looks at me and goes, "Oh shit, you're in Boom Chicago! Come on in."

Andrew Moskos: I didn't get that treatment when I was at the consulate for a passport. When they asked me to empty my pockets and put my jacket through an X-ray machine, I felt what might be a pen in my jacket. But it wasn't a pen. On the tray alongside my wallet, keys, phone, and a roll of Mentos, I had a prerolled joint from Rookies.

Seeing the joint, the Dutch guard said, "Sir, you can't bring that in here." And I was like, "Okay, sorry about that. Please throw it away." I was being respectful, but struggled to pretend that this was a serious issue. I wasn't asking to take weed inside; I was asking to throw it away. But he wouldn't do that, or take me up on my second offer: check it like a parcel and give me a claim ticket. Now he wasn't letting me in at all—instead telling me I have to make another appointment. As I'm escorted out of the gate, he pulls a *gezellig* Dutch move and gives me my joint back. Uh, thanks, Dutch bureaucracy?

Suzi Barrett: I've experienced Dutch bureaucracy in its purest form. I went to the ABN AMRO bank one time and waited in a long line. When I got to the teller, I said, "Hi, I need to get a new ATM card." She said, "You need to fill out a form. *He* has the form you need" She points to the teller next to her, with his own long line. "Uh, can't you ask him to just hand you the form?" I asked. Her answer was immediate: "That is not possible."

Pep Rosenfeld: "*Dat is niet mogelijk*." What it actually means is, "That *is* possible; I just don't feel like doing it." I vividly remember this coming up during an interaction at a frozen yogurt place:

> *Pep: Can I get a vanilla shake with strawberries and banana?*

> *Dutch Frozen Yogurt Minion: That is not possible.*

Pep: Why? You have those ingredients.

Dutch Frozen Yogurt Minion: We can add strawberry or banana to a shake. But not together.

Pep: Is the shake premade?

Dutch Frozen Yogurt Minion: No, we put all the ingredients in fresh.

Pep: Well, can you just put half a scoop of strawberry, and then half a banana, into my vanilla shake?

Dutch Frozen Yogurt Minion: No, that's not possible.

Pep: Okay. Charge me for two shakes, one strawberry and one banana, but put them in one.

Dutch Frozen Yogurt Minion: [Thinks meaningfully for a second.] No. I do not believe they will taste good together.

Steven Svymbersky: In addition to a new runway, 2003 brought a new wave of players into Boom's cast—folks like Jim Woods, Heather Campbell, and Suzi Barrett.

Suzi Barrett: Yeah, 2003 was my first year at Boom. When I got hired in October, Boom said, "We'll bring you out the day after New Year's." "Okay, but I can't come that soon," I responded. "I'm opening a show on January 20." And they said, "You have to cancel your show. We really need you then." So I did.

Jim and Heather came out the same day as me. Jim was also hired out of Chicago, and Heather was hired out of LA. We ended up on the same flight—meeting at a layover in, like, Iceland. The three of us sat in the same row, going over scripts we were supposed to memorize. We'd never met, didn't know what was happening to us, and we were already running lines on the plane. One script was from "Europe: We've Created a Monster." Every person played a different country, so we'd have to do, like, a Russian accent, and a French accent, and then a German one. In these broad, unpracticed accents, we were saying very politically charged things. I felt weird doing that on an international flight. We didn't know if, say, Germans were sitting behind us while we made Hitler jokes.

We landed at Schiphol. After taxiing for twenty minutes, we were like, "What the hell?" Months later, I'd learn we'd landed on the *polderbaan*. Pep picked us up. As we got into the car, he told us how excited Boom Chicago was to have us in the cast.

In no time, we'd pulled up to an apartment building near Surinameplein. Joe Kelly and Randall Harr lived in our apartment before us. It was filthy—like a freshman dorm in a third world country. No part of the carpet was unstained; the stains had stains. "Which bedroom do you want?" was a loser coin flip for any of us. Jim's room had just a bare mattress on the floor; in my room, I found a rickety bed next to a half-full Jägermeister bottle and a shoebox full of bloody Kleenex. Still, it was so exciting. I remember feeling, *Oh, this is going to be great.* I was twenty-three, out of college for a few years while living in Chicago. Now we got to be adults who were kids again: we didn't have to give a fuck about accidentally spilling wine on the coffee table. Rehearsals started shortly after my arrival. I was terrified: our first show was in a week.

Heather Anne Campbell: A week? I was put into a show the very first night I arrived! It was the first time I'd ever left the country. I immediately discovered Americans and Dutch navigate public spaces differently. Walking past someone, Americans instinctively go right, while the Dutch automatically go left—so

I was constantly running into people. The next day, Brendan took us on a bike tour of his favorite spots in Amsterdam, and that was a miracle. I was working with the most talented people, at a theater where actors went on to *MADtv* and *SNL*. It was blowing my mind.

Suzi Barrett: Those first few weeks, there was a steep learning curve taking in all the Amsterdam current events, European references, and inside details that would make people laugh.

Heather Anne Campbell: When I first met Pep, he said, "Heather, if you're going to do this, you have to subscribe to the *Economist* and read the *International Herald Tribune* every day."

Suzi Barrett: It worked. I was confused for so long. One thing that helped was that Andrew taught us great go-to responses for hecklers. He said whenever someone heckles you, ask where they're from. No matter what they say, you go, "Oh, *that* explains it." That would fucking bring the house down! It was so bizarre—just one of many cool lessons in crowd psychology I'd learn. Another was if half the audience was already laughing, the other half wants to seem smart and laugh too. Even if people didn't actually get a joke, they still might laugh. I mean, *I* didn't always get the joke I was making.

Unlike many improv shows in the States, the audience was mostly comprised of people I didn't know and would never see again. At Boom, it's like you can work on your craft in public anonymously. You're very much in public onstage there, but it's not the United States: no one you know is going to see it. So you work in this bubble, the only judgment being the reaction of that night's audience.

Jason Sudeikis: Boom Chicago would offer this opportunity for people who had an innate sense of, like, *Whatever the fuck.*

Suzi Barrett: It was a weird time. Two months after I landed in Amsterdam, George W. gave Saddam his ultimatum that led to the invasion of Iraq. Immediately, being American made you the scourge of the planet. This was impactful, having grown up in American suburbia. I saw a sheet hanging out a window that had *Yankee Go Home!* painted on it. It was a tough lesson to learn that America doesn't deserve the innate arrogance we have: sometimes Americans need to shut up, read a book, and leave everyone alone.

Pep Rosenfeld: The vibe in Amsterdam was changing; the vibe onstage was also changing. A big part of that was that in 2003, Boom alumni started getting hired for TV shows. Suzi, Jim, and Heather arrived after Ike and Josh and Nicole went to *MADtv* and Seth was already doing *SNL*. The new cast had just started working with Jordan when he was flown to LA for his *MADtv* audition.

Josh Meyers: Ike and I were the first Boomers to get hired on *MADtv*. We knew Jordan and Nicole Parker were coming to the end of their time at Boom, so we told our new bosses, "You guys should look at these guys—they're remarkably talented."

Jordan Peele: The beauty of it was, because Ike and Josh vouched for me, I got the offer to go to *MADtv* while I was still living in Amsterdam. That was kind of unreal. I could've stayed forever at Boom; I loved what I was doing, and was excited about the quality of our work. But curiosity about whether I could've taken things to the next level would've killed me. My initial dream was to work my way up in Chicago's comedy scene. I felt like I needed to continue the climb, and if I stayed in Amsterdam, I'd stay there forever. But when I went to *MADtv*, I quickly learned that it was not going to be my Everest.

I thought *MADtv* was going to be a dream come true. But

after doing Boom, my entire time there was spent in mourning: *What have I done?* I'd literally found and loved the best place to follow my passion. Then I came to a place where I didn't have the same freedoms. *MADtv* was all about constant compromises and auditioning for screen time. I went from working six nights a week at Boom, doing any kind of humor I could possibly want to explore, to *MADtv*—where you were lucky if you got in one sketch a week, and then there was a two-week hiatus. I went through long stretches thinking, *I just can't wait three weeks to play Ja Rule for four minutes.*

Heather Anne Campbell: I felt similarly to Jordan. Writing for *SNL* after Boom was the worst working experience of my life. I was only writing one or two sketches a week. That's crazy: I can put out sixty! Why were we limiting ourselves? I made lifelong friends there, and the people are among the most talented you'll ever work with. I felt the way that *SNL* was produced was based on a culture of drug use that no longer existed. There's no reason to run it as if everyone's doing coke all night, because nobody was doing coke anymore. Just run it like a regular fucking comedy show! This reverence for lost magic created a toxic working environment. Someone who got hired around the same time as me started having major health problems. Their doctor asked about their work schedule. They said, "Every Tuesday, I stay up all night and don't go to bed until Sunday." And the doctor said, "Well, you can't physically do that to a human body. That's why your hair is falling out and you've got subsurface bruising."

Liz Cackowski: After leaving Boom, I finally got onto the Second City mainstage after a couple years. One night, I had the Cinderella thing of, "*SNL* is in the audience." They liked me, so they flew me out to see a show. Then Lorne Michaels interviewed me at the after-party. At four a.m. Sunday morning, they told me, "You start on Monday." Jason and I were on *SNL* together—he was a writer first before joining the cast, and was just so fucking funny; Joe Kelly got hired later. Lorne apparently felt *SNL* had too many cerebral *Harvard Lampoon* types who treated comedy as math. They just weren't writing characters, which is *SNL*'s bread and butter. I mean, all I did at Boom Chicago was characters. So *SNL* went to Groundlings and Second City to find people who made you feel the comedy more in your body. It's funny: I was writing then at Second City, but considered myself more of an improviser and comedian who performs. But then I ended up writing for *SNL* for three years, and really felt like I fit in there.

Of course, the producers were like, "Oh, so you know Seth?" Seth kind of gave me the nod and became my buddy there. Seth and I wrote together a lot, which was really fun, and became best friends; he really was like a brother to me. The recurring characters that I wrote with Seth and Amy Poehler were the Needlers, this couple that should be divorced, but weren't. Another sketch I liked was one we did when Catherine Zeta-Jones was hosting. She and Seth played this couple where he's this super-straight, fratty guy and she takes him to a party with all her boho dancer friends. The whole sketch had essentially no dialogue, and was super visual—just all people doing weird Bob Fosse moves, with Seth not knowing what the hell to do. That bit would've killed on the Boom stage.

Andrew Moskos: Having Boom alumni on *MADtv* and *SNL* did change the vibe some. Newer cast members arrived in Amsterdam seeing Boom Chicago as a stepping stone, not a detour. They didn't work any less hard, and they weren't any less funny than those who came before them, but they had more of a career focus: *As soon as I get out, I'm going to work in television on a big show, and start making a lot of money.* People started acclimating to Dutch society less, and reading *Variety* a bit more. There was less figuring out how to stay in Amsterdam, and more trying to follow in the footsteps of recent graduates like Jordan and Nicole.

We'd like to think that when Jordan and Nicole left Boom for *MADtv*, their planes took off from the *polderbaan*—departing Holland from a runway named for the spirit of Dutch compromise and victory over the elements. They'd bring that spirit with them to LA and beyond, changing comedy in their wake. Meanwhile, a new generation of superstars was arriving.

Tarik Davis: I'd just graduated college, and was living in my parents' basement in New Jersey, working at a comics shop. Colton and I were on the same Harold[34] team at UCB. Without asking permission, he'd signed me up for a Boom Chicago audition. When I got home, my mom said, "Some man called and said you got a job in Amsterdam, baby!" Not knowing what to do, I turned on the TV. Bill Moyers's *The Power of Myth* came on, talking about how to become a hero, you must leave home. I thought, *That's the sign!*

My dad's tough, but at the airport he broke down. My parents were like, "Our baby's leaving—but it's time." Pep met me at Schiphol wearing a black leather trench coat and weird cowboy hat. I was like, *Why the hell is Crocodile Dundee picking me up?* On the tram, I noticed an ad featuring Boom's cast; maybe this *was* significant. Watching that night's Boom show was an immersive experience: David Copperfield, but with comedy, pyrotechnics, acrobatics, rapping, singing . . . I thought, *What the hell is this?* I was supposed to do all that? Maybe they'd hired the wrong guy. This was a *problem*.

Later that night, Boom had a New Year's party welcoming in 2004. This was my first European party—filled with beautiful women, fireworks going off everywhere, and people getting high in ways I wasn't used to. It was too wild, too insane: I remember thinking, *Mom, make it stop—I want to get off!*

---

34 "Harold" refers to a structured format used in long-form improvisation. We don't generally do much of that at Boom Chicago . . .

CHAPTER 12
2004

DAY OF *DE LAMA'S*: DUTCH PROVEN TO BE ACTUALLY FUNNY, BOOM CHICAGO TAKES THE CREDIT

The Netherlands never really had a sketch comedy show that was a cultural phenomenon the way *Saturday Night Live* had been for the United States. A Dutch comedy icon like Arjen Lubach has the influence, sure, but his show does not feature impressions or sketches. In the United States, though, many of the country's funniest writers and performers have inevitably come out of *SNL*. In fact, *SNL*'s been so influential that you really have to talk about it in terms of different eras.

The *SNL* of the 1970s was dominated by legends like Bill Murray, John Belushi, Dan Aykroyd, Chevy Chase, Laraine Newman, Garrett Morris, and Gilda Radner. The 1980s produced titanic talents like Eddie Murphy, Dana Carvey, Julia Louis-Dreyfus, and Robert Downey Jr. (well, sort of). The 1990s, meanwhile, featured Tina Fey, Chris Rock, Mike Myers, Will Ferrell, and Adam Sandler. All these people were unique and talented—well, except for Adam Sandler. As a comedian, Adam Sandler is an excellent guitarist . . . And yes, the 2000s brought us many innovative funny people bursting forth from the forehead of Lorne Michaels. An incomplete list would include Seth Meyers, Amy Poehler, Jason Sudeikis, and Kristen Wiig.

Whatever the era, *SNL*'s political impact was felt most in

its "Weekend Update" news segment and the show's traditional "cold open" before the opening credits about the week's most noteworthy topic. These segments are often discussed all over the US media the following week. In addition, *SNL*'s trenchantly funny, painfully accurate portrayals of America's sitting presidents and political candidates have influenced how American citizens perceive both their current and future leaders. The show's memorable impressions of Clinton, Bush, Trump, and Biden have become part of the ongoing political discussion. The only president they couldn't play well was Barack Obama. We are proud that Jordan Peele is usually recognized as the best Obama impression by a popular comedian, although he was never on *SNL*.

The Netherlands, of course, has great comedy too. Still, there was never a show with the impact of *SNL*. That influence has been spread for a long time over many shows and groups. Comedytrain is truly the most influential group of comedians in the Netherlands. They are a who's who of writers and performers, from the established Hans Teeuwen and Theo Maassen, funny and fresh voices like Peter Pannekoek, and up-and-coming thinkers such as Tim Fransen.

Before Comedytrain, the Dutch comedy scene was dominated by cabaret, which does share some elements with stand-up. By the 1990s, though, the cabaret format was feeling slow, dusty, and strangely restricting. A cabaret show had to not only be funny, it had to have "serious" moments as well. No cabaret show was complete without an earnest song or two exploring the human condition in an ironic way. Comedytrain was a breath of fresh air in that it *didn't* do that. They proved you didn't need to study art at an accredited institution or conform to established rules to be funny—although watching Tim Fransen's cerebral show, it is clear that their tent is big enough to include those who had.

Perhaps the most important non-Comedytrain comedian is Arjen Lubach. After many false attempts over the years, his comedy commentary show format finally succeeded in Holland in 2014. Lubach quickly defined humorous political discourse on his weekly *Sunday with Lubach*. It was not only laugh-out-loud funny, but each week his long-form dive into current topics like the NRA and the pollution caused by cruise ships remain part of the political discourse long after the shows air. Arjen upped his game in 2022 when he started a four-night-a-week show, *The Evening Show with Arjen Lubach,* which continued his commercial and artistic success streak.

Back in 2004, another influential show began: *De Lama's.* The show would have a triumphant four-year run as one of the country's highest-rated prime-time programs ever, and was ultimately honored in 2006 with Holland's top award for a television show, the Gouden Televizier-Ring. And unlike anything that had been on Dutch television before, it was all improvised.

De Lama's—incongruously taking its name from the fuzzy, long-necked, spitting animal—started as a Dutch remake of the hit British show *Whose Line Is It Anyway?*—basing the humor solely on interactive improv games. *De Lama's* quickly transcended its origins, however, and became bigger than the IP that BNN had purchased to base it on—all due to the talent, charisma, and innovation of its stars. Like *SNL, De Lama's* created and cemented the fame of the show's core quartet of players: Ruben van der Meer, Tijl Beckand, Ruben Nicolai, and the already popular Jeroen van Koningsbrugge.

The four comedians—plus Arie Koomen (a player in the show's early years) and frequent guest Horace Cohen—made Holland laugh with routines that were sometimes irreverent, often absurdist, and frequently involving lowbrow dick jokes. *De Lama's* greatest innovation, however, was introducing an entirely new concept to Dutch audiences: the troupe's incorporation of improv comedy styles that had evolved out of American laughter institutions like Groundlings, Comedy Sportz, Upright Citizens Brigade, Second City, and—*ahem*—Boom Chicago. Cohen and van der Meer not only took inspiration from Boom Chicago's format and studied improvisational technique with members of its cast—they actually became the first Dutch comics to perform regularly there. In the process, they helped Boom Chicago attract a bigger local audience beyond expats and English speakers visiting Amsterdam.

Ruben van der Meer: Boom Chicago influenced me personally and *De Lama's* with their games and improv style.

Carice van Houten: *De Lama's* was a complete rip-off of Boom— but in a really good way. I do remember thinking, *Yeah, but it's not Boom Chicago.*

Horace Cohen: The first time I saw Boom was when Rob and Andrew invited me to a show. I fell in love with it right away, partially because of my American roots. My parents met because my father was a Brooklyn guy who'd come to Amsterdam for the drugs.[35]

Ruben van der Meer: I'd seen some early Boom shows when I worked at the Lijnbaansgracht theater—but then I went to see them at the Leidseplein theater. That's when I really started drinking the Boom Chicago Kool-Aid. Their sketches and games were so awesomely well-performed by this crew of talented people onstage. It was definitely one of the best casts Boom Chicago ever had.

Horace Cohen: Incredible. Jordan Peele, Brendan Hunt, Rachel Miller . . . Jim Woods, Suzi Barrett, and Heather Anne Campbell had joined the cast the year before too, and were still rocking. Heather was so fucking funny. And then in 2004, Amber Ruffin came out with Ryan Archibald, and later Tarik Davis and Tim

---

35 See? It's not just us.

Sniffen showed up. That year, I remember seeing Brendan's last night at Boom too. Wow.

Tarik Davis: I was the last of the new class of '04. I'd heard of Amber, and when I met her and Ryan Archibald, we immediately bonded. I actually remember the moment when I realized that Amber was going to be huge. It was during a show where she ended an improv game with a song. The audience was already in love with her, but then Amber sang, and just took it to another level. Amber has an *amazing* singing voice, and ignited the whole space. Everyone was blown back in their chairs: she literally blew people away. Seeing that, there was no doubt in my mind Amber was a star. If you can get a room of people from all over the world to react like that, you've proven your undeniable talent. All the actors we were playing with were thoroughbreds, but that night Amber was just a little *extra*.

Andrew Moskos: That was also the first year David Schmoll composed music for Boom.

Ruben van der Meer: 2004's shows were just mind-blowing. I played with Brendan, Amber, and Ryan when they taught improv classes too. Man, was that educational.

Amber Ruffin: It was awesome to work with Dutch actors. Arie Boomsma took one of those classes too. He was the tallest man alive and very good-looking. It made me nervous to have to teach him. Dutch celebrities were quite intimidating to us kids fresh off the plane.

Horace Cohen: I was less tall. When I first talked with Andrew, he said he really liked the show and our sketches. He said it was actually the first time he thought Dutch sketch comedy was good. He meant that as a compliment.

Ruben van der Meer: "For Dutch comedians, you're pretty funny." It was true. There were not a lot of funny sketch shows in Holland then—nor actors who could improvise in the modern style.

Horace Cohen: I understood what Andrew meant. Until then, Dutch comedy *was* still totally old-school and character driven.

Ruben van der Meer: They really impressed us. The integration of tech at Boom Chicago was so smooth. Boom could always find something topical online to back up what the actors were doing onstage. Now it's normal, but back then this was magic. And they did it so fast, in real time.

I asked our techs to try some clever Internet stuff like Boom's, but it didn't work out great. I would start a joke about how I went to a Michael Jackson concert—but instead of the techs getting Michael Jackson onto the screen behind me, we'd get the spinning QuickTime buffer. We could never get clips to sync right, whereas Ken and Steven at Boom were seamless. We knew it was technically possible, but at *De Lama's* we just couldn't do what Boom Chicago did.

Before us there had been a few attempts at improv on Dutch television, but these shows didn't usually come alive in a studio environment. You either had to do "man on the street" ambush-type stuff, or play live in theaters in front of audiences. Until *De Lama's,* it just didn't work.

Horace Cohen: When they really found their footing, *De Lama's* laid the foundation for the next big waves in Dutch comedy.

Ruben van der Meer: We felt like we were a new force in Holland. The way the comedy revolution was happening in the States, we tried to represent that spirit here.

Andrew Moskos: What was interesting about improvisation on TV was that comedians weren't playing recurring characters. It was just these guys being funny. That's what's great about improvisation: you get to know players' individual styles. Compared to written shows then, it felt way more exciting and alive. After *De Lama's* went off the air, there was usually a new but similar improvisation show on TV with at least a Lama or two. These were examples like *De Budget Show* and, perhaps most successfully, *De Grote Improvisatie Show* (aka *The Big Improv Show*), which ran from 2013 to 2017.

Ruben van der Meer: BNN had bought the rights to the format of *Whose Line Is It Anyway?*—which was stupid because it's improv. It's like buying the recipe to make french fries. The French won't sue you, but BNN might. The minute *De Lama's* members got their own fame and started doing stuff outside the show, BNN and the producers were like, "We own the rights for this. We paid for them. You owe us money."

That's unfortunately how Dutch television works. If we'd come to the network and said, "We've got an idea for a show: we'll have four players and a host, and they're going to do improvisation games," they'd inevitably say, "It is not possible." But then they're like, "Hey, we've bought the rights to this very popular show on the BBC." That's what's important to Dutch TV executives: success elsewhere.

As a result, we have to pay if we do anything *Lama's* related now. We did a bunch of sold-out comeback shows last year at the Ziggo Dome, and were told we couldn't use the name *De Lama's* unless we paid the network and producers of our old show. For what? Making up scenes on the spot and doing improv that they had nothing to do with? It's horrible. We had to pay a big price because they still had the intellectual-property rights: "Oh, you're playing the Ziggo Dome? Okay, pay up!"

They wanted like thirty thousand euros per show to do *nothing*. Fuck the name *De Lama's*—because of that robbery, we'll never do another official reunion again.

Rob AndristPlourde: Let's go back a few years to before *De Lama's*. Andrew said to Horace and Ruben, "Why don't you guys do a late-night comedy show once a month and bring your friends?" I directed "Late Night" from 1997 through 2012, when it became "Shot of Improv." The regular "Late Night" show typically featured Boom's entire artistic department, and sometimes special guests from America. But with "Late Night Massive," the idea was to invite Dutch actors, singers, or politicians: that's what made it massive. We even had the mayor of Amsterdam once. That was crazy. It created a different excitement with Dutch guests onstage. Ruben and Horace were the first Dutch comedians at Boom to play there on a regular basis.

Amber Ruffin: It was always exciting when Horace and Ruben came to play. They brought a uniquely Dutch comedy vibe to the show. We learned a lot from them.

Horace Cohen: Who did we have at "Massive"? Mimoun Oaïssa. One night, Jeroen van Koningsbrugge showed up, Najib Amhali . . .

Ruben van der Meer: Alain Clark came to sing. Carice van Houten didn't play onstage ever, but she was always there hanging out with Josh Meyers. Who was the Dutch rapper? Def P?

Horace Cohen: No, Pete Philly. They were crazy times! It was nice because you'd have American tourists interacting with a mix of our friends who'd come to watch, and then other Dutch people.

Ruben van der Meer: As the show started, we'd go to the Boom actors' office called "the Shiny"[36] to prepare. It was this little attic room upstairs. I loved walking in there and yelling, "Look, there's a Jewish family in here!"

Rob AndristPlourde: Anne Frank jokes really never do get old.

Carice van Houten: Oh my goodness, the Shiny—what a crappy place! There were mousetraps everywhere.

Ruben van der Meer: I remember Pep pulling me aside in the Shiny before my first "Massive" show: "Hey, great that you're here, Ruben. So, this is what we're going to do." Then he gave me a piece of paper with the show's lineup and said, "We're going to start with this game. You know this one?" And I said, "No, I don't know anything. This is my first 'Late Night.'" I didn't understand what Pep was asking me to do. He'd explain everything so quickly, talking so fast, and I didn't really know what was going on. And then the first scene started. I was just like, *Okay, let's see what happens.*

Rob AndristPlourde: Pep calls this baptism by fire "cowboying." Arriving onstage a bit underprepared? Just cowboy it! Cowboying became a Boom Chicago tradition. But not everything was cowboyed. For the "Massive" intro, we made a boy band–style MTV video. We'd come out and explain, "Okay, these are the rules. For those of you who haven't seen us before, this is an improv comedy show, and it's all made up on the spot." And then we'd start doing dance choreography and singing a cheesy pop song we'd written, not on the spot, all about how the performance we were doing was completely spontaneous.

---

36 The Shiny was the ironic name of our very dirty artistic office/hangout past the beer tanks. There was nothing shiny about it.

Ruben van der Meer: The chorus was *[sings]*, *"Everything we do is improvised, nothing is rehearsed . . ."*

Rob AndristPlourde: And then *boink*. As we exited stage right, a soft-focus music video we shot for the song came up on the screen: in it, we'd transformed into an actual boy band dancing and wearing white Backstreet Boys–style costumes. After the video, the lights came up.

Horace Cohen: "Welcome to the 'Massive'!" What also brought a whole lot of humor to the show was us not being American, or native English speakers. Well, Ruben wasn't an English speaker at all, really.

Ruben van der Meer: I'd try to translate jokes in my head as they were happening. That made my answers funnier.

Rob AndristPlourde: The most hilarious moments were when neither Dutch nor English would work to express something— but we all knew what Ruben was trying to say. That's what made the "Massive" work—that combination of Dutchies bringing their native humor (and sometimes hilariously poor English skills) to what is a very American space. We had special guests like Mimoun, a classically trained actor who had real difficulty letting go. But he was still fun to play with.

Ruben van der Meer: Mimoun didn't smoke or drink. Luckily, we didn't make him play "Sure, Drink."

Rob AndristPlourde: "Sure, Drink" featured two teams of two. Backstage, on camera, was a table with four pitchers of beer— one for everyone onstage. A scene would start with two players and two relief players. The relief players would slam a pint down and then tag their teammate to continue the scene onstage while their partner now went backstage to drink. When the player backstage finished their pint, they tagged back in. The first team to finish both pitchers was the winner. It's fair to say the scene was not that important. Brian Jack once made his entrance back onstage so drunk, he couldn't make his mouth form words.

Ruben van der Meer: It was ridiculous. I saw that and thought, *This is really what makes the "Late Night Massive" show great.* It was wild and unpredictable, a place where anything could happen.

Rob AndristPlourde: "Sure, Drink" wouldn't be the last game of the night, either—more third-from-the-last game. The players had more scenes to do after having downed four to six pints. Because the audience knew them and liked them from the first two-thirds of the show, the crowd stayed with them, even when they were utterly impaired.

Horace Cohen: My favorite "Late Night Massive" was in 2006, when we celebrated three decades of friendship between Ruben and me.

Ruben van der Meer: That was my absolute favorite "Massive" too. Horace and I have known each other since we were babies, so we decided to have a thirtieth-anniversary party celebrating our friendship. That night was also the night of the Televizier-Ring award—the Dutch Emmys, basically—for which *De Lama's* was nominated.

Horace Cohen: Ruben went to the awards show in his tuxedo— and *De Lama's* won the Ring.

Ruben van der Meer: I had to leave immediately after the show because I had to do "Late Night." We'd invited all our friends, and everybody I ran into at the awards show too. We told our friends to come dressed as me and Horace. My girlfriend at the time and her friend came as the twins from *The Shining*. One couple became the designers Viktor and Rolf; another was Olive Oyl and Popeye. Two friends came dressed as the World Trade Center's Twin Towers: they're very tall. It was great seeing all these TV stars and people from the industry dressed up in tuxedos and evening gowns mingling with costumed lunatics, and the regular "Massive" audience.

It was a great show. We did a scene where Horace and I played each other. I came in on my knees, with big furry eyebrows like Horace's, saying, "Hey, I'm Horace. I'm from America originally." We put on each other's shirts too. Horace had a big pillow stuffed under his shirt for my stomach. I don't know why.

Horace Cohen: And I laughed really loudly at everything.

Rob AndristPlourde: The whole show was fabulous. It was sold out, and the house was totally packed.

Ruben van der Meer: That night was filled with love. We closed the show with Horace giving a speech. He was really terrible at it, but he kept going on and on. And then my friends Trijntje Oosterhuis and Edsilia Rombley, who are professional vocalists, sang "That's What Friends Are For." The craziness continued all night. We took the tables away to make a dance floor. I'm a big Michael Jackson fan, so I had a friend perform who was the winner of the Dutch Michael Jackson impersonator contest when he was fourteen years old.

Rob AndristPlourde: At that moment, the rest of *De Lama's* strode into Boom in their tuxes, holding this giant golden trophy they'd just won. Ruben Nicolai was walking on top of the tables, holding the Ring award aloft; then they all came onstage together, and everybody was hugging. That was the best "Massive" ever—and maybe even the best "Late Night," period. I have never seen that much joy, friendship, and laughter mixed together in one place before or since.

Andrew Moskos: "Late Night" was already a zone where—driven by beer and bravado—Boom's cast members could get their comedic freak on well beyond anything even super-freaky Amsterdam had ever seen. Then "Late Night Massive" took that unhinged format to another level, bringing in avatars of Dutch pop culture as guests. In the process, Boom Chicago fully transformed from an American expat phenomenon into a native Dutch comedy institution once and for all. I was proud of that.

Pep Rosenfeld: With Horace and Ruben as regular guests, they influenced Boom Chicago and vice versa. And when Ruben joined *De Lama's,* he raised the improvisation bar.

Andrew Moskos: *De Lama's* in turn introduced improvisation to the Dutch who didn't know Boom Chicago—stimulating the world-broadening internationalization of the global comedy community in the Netherlands. *De Lama's* solidified a greater appreciation of contemporary comedy in Holland. Shows like *De Lama's*—combined with the talent of Comedytrain and the reach of the Internet bringing foreign comedians to Dutch audiences—ushered in a stylistic revolution for Holland, pushing Dutch comedy beyond traditional cabaret into the faster, fresher big tent it is today, all while making the Netherlands safe for a whole new generation of fart and dick jokes.

Ruben van der Meer: I've never stopped doing improv, and we're still going strong with *De Lama's* (although for legal reasons, we had to officially change our name to *TAFKAL—The Artists*

Formerly Known As Lama's). In recent years, we've played the Ziggo Dome six times, did a sold-out tour, and made our comeback on TV, which is going great. Last weekend, we played two nights in Rotterdam, drawing 1,700 people each night. And we try not to let cancel culture affect us too much. But that's what's nice about improv—saying sorry for everything is sometimes even more funny.

CHAPTER 13
2005

BITE THE BULLET: BOOM GETS POLITICAL, HOLLAND GETS THE EURO, WE ALL GET FUCKED

Boom Chicago has always been on the side of a bigger, better Europe. More trade, less war. More English, less French. More euros, less annoying currencies you had to buy at the border. We loved European life with all the different flavors, but less hassles. That was what a tighter Europe meant to Boom Chicago.

When we occasionally suggested caution onstage, you could tell we didn't really mean it. For example, in 2001's "Europe: We've Created a Monster," Boom had a scene that asked, "Why is everybody going so fast to create the European Union?" Instead, we suggested perhaps trying out some "smaller unions" first, whose reimagined flags we put up on the screen:

France and Italy merge to become: Fritaly! Where men are hairy, and women are hairier.

Greece, Spain, and Portugal will merge to become: Club Med!

Germany, Austria, Poland, the Czech Republic, Slovakia, and Hungary merge to become: [slide of swastika flag from the Third Reich] Oh, how did that get in there?! We meant, uh, "a happy place where people are similar!"

Joking aside, Boom's philosophy was: *Mo' Europe, mo' better*. So imagine the disappointment on the slightly older, wiser faces of Boom's founders when, in June of 2005, the Dutch voted down a referendum on whether or not the Dutch government should ratify the European Constitution. In perfect Dutch form, the referendum was nonbinding: the classic meeting-to-plan-the-meeting-for-the-actual-meeting bit. Still, it would be hard to ignore the 61 percent–to–39 percent defeat. That wasn't close: that was a thumping. The Dutch government promised to abide by the vote. Coming just three days after the French voted the same way, it was hard not to smell something in the air. Were Europeans starting to get a slight case of merger's remorse? Was this the beginning of the "Screw Europe—what about *us?*" phase?

The Netherlands prides itself on its reputation as a tolerant society. But in 2005, our latest Boom show made clear that, just because the Dutch tolerate you, it doesn't mean they *like* you. The slow rise of far-right political parties had shifted into high gear. Four years earlier, anti-immigrant sentiment came with an impeccably tied tie: Pim Fortuyn, the bald, flamboyantly gay politician from Rotterdam. He might not have looked like a classic far-right populist, but sometimes he sure sounded like one. Fortuyn claimed he had nothing against immigrants. Indeed, he noted, some of his favorite lovers were Moroccan! It was more that he refused to accept immigrants who were intolerant of homosexuality, among other things. If you can't absorb long-held Dutch norms and values, Fortuyn explained, then perhaps the Netherlands wasn't the right place for you. Fortuyn was then assassinated in May 2002. Had he not been killed, he may well have become prime minister of the Netherlands. His party, the LPF (for "List of Pim Fortuyn"), was polling scarily well in that election.

Boy, do the Dutch love political parties. *And there are so many*. America effectively has two parties. The Netherlands, meanwhile, has ten normal parties, plus another ten that will never actually get into the government. Then there are new, crazy parties that inevitably pop up with every new election, like, say, the Pirate Party, and the Pedophile Party. (Both are real.) And then there are some politicians who are too nutty for any of the existing parties. Those folks sometimes form their own parties, as Pim Fortuyn had.

After Fortuyn's killing, right-wing nativists got less classy, more angry. Rita Verdonk's Proud about the Netherlands Party in 2007 was less about intolerance of intolerance and more just classic xenophobia. Her Trumpy slogan to describe Holland was, *Full is full.* Geert Wilders's Party For Freedom followed this line even deeper into the ideological gutter. You don't get a bunch of racists chanting about reducing the Muslim population unless you're a bit of a dick, right? The Freedom Party offered a funny kind of freedom in its gaslighting platform: *Can I be a Muslim? No! Can I wear a headscarf? No!* Ironically, if anyone in the Netherlands could benefit from wearing a headscarf, it's Geert Wilders. It would cover up those dark roots.

Greasing the wheels of 2005's European Union rejection— and the accompanying nationalism—was the murder of Theo van Gogh, a prickly Dutch columnist, artist, and filmmaker. Above all, van Gogh—who egregiously touted his familial origins with some painter named Vincent—was a provocateur: he made his living enraging and offending, all while speaking truth to power—or at least speaking truth to the already very angry. Van Gogh actively tried to piss people off, usually succeeding. When Fortuyn's assassin turned out to be an animal-rights activist, the nation collectively breathed a sigh of relief that at least he wasn't a Muslim extremist. The opposite, however, was true when van Gogh was killed in 2004. The note stabbed to the dying man's chest was quite clear on that front. It also named the next target: politician, filmmaker, and truth-stretcher Ayaan Hirsi Ali. Ali had made her reputation repudiating and antagonizing Islam—most provocatively in the controversial film made by van Gogh that would lead to his killing. Afterward, she was forced to live under constant protection, eventually emigrating to the US.

Meanwhile, Boom Chicago leapt at the chance to inject more politics into our new shows at the Leidseplein theater. In 2003, we'd already taken Bush and his War on Terror by the horns. In 2004, Greg, Pep, and Andrew followed that up with "Mr. America Contest," the first of what became a quadrennial[37] Boom Chicago tradition: shows about the concurrent American presidential election. And as the whole vibe in the Netherlands shifted from go-go 1990s to hark-who-goes-there mid-2000s, Boom Chicago continued to do what Pep and Andrew loved doing best: breathing comedic life into politics.[38]

Steven Svymbersky: Andrew was excited when Holland switched from guilders to the euro. I think he was more excited to use it as source material. Boom made a video about the occasion. Almost everybody who worked at Boom was in it, including my daughter. It was called "The Guilder's Nightmare." We dressed up actor Randall Harr in a giant ten-guilder costume. He started off happy and smiling, but things changed for him the next day. Now he couldn't get into his regular bar. The bouncer pushes him out, pointing to a freshly painted sign that explicitly stated, *No Guilders.* After enjoying a street musician's performance, Mr. Ten Guilder hops in the open guitar case as a donation, but the musician shoos him away. His surreal nightmare continues as he descends into a forest of scary euro notes. The final indignity comes when he encounters a guy in a bathroom where the toilet paper is a roll of guilder bills. The final sound is a toilet flushing.

---

37 Yes, that's a real word—look it up. We did.

38 A point made by Ryan Archibald at one of Boom's traditional farewell roasts, in which he noted, "Andrew and Pep have spent their lives turning articles from the *Economist* into comedy sketches."

Andrew Moskos: Bye-bye, guilder! It was a fun video to make because, hey, you only change currencies once in a lifetime. One day, the prices just changed. Suddenly, instead of spending two guilders for something, you're spending less than one euro. Americans would never give up the dollar for that hassle.

Pep Rosenfeld: It's true. Think about the 1970s, when smart people in America were like, "Hey, let's switch to this new metric system. It's way easier, and it's what the rest of the world uses." And Americans were like, "No thanks. Inches forever!"

Andrew Moskos: We Americans might not know how many pints are in a quart, or how many yards are in a mile—but you can be damn sure no European scientists are gonna make us change. You can pry the yardsticks out of our cold, dead hands.

Suzi Barrett: They were already on euros when I got to Boom. I was there for three years, my heyday being year two, 2005. The first year you're learning so much just getting acclimatized—how to walk, basically. But then the second year was so much fun. You know how to do the job, so then you can start really owning it and making it your own. Plus, Boom got tons of great new cast members that year: Tim Sniffen, Ryan Archibald, Tarik Davis, Amber Ruffin, and then Matt Jones arrived right at the end of that.

Ruben van der Meer: Badger!

Steven Svymbersky: Matt Jones went on to fame playing Badger in *Breaking Bad*. Heather knew Matt from LA, and he came into Boom when he was touring Europe.

Rob AndristPlourde: Heather told him, "You should come to

Boom and do a show." So Matt did a "Late Night." Afterward, he gave Pep his résumé and said, "I'd like to audition for Boom."

Pep Rosenfeld: I said, "Um, I'd say you already did. You're hired."

Andrew Moskos: Matt came to Boom just in time to help us create "Bite the Bullet."

Steven Svymbersky: That was one of our best shows. "Bite the Bullet" was Boom at its most controversial—dealing with religious strife and everything else that was affecting us in Europe and globally. It was a little edgier than typical Boom material. Andrew was really pushing for that. There was a song called "Be Skeptical" that made the audience gasp in shock: *OMG, I can't believe they're saying that!* It began in Jerusalem with a song that Matt and Heather did about a Jew and a Palestinian standing next to each other at a bus stop:

> *For centuries Jews and Arabs fought over this Holy Land*
> *Hey guys, it's a shit-hole, surrounded by sand*
> *Focus instead on the things you share a stake in*
> *Like . . . you both hate gays and bacon!*
>
> *Be skeptical, be skeptical*
> *Don't be a religious receptacle*
> *If you believe anything 100 percent*
> *You're a moron! You're a stupid, fucking moron . . .*

Heather Anne Campbell: My favorite thing I did at Boom was "Be Skeptical"—it's actually the first song I ever wrote. I wanted it to be about the religious takeover of politics that was happening: I felt that was important to comment on, as an atheist and former Christian. The first time we performed it, a couple people actually walked out. I thought that was great. To me, the goal of comedy is to go right up to that line.

Pep Rosenfeld: Heather was really one of Boom's most political writers.

Heather Anne Campbell: The stuff that I was thinking about and wanted to write was encouraged. When I was in high school, I would write political diatribes on the chalkboard. And I'm a news hound: talking with Pep about politics was my soul food.

Steven Svymbersky: "Bite the Bullet" was different in several ways. Usually we ended with a big musical number featuring the whole cast. Not this show, which closed with another song by Matt called "Who Should I Believe?" That was weird by Boom standards because it really was just Matt coming out by himself with the guitar, singing a song questioning what he did and didn't believe in life and religion:

> *Ladies and gentlemen, you heard a lot of opinions here*
> *tonight and I'm left with one question*
> *Who should I believe?*
> *Rock music tells me to commit suicide*
> *Rap music tells me to pimp my ride*
> *Country music says I should live in a double-wide*
> *Who should I believe?*
>
> *Muslim imams tell me it's evil to dance*
> *Catholic priests tell me to drop my pants*
> *Hindu holy men have eight more arms than me*
> *Who should I believe?*
>
> *Turkey says that they are European*
> *Europe says no fucking way*

Americans don't even know where Turkey is . . .
Who should I believe?

What lies are true?
Do I believe the angry Muslims or the angry Jews?
Somebody tell me, what would Jesus do?
Who should I believe?

Pep Rosenfeld: The show's topics and scenes were definitely flavored by Theo van Gogh's murder.

Steven Svymbersky: 2004 was very traumatic for the Dutch psyche. I biked past where van Gogh was murdered that same night, and it was gut-wrenching: there was still blood on the street. Everybody was sobbing and leaving flowers; it was a really emotional scene. People still hadn't gotten over the assassination of Pim Fortuyn in 2002. I mean, two divisive political figures killed on the street in cold blood, just two years apart? That's heavy. The soft populism of Pim Fortuyn already led to Geert Wilders, and Theo van Gogh's killing really unleashed those right-wing feelings that were coming out more in the mainstream. Pim Fortuyn maybe wasn't as bad as Geert Wilders, but he was saying lots of anti-immigrant things. That's when I started realizing, *Oh, there's a far-right faction in Dutch politics.*

Ruben van der Meer: Geert Wilders is a *real* far-right guy. He was on *De Lama's* once as a guest. The day before the shoot, security guys came to check the exits. I asked them, "How many security people are coming?" He said, "Ten guys—well, ten that you see, anyway. There will be more, but you won't know if they're part of our team." I felt sorry for how he had to live his life.

Pep Rosenfeld: The first time Boom Chicago did an election show was 2004. Greg and I did a two-hander about the election. In the show, Greg was John Kerry and I was George Bush.

Greg Shapiro: On Election Day, because of the time difference, we were booked for gigs all through the night. We started with "Coffee Time," a pleasant afternoon show for housewives that came on during, you know, coffee time. Then we did our own show at eight p.m., which on election night always meant a passionate crowd of newspaper readers and late-night talk-show watchers. Then there was an appearance at an election-night event at the Melkweg. We then jumped in a taxi, heading to the taping of the biggest late-night Dutch TV show at the time— ready to go all night with election commentary and comedy from us. They even hired American-style cheerleaders and football players from the then-active NFL Europe team Amsterdam Admirals.

Pep Rosenfeld: Unfortunately, Election Day that year—November 2, 2004—was also the day Theo van Gogh was killed.

Greg Shapiro: While as Americans we're hyper-focused on the election, the rest of Holland begins processing van Gogh's devastating, brutal murder. Holland was under attack—and oh, by the way, there's an American election too.

Pep Rosenfeld: They didn't send anyone home. Everyone at the table talked about the future of Dutch society . . . and then it was time for an election update. With cheerleaders! We were trying to do comedy bits around what had become a somber night.

Greg Shapiro: Election Day is like Christmas for us, and that's all we were thinking about. The full significance hadn't sunk in: *Sure, something bad happened—but this might be the night we get rid of George Bush.*

Pep Rosenfeld: We really didn't know how the election was going to go. It wasn't like 2016 when Hillary was *totally* going to win. Until, you know, she didn't.

Greg Shapiro: By then, we were seeing the headlines: Bush won again. Even after Iraq. Kerry had blown it. Sure we made jokes about how Kerry was boring. But he wasn't supposed to *lose*.

Pep Rosenfeld: Kerry was more secretary-of-state material: smart, efficient, and dull. Hillary too. Same-same. Those types never win. It didn't feel that funny. Everybody was in mourning.

Greg Shapiro: When we finally saw the day's headlines, they weren't, like, "Idiot Reelected as US President," but instead, "Theo van Gogh Murdered in the Oosterpark." No one gave a shit what a bunch of expats thought about the American election. The Dutch had their own problems to worry about.

Pep Rosenfeld: We were like, *Riiiiight*—that *happened yesterday too*.

Andrew Moskos: Even though the European Constitution was officially dead due to Holland's and France's "no" votes, the ideas of the constitution were later merged into existing treaties. Other elements were passed two years later, without any pesky popular votes, in a document that became known as the Lisbon Treaty. Boom Chicago got a mo' better Europe, and those who thought they could stop Europe at the ballot box learned to be skeptical, as Matt Jones had memorably sung on Boom's stage. But the shine had really come off the European project.

In the Netherlands, tensions simmering for years under the cloak of "tolerance" had finally boiled over, leading to even more right-wing populism. Upcoming financial and immigration challenges were not going to make Europe any calmer, either. No. Instead, more and more people would begin to wonder, *Who should I believe?* In 2005, we believed in Matt Jones . . . Not everything we did that year was political. As such, Matt Jones had a genius bit that really goes down in Boom Chicago history in terms of laughs-to-gag quotient. It was a video where Matt lip-synched the James Blunt song "You're Beautiful" to himself in the mirror . . .

Steven Svymbersky: And when it gets to the end, the camera pulls back suddenly, and Matt is . . .

Pep Rosenfeld: Totally bare-assed naked from the waist down. That's what they laughed at—Matt's smooth, white ass.

Andrew Moskos: *[Singing]* *"You're beautiful . . ."*

CHAPTER 14
2006

FOR YEARS, THE DUTCH HAD RACIST CANDY NAMES. WE CAN'T MAKE THIS SHIT UP, PEOPLE . . .

Do you know what year women got the right to vote in the United States? 1920. And when was the first gay kiss on American TV? 1991. If you're like us, you figured that stuff happened way earlier. So, one might be shocked to learn that it took until 2006 for Holland's iconic Van der Breggen candy factory to yield to less openly racist contemporary sensibilities and change the name of a popular confection from *negerzoenen* to *zoenen*. *Neger* means "Black person." *Zoenen* means "kisses": put them together and you get a bite-sized chocolate-covered marshmallow treat. When a Dutch person says *neger*, technically they don't mean the N-word. Okay.

It was a classic argument of two polarities: "We've always done it that way" versus "You cannot name candy after Black people." And like the steady march of better restaurants with late hours, shopping on Sunday, and coffee served in a to-go cup, this was another example of internationalism butting heads with traditional Dutch society.

Pep Rosenfeld: Dutch people are childishly stubborn about some things. They changed it to *zoenen*. But some Dutch people still call them *negerzoenen* because they don't like to be told to change.

Greg Shapiro: And you know who realized that? The grocery chain Albert Heijn. Right after the change, they changed the name of *their* version of the candy to *negen zoenen*. Because *negen* is the dutch word for "nine." And there were nine cookies in the box. So any similarity between *negen* and *neger*, you see, was obviously unintentional. Albert Heijn could plead innocence. And yet old racist Dutch grandmas could still squint and see *negerzoenen* if they wanted to. *[In Dutch accent]* "No, no—it's not what you think. A *negerzoen* is a little kiss from a Black person. And if you take a bite, you're eating some of their flesh. It's not racist, see?" It should be more about owning the cannibal space.

Pep Rosenfeld: The shit just writes itself. I mean, there are also *Jodenkoeken*, which means "Jew cookies": "Get your delicious Jews here—fresh out the oven!" What's the matter with you people? Does everything delicious have to have a horribly offensive name? "Oh look, I'm a Dutch chef, and I just invented a new cookie. It's vanilla with chocolate sprinkles; I'm going to call it the Lazy Moroccan."

It's hard to process this stuff as an outsider. I feel like the Dutch are not racist at all until dessert—and then all bets are off. Unless you're betting on them being racist. Then all bets are on. And, of course, lest we forget—the most racist Dutch national tradition is also the biggest and most beloved of them all: Zwarte Piet, which takes place in the three weeks up to December 5 each year.

In America, of course, we've got Santa Claus and his elves to symbolize Christmas cheer. And in formerly colonial Netherlands, there's Sinterklaas and his army of Black slaves called Zwarte Pieten, which translates to "Black Petes." I mean, nobody else in the outside world sees a lazy white man on a white horse followed by dozens of Black dudes doing all the work without seeing it as racist. Dutch people, meanwhile, are like, "No, we can't be racist because, unlike you Americans, Dutch people never owned slaves."

Jordan Peele: No, they just bought and sold them to everyone else, including the Americans. This distinction always rubs me the wrong way: "We would never keep slaves ourselves. We just sold them, okay? That's all." I mean, back in the day, the Dutch East India Company basically *invented* slavery.

Pep Rosenfeld: As a result, over the years there's been an ongoing national debate in Holland about whether Zwarte Piet is racist.

Jordan Peele: We lived in Amsterdam, which was different from the rest of the country. I mean, Dutch tolerance is great—but really, they're not *that* tolerant when you get into the more right-wing areas. Some of these small towns feel a bit like the American South. It's like they don't understand their relationship to racism; in a weird way, I don't think they really *believe* in racism. I think to them it's like, "Oh, racism—that's some American thing. We don't care about that. We're tolerant of everything."

Tarik Davis: Whenever we'd travel to the Netherlands's equivalent of, say, Kansas for a corporate event, it felt like new territory. We'd encounter crazy things like being called the N-word in public. Not to take anybody off the hook, but there was a slightly different emphasis than you'd find in a similar place in the US. I don't think there's an innocent way one can say the N-word, but these rural Dutch people would be like, "Isn't that what you people say to each other? I hear that word all the time on MTV in rap music. Is it wrong?" Amber and I would have to educate them in the moment—"No, that's not an appropriate word to use around us"—and they'd be truly shocked and apologetic.

Amber Ruffin: I gave up on explaining this stuff to Dutch people.

Tarik Davis: I mean, when I first got off the plane in Amsterdam, there were people in Blackface at the airport. I was like, *What's happening?* I had no idea about the Zwarte Piet tradition. I shouldn't laugh, because it's fucked up on every level—but stepping away from it, the whole thing was hilarious. In terms of the narrative of that young man who was me then, it was like, *Of course you're going to come to this new country and immediately see people in Blackface, and then be picked up by a man dressed like a cowboy vampire pirate.*

Dutch culture is a little schizophrenic—perhaps a little insane, even—in this regard. Come Christmastime in the Netherlands, walk into a store and suddenly everything is N-word this, N-word that. That was wild! We used to joke about how 364 days of the year, Holland is a pretty okay place to be a Black person—and then there's that one day when the Dutch let all their racism out.

Dave Buckman: I experienced this culture shock on my first day in Amsterdam. My roommate was Ike Barinholtz. While he was making dinner, I was relaxing on the couch, watching TV— desperately looking for something I could remotely understand. Flipping channels, I came across an obviously blond, obviously white lady in Blackface. Shrieking like I'd just seen a live rat, I yelled, "Ike, get in here!" Panicked, Ike came running in, thinking I'd hurt myself or something. I pointed at the screen and said, "What is *that?*" Ike was like, "Oh, Dave—that's Zwarte Piet. Welcome to the Netherlands." I'd just never heard of or experienced or been to anyplace where appearing on television like that would be okay.

Ruben van der Meer: It's difficult for people who grew up here to see this as a bad thing. Everybody's grown up loving Zwarte Piet, but now they're supposed to say, "I see that it's racist."

Amber Ruffin: I was very interested in the whole Zwarte Piet thing. While I was at Boom, we went to the Sinterklaas parade, from which I did a "woman on the street" video report. In it, I walked through the parade with a microphone, hitting on everyone dressed like Zwarte Piet. I'd say to them, "December in Holland is when Sint brings Black men to all the Black women—so who's been sooooo good this year they get to take me out tonight?"

Jordan Peele: That's just so subversive on Amber's part. She's amazing.

Amber Ruffin: In the video, every single Zwarte Piet in Blackface I could get my hands on, I asked them all on dates. Only one of them agreed to go out with me.

Pep Rosenfeld: And she married that Piet.

Steven Svymbersky: That's not true—but Amber did marry a Dutch guy. She even wrote a TV pilot about a Black woman who marries a Dutch man.

Pep Rosenfeld: That wasn't our first Zwarte Piet/Sinterklaas video. That was in 2002, when "Zwarte Piet Revolution" made its debut. It featured Jordan and Colton as Zwarte Pieten who get fed up with Sinterklaas and take over.

Colton Dunn: I loved doing the "Christmas in Holland" video and being able to comment on the Zwarte Piet phenomenon. The Dutch were able to laugh at it and not feel like we were calling them all racists, you know? The point was to get people to connect with us through humor, and then make them think.

Andrew Moskos: I remember when Jordan first met Colton, he was concerned that he'd been replaced—that there was only room for one Black guy at Boom Chicago. We've been institutionalized to expect that—kind of like how one immediately assumes the Black guy is going to get killed first in a horror movie.[39] But, uh, at Boom we can have *two* funny Black guys in the cast at the same time, no problem.

Tarik Davis: For Black performers, I call that "being a Highlander": there can be only one.

Jordan Peele: Of course, there can't be *two* Black guys at Boom Chicago at the same time! I don't remember that, but that's really funny. Colton's one of the greatest human beings of all time, and another instant bond. He actually became my best buddy when he got to Boom.

Colton Dunn: I've heard that story. Clearly that wasn't going to happen, because Jordan's much more talented than me. Once Jordan saw me perform, he was like, *Okay, I'm fine* . . . We very quickly became friends, having very similar upbringings and obviously both really loving improv. We weren't necessarily in the same shows at the same time, though. If Jordan was doing the theater show, I'd usually be out touring, or vice versa. We didn't really perform together much unless it was a "Heineken Late Night" gig or the "Christmas in Holland" video.

Pep Rosenfeld: "Zwarte Piet Revolution" came about as I was going back to the States for Thanksgiving. Our video director Jamie Wright said, "We should totally do a Zwarte Piet music video." I was like, "Oh, do you mean we take 'Christmas in Hol-

---

39 Tarik Davis even made an acclaimed short film exploring this topic, *Page One.*

lis' by Run-D.M.C., but instead it's 'Christmas in Holland,' and then Zwarte Pieten rap about how Sinterklaas sucks?" And he went, "Yeah, exactly!" So I wrote this thing on the plane, and I think if I wrote it today, everybody would say, "You can't write 'urban' lingo for Black actors. It's offensive." They might have a point. There's one particular cringe line in "Christmas in Holland": *"Throw him in the sack / We'z the boss."* Yes, I actually spelled it with a "z." I bet Colton and Jordan would both say, "Yeah, we thought it was weird how this white Jew wrote rap-speak for us."

Andrew Moskos: Don't feel too guilty, white Jewish guy. That video is in the Tropenmuseum in their exhibit about race and racism in the Netherlands. The Holy Grail isn't even in a museum, despite Indiana Jones's best efforts.

Jordan Peele: We did that Christmas rap as Zwarte Pieten. It was fun but strange—this feeling of awkwardness with Dutch people dressing up in Blackface, but having no context as to why that's not cool. I mean, *kids* love these colonial "helpers" of Sint!

Rob AndristPlourde: "Helpers"—a Dutch euphemism for "slaves."

Ruben van der Meer: In America, all the boys want to be Superman, Batman, Spider-Man. Here in the Netherlands, everybody wants to be Zwarte Piet—*he* was the hero. I mean I had a Zwarte Piet suit: I wore it to school every day for three weeks during the holidays. I basically waited to see Zwarte Piet all year. Really, Sinterklaas was just an old guy on a horse. Zwarte Piet did all the work, and was athletic too: he could climb up the chimney and run across the roof. It was like doing parkour—but carrying a big bag of presents while wearing a nice velvet suit and a feather earring.

Steven Svymbersky: We started doing a Zwarte Piet show in 2011 because we wanted to tackle all that stuff. Boom was one of the first institutions to really publicly go there and say, "This is bad." In that show, they came up with a solution that was later adopted. Boom was ahead of the conversation on that one.

Pep Rosenfeld: In that show, we pitched what we thought was the most practical solution: a soot-faced Zwarte Piet. We would always say "Sooty Piet" shouldn't look like he's in Blackface. He should be more like the chimney sweep from *Mary Poppins*. He's just dirty from all that chimney soot.

Steven Svymbersky: And then voilà—you've solved the problem. Of course, you have to take away the massive red lips and crazy ersatz-Afro hairdo as well.

Pep Rosenfeld: Zwarte Piet covered in soot from going down the chimney makes narrative sense. But with the current iteration, he has very dark soot all over his face . . . and yet nothing on his clothes. Wow, Sint must have given him some magic soot-proof clothes. And how again did the chimney make his lips so red, and cause his ears to sprout giant hoop earrings?

Let's go further here: Jewish people like me should get to enjoy the same oppressive fun that Black people have with Zwarte Piet. How about a new helper for Sint: Hebrew Harry! Hebrew Harry's not an anti-Semitic stereotype. No, he just banged his nose in the chimney. That's why it's swollen up so big. That's not a stereotype. Not at all!

Greg Shapiro: Not all Dutch people were amused by our insights regarding their native seasonal traditions. A lot of people told us their views at the bar after the show: it's not racist—it's tradition. And it's for the kids.

Andrew Moskos: It's funny how many adults feel very strongly, but present their personal feelings as if they come from their kids, who don't care at all.

Greg Shapiro: There's a YouTube video of some Dutch kids in New York celebrating Sinterklaas, and you don't see any Blackface Zwarte Pieten. And the kids were still excited when Pieten arrived and took candy and presents from them, despite the fact that they were white.

Pep Rosenfeld: If anything, these kids needed a refresher course on not taking candy from strangers.

Andrew Moskos: A few years later, we developed a project with the Dutch airline KLM where we did a Sinterklaas show in a 747 flying from Amsterdam to Chicago. Twenty people got an upgrade to business class, which they'd dolled up to feel like a comedy club, where we did a show during the flight. If they didn't want the comedy show, they could go and sit in the economy section in silence, but no one took that option.

Pep Rosenfeld: It was super fun. The passengers were so into it.

Greg Shapiro: Pep played Santa Claus, and I was Sinterklaas. The gig had the potential to go incredibly badly, but it was a huge success. The flight crew loved it especially—my God, so many selfies. It really did turn out to be fun. We didn't have to bring any Zwarte Pieten. KLM knew that was not a good international move to play; they were kind of cutting edge in that way.

Pep Rosenfeld: They didn't want to be rebranded as KKKLM.

Andrew Moskos: I'm happy to report that since 2020, there are no Blackface Zwarte Pieten to be found in Amsterdam— only rainbow and soot-faced Pieten. By the time you read this, they might even be extinct in the less sophisticated parts of the Netherlands as well. I'm not taking credit for these evolutions, nor does Boom Chicago believe it sparked this social upheaval. Unfortunately, our brilliant idea of "Sooty Piet" fell mostly on deaf ears. But we did say something before most everyone even registered the problem.

Pep Rosenfeld: For Boom Chicago, 2006 was probably more about receiving the gift of a great new cast. Joining Boom that year were Lauren Flans, Ryan Gowland, Laurel Coppock, Hilary Bauman, Brian Jack, Dan Oster, and Michael Orton-Toliver, aka Mike OT (or just OT). And Michael Diederich, the longtime friend of Boom, understudy, coach, and teacher, who had been lowered from a cage when we opened the Leidseplein, became a member of the ensemble. Vladimir Berkhemer joined the music team, while Becky Nelson joined the video team.

Andrew Moskos: We were diving into Internet content, the "mobile space," and other trendy, exciting buzzwords. All global entertainment companies were looking for online content. That was before everyone realized online content was the same as regular ol' content. We jumped into this, making videos for Atomic Wedgie, which sounded exactly like what it was supposed to be: a fun, young, and irreverent daughter company of super-corporate FremantleMedia. The name might've been silly, but Atomic Wedgie had good budgets, and we were happy to spend them.

Pep Rosenfeld: We had some hits and some, uh, misses. My favorite was Brendan Hunt and Matt Chapman doing "The Unlikely Fan." It was a daily series about the 2006 World Cup as it was happening. They made one video about streaking where

Brendan ended up running naked across an empty football pitch. I played the cop who tackles him and cuffs him. That was Brendan at his best: charismatic, funny, knowledgeable about football, lying facedown naked in the grass . . .

Andrew Moskos: We also made two other series. "Full Frontal News" with Greg Shapiro was about current events (and yes, we had the title before Samantha Bee). We also made "Slacker Fantasy Football" with Mike OT and Brian Jack in the lead roles. OT would go on to set up the Free Association, London's premier improv school, as well as create the UK TV smash *Borderline*—directed by Matt Jones.

Greg Shapiro: Early on, Andrew was saying this Internet thing was groundbreaking, and so Boom Chicago was ahead of the curve on that too. Web content was a part of our show early on. We even made tech the theme of the show that year.

Andrew Moskos: "Me, Myspace, and iPod" was my favorite show title and we got some really good reviews. Merijn Henfling said in *Het Parool,* "We are once again grateful that [Boom Chicago] decided to make Amsterdam their home." Henk van Gelder wrote in *NRC Handelsblad* that we "created an entirely new form of theater; call it 'digi-comedy.'" Sure, "digi-comedy" didn't exactly stick, but I'll still take it . . .

Pep Rosenfeld: I love that two of the three parts of that oh-so-topical title are now gone. *Poof!* Nobody has an iPod anymore, and Myspace vaporized during the run of the show. How weird is that?

Andrew Moskos: Hey, digi-comedy is a constantly evolving mistress.

Pep Rosenfeld: "Me, Myspace, and iPod" had a great finale. We sat a couple on a couch and used them in a scene about identity theft and Internet fraud. Back then, people were asking if it was safe to buy things online. Before pin codes, you just gave your credit card to, like, every restaurant and, um, comedy show.

So we took the guy's credit card and "rented" them a limo, then showed them and the audience a fake receipt that Steven had made during the intermission. "We've also reserved a luxury suite at the Amstel Hotel with your credit card. But you can still cancel it. So look at your wife and ask, *Is she worth that much money? Or should we just cancel?*" Awkward. Hilarious. Smart point. Classic Andrew.

Andrew Moskos: Since we knew they were at the show, that meant it was likely no one was present at their home. So we showed a Google Earth view of their house. People thought they were at the show anonymously, and then were shocked when we put a picture of their home on the screen. Back then, most people hadn't seen that before. At the end of the scene, we put on masks with the guy's face printed on it and did a final song about taking his identity and living in his house.

Pep Rosenfeld: None of the actors wanted to do it. Matt Jones was worried that an audience member would punch him in the face. I was like, "Yeah? Tell you what: I'll try it at 'Late Night' tonight. And when it kills, you can do it in the show tomorrow." It did, and he did, and from then on, he loved to do that role.

Greg Shapiro: At Boom, actors have to educate themselves about a situation, then quickly turn it into comedy. It's a valuable skill. I mean, I had never heard of *negerzoenen* until I had been here awhile. Now Pep and I do whole shows inspired by racist candy. That's what Boom does: learn fast, and then turn what you learn into jokes even faster.

One of the things that keeps making shows fun for us is connecting with news and pop culture. Whether political, social, or technological—as long as people are talking about it, it's fair game. It's even better if they aren't talking about it, and say, "Wow, I learned something!" The Zwarte Piet debate was a perfect storm—a topical, important issue that inspires passion on both sides. Thankfully, some cultural phenomena are just so ridiculous that you *have* to make fun of them. I mean, when we hold up a mirror to Dutch people, and they see themselves eating treats named after kisses from a Black person . . . they have to either laugh, cry, or apologize. Or all three.

Suzi Barrett: I think of all the knowledge I gained about international politics and history just from living in Europe. In that environment, our horizons were expanding, whether we wanted them to or not. I was so thankful to finally experience my own American ignorance like I never had before. At the same time, I missed home too.

Rounding into my third year in Amsterdam, I started feeling like it's time to return home. In no way was that a negative reflection about my Boom experience. I wanted to use what I'd learned at Boom on new stages. I wanted to be challenged again by utilizing this new knowledge and sophistication I had. And there's only so many sketches one can write about Albert Heijn; I'd hit my maximum. Still, there was no denying I was now much better at everything I'd always dreamed of doing: writing, acting, directing, improvising . . . By the end of your Boom career, you know you're able to grab the audience's attention and hold it. I left my time in Amsterdam confident I could now handle a room full of unruly people who spoke eighteen different languages and didn't know what the fuck I was talking about—and still make them laugh. I came home from Boom feeling like I could host the Oscars.

Holly Walker: I was the first cast member of color at Boom Chicago. I'm incredibly proud of all the cast members of color who came out of Boom—and let's not forget rock-star Boom alum Carl Tart too. But each of them were super talented *before* they got to Amsterdam. Clearly, Boom saw that, or they wouldn't have been hired.

I can only speak for myself, but living outside of the US may have played a role in allowing me to cultivate my own voice. It could be that no one knew me in Amsterdam and I got to reinvent myself. It could be that I didn't feel racism as acutely in Europe. Don't get me wrong, there's definitely racism in Amsterdam—but maybe the recess from the particular kind of racism I grew up with let me breathe a bit and flourish. Boom definitely helped sharpen my skills by the mere fact that we did 200+ shows a year. But living in Europe played a huge role there too. It broadened my horizons—and I don't just mean the drugs (which I cannot confirm or deny that I took). Let's just say, there were definitely a lot of influences in the mix. Thankfully, what happens at Boom Chicago stays at Boom Chicago. ;)

Tarik Davis: After being in Holland awhile, I realized we're all part of this thing, and a lot of that was about me finding my identity as a Boom Chicago performer. Being Black in Amsterdam had a different weight, especially with Colton, Jordan, and Amber being part of it—that really marked my full transition. For a year, people kept calling me Colton or Jordan. The audiences were so brutally honest, so someone would always say after the show, like, "Colton, wow, that last scene sucked," or, "Hey, Jordan, you were pretty good tonight." And then one night, someone said, "You really rocked it, Tarik—that was incredible!" Once that happened and people started calling me by my name, I was like, *All right, I'm here—I've arrived.*

In the Netherlands, I was very aware of my Blackness being sometimes secondary to my Americanness. That was a trip. Of course, I'm not alone in feeling this way. I think of James Baldwin and other Black Americans who'd traveled from the States to spend considerable time in Europe, having this experience of cognitive dissonance—where race isn't considered one's entire identity.

Really, the hypervisibility of my being Black in the Netherlands just felt lighter. This was especially powerful coming from Upright Citizens Brigade, where Colton and I and one other person were the only Blacks in the company. UCB was a very white space then. I had already been reprimanded for being too Black at UCB before, and was always aware of my place in that system—who I was in it, how to navigate it. But then at Boom, I was able to be more of myself than I was performing at UCB. There's a larger-than-life style of play at Boom, and I was always a very big, theatrical performer, so I was able to incorporate my Blackness on that stage in a way that would get me booed in New York unless I went to the place of being a stereotype.

Weirdly, I was able to be my more authentic self in a European country than in the States. I had new insight into how jazz musicians had found success in Europe that was unlike the success they had back home. Europe has an appreciation for new flavor, and the more authentic that flavor, the bigger the appreciation. There's something specific about the experience of being a person of color at Boom. I felt like in New York, improv was about being cute and trying to impress certain people, and authenticity kind of gets left at the door. At Boom, though, I found I could be very much who I am onstage and share my experiences from where and how I grew up in a way that I couldn't in the white safe spaces of UCB. Boom Chicago wasn't interested in creating a safe space for white people: on that stage, they wanted us to try and *ignite* something.

I was very humbled to be in this class at Boom with people like Lolu Ajayi and Holly Walker, who are just incredible, and the other great performers of color who came out of there with us. I didn't understand what Boom had seen in me at first, but by the time I'd flourished and found my voice there, they were very trusting. I'll be forever grateful to them for not just picking me, but placing that trust in me—that created a very warm home where I felt like I could do anything and get my Malcolm Gladwell ten thousand hours in.

Amber and I always joke that Boom was like the comedy version of the Beatles in Germany. Between us, we probably did over a thousand shows—most of them great, some of them very difficult. By the end of my time there at Boom, I literally felt like I could fly onstage: I could do anything, and there were no rules holding me back. It always seemed ironic to me that the first image I saw walking into my Amsterdam apartment was this mural of Neo from *The Matrix* dodging a bullet on the wall. Seeing that, I was like, *Oh, that's what this place is. Here at Boom, we break the Matrix!*

CHAPTER 15
2007

EVERYTHING IS LOVE: MOTHERFUCKING BURT REYNOLDS TAKES THE BOOM STAGE, AND OTHER TRUE TALES

Since arriving in the Netherlands, Boom Chicago has always been interested in following Dutch cinema. It's kind of a thrill when you move to a new place, and then see that place in a movie. For example, we remember when the Dutch movie *Antonia* won the Oscar for best foreign film in 1996. It being of Dutch origin was enough to tickle us when we saw it at a Chicago art cinema during an early off-season. The movie was called *Antonia's Line* in America because . . . uh . . . yeah, we don't quite get it. We swooned to hear Dutch in a movie in Chicago. We were also delighted by the sex and nudity—which, along with endings that weren't always happy, came to define Dutch film. From Boom's point of view, anyway.

The best example in cinema that highlights the different outlook of Dutch filmmakers versus their American peers is 1988's *Spoorloos* (pronounced "spore-lohs")—remade by Hollywood five years later in English as *The Vanishing*. The stories were basically the same (and we won't say "spoiler alert," as surely the statute of spoiler limitations runs out after thirty years). A man and his girlfriend are on a road trip. She's kidnapped by a creepy nut. Naturally, in *Spoorloos*, the creep is Belgian; in *The Vanishing*, he's Jeff Bridges, so it kind of evens out. The creep abides . . .

In both versions of *The Vanishing*, the boyfriend goes nearly insane looking for his girlfriend. In each film, he's contacted by the creep, who basically tells him, "If you want to learn what happened to her, I can't tell you. You have to experience it." The protagonist agrees with the creep, putting his face into a damp cloth doused in knockout sauce (which still seems pretty weird). And in both films yet again, the protagonist wakes up in the dark—only to light a lighter (a Zippo in *The Vanishing,* a Bic in *Spoorloos*) and discover he's sealed in a coffin, buried alive.

In *Spoorloos,* that's it. The hero screams, and then it cuts to the Belgian creep shoveling dirt on the coffin. Roll credits. *Yikes.* It creeps us out just thinking about it. In *The Vanishing,* however, Hollywood takes a little more license with the ending. Our hero's screams are heard! Sandra Bullock, who has become his not-quite-love interest, frees Kiefer Sutherland. Then they kill Jeff Bridges, and the music swells. Jack Bauer lives to later fight terrorists twenty-four hours at a time! *USA! USA! USA!* You think Americans can stand the idea of Kiefer Sutherland dying? No way. We need a happy ending—and add a double order of violence, hold the nudity. Oh, and remove the twist that was the whole reason the original was so effective.

Dutch cinema really was different from typical Hollywood multiplex fare. Bad, sad things happened in Dutch movies. People who had sex with each other didn't always wake up in full makeup and a bra, or die. To us it seemed a bit more . . . relatable. At least it did for a while. But just as Santa Claus began encroaching on Sint, Hollywood style was steadily creeping into Hilversum filmmaking. And that trend hit a shark-jumping head in 2007 with the release of *Alles Is Liefde.*

Alles Is Liefde ("Everything Is Love") felt like a Hollywood film. We mean that literally—it felt like *Love Actually,* actually.[40]

---

40 Technically, *Love Actually* was made in the UK. And yes, some of the jokes feel more British than American. But come on—that shit is *so* Hollywood: the plot, the music—even the British actors in it had already split the BBC for Hollywood years ago. Keira Knightley was in the *Pirates of the Caribbean* series; Alan Rickman was Hans Grüber in *Die Hard*; Hugh Grant got busted on Sunset

Both feature a big mixed bag of famous actors whose characters' romantic stories cross paths in a fun way. These "meet cute" archetypes include, naturally, a lovable goofball (Rowan Atkinson/Paul de Leeuw) and a high-status dude (prime minister/prince) who falls for a low-status woman (political staffer/department-store salesperson). Both movies center around a December holiday (Christmas/Sinterklaas). Both begin with a monologue about what love is all about. But *Alles Is Liefde* wasn't a direct remake of *Love Actually,* per se. It was more like a Dutch rip-off—as if some Dutch producers were like, "Okay, we want a movie with that *Love Actually* vibe, but we would *love* to not *actually* pay for the rights. Oh, and get Carice van Houten to star in it."

Ruben van der Meer: Of course I remember *Alles Is Liefde*—I was in it! I only had a small part, though. My character didn't even have a name: I was "the Barman." I auditioned for other parts in the movie, but I didn't get anything. The guy who got the part for the role I was auditioning for, Thomas Acda, went on to become a huge star.

Pep Rosenfeld: At Boom, of course, we were totally psyched to see Carice van Houten on the poster for *Alles Is Liefde,* because we've always been massive fans of the van Houten sisters. Before she blew up too, Carice's sister Jelka worked for a while at Boom Chicago as a bartender. There's still a character named after her in the *Best of Boom* scene "Dutch Date."[41]

Greg Shapiro: We first encountered Carice when she was just studying at an Amsterdam theater school. She started dating

---

Boulevard with a prostitute in his car. Those Brits rock some hard-core Hollywood bona fides right there.

41 If you squint, it's perhaps a sweet tribute to an old friend who worked at Boom during the time it was written. If you look closely, it might be evidence that one of the actors was trying a little too hard to impress Jelka.

Josh Meyers for a good long while—they were a cute couple. That was right around when we started knowing people who'd started getting a name for themselves in the Dutch scene.

Carice van Houten: My sister Jelka had a job at Boom behind the bar, and she said that there was a guy working there who she really liked and thought might be sort of something for me.

Pep Rosenfeld: So Jelka played matchmaker with you and Posh?

Carice van Houten: Yeah. It's not that Boom Chicago wouldn't have otherwise interested me. I just didn't ever know about the possibility of English-language theater in Amsterdam. It was exotic and terrifying, but it had something: I felt so compelled to hang around because there was so much talent there. Boom really opened up a whole world for me that I found myself drawn to. What attracted me was that there was no room for ego, doing comedy in a group the way Boom did. And it was a good group. The individuals were very funny in themselves. I was just early in theater school, so I really admired the guts of the actors, and how they were flexible in dealing with things that fell flat. The sharpness and quick recovery, making jokes about your own stuff—that all felt very refreshing.

Andrew Moskos: Jelka really brought Carice into Boom's orbit. We remember seeing Carice early on in the play *Het Bewijs*, which was the Dutch version of *Proof*—the acclaimed dramatic play by David Auburn about a math-nerd set in Chicago (which especially appealed to Pep, being a math nerd from Chicago). Jelka also memorably starred in the MTV production *Sexual Perversity*—also a Dutch version of a play, David Mamet's *Sexual Perversity in Chicago*. And who didn't love watching actual sisters Carice and Jelka play actual sisters in *Jackie*? Jelka also starred in a pizza video with Pep, which required getting a gluten-free Domino's pizza, which he says was surprisingly tasty. So the van Houten sisters, yes, they're longtime friends now, and still regulars at Boom Chicago premiers.

Pep Rosenfeld: Indeed, we remain lifetime fans of our dear friends, the van Houten sibs. But *Alles Is Liefde*—even with Zwarte Pieten running around in it—feels like the least Dutch, most Hollywood thing either one of them has ever done. I mean, Carice's résumé is full of very Dutch stuff. The BAFTA-nominated *Black Book* was about the German occupation (and featured an incredibly intense, high-stakes performance by Carice that won her international accolades). *Minoes* was based on a book by Annie M.G. Schmidt. *De Passievrucht* was chock-full of sex, nudity, and depression—the main hallmarks of a Dutch film!

Carice van Houten: People are so cramped in America about nudity. It's completely opposite here in the Netherlands. In retrospect, I've thought to myself, *Was that normal? Is that a Dutch culture thing? Or is that just patriarchy going way too far?* I've done films where there was so much unnecessary nudity, and it didn't even cross my mind—not once. That's probably a mixture of me being comfortable in my own skin and not feeling very precious about it, but also conditioning that's hugely cultural.

Pep Rosenfeld: In the Hollywood-made *Valkyrie*, Carice starred alongside Tom Cruise, helping him try to kill Hitler—perhaps the most Dutch fantasy of all.

Carice van Houten: There's a bit of a history there. We grew up with so much German hatred, and of course it didn't help with football extending that hatred. Actually, I really like the German football team. I once dated a German man and really saw this from a different perspective. I was like, *Wow, they've been carry-*

ing this guilt for so long. When the German team won the World Cup, he told me this was the first time Germans actually felt like they deserved to wave their flag again.

Valkyrie was my first real introduction to a Hollywood-vibe kind of film too. That was also not normal, I guess, because it's a Tom Cruise movie. That meant it was the most luxurious shoot I've ever been on. If I had to walk a hundred meters somewhere, they'd send a limousine. It was insane: I felt hugely spoiled, but the sustainability factor was zero minus one thousand.

Pep Rosenfeld: Did Boom Chicago prepare you for the nerdy comedians you would encounter when you guested on *The Simpsons*?

Carice van Houten: Boom Chicago introduced me to *The Simpsons*; I didn't really know about it before. But I'm a complete nerd, and I've always been attracted to nerds.

Pep Rosenfeld: Oh really?

Carice van Houten: I would not have been in *Game of Thrones* if Seth hadn't told me it was a great nerdy show and cool series of nerdy books. But I mean, I'm not so nerdy that I *read* all the books.

Pep Rosenfeld: Did you read *any*?

Carice van Houten: Any? Hmmmm . . . No. But when I went to LA for the first time, people were asking me, "Where do you want to be five years from now?" The only thing that came up in my head was, "Be a voice on *The Simpsons*." That came true, so that's pretty good.

Pep Rosenfeld: Even when Carice was on *The Simpsons,* she played an authentically Dutch character. But is *Alles Is Liefde*

more Hollywood than Dutch? Think about it. Happy ending?
There are several, yes. Nudity? None that we remember, alas.
Annoyingly catchy pop song whose chorus is the name of the
film? Thanks for nothing, Bløf (and that goes for the weird
slash-through "o" in your name too).

Andrew Moskos: Once Hilversum—the Dutch equivalent of
Hollywood—scored a smash box-office hit with its first *rom-
kom*, they kept milking the formula.

Carice van Houten: *Alles Is Liefde* was a curse and a blessing.
We were really ready to show that we could do a good comedy.
But then it sparked people to think, *Oh, wait a minute . . . If we
put hearts in the title and make it about a couple in Amsterdam,
that's going to score!* And then it degraded to the point where
the whole genre has gone to shit.

Andrew Moskos: Each successor has one of those we-could-
never-fall-in-love-until-we-can plots that boyfriends all over the
USA sit through in order to get laid. "We could never fall in love
. . . because you're a prince!" "We could never fall in love . . .
because I work for you!" "We could never fall in love . . . because
you're the jerk next door!" "We could never fall in love . . . because you're being paid to pretend to love me by my mother!"
Blecch. It's enough to make us watch *Love Actually*'s Alan Rickman in *Die Hard* again.[42]

Pep Rosenfeld: Why stop? There's no reason Dutch ladies who
go to movies on ladies' night should have to sip prosecco while
watching an *American* chick flick. Anything Americans can do,
the Dutch can do just as well, and on a more practical Dutch
budget. In their movie trailers, Dutch filmmakers prove just as

---

42 Don't get this reference? You should've read the previous footnote. Wait, did
you read this footnote but not that footnote? Weird.

capable in their ability to signal the arrival of a game-changing plot point with an annoying needle-scratch sound effect that's as good as any Hollywood filmmaker's. In our show, we improvised a stereotypical parody of a movie trailer from one of these movies. From audience suggestions, we'd improvise the American version, and then flip it to make fun of the Dutch:

> Host: So when an American rom-com comes out of Hollywood, you all make fun of how bad it is, but we all know the same kind of crap comes out of Hilversum. So based on your suggestions, here's the trailer for a Dutch remake of that American romantic comedy.
>
> VO: This summer, Carice van Houten is a woman who's too busy for love.
>
> Actress as Carice: I used to be a [job suggested by audience], but right now I'm unemployed with generous Dutch benefits.
>
> VO: And Antonie Kamerling is the loneliest man in Amsterdam . . .
>
> Actor as Antonie: [Sad/bored] Hè-hè.[43]

Andrew Moskos: When we took a step back, we saw the growing similarity between Hollywood and Hilversum as a symbol of the blurring lines between United States and Netherlands cultures. By 2007, the world could see the light at the end of the George Bush tunnel, and the *Yankee Go Home* signs were

---

43 Unfortunately, our naming Dutch movie star Antonie Kamerling the "loneliest man in Amsterdam" proved sadly prophetic. Antonie committed suicide in 2010 while this scene had a place in *Best of Boom*. We changed the name in the scene to Thijs Römer, and, as they say, the show went on . . .

finally coming down. In the States, an inspiring senator named Barack Obama announced his candidacy for president—though everyone knew he would be beaten by Hillary Clinton. Shit, her victory was a sure thing! During that era, we even titled a show "Yankee Come Back," to celebrate that Americans could come out of hiding and feel welcome in the Netherlands again.

Pep Rosenfeld: It was a great time for Americans to travel to Europe again. This included new members of the Boom team like Andĕl Sudik, who now directs at Chicago's Second City, Nigerian Amsterdam local Lolu Ajayi, and James Kirkland, who loved to tell you how 9/11 was an inside job. (Kirkland would later be featured on a poster as a literal tree hugger: *If the tree doesn't want to be hugged, is it rape?* This was clearly well before #TreeToo . . .) Now when we asked audiences, "Are there any Americans in the house?" they'd cheer like it was 1998—instead of silently sipping drinks while sitting on their hands like, say, the perennially guilty Germans.

Andrew Moskos: We love our Dutch audiences (who typically raise their hands politely when we ask them to cheer), but it was nice having whooping and hollering Americans back in the house again. And we have to admit it: even though more and more of our alums went on to fame and fortune in the States, we were tickled when we'd discover people whose work we were fans of in the audience at Boom Chicago.

Pep Rosenfeld: We still get a kick out of it when Dutch stars and internationally famous American celebrities randomly show up at Boom to see the show and hang out. Like, say, our favorite hip-hop DJ . . .

Andrew Moskos: I had a great night with Jam Master Jay once. We were super Run-D.M.C. fans, having been huge rap fans since 1984, when our white friends didn't know what hip-hop was. You can imagine how psyched I was when I learned the Jam Master himself was coming to a Boom Chicago show.

A Boom Chicago promoter, Caroline Ementon, had gone to see Run-D.M.C.[44] at the Paradiso one night in the summer of '98. After meeting Run-D.M.C. after their show, the group asked Caroline and her friends to be tour guides and show them around Amsterdam. After getting the members of Run-D.M.C. high on mushrooms, Caroline hyped up Boom Chicago to them, offering them tickets to the next night's show.

Rob AndristPlourde: I wasn't supposed to perform that night. I called Jill Benjamin—who was actually in that show—and said, "Jill, if Depeche Mode ever comes to see a show, I will switch out and you can play it." So, yeah, I got to perform for Jam Master Jay. During intermission, we heard Jay was outside, so we went outside too. Andrew and I were pie-eyed puppy dogs standing next to the man.

Andrew Moskos: Run-D.M.C. ended up loving the show. Afterward, we had some beers with Jay, which made it one of the all-time great nights for us. And apparently he had a great time too. A year later, I was in New York at the book release party for *The Vibe History of Hip Hop*[45] and Jam Master Jay was also there. As the party was breaking up, I went over to him and said, "You might not remember me, but my name is . . ." And he said, "Andrew! We met in Amsterdam. Comedy show. Boom Chicago!" Inside, I was like, *Holy fucking shit, Jam Master Jay*

---

44 At the time, Run-D.M.C. was experiencing an unexpected revival of popularity following the release of Jason Nevins's smash club mix of their 1983 single "It's Like That." Nevins's remix would top charts in the Netherlands and fifteen other countries in 1998—ultimately selling over five million copies globally.

45 We were invited by this book's coauthor Matt Diehl, who had written a chapter in *The Vibe History of Hip Hop*. Jay's murder was also eventually solved in *Notorious C.O.P.*, a book Matt coauthored with Derrick Parker, the detective who started the NYPD's "hip-hop surveillance unit."

knows my name! But I played it cool and asked where the next party was. He told me he was on his way to a record-release party for rapper Rakim. I reported to my friends that not only did JMJ remember me, but I knew where Rakim was throwing a party. For a second, I was *the man.* So the four of us got into a cab and headed there. When we arrived, Jay waved us over to the front of the line. At the velvet rope, a white record exec with a clipboard was happy to see him: "Jay! How you doin'? So, how many are in your group that need to get in?" Jay said, "Eight." Record-exec guy shoots a disapproving look at Jay and says in a *Come on, dude* tone, "Jaaaaaaay . . . you're killing me. You can bring in four only." Jay just looked at us, shrugged, said, "Oh well, I tried," and then went into the party.

Pep Rosenfeld: Looking back, how come Jam Master Jay *couldn't* get eight people into a party? He's Jam Master Jay.

Andrew Moskos: *"Goddamn, that DJ made my day."* Well, almost.

Pep Rosenfeld: We did make P!nk's day when she hung out after a "Late Night" show. That was also a pretty great night. P!nk came to see the show with a posse of a dozen people. Afterward, they just chilled in the balcony, drinking with the actors and listening to music; it was outstanding—just a fun night that felt like a house party, with people dancing, talking, and being flirty, and a pop star with an exclamation point standing in for the "i" in her name along for the ride. That's what "Late Night" feels like at its best. I found it extra cool because I'd been a fan of P!nk's ever since she accepted the MTV video award for "Lady Marmalade." At the podium, she said something like, "Well, if you gave us this award, you must've thought we did a great job playing whores." It was such a great zing on how women are portrayed in videos.

Steven Svymbersky: But the best celebrity-at-Boom story is the one about Burt Reynolds. Burt Reynolds was filming a movie in Amsterdam and showed up one night.

Pep Rosenfeld: For the kids, Burt Reynolds was a 1970s movie star who got famous as a good-looking, hairy-chested good ol' boy. Burt went from fun and funny in his car-crashing youth to a legit serious career in middle age, followed by a late-career revival thanks to his ironic stunt casting as a porn auteur in 1997's *Boogie Nights*. I'm not actually sure what brought him to Boom that night.

Greg Shapiro: Must've been that apocryphal *Boom Magazine* that Quentin Tarantino took home in 1993.

Steven Svymbersky: During intermission, Andrew went over to Burt's table and asked if he'd appear onstage in an upcoming improv scene. Some stars are cautious in such instances. They could fail. They could look dumb. They could've been drinking too much. And onstage at an improv show, you never know what might happen in the moment. But Burt's answer was immediate: "Hell yes!" He showed no doubt, no fear.

Andrew Moskos: So when I started the second act, I asked for a volunteer from the audience. Some guys near the stage were shouting for me to choose their friend. I walked over to the group and asked his name; they screamed back in unison, "Antonio!" "Well, I'm sure Antonio is a really cool guy," I intoned into the mic, "but he's not as cool as motherfucking Burt Reynolds!"

Steven pumped the music as he hit Burt with the spotlight at his table. The crowd couldn't believe it. Motherfucking Burt Reynolds just flashed his big, expensive-looking white smile. He looked tan and fantastic for his age, and when he stepped onstage, the crowd went wild. When I shook his hand, Burt gave me a satisfyingly firm, meaty *Smokey and the Bandit* handshake.

Steven Svymbersky: Burt didn't disappoint. As soon as Andrew started interviewing him, someone in the audience yelled, "Burt, is that your real hair?" Of course, he was wearing a toupee that evening, as he was famous for doing.

Andrew Moskos: Burt got serious immediately. He grabbed my microphone, pointing it in the direction of his heckler. "Who said that?" he demanded. No one answered, so Burt barked his order again: "I said, who *said* that?"

Resistance at this point was futile; this was motherfucking Burt Reynolds. A pale, beefy Brit lunkhead meekly raised his hand. "What's your name?" Burt snarled. Abashed, he quietly responded, "Um, I'm Simon." "Well, get up here, Simon," Burt commanded. Simon the outed heckler made his way to the stage awkwardly, clearly intimidated: he was no longer the class clown he was just seconds ago. He was going up against motherfucking Burt Reynolds. No one knew what was going to happen.

Steven Svymbersky: The guy was just shaking with fear as Burt Reynolds, now standing right next to him, looked straight into his eyes. "Yeah, it's my hair all right," Burt snapped. "And you know how I know it's my hair?" Simon shook his head no. "Because I paid five thousand goddamn dollars for it!" Burt yelled, at which the crowd exploded in laughter.

Pep Rosenfeld: He *owned* it—copping to rocking a toupee while being like, *Fuck you, I'm Burt Reynolds.* That was a great lesson from Burt: you gotta own your shit onstage. That, and never go on a rafting trip with Jon Voight and Ned Beatty.

Andrew Moskos: But Burt wasn't done. Staring down poor Simon, he got super intense: "And you can have my toupee if you can grab it off my head . . . before I drop you to the ground. Wanna try?"

Steven Svymbersky: And then he flinched at the guy like he was going to hit him, and the guy recoiled in terror. Game over. Burt Reynolds: 1, Brit Lunkhead: 0.

Andrew Moskos: Burt starts laughing and says, "Hey look, I want this to end well. So let's give this English twerp a round of applause!" He gamely put his arm around Simon, then sent him off as the crowd went crazy. This was a master class in classy. Burt controlled the whole encounter, and brought it to a win-win end for everyone. Another great improv lesson from a man who knows what he's doing onstage: always end an awkward beat with a bang. So once again I yelled, "Motherfucking Burt Reynolds!" and the crowd went even more nuts. That was such a great night, thanks to that most unexpected guest.

Pep Rosenfeld: You want to talk unexpected? How about Maurice de Hond going from Boom Chicago superfan to costarring in a show. Maurice is the biggest political pollster in the Netherlands. After seeing a Boom show, he was hooked. Maurice started coming to every premier and became quite an, uh, honest critic.

In 2004, Greg and I did our first show about the election. In one improv bit, we had an audience member run for president instead of John Kerry, who we declared was too boring to beat George Bush. So we had this new candidate answer questions from the audience. Whatever they'd say, I would spin it into a reasonable political point. Fun game, right? But the surprise was when we said, "Well, to see how that answer appealed to the voters, let's go to our pollster, Maurice de Hond." Maurice had made these little videos where he's like, "That answer was a little too much for the American people. They can't handle your honesty. I'm afraid you're down 5 percent." The audience couldn't believe that *the* Dutch pollster was in the show. And neither could Maurice! He was psyched, and caught the performing bug a bit. He wanted to do more, and wanted to do it live—no safety net. So in 2010, Maurice, Greg, and I did a show called "Political Party." It was one part Greg and me doing stand-up about Dutch politics, and one part Maurice interviewing an actual Dutch politician whom he'd convinced to appear in the show.

Greg Shapiro: Maurice brought heavies like Femke Halsema, who's now the mayor of Amsterdam.

Pep Rosenfeld: Three mayors of Amsterdam have come to Boom Chicago and participated in the show. I remember the last one was running late, so we did whatever we could to stall starting the show. Finally, peeking outside, I saw the mayor furiously riding up on his bike. I got onstage and said, "I have an official report: we are going to hold the start of the show for five more minutes while the mayor of Amsterdam locks his bike."

Andrew Moskos: Now *that* would've never happened if we'd stayed in Chicago.

Greg Shapiro: We tried for Geert Wilders too—but not even Maurice could make that happen. My favorite part was the scene where I'd dress up like the politician guest, the guest would dress up like their political opponent, and Maurice would dress up like an audience member. All three of us took questions from the audience while Pep kinda made fun of whatever any of us said.

Pep Rosenfeld: Maurice was getting honest laughs, which he loved. He's funnier than you would think (although slightly less funny than *he* thinks). And the politicians enjoyed making fun of someone they didn't like. And there was Greg: seated right next to the guest, dressed up like the guest, *making fun of the guest.*

Greg Shapiro: It was meta. The best part was seeing politicians let their hair down. Something about speaking in English made it work. Being out of their Dutch-language comfort zone actually made Dutch people feel more comfortable and be more honest onstage. We certainly got fewer prepared answers and talking points than you'd expect from seasoned politicians.

Pep Rosenfeld: We've had some guests tell us they were worried about sounding stupid in English. I know that I find it harder to be funnier in Dutch, so I get it. Speaking of funny Dutchies, out of the blue one afternoon, Carice asked me to run lines with her before an audition in Hilversum. It's not like I'm her usual scene partner; she wanted an American for this because it was an English-language movie she was up for. So while chatting on the way to Hilversum, Carice happened to ask me, "What do you think of the latest season of *Game of Thrones*?" I had to confess that I'd stopped watching it.

Seth Meyers: Pep didn't watch *Game of Thrones*? What the hell is wrong with him?

Pep Rosenfeld: Well, it became so . . . unpleasant. Remember the cut-off-the-guy's-dick season? I told Carice I felt unhappy whenever I watched it. She was like, "That's fair."

Andrew Moskos: To compensate for Pep's faux pas, we installed a *Game of Thrones* pinball machine at Boom Chicago.

Carice van Houten: My character's image on the pinball machine doesn't look like me at all.

Andrew Moskos: During play, Carice's voice on the soundtrack says, *"The night is dark and full of terrors."* Apparently, she's not sure she got paid for that.

Carice van Houten: I don't remember if I agreed to it. I definitely would've if they'd given me one. There was a time when I played pinball a lot, especially at Boom Chicago.

Pep Rosenfeld: Hey, they paid her in love. And *liefde is alles* . . .

Seth Meyers and Jill Benjamin in promo photos for "Pick Ups & Hiccups" (1999).

Brendan Hunt and Jordan Peele in "Here Comes the Neighborhood" (2002).

Boom Chicago's first cast, posing on a public urinal (1993).

Closing night 1993 at Iboya; Doreen Calderon, Andrew Moskos, Neil McNamara, Ken Schaefle, Pep Rosenfeld, and Pam Gutteridge hold flowers onstage.

Underwear Dinner at Blasisusstraat; Andrew Moskos, Saskia Maas, Pep Rosenfeld, and Ken Schaefle "looking like a cast of a porn movie, and that's a compliment"—per Ken (1994).

The Boom Chicago theater on the Lijnbaansgracht. Boom moved from Iboya to this 180-seat space in 1994.

Andrew Moskos, Michael Diederich, and Pep Rosenfeld ride a merry-go-round at the Efteling amusement park (1996).

Full cast of the 1997 company including Rob AndristPlourde, Phill Arensberg, Pep Rosenfeld, Lisa Jolley, Andrew Moskos, Josie O'Reilly, Gwendolyn Druyor, Shane Oman, Seth Meyers, Pete Grosz, Allison Silverman, and Greg Shapiro.

Gwendolyn Druyor, Allison Silverman, and Greg Shapiro direct traffic to the Leidseplein theater (1997).

Jill Benjamin is shocked about the customer data that grocery employees Seth Meyers, Andrew Moskos, and Josie O'Reilly know about her. Greg Shapiro plays supermarket magnate Albert Heijn (1998).

Rob AndristPlourde lights a cigarette with a blowtorch during the renovation of the Leidseplein theater (1998).

Brendan Hunt, Kay Cannon, and Jennifer Bills sell the deliciousness of shawarma. Ike Barinholtz is the rotating shawarma (2000).

Dave Asher tries to sell a photo and roses to the happy couple of Holly Walker and Brendan Hunt in "Live at the Leidseplein: Your Privacy Is Our Business" (2000).

Ike Barinholtz, Greg Shapiro, and Jennifer Bills promotional photo for "Live at the Leidseplein: Your Privacy Is Our Business" (2000).

Fellow sheep and cows Pep Rosenfeld, Nicole Parker, and Lauren Dowden try to hide Jordan Peele's mad cow disease in "Europe: We've Created a Monster" (2001).

Josh Meyers (England), Holly Walker (France), Nicole Parker (Holland), Brendan Hunt (Italy), and Greg Shapiro (Frankenstein's monster) in a promotional photo for "Europe: We've Created a Monster" (2001).

Brendan Hunt, Josh Meyers, Rachel Miller, Lauren Dowden, and Jordan Peele behind the scenes (2001).

Jordan Peele and Colton Dunn started the revolution against Zwarte Piet in Boom Chicago's "Christmas in Holland" video from 2002.

Andrew Moskos, Kay Cannon, and Jason Sudeikis behind the scenes (2002).

Heather Anne Campbell and Colton Dunn behind the scenes (2003).

Jim Woods, Jordan Peele, and Brendan Hunt pose, promoting the 2003 production "Boom Chicago Saves the World (Sorry about the Mess)."

Luke Hilton and Amber Ruffin pose with water guns for the cover of *Boom Magazine,* Volume 11, Issue 3 (2004).

Heather Anne Campbell, Jim Woods, Matt Jones, Amber Ruffin, and Rob AndristPlourde performing "Bite the Bullet" (2005).

Amber Ruffin and Jordan Peele improvising on stage (2005).

Michael Orton-Toliver, Amber Ruffin, Matt Chapman, and Jessica Lowe in a promo picture for "Social Media Circus" (2011).

Michael Orton-Toliver, Greg Shapiro, and Pep Rosenfeld for "9/11 Forever" (2011).

Andrew Moskos and Saskia Maas with Barack and Michelle Obama at the White House Correspondents' Dinner in April 2011, at which Seth Meyers was the keynote speaker.

Rob AndristPlourde being "Branded for Life" (2012).

Alumni return for twentieth-anniversary "Best of Boom"; Andrew Moskos takes center stage with Jim Woods, Ryan Archibald, Pep Rosenfeld, Matt Jones, Michael Diederich, Sam Super, David Schmoll, and more (2013).

Seth Meyers returns to do stand-up at Boom Chicago on April 22, 2013.

Rob AndristPlourde and Lolu Ajayi break it down on a tour show in 2014.

Pep Rosenfeld and Greg Shapiro perform for Google's annual most-searched-for-in-Holland video, this year represented in stand-up comedy (2017).

At the Boom Chicago twenty-fifth anniversary/reunion in 2018. Top left, Amber Ruffin and Greg Shapiro; top right, Suzi Barrett and Kay Cannon; bottom left, Holly Walker, Amber Ruffin, and Sam Super; bottom right, Ruben van der Meer and Greg Shapiro.

Tyler Groce and Lizz (Biddy) Kemery perform at "The Future Is Here" (2019).

Andrew Moskos tries to rescue a hostage with his police "partner," an AI-powered robot, from "The Future Is Here and It Is Slightly Annoying" (2019).

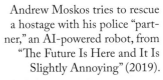

Matt Castellvi, Lizz (Biddy) Kemery, Simon Feilder, Stacey Smith, and Simon Lukacs perform in "Sitcom" (2020).

Simon Lukacs, Stacey Smith, Matt Castellvi, Terrance Lamonte Jr., and Katie Nixon perform "Meta Luck Next Time" (2022).

Jason Sudeikis and Brendan Hunt, in Amsterdam for the filming of the third season of *Ted Lasso*, returned to Boom Chicago to improvise together (2022).

Andrew Moskos with King Willem-Alexander (2022).

Saskia Maas, Pep Rosenfeld, and Andrew Moskos with Prime Minister Mark Rutte (2018).

Andrew Moskos, Saskia Maas, and Pep Rosenfeld (2008).

CHAPTER 16
2008–2009

CRISIS? WHAT CRISIS? BOOM GOES
CORPORATE AS WORLD ECONOMY TANKS

2008 was a dip for comedy. Few big films that year were comedies. After three great *Jackass* movies, Johnny Knoxville and Spike Jonze made *Bad Grandpa*—the worst grandpa movie until Robert DeNiro came with *Dirty Grandpa*. Memo to moviemakers: putting *Grandpa* in your title is the kiss of death. There were comedy bright spots though. Seth Meyer's favorite film, *In Bruges,* was released that year. Don't get him started. *In Bruges* is actually set in Belgium, making it even more remarkable as a comedy achievement.

Back in Amsterdam's comedic universe, Hans Holsen and Liz Bolton arrived as the new blood in the Boom cast, while Ryan Archibald and Amber Ruffin came back to play for a year. Behind the scenes, Julie Nichols joined David Schmoll in creating Boom's music.

2008 also brought the financial crisis, which challenged many small businesses—Boom Chicago included. We diversified into haunted houses and escape rooms, and opened the Chicago Social Club—arguably the coolest club in Amsterdam during the late aughts. The crisis would eventually lead to our current venue on the Rozengracht as well.

2009 sucked like 2008—except a lot worse. No matter what else happened that year, it was hard to drag oneself out of the shadow of the economic crisis crippling the dawn of the following decade. As 2009 wore on, stressors on global financial health seemed to grow exponentially. Living through it made it hard to think about anything else. Failed attack on the royal family on Queen's Day? *Don't remember it.* Discovery of ice on the moon? *Doesn't ring any bells.* Gordon gets into a fistfight with René Froger after a Toppers concert? Okay, we just made that one up, but it certainly *could've* happened. No, the news was always ever-tightening budgets, canceled bonuses, and disappearing loans. It was an economic period crappy enough that you can just call it *[cue scary music]* "The Crisis," and everyone knows what you mean.

The Crisis *[cue scary music]* probably started in 2007. You know the story: there was this housing bubble, and then banks that were too big to fail started to fail, and the less said about those subprime mortgage bundles the better . . . If you want to learn the background of The Crisis in a bit more Academy Award–nominated detail, you can watch *The Big Short,* or *Inside Job,* or *Margin Call*—it's a cinematic genre unto itself. Suffice to say, the economic shitshow that started in 2007 and really hit its stride in 2008 had become an invasive species that, by 2009, couldn't be stopped. The Netherlands and the rest of the world were all now knee-deep in *[cue scary music]* The Crisis.

While The Crisis was spreading internationally, the United States under the Bush administration uttered a collective stammer. No one knew how to handle something of this magnitude. These fucks couldn't help people out during a hurricane; they certainly wouldn't know what to do about a global crisis they didn't understand. They couldn't even start a war against it. *Shock and awe, bro!*

In fall 2008, the American presidential election took a weird turn thanks to The Crisis. The rival candidates—famed maverick senator John McCain and freshman senator Barack Obama—were in the midst of intense campaigning as the headlines began proclaiming the next Great Depression was on the horizon. In

September, McCain suggested the presidential candidates suspend their televised debates to work out the details of a bailout bill: "I am calling on the president to convene a meeting with the leadership from both houses of Congress, including Senator Obama and myself . . . It's time for both parties to come together to solve this problem."

Obama wasn't having it. He responded with the best political mic drop since Lloyd Bentsen told Bush 1.0's lame vice president Dan Quayle, "Senator, you are no Jack Kennedy." As 2008's change candidate noted, "Part of the president's job is to deal with more than one thing at once . . . This is exactly the time when people need to hear from the candidates."

Zing! Here in the Netherlands, The Crisis proved the worst fiscal dream come true for the pessimistic Dutch. It was the financial equivalent of Holland's North Sea flood of 1953, an unbelievable disaster. As with the flood, The Crisis was a calamity that the Dutch were uniquely qualified to deal with. All the traits for which the Dutch get made fun of proved to be just what the stalled economy called for. Do Dutch banks know how to tighten credit? *Ja!* Does the government know how to cut budgets when necessary? *Jawel!* Do people yearn for something to complain about besides the weather? *Ja hoor!*

Saskia Maas: By 2009, Boom Chicago had become less dependent on tourism, but it still represented significant amounts of our revenue. Ticket sales were down, but we'd gotten through dips before. We assumed things would work out and eventually we'd find a way to turn the business around. Unfortunately, The Crisis didn't just affect tourism. Everyone was spending less on going out, period. On the business side, corporate budgets were now getting slashed willy-nilly: our corporate gigs just started vanishing. It turns out that, during an economic downturn, the first things to get axed are expensive improv comedy team-building projects.

Pep Rosenfeld: We had two new actors in the cast: video director–turned-performer Matt Chapman and Jessica Lowe. Jessica arrived just in time for September 2009, when drops in corporate and in-theater business had us up against the ropes. That might actually be my least favorite month at Boom Chicago.

Andrew Moskos: But that's when we came up with a new show/workshop combo for business events, "The Future of Your Organization." It was a seventy-minute show in three parts. First, it served as a conversation about where a particular company was, and where it was going. Second, we used improv and interactive activities focused on communication to help teams innovate and work together better. Lastly, we wrote tailored comedy sketches about everything they were worried about.

Pep Rosenfeld: That was really when our more integrated business stuff began—when we stopped being providers of "funny comedy at your event" and became "thinking comedians who help deliver the message of your event." We started working with companies using comedy and improv to deliver their messages better, while training execs how to actually be funny in public speaking engagements.

It makes sense that this stuff caught on during The Crisis. People were scared. They felt like what was happening was beyond their control—which a lot of it was. We gave them tools to use teamwork to find new ways out of these holes, and at the same time helped them laugh at what was going on. I mean, there's a reason that gallows humor exists. In 2009, all you could really do was laugh.

Saskia Maas: It got so bad in 2009 that ING bank asked their top 1,200 employees to return their bonuses so they could keep the lights on.

Pep Rosenfeld: Yes, *bankers* were expected to give money back that they'd already been paid. Free-market surrealism at its finest.

Andrew Moskos: Sometimes companies wanted Boom Chicago to make the bad news everyone knew was coming go down just a little easier: "So, you might've heard your company's restructuring . . ."

Pep Rosenfeld: We definitely had some weird briefs. There was literally one time when a company asked us, "Hey, can you help announce some layoffs?" I don't know how they thought that impending layoffs would somehow be funny. We couldn't do it. I imagined there were only a couple of joke options, like:

HR: Knock-knock.

Employee: Who's there?

HR: Not you anymore. Martin from security will help you clean out your desk and escort you from the building.

Steven Svymbersky: One show *really* didn't go so well. It was a pretty tough brief: Greg was hired to go onstage and pretend to be the CEO of the parent conglomerate that had taken over a clothing company. Using humor, Greg would prep employees for big changes coming in a light, humorous, self-deprecating way. Kinder, gentler layoffs, if you will.

Well, I've never seen an audience turn on someone so fast. Once I had the show up and running and Greg had started his fake CEO monologue, I had to run out because my car was illegally parked. When I returned after a few minutes, the audience was throwing fruit at Greg. For real. Throwing fruit like in cartoons from the 1940s.

I got on the mic and told the crowd, "This is all a joke! He's not really the new CEO—he's an actor . . ." Then they just started throwing food at both of us. To end on a high note, we did one last improv game and then got the hell out of there. Looking back, it's insane that we thought doing one more bit was a good idea: "Oh, you hate us? In that case, please shout out a location where two people might meet . . ."

Saskia Maas: Our philosophy is using comedy to tackle tough issues head-on. Your employees are talking about this stuff anyway: you can either lead that conversation, or not. In preparing for these events, we learned a lot about companies. Our next book should be a tell-all called *Really, You Should Have Made Us Sign an NDA.*

Andrew Moskos: Intriguingly, many Boom people who wrote the best corporate shows have proven successful in later entertainment careers. Michael Orton-Toliver wrote Boom's corporate scripts before he created the hit show *Borderline* in the UK and the e-sports docufiction show *Players*. Kay Cannon ran Boom's corporate shows before she went on to huge success as a writer/director with *Pitch Perfect*, *Blockers*, and *Cinderella*. Joe Kelly's a successful TV writer who—along with Seth, Pep, and other alums who went on to television success—started out crafting sketches about the likes of ING and Friesland-Campina for Boom Chicago long before he ever did so for *SNL, Ted Lasso,* and *How I Met Your Mother.*

Ike Barinholtz: Seth Meyers's success is a great example. He was always up for the corporate gigs. Seth's attitude was basically, "You don't get good by *not* doing things."

Joe Canale: Seth works as hard as anyone I've ever seen—never missing anything. This work ethic was evident early on. While we'd all be out partying, he'd knock out corporate scripts for a couple hours before meeting us wherever we'd gone to dance. I was really impressed by his focus and ability to stay sober for that long in the face of temptation. Jordan was another one with a crazy work ethic. I mean, we can start doing the math here, right?

Seth Meyers: For me, the real gift of corporate work writing those scripts was how I made money when I came back to the States—up until I got on *SNL*. The week I got hired at *SNL*, I felt terrible that I had to tell Saskia, "I'm sorry, but I don't have time to write these corporate shows anymore."

Pep Rosenfeld: Saskia's assistant thought Seth might be able to do both. She kept trying to think of ways he could write for us in his off time. I was like, "I think you better find a plan B here . . ."

Andrew Moskos: I actually like doing the corporate stuff—not just as a means to an end. I really enjoy all aspects of it. A three-day event in Cannes for a company developing measurement devices for infrastructure projects? I'm in! A photocopier company shifting their business from selling boxes to selling "services"? Bet there's something funny there! A German medical supply company that makes operating room equipment? I mean, medical supplies and Germans—what could be funnier?

Pep Rosenfeld: Maybe the fact that, during said German medical-supply gig, our jokes were simultaneously translated live into *Deutsch*.

Andrew Moskos: Although this was for an international company, it was a very German international company—so German, they'd set up live translators to take whatever event speakers said in English (the company's official language) and render it into

German (the language most employees spoke every day). About one-third of the audience opted for the wireless headphones receiving real-time *korrekt Deutsch* translation, performed by two stern-faced *frauen* sitting in the back. Walking into that setup, we thought, *This cannot be good for comedy.*

Pep Rosenfeld: But it went great. Andrew invented a comedy bit that used the poor translators to our advantage.

Andrew Moskos: I said into the mic, "Hello, this is the translator speaking. I'm right behind you, but don't turn around. I've turned off all the other headphones, and now I'm just talking to you." We heard a murmur from the headphone wearers as the translators dutifully performed their job. I continued: "I'm not supposed to fall in love with my clients, but when I saw you during the break, I couldn't help myself. You're a real German, who speaks German, like me . . . I feel like I can be myself speaking with you. Besides, it's nice to take a break from translating these jokesters. Could they be more American? Everything they say sounds like, 'Yee-haw, I'm a fat cowboy!' Unlike you, so handsome and classically German in your features . . . I would have no problem introducing you to my mother back in Bavaria."

Pep Rosenfeld: People started getting hip to what was happening. If you were wearing headphones, it was funny; if you weren't, you realized no matter what Andrew said, these very serious German-translation professionals would never break character, no matter what. While he spoke, Andrew stared at the translators in the back, maintaining intense eye contact . . .

Andrew Moskos: "I love you . . ." *Ich liebe dich* . . . "No shit." *Keine Scheisse.* Then I waited a few seconds and said, "Fuuuuucck!" Everyone waited to hear how the translators would cope.

Sure enough, after a short pause, we heard *"Fiiiiiiiiick"* from everyone's headphones. They loved it.

Pep Rosenfeld: German audiences are surprisingly awesome. They have a great sense of humor. They love laughing at themselves—and, of course, you get the entire well of accurate German stereotypes to draw from.

Andrew Moskos: Germans are never like, "Zat is not fair." *Zey* know it's all fair. *Zey* have zero attitude.

Kay Cannon: The corporate shows were a great way to see other countries and different parts of Holland. We performed in caves, castles, restaurants . . .

Heather Anne Campbell: I remember doing a corporate show in a bullring. As in a literal bullring. In Spain.

Kay Cannon: I'll never forget an international show we did for Wells Fargo in Cyprus, which was incredibly well received by an international crowd of extremely fun people. After we finished, togas tailored in our exact individual sizes were delivered to our rooms for us to wear to the after-party. Late in the night, a well-intentioned Russian man yelled, "Throw the American girl in the pool!" That American girl, dressed in a toga, was me. After I was tossed in, everyone jumped in the pool. Instead of the hotel kicking us out, the staff kept bringing stacks of towels—just stacks and stacks of fucking towels. It was so great.

Pep Rosenfeld: My takeaway from the international corporate-comedy circuit is that most cultural stereotypes are at least a wee bit true. In Dublin, the Irish heckled us at a sales event . . . a *sales event*. In Spain, we performed at an outdoor beach festival involving enormous beers, jumping over bonfires, and running aflame into the sea. In Russia, we drank straight vodka all night . . . although technically that was our choice, not theirs.

Amber Ruffin: I went to Dubai with Shane Oman, Robbie AndristPlourde, and Hans Holsen for a Boom corporate gig. At the hotel, they tried to stop us from going to our rooms because they saw a Black woman with three white men and assumed I was a prostitute. I will never forget Robbie convincing me to let it go. Otherwise, I would still be there. In jail.

Andrew Moskos: That was during the World Cup. In Dubai, we were looking for a place to watch the Dutch national team play. We called a few places and one guy was like, "Yes, here you can watch the World Cup on a huge screen with two hundred other people, all while enjoying a five-course, authentic Middle Eastern dinner." Sounds great, right? But then he adds, "And because it's an authentic experience, absolutely no alcohol will be served."

Pep Rosenfeld: Needless to say, we watched the World Cup with a less-authentic experience.

Andrew Moskos: These days, our reputation gets us high-stakes events with internal buy-in, where we can really shine. But in the early days, not all corporate shows were dreams come true.

Ike Barinholtz: It was hard not to crack. In 1999, we went to some castle two hours away to perform for a wedding. This show didn't go well, and the guests were drunk and rude. Afterward, we had to pack our equipment ourselves, and Andrew—not one for any kind of physical labor in the first place—was trying to drag out a heavy piece of the stage which had gotten stuck. At this moment, the mother of the bride came over, tapped Andrew on the shoulder, and gave him a command: "Now you and your group will sing 'You'll Never Walk Alone.'" Andrew dropped the big chunk of stage onto the floor, turned to her, and snapped, "Why don't *you* sing 'You'll Never Walk Alone'?"

Pep Rosenfeld: Boom alumni still trade horror stories about the corporate shows. There's even a Facebook page for Boom Chicago players' worst corporate-show experiences. The Mexx-Philips iron gig is one that's still talked about. It's become a ghost story, really—a twisted fairy tale we tell little children to scare them. And by "little children," I mean "full-grown adult actors."

Suzi Barrett: The story of Mexx-Philips? Well. Once upon a time, we had to do a series of improv "shows" inside the store windows at Bijenkorf department stores across Holland. They hung speakers outside the store, and we performed in the front window facing onto the shopping street. The whole thing was a cross-branding campaign that combined—wait for it—Mexx clothes and a new Philips iron. So we wore freshly ironed Mexx outfits while we tried to play improv games with an iron. It went as well as you would think—that is to say, it was the worst corporate show of all time. Then we went to different cities and repeated our sad little Mexx-Philips show, over and over.

The shows were meant to be interactive—so while shoppers hurried past, we hollered requests for improv scenes at them. Imagine you're trying to shop—and all of a sudden, two people pop up in the store window like talking mannequins and say, "Hey, can you suggest a relationship between two people?"

Heather Anne Campbell: Shopping for clothes is already such a vulnerable, fraught experience. You certainly don't want to walk into a store and find a bunch of fucking comedians in the window trying to talk to you. It was bonkers.

Suzi Barrett: Passersby would tap on the glass like we were zoo animals. But then again, we *were* zoo animals. We hoped any-one would linger just long enough to hear a full sentence come out of our mouths. There were two people who did: a teenager who'd stopped to bang his middle finger against the window over and over again, and a homeless man who actually crawled inside the display case with Tarik and me.

Tarik Davis: And instead of freaking out or calling security, we were like, "Hey, buddy!" We just incorporated him right into the scene without batting an eye.

Suzi Barrett: On the upside, I did get a Mexx suit out of the deal. And an iron. That suit is gone, but the stories last forever. And I still have the iron. It's a good iron. All it cost me was my soul.

Pep Rosenfeld: I kept hearing stories about how bad these Mexx-Philips shows were—so naturally I *had* to do one myself. I wanted to be able to say, "Guys, come on—these shows aren't that awful." But they were. Oh God, they totally were.

Tim Sniffen: At the end of one Mexx-Philips gig, the store asked us to sign their wall with paint. "Why did you write on the wall?" a confused, angry store manager screamed at me. It turned out that the employee who asked me had gone rogue. Wonderful.

Pep Rosenfeld: That manager called me to complain, not real-izing that I was both the extremely responsible artistic director of Boom Chicago *and* one of the illicit painters. I told him, "Of course we had permission. We didn't decide on our own to paint on your wall. And how could we expect to get away with it—since we wrote our names?"

Ike Barinholtz: Boom corporate shows could be brutal. Once, we had a corporate gig in this random office building near Schiphol.

Kay asked our company contact, "Where's the dressing room?" And the rep responded, "The disabled toilet will serve as the actors' area." So we're all stuffed among handicapped stalls thinking, *Ah, that's real showbiz.*

Josh Meyers: The day I landed in Amsterdam, I went with Andrew to do a corporate show in Deventer. Welcome to Holland! This was a true Boom Chicago trial by fire, cowboying at its best. I just hit the ground running like, *Fake it until you make it.* I was still clueless. While sound-checking my mic, I started doing a riff: "Testing! Check one, two . . . I just landed, fresh off the boat from the United States. This is my first job out of school, and my first show with Boom Chicago. I'm super excited to be here to entertain you Dutch people . . ." And then Andrew ran up, growling through gritted teeth: "*Shut up!* You can't say that this is your first show. The clients are here—they can't know you have absolutely no experience doing what they've hired us for."

Pep Rosenfeld: That's one of the great lessons of Boom. Hire talented people like Josh, have them bite off more than they can chew, and they rise to the occasion. They cowboy.

Ike Barinholtz: Boom Chicago was my first legitimate paid job in showbiz. It taught me that even when it's not glamorous, you should still feel lucky you're getting paid to work in entertainment. You're not a coal miner. You're not getting shot at. You don't work as a debt collector—although you just might end up performing at a debt collector's holiday party. Just doing the job teaches you to love what you do. That's what it did for me.

Jordan Peele: One of the biggest corporate-show bombs of all time was a London show I did with Nicole Parker. All I remember is that the audience was all wearing hats. We were doing some kind of musical-rap thing, and it was just not landing. They didn't even hate us: it was like we didn't *exist*. It was so dead, it became perhaps the most miserable experience I've ever had onstage. But there was camaraderie in that shared agony. The hardest of those moments were really formative.

Seth Meyers: I thank the lucky stars that we had the corporate shows. I think doing them kept us tethered to the real world. Without corporate shows, we would've all just turned into insufferable club kids, wearing reflective stripes and going down K-holes, never to be heard from again . . .

As a check and balance, every now and again we'd leave Amsterdam to go to, like, Helmond, Hengelo, or Hoorn—reminding us that the whole world wasn't as in love with us as we thought they were. I'd crashed onstage before I went to Amsterdam, but I never fucking *died* like I did at some corporate shows. I did one once where we drove in a van to a construction site. In a prefab lunch hall, we performed a noon show about safety regulations for the kind of Dutch people who don't ever go to Amsterdam— who grew up in the shadow of windmills. They were busy eating their daily lunch of hard sausage and a carton of milk—the last thing they wanted was to watch *us*. I could tell because they didn't. So now, when I walk out onstage to do something like host the Golden Globes, I think, *Hey, this can't be worse than the safety-regulation corporate show I did in the middle of a muddy construction site in Hoorn.* The thing about corporate shows is that, if it wasn't us doing it, their entertainment would be, like, Jan from accounting. At least we provided some variety to their workday.

Andrew Moskos: I recently had a better safety-day experience. Last year, I was hired by Shell IT in the Hague to lead a discussion at their annual safety day—clearly a big deal for Shell. This was a global event where all 90,000 employees spanning oil rigs to office cubicles would participate. My piece involved 150 people from the IT department. In the briefing, my contact's boss asked for a one-on-one call with me. He was concerned that a comedian would screw this up, with the fallout blowing back on him. I assured him I understood the stakes. Of course, this being a Dutch workplace, after the event wrapped up, the company organized a room at a local bar for post–safety day commiserating and networking over *biertjes*[46] and *bitterballen*.

Liz Cackowski: *Biertjes* were so delightful—just perfect. My preferred intoxicants at Boom Chicago were definitely pot and *biertjes*.

Colton Dunn: I definitely miss *biertjes* too. It's the perfect size beer. I miss those so much.

Andrew Moskos: I ended up walking with the once-concerned boss to where the post–safety day fiesta was being held. Where he'd been super stressed before, he was now totally giddy. The event had gone so well, he was being praised by his superiors for "reinventing safety day at Shell." The whole thing had been so successful, he told me, he might get a promotion.

Seth Meyers: I distinctly remember the feeling of driving back to Amsterdam, pretty sure that Saskia was going to tell me, "They called and refused to pay us because of how badly it went." But more often than not, Sas would say, "They said it was the best event they've ever had."

Pep Rosenfeld: These days, those shows almost always go great. The good news is that we're not competing with Jan from accounting for gigs anymore. Now it's the Dutch Albert Heijn su-

---

46 *Biertje* refers to what's known as a "small beer"—a distinctly Dutch tradition of serving beer in small glasses.

permarket chain merging with Belgium's Delhaize conglomerate and wanting to create a common culture—so they call the Boom Chicago experts to explain it companywide in a fun, creative, inspiring way. If we can help get their teams more nimble on their feet, better able to communicate with each other, and learn to laugh together, we might actually be getting them prepared for *[cue scariest music yet]* The Next Crisis. Worse comes to worst, we're helping them laugh about things as they try to create meaningful change.

Andrew Moskos: For so long, the slump of The Crisis seemed to weigh down every decision. Should we invest? *Hold off.* Do we buy that new thing we need? *Not right now.* Should we take a holiday? *Better wait.* Should we hire that comedy company to perform at our new strategy announcement event? *Maybe we'll go with Jan from Accounting this year.*

Pep Rosenfeld: But if necessity is the mother of invention, then totally-broke-ass necessity is the birth of a new business model. We stretched to help other companies get out of their slumps, while keeping *our* lights on—pushing ourselves on those corporate stages so when the business returned, we'd be ready.

Liz Cackowski: Awkward corporate shitshows delighted me because they're so fucking weird: *I'll remember this bizarre, failed Tommy Hilfiger Christmas event forever.* When Will Ferrell hosted *SNL*, my friend Emily Spivey and I wrote a sketch based on Boom corporate shows; it actually ended up on one of Will Ferrell's "best of" DVDs. Will plays the host of a corporate event for Oracle where nothing works. As an improviser troupe sings "Gloria" by Laura Branigan—substituting "Oracle" for "Gloria"—he tries to get everyone riled up, then falls off the stage.

Ike Barinholtz: In those moments, you just do it. It's your job. And you get to perform. I'll tell you this much, Boom corporates ultimately prepare you for what show business can *really* be like.

CHAPTER 17
2010

FACEBOOK, MYSPACE, AND, UM, HYVES?
DUTCH FAIL EARLY IN SOCIAL MEDIA ARMS RACE

There's a T-shirt Dutch people wear to be (barely) funny that says, *As a finishing touch, God created the Dutch*. The shirt basically makes two things clear: (1) Dutch people are special, and (2) "touch" rhymes with "Dutch." That first part is an important component of Dutchness. As in most countries—except the USA, of course—Dutch people have a false outer shell of modesty, but an inner core of national pride. Dutch people *say*, "Oh yes, we're so cheap." What they're really thinking is, *We're smart with money—you're dumb with money*.

Dutch people also *really* like Dutch things. The Netherlands is a truly international country—one that values travel and global trade, and encourages the learning of foreign languages by its citizens. But boy, do Dutch people like *onze eigen* things. *Onze eigen*, in case you forgot, means "our own"—as in, "Other airlines are okay, but we like *onze eigen* KLM. We also support *onze eigen* Philips, *onze eigen* Hema, and *onze eigen* Dutch Treat." So when Facebook was on the rise in the late 2000s, Dutch folks proudly stuck to *onze eigen* Hyves—a homegrown Dutch social media network founded in 2004 by Raymond Spanjar and Floris Rost van Tonningen that you've probably never heard of.

Hyves. Hyyyves. *Hyyyyyyyyyyyves*. Just rolls off the tongue, doesn't it? Of course, they originally wanted to call it "Hives"—

alas, hives.nl was already taken. But Floris and Raymond, guess what: in 2023, hives.nl has now become available! Your domain-name dreams can finally come true. But forget hives. org—ain't happenin'. Hives.org is a website established by Dr. Tiffany Davies, who has been helping people suffering from hives, i.e., the skin rash, for years.

So, yeah, that's a pretty fucking weird name for a social media platform! But by May of 2010, Hyves had over ten million accounts. Of those accounts, we can safely assume that all ten million belonged to Dutch people. That's almost two-thirds of the country—not bad penetration for two *jongens* from Laren.

The rest of the world, meanwhile, had already jumped ship from Tom Anderson's Myspace to Mark Zuckerberg's Facebook. Myspace was the most popular social networking site in the world from 2005 until Facebook overtook it three years laer with almost 100 million members. By the end of 2010, it was over five times that. And that's when Facebook fired the shot across Hyves's bow. Zuck & Co. announced the opening of an Amsterdam office. Hyves was not concerned: *Doe je best sukkels!* ("Do your best, suckers!")

The rest is history. One day, everyone got a message from a super-social friend that had joined Facebook. *Well,* that's *weird,* we thought. *What's wrong with* onze eigen *Hyves?* A few weeks later, we made our own Facebook profile page. One month after that, we were posting and uploading pics first to Facebook and then Hyves. Almost immediately, people stopped going to Hyves. Only our younger siblings remained on Hyves; soon, they, too, made new social media moves. When Haley Mancini, who now writes for *Powerpuff Girls,* arrived at Boom Chicago in 2010 as a new cast member, Hyves was as much a thing of the past as guilders—and, apparently, only slightly more valuable.

In 2010, Hyves was bought by the Telegraaf Media Group, owner of *De Telegraaf,* the newspaper least associated with Dutch young people who actually used social media. *De Telegraaf* wanted to prove it was not a tired old newspaper read mostly by taxi drivers and small-town hairdressers—repositioning itself as a forward-looking tech-media company with an eye on youth and The Future! But TMG also valued its innate Dutchness, and therefore decided their brand should acquire something *onze eigen* for their entrée into social media.

By 2010, Hyves was already over. It turned out that TMG was actually a print-led media organization run by old people who were not only unable to see the future, they couldn't see the present, either. In 2013, Hyves, finally admitting what was clear to the entire country, shut down its social media operations.

Horace Cohen: A lifetime ago, I was on Hyves because I played poker with the guy who started it. And whenever I'd win, I'd go, "High fives!" Pronounced like Hyves, get it? Okay, nobody laughed, but I thought that was really funny.

Rob AndristPlourde: Hyves was more for children. Parents would ask, "What are you kids up to on the Internet? Oh, Hyves, okay . . ." They didn't realize seemingly benevolent Hyves was actually the gateway drug to the rest of social media.

Andrew Moskos: The Hyves user interface was so ugly. It resembled a dot matrix–printed menu from an Egyptian shawarma stand. Then Facebook came along looking like the Apple store.

Ruben van der Meer: It took longer for Holland to pick up on social media for some reason. Now the Netherlands has become one of the leading Twitter countries. We just love to shout out angry stuff anonymously.

Pep Rosenfeld: Everyone got hooked on social media. That led to dating apps, which were scoffed at initially—until everybody started using them.

Andrew Moskos: Tinder started off as Grindr for straight people—a platform primarily for empty hookups. But as more respectable people came on board, Tinder slithered out of the digital shadows into the mainstream. Now, of course, we have other dating apps, each with a unique angle: curated, not curated, women make the first move, pervs only, Jews only . . .

Ruben van der Meer: The whole dating aspect of social media took a minute to catch on here. That's due to differences between the Netherlands and the US. In America, both on- and offline, there's this dating dance you have to do. Dutch courtship is more like, "Let's go back to my house to have sex right now." As a result, mixing the two approaches can sometimes lead to misunderstandings between cultures. When I was twenty, I worked as an au pair in New York City. When I'd ask American women out on dates, they'd ask me, "Where should we meet?" I'd say, "Well, let's go for a drink near my place, so we can walk back afterward." And these women would say, "Do you think I'm going to have sex with you on the first date?" To which I'd respond, "Why wait? We could be dead tomorrow."

Horace Cohen: Such a charming motherfucker, this one.

Pep Rosenfeld: At least Ruben's honest. He can't help it: he's Dutch.

Josie O'Reilly: I never came close to dating Dutch men. They were tall, desperately good looking, and way out of my league. In my mind, they saw me as a bit of an Oompa Loompa from Oz.

Amber Ruffin: I married a Dutch man in 2010, and I can't get enough of that Dutch honesty. It does a lot of the work in your relationship for you. Unbridled Dutch honesty is a billion times better than what I've gotten from American liars I've dated.

Greg Shapiro: During my first year in Amsterdam as a Boom cast member in 1994, I was twenty-five, footloose, and fancy free. One night, I met a woman who said she loved the show: "I've never seen anything like this before! It's so inspiring, your work. You have to come over for dinner." I was thinking, *Okay, so this is how you do it here: dinner first . . . then it's on!* So we dined and chatted a bit about ourselves. Then, after dessert, she showed me the door. Seeing my face fall, she said, "I was inspired by your show, wanted to get to know you, and share a bit about Dutch culture. But I don't want to have sex with you."

Saskia Maas: Dutch people are much more casual—they don't see going out with someone as a "date," with all the expectations attached to it. That's also why you can go out with a Dutch girl and then she might announce she has a boyfriend. Like, WTF?

Greg Shapiro: Dutch women are just very clear about what they want and don't want. Other Dutch women were like, "You look like fun in bed. Let's have sex now." Resistance proved futile. That was very different from the United States. Once, I'd invited a couple Dutch women to see the show. Talking afterward, they told me about an American girlfriend of theirs. They were mocking her because she'd said, "I've been dating this guy for like two weeks, and we have our third date tomorrow. It might be just the right moment to invite him into the bedroom." They thought that was hilarious: "Why would you waste two weeks of your life on a guy if you don't know what he's like in bed?"

Horace Cohen: Dutch people find that out the first night, then move on.

Ike Barinholtz: They are so efficient. If there's no sexual compatibility, why waste the time? That perfectly encapsulates the Dutch mentality: practical, even in romance.

Tarik Davis: Dating in Amsterdam was a trip. I went on a lot of dates—each one a nightmare. Women would be like, "Let's do a bag of cocaine, then go to the Red Light District." I'd be like, "Well, um, what's your name? What do they call you in Slovenia?" They assumed that because I'm an American actor in Amsterdam, I'd be into all that. I was more, "Actually, I really just want to chill and get to know you . . ." I remember going on a date with a *Playboy* model and thinking, *Okay, this is a little fast.* My life before was so Jimmy Stewart. I'm from a small town in New Jersey, and now suddenly everyone's, "Yeah, let's fuck!"

It was a lot to take in. Every European woman I met was so much more mature and worldly than I was. Finally, I met someone who was just a cool person going at the same speed. She was half Dutch, half Australian: she spoke English, but being with her also gave me a chance to practice my Dutch with her mother and family. I now had someone I could learn the country, the language, and the landscape with who wasn't driving two hundred miles an hour.

Michael Diederich: One night after a show, I was smoking weed with Ike and a group of crazy, wild women. It didn't take long to realize that each and every one of them wanted to fuck Ike. They were not subtle about it at all, bragging about how good they would treat him. It turned out they were in town for a sex convention and were all dildo testers.

Alas, Ike wasn't interested, and told them so. As a last ditch, one lady offered him a pile of guilders for the night. I wouldn't have believed it had I not been standing there. Even more unbelievable, Ike actually turned them down. I mean, I'm gay and *I* would have done it for that money.

Ike Barinholtz: I am not for sale! Besides, there were so many great Dutch women. Dutch women are very dynamic, funny, and love to dance. As for Dutch guys, well . . . My stereotype of Dutch males was personified by the guys Brendan roomed with above McDonald's. Each one of these ten Dutch dudes was a class-A alcoholic. They worked at banks, drank, and watched Ajax games—that was their entire existence. It's a gross generalization, but Dutch men mostly want to do two things: watch football and get drunk. After those, sex is maybe number five on their list of priorities.

Saskia Maas: American men *are* more tuned in to what women want, due to their training in the US dating dance. Of course, that's all about getting into someone's pants, so who are we kidding?

Carice van Houten: It's true, Dutch people don't date. I'd never considered holding hands in the cinema, all that stuff. I've only dated one American, but it was a bit more old-fashioned and romantic. Now, Josh is not your average guy. He's very special: I remember him giving me flowers when I had my periods. I was like, "Wow, that's not a Dutch tradition at all."

I also remember when we started dating that, all of a sudden, we always smoked from bongs, which I'd never done before. One day, Josh and I were watching TV while smoking a bong. There was a show about serial killers who'd never been caught; in it, they profiled this white guy from the East Coast. I just looked next to me and thought, *Fuck—it's him!* Josh is possibly the nicest person in this world—I mean, he talks to plants, he's so nice—but in that moment I was convinced he was a serial killer.

Pep Rosenfeld: That was clearly the bong talking. I mean, Joe Canale could've been a serial killer—but not Josh.

Jordan Peele: Dutch women are in control. They know what they want. They can sense bullshit.

Greg Shapiro: In America, women are like, "Take me to dinner, and if that goes well, maybe you can take me to bed." Whereas here in Holland, Dutch women are innately "I can open my own door, thank you" feminists. They're more like, "I'm taking you to bed, and if that goes well, maybe you can take me to dinner—but I'm paying for half." "Going Dutch" is a real thing.

Saskia Maas: Dutch women are powerhouses who have no problem having sex when we want to—but a relationship is a commitment. Ha ha!

Brendan Hunt: In Amsterdam, no one judges anything—especially that women are also sexual creatures who have their own individual appetites. They might want to have sex with you, or they may not; their call. They're also better at drinking than you because they've been able to drink legally since they were teenagers. People can get messy, but it's not like Las Vegas, know what I mean? In Vegas, repressed people go crazy and act out; in Amsterdam, people aren't repressed—they just enjoy themselves. This wonderful attitude was so much healthier than the American bullshit.

Greg Shapiro: I was pleasantly surprised to learn that, in many ways, Holland was more civilized and advanced than what I'd experienced in the States. "Culture shock therapy," again, where you're forced into the realization that the European lifestyle is just better in so many ways. Onstage, I often tell the story of going to a sauna for the first time in Holland. The big reveal is the first person who took me to a Dutch sauna was my boss at the time, a woman. She was like, "I've seen you staring at my tits in the office. Well, here they are." And then after that, everyone relaxed. This seemed a more sensibly adult approach: recognizing and treating sexuality as a normal part of the human experience.

Saskia Maas: That Dutch boss was *me*. I don't think those were my words, exactly—but it's a fact that Dutch women are much more comfortable with their bodies and sexuality than Americans. Most Dutch women walk around naked totally without shame. It's this down-to-earth society we grow up in that produces a culture of normalcy around nudity.

Ike Barinholtz: For me, dating in Amsterdam was much easier. You're onstage five nights a week, and if you're an American guy who's not completely disgusting and is nice and respectful, you can do very well. In Amsterdam, it's easy, friendly, and cool. Everyone's taught about sex at an early age, so they have healthier attitudes about it. And it feels safer. Everyone there wears condoms—they practically throw condoms at you when you get off the plane.

Andrew Moskos: There's a story—possibly apocryphal—where we had a new bar manager, and he'd called a meeting of the bar staff. At some point, he asked how many of them had slept with Ike.

Pep Rosenfeld: One hand goes up. Then another. And then another . . . Soon, all hands are raised. It's like, "I am Spartacus!"

Ike Barinholtz: That can't be true. That story is . . . impossible.

Seth Meyers: This is back when it was considered socially acceptable to ask people who they slept with.

Brendan Hunt: What a time to be alive! I tried to avoid dating at

Boom, although sometimes you couldn't help it. Boom Chicago felt like an open relationship with twenty people. There was no telling who might pair up with whom on a given night. But outside of Boom, I had sex with several female friends of mine, and they remained friends after. It was like, "Okay, thanks—see you tomorrow."

The first one-night stand of my life was in Amsterdam. She took me to her place, and it escalated quickly to the sexy time, which was her clear intention. I didn't have condoms on me, so she grabbed one from her stash, which she pulled out of a branded metal tin. There were maybe thirty condoms in there. I could never have imagined that before. In my experience up to that point, an American girl would never do that. If she had condoms—which is obviously a smart thing to do—she'd be like, "You know what? Let me go check and see if I have any. I'm not sure . . ." But then this visionary Dutch woman took out the jumbo box of forty and was like, "It's *on*." That was a much healthier attitude to sex than I'd encountered up to that point.

Ike Barinholtz: I'm very happy that I was able to get that all out of my system, so when I met my wife, I was ready to say, "Let's have kids and spend the rest of our lives together." Before that, though, dating in Amsterdam really set me up for failure and disappointment when I moved to Los Angeles with Jordan and Josh to be on *MADtv*. I didn't do well with women for a very long time.

Jordan Peele: Ike's game in Amsterdam was unreal. But the idea that Ike had problems meeting women in Los Angeles . . . that's ridiculous. Believe me, he did absolutely fine.

Pep Rosenfeld: Ever since there was social media, we've been trying to use it in the show. The way people were dealing with the world was also the way we were dealing with the show. We started that in the Hyves era with "Me, Myspace, and iPod" in 2006. We'd have an audience member sign into their Myspace onstage and then look at their friends. Then we would dress up like those friends and show the dark, seedy underground of social networks by improvising a soap opera about them. Halfway through the season, we had to switch from Myspace to Facebook.

Andrew Moskos: Myspace was so hot in 2006 that we put it in the title of the show. Nine months later, it was gone. No one wanted to be friends with Tom anymore. So we'd do the exact same bit—just substituting Facebook for Myspace.

Pep Rosenfeld: Facebook came up again in 2011's "Social Media Circus." The idea was that we have too many friends on Facebook. How many are real friends, really? So we'd have audience members defend their Facebook friendships onstage. If we or the audience didn't buy it, we would unfriend them from those friends. We weren't pretending to unfriend them, either. We actually did it! "Oh shit, can you believe they did that?" One time during a show, Greg Shapiro was playing, and I unfriended the legendary writer/director Adam McKay from his Facebook account. I still feel bad about that.

Andrew Moskos: Greg's friends with Adam McKay?

Pep Rosenfeld: Facebook friends. Dude, *I'm* Facebook friends with Adam McKay, but he doesn't exactly call me up on the reg for my notes on the latest episode of *Succession*. Boom also tried to use Twitter in shows, usually to get ideas from the audience. But back then, I was more into Twitter than our audience.

Andrew Moskos: We used Instagram in 2016's election show,

"Angry White Men." The idea was Hillary Clinton was so cold and methodical, she wasn't capable of creating a convincingly human-feeling Instagram. So Bill Clinton arranged to use pictures of real people from the audience's Instagram accounts and pretend they were Hillary's friends.

> *Hillary: See, here I have friends who go to the beach— and they're all smiling and laughing together because I have friends and they enjoy my warm, genuine company.*

> *Bill: I like to be friends with Hillary's friends. Especially the one on the left. I see she'll drink a margarita or two at lunchtime, which means she's up for a party. So is Bill, by the way . . .*

Pep Rosenfeld: It was Greg's A+ Bill Clinton impression that made it work. My Hillary was a C-.

Andrew Moskos: We also invented a great improv game involving e-commerce. We'd find three crazy items for sale on eBay, and then ask audience members to vote on which we should buy. Then we'd call the seller live and put the conversation over the sound system—keeping them on the line while incorporating suggestions from the audience: "You see, I'm an astronaut . . . well, an astronaut in training is more accurate. And I am very interested in your African statue. Has it been to space?"

After doing this game for six months, we were on one of these calls and after sixty seconds, the seller asked, "Is this Boom Chicago?" The audience erupted. We'd called so many people that year, we'd hit a seller twice!

Saskia Maas: By this point, Boom Chicago was now drawing primarily Dutch audiences, with two-thirds of the crowd comprising locals. Part of this was due to, yes, social media and online marketing—even more impressive considering how primitive social media was back then.

Andrew Moskos: In 2010, Google Street View was still a novelty to use on your phone; eBay wasn't on your phone. Hyves was not on your phone. Even Facebook didn't have a mobile strategy initially. Investors worried that if Facebook couldn't make the jump from personal computing to mobile devices, it would join Myspace in the digital ash heap of history.

Pep Rosenfeld: At the beginning of the year, we created this show called "Your Worst Fears," which evolved into the next year's show, "Social Media Circus." The concept behind it was to ask, "What are you going to do, now that social media runs your life? How are you going to retrench when the shit hits the Facebook?"

Andrew Moskos: That concern seems cute now. Facebook and Instagram are a huge part of our lives. How did we ever wait for an elevator without them? The issue today is more about Meta growing too big, unwieldy, and intrusive. Back then, we didn't grasp that Facebook would become one of the world's most powerful companies. We thought it was just a place to post dog pics and send messages to your friends. We thought it was . . . just like *onze eigen* Hyves.

Pep Rosenfeld: Social media was really just getting going. It was to be an era of new promise, new challenges, and new avenues of digital nefariousness. What, pray tell, could go wrong?

Andrew Moskos: *Doe je best sukkels!*

CHAPTER 18
2011

THE DUTCH TEAM WINS THE BASEBALL WORLD CUP. WAIT, THERE'S A BASEBALL WORLD CUP?

A dmit it—you didn't even know there was such a thing as a Baseball World Cup until you read the title of this chapter. Even now, you're wondering, *Is this whole thing a bit? Maybe this introduction is just an elaborate attempt to pull one over on me . . .*

Of course there's no Baseball World Cup. That's the thing about baseball: It's only *really* played in North America. And, we're told, Japan.

No, seriously, there's *totally* a Baseball World Cup. The idea that we made it up as a bit *was* the bit. We tried to fool you, but you didn't fall for it. You knew there's a Baseball World Cup— or is there?

There isn't.

There totally is.

Not . . .

Gotcha! Of course there's no Baseball World Cup.

Actually, there *is* a Baseball World Cup, and in 2011 it was held in Panama. The weather was terrible: games got rained out constantly. Some had to be played the day after they were scheduled, so teams were forced to slog through endless doubleheaders. Back-to-back games needed to be shortened to seven slightly unsatisfying innings. Everyone's least favorite event, the third-place game, was canceled so the rescheduled final could be played. Bronze went to Canada, who proved better than team USA. Cuba took silver—and for the first time since the tournament began in 1938, the Baseball World Cup gold medal went to a European team. You guessed it: the 2011 *honkbal* world champion was the Netherlands!

Ruben van der Meer: The Dutch baseball team beat Cuba to win the Baseball World Cup. Yeah, that happened—but the cultural impact was, like, 0.001 percent.

Steven Svymbersky: In Chicago, baseball is even more the opiate of the masses than religion. But I never knew there was a national baseball team when I was living in Holland.

Joe Canale: For my very first Boom Chicago show in 1999, I'd just come from Chicago. Albert Belle played outfield for the Chicago White Sox. He was a massive baseball star, set Major League Baseball records for home runs, and was the highest-paid player ever at one point. So during my first show ever at Boom, I made an Albert Belle reference and . . . zero reaction from the audience; I mean, *crickets*. I'd died for the first time onstage in Amsterdam with a joke that would've brought down the house at Improv Olympic in Chicago. It was an auspicious beginning . . .

Andrew Moskos: Baseball is a fraction as important as darts here. It's even less important than e-sports, or as it used to be called, watching people play video games.

Ruben van der Meer: I have some friends who are into baseball, but they're mostly expats. The only real Dutch baseball star I can think of is Rick van den Hurk. People were like, "This guy Ricky is good enough to go to America."

Rob AndristPlourde: Ricky played on Major League Baseball teams like the Florida Marlins, the Baltimore Orioles, and the Pittsburgh Pirates.

Ruben van der Meer: So when you see someone like Ricky doing well in baseball, you say, "Hey, this is nice." But nobody cares really, because in the Netherlands baseball is kind of a weird sport. I think its weirdness is best demonstrated in John Turturro's scene in that Adam Sandler movie *The Ridiculous 6*. Turturro explains baseball something like: "Okay, now you got two strikes; now you have to throw the ball between the knees and the shoulder." Every time he loses, he comes up with a new, bizarre rule—which is, of course, actually a real baseball rule. It didn't make any sense, but that's baseball.

Andrew Moskos: What's funny about the Dutch team winning the Baseball World Cup is that it makes you wonder if there's a World Cup for everything now.

Pep Rosenfeld: I think there is.

Andrew Moskos: Bowling? Is there a World Cup of bowling?

Pep Rosenfeld: I don't know. Probably.

Andrew Moskos: Mini golf?

Pep Rosenfeld: Warning: please don't call it by its offensive Dutch name: midget golf. You see, it's like regular golf, but smaller, so the Dutch named it with a derogatory term for the people who should be best at it: midgets. It's offensive enough that this slur should be used in an Efteling ride. *[Sings] "Midget Cannibale . . ."*

Andrew Moskos: I mean, the so-called "World" Series is just played by teams from the US and one Canuck outlier, Toronto.

So why didn't Holland winning the Baseball World Cup make a bigger impact? Why didn't baseball terms start entering the Dutch language?

Pep Rosenfeld: I constantly stop myself from saying "home stretch" because I know it's a baseball expression that *Nederlanders* won't understand. But it's a super good one: "in the home stretch" means "we're almost done." Super useful, right?

Andrew Moskos: Not if Dutch people don't get it.

Pep Rosenfeld: That's totally my point. If they're so good at baseball, they should know what the home stretch is. Maybe it's about them calling the game *honkbal*. Maybe home base isn't called home base in *honkbal*. Maybe it's got some charming Dutch name like *de honk*?

Andrew Moskos: No, it's called home base, *thuishonk*. My oldest son Finn played *honkbal*. The catcher plays on the *thuishonk*.

Pep Rosenfeld: Is the catcher actually called a catcher?

Andrew Moskos: Yes. Pronounced "ketcher." As in, *Trow de bal to de ketcher*.

Pep Rosenfeld: I'm totally saying "home stretch" from now on to Dutch people.

Andrew Moskos: Wait, hang on. That isn't a baseball expression at all. It's horse-racing jargon referring to the last part of a horse race.

Pep Rosenfeld: We should probably cut all this.

Andrew Moskos: Ah hell, let's leave it in. It's meta, like *Captain Underpants*. Anyway, this whole *honkbal*-versus-baseball thing is a perfect example of one of those little differences between Amsterdam and America that John Travolta was talking about in *Pulp Fiction*.

Pep Rosenfeld: You can't bring up *Pulp Fiction* or they'll cut the whole story and move it to the *Pulp Fiction* chapter.

Andrew Moskos: It's our book, and this is clearly a story about the Dutch team winning the Baseball World Cup.

Pep Rosenfeld: So, you were saying, the little differences . . .

Andrew Moskos: Like PAL versus NTSC.

Pep Rosenfeld: Yes! Two slightly different TV formats, which meant the NTSC VHS tapes we brought from home didn't work on the PAL Dutch VHS player in our apartment.

Andrew Moskos: VHS was how we watched video in olden days. Before streaming, before video subscriptions, before DVDs, before Blu-ray even, there were videotapes. And in the United States, videotapes were almost entirely in the VHS format.

Pep Rosenfeld: So our first summer, we brought all these VHS tapes loaded with episodes of *Star Trek* and *The Simpsons* with us to the Netherlands to help us feel connected to home.

Carice van Houten: This is when I got introduced to *The Simpsons*.

Andrew Moskos: We did find *Star Trek* episodes on German TV dubbed into German, but *Raumschiff Enterprise* . . . it just wasn't the same.

Pep Rosenfeld: By the time Boom's class of 2011 actors landed at Schiphol—Drew DiFonzo Marks, Laura Chinn, and Cari Leslie (our first ever full-time Canadian!)—they'd arrived into a world already streaming, bit torrenting, and Netflix and chilling.

Andrew Moskos: They'll never know the hardship of waiting for snail-mail delivery of VHS tapes.

Pep Rosenfeld: No they won't. But our hardship got worse: we had to find a place to convert our NTSC tapes into PAL so we could actually watch them.

Andrew Moskos: But where does one go to convert video as such?

Pep Rosenfeld: I mean, it's not the most legal thing . . . but it's not the most illegal thing, either.

Andrew Moskos: Exactly. So who could perform this gray-area service in our new town? What industry in Amsterdam would have an urgent need to maintain video transfer technology as we transitioned from one format to the next? Porn, of course! We figured there must be a guy in the Red Light District who converts videos to make copies "for private use only."

Pep Rosenfeld: Yes, those who sell tapes of people having sex with animals probably aren't too worried about copyright violations.

Andrew Moskos: So whenever Pep's mother would send us new *Star Trek* episodes, we would go over to Charlie Porno to convert them. His name was Charlie, so of course we called him Charlie Porno. He was a big guy, and his office was literally stacked with porno tapes. Like in five-foot-tall stacks. Navigating these stacks was like entering a labyrinth. If you made a wrong turn, you'd find a shirtless porn minotaur.

Pep Rosenfeld: The Pornotaur! And that would be Charlie Porno, holding court from the center of his porn-tape maze. Charlie the Pornotaur was always weirdly happy to see us. He'd be like, "Hey, Mister Boom!" I always thought it was weird that he called me Mister Boom, but I guess we called him Charlie Porno, so . . .

Andrew Moskos: Years later, when Amsterdam was trying to clean up the Red Light District, I was reading about the underworld kings getting pushed out. This article described a man called Dikke Charles, aka "Fat Charles." Immediately, I was like, "Wait, Fat Charles *is* Charlie Porno." Our *Star Trek* PAL pal was a famous Dutch gangster! Gangster enough, anyway, to have a nickname that started with "Fat," but respectable enough to keep "Charles." Like VHS tapes and *honkbal,* these little differences inspired many Boom Chicago shows—from 1995's "Culture Shock Therapy" to 2013's "Seven Deadly Dutch Sins" and beyond.

Pep Rosenfeld: Do we have time for one more baseball story? Because I feel like it's time for the ending, one that calls back the "home stretch."

Andrew Moskos: Why yes, of course we do.

Pep Rosenfeld: Good. My Dutch wife Tamara is obsessed with the Chicago Cubs. She's now a fan with a capital "F."

Andrew Moskos: And that's the whole story?

Pep Rosenfeld: Yeah. There's not really a story; I just wanted to end by bringing it back around to baseball and "the little differences."

Andrew Moskos: That's good, because this chapter was well past the home stretch . . .

CHAPTER 19
2012

"GANGNAM STYLE" BRINGS K-POP TO THE MASSES; BOOM CHICAGO BRINGS YESTERDAY'S NEWS TO COMEDY CENTRAL

The letter "K" makes for a most interesting prefix. Put in front of "car," you get the K-car—a blah line of automobiles from blah Chrysler, spawned during the most blah moment of the blah 1980s. Pair K with the word "hole," and you create a "k-hole": an infinite void into which mind and body sink after being spun out by the '90s rave drug/horse tranquilizer, ketamine. Combine K with the number three—and voilà! This hybrid produces K3, the Dutch/Belgian girl band. And placed in front of "pop," you get K-pop—the bright, sugary musical export that put South Korea on the pop-culture map.

With the likes of BTS and Blackpink attaining widespread global fame far beyond their homeland's borders, K-pop demonstrated to the wider world that Korea has something pop-culturally vibrant and fresh to offer the world—something that much-larger China has never successfully done. Even if K-pop offends serious music critics, their children disagree. Korea's entrée into pop culture's spotlight can be traced to 2012's most unexpected pop smash, "Gangnam Style"—a nuclear earworm propelled into public consciousness by the rapper-musician–YouTube savant known as Psy.

Oppan! The "Gangnam Style" video went viral in a major

way in 2012—a most unlikely success, this funny rap song featuring a stocky Korean dude in weird sunglasses rocking odd "I'm riding a horsey" dance moves while exuding too-cool-for-school ennui. "Gangnam Style" would top charts pretty much everywhere (except for the US, where it stalled at #2). In the process, "Gangnam Style" basically became the "Macarena" for a new era. Even a decade-plus later, good luck going to a wedding and not hearing fucking "Gangnam Style." No one would've ever predicted this song would become such a cultural phenomenon, its video reaching over three billion views on YouTube. That's billions as in *three thousand millions*. Take that! K-pop had clearly arrived.

The song paid tribute to—and also mocked—Gangnam, the wealthy neighborhood that's basically the Beverly Hills of Seoul. The lyrics made fun of the over-the-top culture of the people who live and party there. For us adopted *Nederlanders*, it would be as if DJ Sven and MC Miker G of "Holiday Rap" fame made a song in Dutch about chillin' in Wassenaar: "Heeeeeey, sexy dame! *O-O-O-O! Oppan Wass'naar stijl!*"

"Gangnam Style" was a YouTube hit. And YouTube hits created YouTubers, a new kind of celebrity who made bite-sized servings of wacky content. Who would have thought unboxings would ever be, like, a *thing?* Suddenly, the dream of young creatives changed from "get on a TV show" to "make videos of me playing Xbox and getting rich."

Back in Amsterdam, Sam Super, Marcy Minton, and musician Sacha Hoedemaker arrived at Leidseplein theater to kick off their European improv adventure. Naturally, Boom Chicago's big show that year, "Branded for Life," explored the wiles of advertising and marketing in an already-volatile climate turned atomic by the digital era. For the 2012 US election, Boom Chicago mounted a new political show, "My Big Fat Greek Election." It featured dueling Obama impressions from Michael Orton-Toliver (as the Black half of Obama) and Greg Shapiro (as the white part), while John McCain was played by Pep (the angry part). Finally, we mounted "Deep Undercover," an unusual mystery that unfolded at locations all around Amsterdam, from Centraal Station and the Red Light District to the new Rokin station on the city's still-in-process metro line.

In addition to Boom's onstage antics, exciting things started happening online. Increased prominence of Internet content altered how incoming actors saw their career vis-à-vis their time at Boom Chicago. When Seth Meyers left Amsterdam at the top of the century, he brought with him a two-man show he'd developed at Boom that served as his de facto audition reel. A decade later, a two-hand show performed in black-box theaters felt less cool as an entertainment medium, and more like an eight-track tape. Now your shit had to be short, fast, and on TikTok. You needed to have . . . *oppan* Gangnam style!

Andrew Moskos: Expectation today is that artists, and especially funny people, should put out a constant stream of free content— YouTube videos, Instagram Live posts, endless tweeting . . .

Ruben van der Meer: For kids today, YouTube and TikTok are what TV was for people my age.

Jordan Peele: With *Key & Peele*, we found out by default how well sketch comedy lends itself to YouTube. Part of it was because we were making a show at the time when all this stuff was still new. We started putting original sketches out as advertising for the TV show. Halfway through, we realized, "Oh wait—that *is* the show." That's how everyone was ultimately coming to our thing, so our digital strategy evolved.

There was an interesting interaction between *Key & Peele*'s Internet stuff and the actual broadcast material. Some things were intended specifically to go online, some weren't. We couldn't put *everything* online—at most, maybe two or three sketches from each episode, max. Otherwise, we'd just be giving away the whole show on YouTube.

I was first exposed to the power of YouTube when Ike, Josh, and I were on *MADtv*. The show hired an early YouTube star, Lisa Donovan, who didn't have a background in sketch comedy like the rest of us. Instead, she'd gotten noticed from these really funny, spontaneous YouTube videos she made doing hilarious impressions. She wasn't used to working on sets, and the *MADtv* executives had trouble figuring out how to mix her aesthetic with the show's. They eventually chose to let Lisa go. Of course, Lisa went on to form Maker Studios—selling it for, like, half a billion dollars to Disney.

Josh Meyers: She's the exception. So few people make any real money off YouTube, but the possibility of streaming mega-success warps their brains. It's like the gold rush.

Pep Rosenfeld: YouTube stuff gets crazy sometimes. A few years ago, a young woman in Minnesota accidentally killed her boyfriend while making YouTube videos. They'd hoped this one video would make them stars—and it sort of did, in a sick way that seems very "now." During a staged stunt, she shot him with an actual gun through a book he was holding in front of his chest. They thought the book would stop the bullet. As I'm telling the story, I'm realizing that while I have no reason to think the book was a Bible, I kinda hope it was.

Josh Meyers: One bummer is that talents who would otherwise be drawn to Boom Chicago are now more motivated to make online content. I was on a panel at the New Hampshire Film Festival with this YouTube-sensation guy. When a young woman from the audience asked about monetizing her online videos better, YouTube-sensation dude was like, "I've never monetized anything; I just put videos up. When they got popular, I started getting jobs that actually paid." I asked the aspiring YouTuber her age. She was fifteen years old: not old enough for a job scooping ice cream—yet existentially concerned about hacking YouTube's monetization policies. I told her, "Everyone on this panel delivered pizzas until we figured out what we did. Stop worrying about money: concentrate on making your stuff *good*."

Ruben van der Meer: The problem with making original YouTube content in Holland is that you'll never get billions of views like "Gangnam Style" or *Key & Peele*. It's especially hard if the content is in Dutch, so people hoping to score viral videos just do stuff in English now. The thing is, you never know what's going to go viral—there's no rule for what gets the most hits. You have to be lucky: somebody has to think, *This is funny*, and then share it.

I made this online talk show called *Apples and Pears*, and it took a bit of work. Then I did a somewhat fancy video with choreography, dances, and production that did, like, twenty-five thousand views. But my most-viewed clip is an iPad video of me doing a sexy dance while making fun of it. In it, you can hear my wife yelling for me to come to dinner. "I'll be there in a minute," I say as I wrap up the clip. In a half-hour period, I shot the video, posted it on YouTube, and ate my dinner—and then *that* became my most-viewed video.

Andrew Moskos: Boom Chicago has been making viral videos for years, beginning in the pre-YouTube era and continuing today. It was in 2000, in fact, when we hired Jamie Wright, our first video director. Jamie made comedy videos for use in shows and online, as well as putting real-time video and images on-screen during live performances. Over the years, Matt Chapman and Becky Nelson were also brought in for their video-making talent.

Pep Rosenfeld: We've had a few videos go viral. The first one was the "Florida Voting Machine" video for the 2004 election between George W. Bush and John Kerry. In the video, we showed someone in Florida trying to vote for Kerry—but the voting machine, made by a company with Republican leanings, will only let him vote for Bush.

Andrew Moskos: "Florida Voting Machine" was funny. Greg and Pep wrote it together, Jamie Wright did the animation, and then Greg really brought it to life with his voice-over. It was simple, funny, and topical. *Time* magazine wrote about it, and it was featured on CNN and news programs all around the world. Four years later, *The Simpsons* did a suspiciously similar thing during the Obama/McCain election. But hey, we've ripped things off from *The Simpsons* over the years, so fair play.

Steven Svymbersky: Early on, we did a video for YouTube called "Put Your Titty Shirt On." The idea was simple: put on the shirt that best shows off your tits. A bunch of Dutch celebrities starred in it—Carice van Houten, Horace and Ruben, and this huge actor/pop star of the day, Ellen ten Damme—alongside Jordan Peele, Colton Dunn, Brendan Hunt, Joe Kelly, and Nicole Parker from Boom. The "Titty Shirt" video was pre-YouTube. The idea was to score an MTV hit as promotion for Boom Chicago. I don't remember it being a huge hit.

Andrew Moskos: In 2002, Boom Chicago tried to create a party hit based on the new fashion trend of fitted T-shirts for women. Until that spring, many women wore blousy T-shirts made for men, just in a smaller size. Then "girly" T-shirts tapered at the waist appeared. Everybody looked great in them, which is why they are still popular years later. Our video, "Titty Shirt," was intended to celebrate this fashion revolution, down to its call-and-response chorus worthy of a Lil Jon crunk anthem: *"Where my titty shirt at? Get your titty shirt on!"*

Carice van Houten: Clearly, this was the pre-#MeToo era.

Pep Rosenfeld: Well, we meant it ironically, and we tried to have a pro-woman message in the lyrics.

Andrew Moskos: Defensive much? We filmed much of the "Titty Shirt" video at the Zebra Lounge, a classy strip club which had opened for a few months while the city figured out a legal way to close it (which they eventually did). We were friendly with the dancers—just being neighborly!—and they were up for being in our sexy music video.

What was funny was that the whole thing was way too tame. Our T-shirts weren't especially tight; meanwhile, having never shot music videos before, we didn't realize where to place the camera to actually get those sexy music-video shots. The dancers knew the game, though—they kept telling us, "Get in there close." But our naiveté and nervousness resulted in something surprisingly modest and chaste. While catchy, "Titty Shirt" didn't exactly stand the test of time.

Nicole Parker: All the women in the cast at that time had to be in the video, wearing the shirts. Yeah, I don't think that that video aged well . . .

Carice van Houten: Humor at this time was very tricky. Some things are just not possible anymore. I'm surprised at how things have changed, and how I look at things differently. It's just very telling how we were all conditioned to find everything like that normal—but not anymore. I think that's a good shift.

Pep Rosenfeld: We also made a rap video in 2002, and Carice did a little guest spot in that too. But surprise, surprise—it was our political sketches that connected online.

Andrew Moskos: Our strength video-wise was when we'd focus on topical stuff. Then we got hired to make our own TV show. In 2007, Comedy Central Netherlands was launching, and they wanted to be more local and relevant, so they commissioned us to make *Comedy Central News*. A satirical show in English about Dutch news, its tag line was "Because Dutch News Is News, Too." Pep took head-writer duties along with Brendan Hunt, new video director Matt Chapman would shoot and direct, and Greg Shapiro naturally took on the anchorman role.

Pep Rosenfeld: When *Comedy Central News* first appeared in 2007, it was a pretty daunting project. We had to feature news from not just Amsterdam, but also from little places all over the country where nothing interesting ever happened. With commercials, we were making a fifteen-minute daily show, but filming only twice a week. That meant we were writing Thursday's show on Monday. We found out the hard way that news ripped from the headlines of a three-day-old paper was *not* a good recipe for topical comedy.

Whereas most TV comedy shows have huge staffs and commensurate budgets, our writers' room was, like, six actors pitching jokes over beers in Boom's backstage lounge. And yet, we pulled it off: Chapman's knack for weird visual shit combined with Shapiro's antics behind the desk proved a winning combo. That hybrid—plus Lauren Flans fearlessly talking to people on the street in reporter mode—made *Comedy Central News* work. Well, for a short time . . .

Andrew Moskos: For our second season, we turned *Comedy Central News* into a thirty-minute weekly show, which was much smarter for content and workflow. Unfortunately, another topical daily show launched at the same time, *De Nieuwste Show*, where Dutch comedian Arjen Lubach got his start doing newsy commentary. Still, *De Nieuwste Show* didn't make much of a splash, and unfortunately, neither did *Comedy Central News*.

Pep Rosenfeld: It's like when Hollywood puts out two earthquake movies at the same time: one's going to get lost in the rubble. We were covering much of the same stuff as Lubach, but in English, making us less essential to Dutch audiences. Ultimately, you could say both of our earthquake movies got left in the dust.

Andrew Moskos: Most days, *Comedy Central News* was the best-rated show on the network—but the best rated show on the tenth-biggest network in a country of sixteen million people meant a nightly audience of around 100,000, max. Those numbers didn't justify the costs. Comedy Central could get pretty much the same ratings with reruns of old *South Park* episodes.

Eventually, the network canceled the show after the second season. They explained that Comedy Central had wanted to create a breakout, must-watch TV show—and to be fair, we weren't that. Greg might've been getting recognized more on the tram, but we weren't growing an almighty buzz.

So many TV projects end badly. There's "If only the network hadn't meddled creatively," and that perennial chestnut, "If only they had supported and promoted us more . . ." But we couldn't complain about Comedy Central, who were great to work with: they believed in us, gave us artistic control, and promoted our show pretty hard. We're probably the only people to get canceled and then say, "We see your point here—continuing the show just doesn't make business sense."

Not long after we were canned, Comedy Central scored the cultural hit of its dreams with *New Kids*. A lowbrow, foul-mouthed show about losers from a small village in provincial Noord-Brabant, *New Kids* would become a hit in the Netherlands *and* Germany, and also spawned two films. While *Comedy Central News* wasn't a hit in either the Netherlands or Germany, we like to think it was ahead of its time. The original team could always be brought back together for a reboot—that is, if the price is right. And we guarantee that, whatever your price is, it's right. So let us know . . .

Saskia Maas: After Comedy Central, we did some more big video projects. Greg voiced the *Zondag met Lubach* "America First, Netherlands Second" video after Trump won the election. That went viral around the world—making it the second-biggest Dutch comedy video of all time.

Andrew Moskos: Number one was Boom Chicago's "Sponge-Bob SquarePants in China" video, which would go on to reach over 100 million views following its release in 2007. Shout-out to the creators Matt Chapman and Dan Oster. It was one of those simple ideas that worked so well: SpongeBob goes on the air in China, requiring a more Chinese government–friendly version of the show. In our take, when SpongeBob looks for information online, he discovers Chinese Internet censorship has restricted his searches.

Pep Rosenfeld: It ends with labor agitator Patrick yearning for freedom and leisure time, hoping to one day make enough money to afford the "hilarious rubber dog poop" they made. Before that can happen, though, SpongeBob & Co. get shut down by the government's thought police. That was good stuff, and still funny today

Andrew Moskos: Although some people commenting thought it was racist.

Pep Rosenfeld: We just gave SpongeBob a classic Chinese haircut and made his eyes look . . . okay, Asian. Is that racist? Asian eyes are normal, although I guess there's a case to be made with "*hirarious* rubber dog poop." We actually got yelled at most for making SpongeBob's teeth look stereotypically Chinese—except we didn't change his teeth at all. That's just how OG Sponge-Bob's teeth look. Dude needs a little fish orthodontist.

Rob AndristPlourde: By 2009, "SpongeBob Square Pants in China" had become the most viewed animation video on You-Tube. It keeps going: every time it offends someone, we get a million or so more views, and it gets a new life.

Andrew Moskos: Viral videos have to touch a real nerve, so we knew "SpongeBob SquarePants in China" succeeded when the Chinese Embassy asked us to remove it from the Internet. We said, "No, thank you." The Netherlands isn't China or North Korea: you don't get to just shut down things you don't agree with.

Greg Shapiro: Speaking of North Korea, never forget Trump's historic—that is, historically dumb and dangerous—lovefest with Kim Jong-un. Maybe now's the time for the inevitable se-quel, "SpongeBob Squarepants in North Korea."

Andrew Moskos: It would be funny enough just to hear Trump mispronounce "Psy." That would be K-razy *hirarious*.

Pep Rosenfeld: Kim Jong-un is always good for a laugh—throw Psy in there for some "Gangnam Style"–era 2000s nostalgia, and you're money. Why stop there? Trump could do Psy's horsey dance at a wedding reception; BTS could join Biden's cabinet as the administration's advisers on K-pop trade policy. That alone would be worth the endless insults in the comments section . . .

CHAPTER 20
2013

KEEP IT CLASSY, BOOM CHICAGO: MOVIN' ON UP TO AMSTERDAM'S LEGENDARY ROZENTHEATER

In 2012, the City of Amsterdam had a problem: one of the most historic, storied theaters needed a tenant.

Since the economic collapse of 2008 had turned into [*don't cue the scary music; it's become a bit tedious*] The Crisis, conservative governments had been able to push through budget cuts that would make even the tightest-fisted Dutch blanch. Taking a page from US culture warriors, this new austerity chic put Holland's public-arts funding directly in the crosshairs. To them, we city slickers looked down on provincial Josef Six-Pack. So they resented us—along with the recently arrived immigrants we urban elites let into "their" country—and their politicians took it out on "our" culture. Putting this into political perspective, circuses—to which presumably our Dutch equivalents of Joe Six-Pack would go—remained at 6 percent sales tax. We're not talking Cirque du Soleil here, mind you,[47] but circuses where audiences could watch real elephants endure real abuse and misery. Sales tax charged on tickets sold by artsy businesses like Boom Chicago that right-wing voters hated, meanwhile, rocketed to 19 percent.

The whole *mishegas* proved a crass cultural play by conservatives, preying on the symbolic divisions between left and right. Between that and de facto higher prices caused by tax

---

47 Full disclosure: the authors of this book are more Cirque du Soleil types.

hikes, many theater companies lost their lifeline to survival: their government subsidy. Smaller, less commercial theaters were especially in trouble. One of those struggling was Amsterdam's Rozentheater. Known for student shows and an annual improv festival, the company relocated after it could no longer afford its original home in Amsterdam's historic Jordaan neighborhood. Their problem soon became Amsterdam's problem, since the city was the Rozentheater's landlord.

In the meantime, Boom Chicago had outgrown its home in the Leidseplein. Looking for additional business opportunities, Boom and a consortium of heavies from Amsterdam's coolest restaurants and nightlife venues opened the Chicago Social Club. In 2010, the idea seemed brilliant: our space had a five a.m. liquor license, and we were only using it until one a.m. at the latest. Why not have Boom Chicago do a show in the evening— and then reopen at midnight as Chicago Social Club? The rent was already paid, and we now had a second revenue-generating business in the same space. Easy!

At first, that's how it worked. After the comedy rush from eight to eleven p.m., there was now a club rush until four a.m. And as the Chicago Social Club grew, it needed more hours. Promoters wanted to set up before Boom Chicago's show ended. And we learned that clubgoers treat public spaces differently than theatergoers. Young clubbers were spilling beer, breaking glasses everywhere, and covering bathroom walls with graffiti, where every toilet handle quickly snapped off from doubled us-age. As a result, the place was aging fast and falling apart at incredible speed. Boom actors were literally dodging shards of broken glass now littering the stage.

In 2012, Boom approached the City of Amsterdam and explained our situation. They showed us the recently vacated Rozentheater, and we immediately fell in love with the space for our new home—it had everything we didn't have with in the Leidseplein. The theater was bigger and well maintained, with high ceilings and a proper lighting grid accessed by a catwalk. The building was large, with lots of office space. The backstage area had the luxury of four—*four!*—proper dressing rooms. There was a bigger bar area, and upstairs space that could serve as a second theater. And the city seemed to be a great landlord: they cared about the building, its future, and preserving its artistic history. Moving to the Rozengracht would solve another problem. Although the always-busy Leidseplein area had incredible foot traffic, it was primarily for tourists. To some, we were seen as putting on shows for tourists, to which Dutch people were also welcome. Boom Chicago actually aspired to be the opposite: shows for locals, where tourists were also welcome.

Excited, we met the city's team that Friday—only to leave dejected after they proposed an impossibly high rent. Thinking that was the end of the story, we called Carolien Gehrels—Amsterdam's alderperson of cultural affairs, who had set up the meeting—and told her how badly it had gone. An hour later, we got a call to return on Monday, where we received a much better offer. It turned out the city was looking for a specific tenant—creative and cultural, not needing a subsidy, and already doing business in Amsterdam. The list of groups satisfying those requirements proved very small. Perhaps that list had just one name on it: Boom Chicago.

So in January 2013, Boom Chicago relocated to the Rozentheater. Boom's new actors—Carl Tart, Ally Beardsley, and Eleanor Hollingsworth—would never know the pleasure of sitting on the giant Leidseplein terrace after a show to enjoy the sophisticated, Heineken-enhanced musings of small-town bachelor parties and tear-gassed football hooligans. Shedding Leidseplein's touristy trappings for the more sedate and authentically Dutch Jordaan location made Boom Chicago suddenly feel more . . . *adult?*

Boom's first show here was "Baby, I Like It Raw"—titled to reflect the unvarnished feel of our new space still under renovation. By spring, we'd made enough improvements to open our first proper show in the Rozentheater, "The Seven Deadly Dutch Sins." Under Andrew's direction, Pep, Lolu Ajayi, and Jim Woods wrote and performed the three-header production, which accomplished two things marvelously. First, it doubled down on what Boom Chicago does so well: holding a mirror up to the Dutch so they could see themselves the way we saw them. Per that brief, "The Seven Deadly Dutch Sins" named seven important characteristics Dutch people might not have realized they were guilty of:

1. *Excessive practicality and pragmatism, to a fault*
2. *Unique, horrible swear words*
3. *Exceptionally boring national cuisine*
4. *Tolerance of scooters and their drivers*
5. *Boring birthday parties*
6. *Leedvermaak (for which in English we use the German word* schadenfreude)
7. *Absurd frugality (i.e., cheapness, see #1)*

That last one was predictable but unavoidable. As Pep notes in the show:

Bad news, Dutch people, the world thinks you're cheap. And the worse news is that you seem to agree. But I admit, this whole cheap thing is complicated. I mean, if you invite me to dinner, you're super generous. It's a huge dinner of wine, appetizers, and coffee—and exactly one cookie. But if I'm not invited to dinner, but I'm there, and the clock strikes six—which for some reason is the National Dutch Dinnertime—I'm kicked out of your place faster than a Dutch cyclist rings his bell at tourists in the bike lane . . .

The sin of Dutch cuisine also had a special place in the show.

Again, we didn't want to beat a dead horse—even one that had been turned into cheap IKEA meatballs that people line up to eat on Sundays in some parts of the country.[48] Still, we weren't afraid to point out the brutal truths of this stereotype:

> *Sure, modern Dutch food is good and we all have our favorite restaurants—but why are there no Dutch restaurants abroad? When was the last time you were traveling and saw a place advertising "authentic Dutch cuisine"? Every other country has their cuisine represented abroad. Even small countries have international restaurants, like Korea, Lebanon, Cuba, and Ethiopia. And Ethiopia doesn't even have food!*

In addition to Dutch social content, the show also used mapping technology—perhaps the first comedy show to do so. This was yet another cool, theater-friendly technology that assimilated early into Boom's comedy toolbox. Uncharacteristically, "The Seven Deadly Dutch Sins" ended not with a final song, but with the actors deceased and wandering through a strange purgatory where they were forced to experience the seven deadly Dutch sins over and over.

Lolu and Pep had big penises projected on them. At one point, Geert Wilders's face was projected onto Jim's crotch, setting up an obvious gag: "That's a big Dutch dick!" But there were more than just high-tech dick jokes (admittedly, no shame there). We set up a secret video camera to illustrate the Dutch sin of taking pleasure in others' misfortune. The audience roared with delight watching live feeds of audience members' unwitting misbehavior. That's the joy of *schadenfreude*: even if it was you being embarrassed a minute ago, you soon get to enjoy other people's embarrassment . . . which somehow makes it okay. It's a very Dutch sin, after all.

---

48 If it's Sunday, it must be Friesland . . .

In 2018, with renovations completed, we relaunched the venue once more as the Rozengracht Theater. As the Rozengracht, the space became an integrated venue serving as the center for all of Boom Chicago's creative activities and outside events, as well as an exciting new sideline in developing escape rooms. On the comedy side, Boom Chicago started our improv training center, the Boom Chicago Academy. The Academy also became home to InterActing, an innovative program that teaches improvisation skills to teenagers with autism to help them better handle and appreciate the randomness of life.[49] The Rozengracht Theater was now more than a mere building or venue: it ultimately became the hub for a community of creatives who laugh, learn, drink, play pinball, watch, and perform live theater together. And yes, make the occasional dick joke . . .

Andrew Moskos: Regarding the move, it hurt some not getting foot traffic from being in tourist central. But our audience had become more local anyway, so moving to a cooler, more historic and beautiful part of Amsterdam proved a huge advantage in the long run. And let's face it—there's more space to put the pinball machines, for which my enthusiasm has not diminished. We now even have two pinball machines, "Dialed In" and "The Godfather," that Boom Chicago actors and I auditioned for and were cast to do characters in each game. My life is now complete, and hey, these games are as good as "Medieval Madness."

Jason Sudeikis: Well, I doubt that—but I'm just glad Boom still has pinball.

Saskia Maas: Fucking nerds.

---

49 Saskia has been the major force behind InterActing and gave a wonderful TED Talk on the subject. The program is especially close to her and Boom Chicago's heart as it was inspired by the journey of her and Andrew's youngest son, Aidan, who is autistic.

Ruben van der Meer: In the end, the Rozentheater was a great move for Boom Chicago. It's a real "Amsterdam" place with an incredible history, and it's just a great theater space, period. And let's face it—anything around the corner from the Anne Frank House is going to seem funnier by comparison.

CHAPTER 21
2014

BELOVED DUTCH ICON SAYS GOODBYE
AS BOOM GOES COMMERCIAL

2014 was all about "out with the old, in with the new." At the movies, *X-Men: Days of Future Past* continued the march of X-Men characters being replaced with younger, newer versions. *Guardians of the Galaxy* proved that Marvel Cinematic Universe could feel as hip and irreverent as Tarantino. *About Last Night*,[50] the 1986 Rob Lowe and Demi Moore–starring sex comedy based on a raunchy David Mamet play, was remade as a Kevin Hart and Regina Hall sex comedy[51] based on a movie based on a raunchy David Mamet play. The old *Teenage Mutant Ninja Turtles* cartoon characters were replaced with new cinematic live-action Ninja Turtles, leaving aging nerds disappointed worldwide. Meanwhile, the disappointment of the Dutch football team taking second place at the 2010 World Cup was replaced in 2014 with an even greater outrage: *third place*. Oh, the horror . . .

But Holland's biggest "out with the old" story that year proved to be Harry Piekma hanging up his blue Albert Heijn jacket for the last time. Albert Heijn (pronounced "hine") is the most ubiquitous supermarket chain in the Netherlands. That's

---

50 Guess what play this movie was based on? Yep, *Sexual Perversity in Chicago*, David Mamet's work that was produced in Amsterdam under the name *Sexual Perversity*, starring Jelka van Houten. And yes, *About Last Night* is probably a more marketable name.

51 Directed, no less, by our old Evanston homey Steve Pink.

in large part due to the brand's TV commercials. These heart-tugging, award-winning ads centered around an iconic character, supermarket store manager Mr. van Dalen, who grew to be beloved by the entire Dutch population (and absolutely no one else in the world). Over a decade, Harry Piekma played Mr. van Dalen in 153 Albert Heijn ads. Other than the hilarious "Two Guys" from those Sonic Drive-In commercials (one of whom was played by Boom alum Pete Grosz![52]), no actor personified a single brand for so long in the public eye like Piekma. Indeed, for most of the Netherlands during this time, Harry Piekma *was* Albert Heijn. And then one day, the Mr. van Dalen the Dutch had come to know and love disappeared from the airwaves, to the shock of a nation . . .

Andrew Moskos: In his valedictory message, Harry Piekma said he wanted to pursue other acting projects. Um, good luck with that! You're fifty years old—not a good age to look for a variety of great roles. Sorry, we'll always see you only as Mr. van Dalen. It's like when you're watching some gritty indie movie starring Daniel Radcliffe and can't help thinking, *What the hell is Harry Potter doing here?*

Ruben van der Meer: Well, good for Piekma. I'm sure he made some good money.

Andrew Moskos: What if Piekma lived next to a Jumbo supermarket? Could the actor who personified Albert Heijn to a generation really shop there comfortably—or would he have to go to the Albert Heijn farther away? It's hard to imagine a

---

52 Peter Grosz: It was a great run with those Sonic ads when they were happening, and yes, it's less great now that it's over. I worked alongside one of my greatest friends, I made a good amount of money, and afterward I wasn't typecast forever as just the "Two Guys" guy. I can't imagine another job I'd enjoy as much, and for so long. And what about Verizon's "Can you hear me now?" actor? Didn't he switch to Sprint?

greater scandal than Mr. van Dalen being revealed as a Jumbo shopper.

Pep Rosenfeld: Dutch *TMZ* would be all over that shit! I'll tell you, if Albert Heijn had been willing to replace van Dalen with, say, Rob AndristPlourde, I could personally guarantee Rob would shop exclusively at Albert Heijn—and that deal still stands. Boom actors have actually starred in some pretty good TV commercials over the years. Tim Sniffen and Jim Woods were in this surreal MTV campaign called "Brad and Eric." In it, there was one smart brother and one dumb brother who'd say ridiculous stoner musings like, "Hey, how come when rocket ships go into space, they don't fall back down to earth?" *Long pause.* Then Eric would say, "What's on MTV?" For a while, Tim and Jim would be recognized on the street. People would just say to them, "What's on MTV?" And then Andrew was in that virtual-reality KLM commercial.

Andrew Moskos: That was a strange one. We shot for a day in a brand-new Boeing 787 Dreamliner, with a plane full of extras. Well, half a plane full of extras. Only the people behind me were people. Everyone in front of me was a balloon on a stick with a wig. The commercial wasn't bad, but I wonder if a single person actually saw it. You really had to make an effort! First, you needed a virtual-reality viewer for your phone—already a small demographic. Then you had to download this incredibly large 360-degree VR file. Only once you jumped through these hoops could you "experience" flying on KLM's new plane . . . in a commercial. Who would do that? People don't especially like watching commercials—I don't know many who would go out of their way to actually watch one. But let's be honest, I'm no Mr. van Dalen.

Heather Anne Campbell: Albert Heijn is a primal part of the

Boom Chicago experience. We were broke fucking comedians. That meant half my meals were grilled-cheese sandwiches from Albert Heijn, and then the other half were more "I guess I'll see what the Dutch take on a burrito tastes like."

Seth Meyers: Sitting in our run-down actors' apartment playing old Frank Sinatra albums on vinyl and drinking cheap red wine from Albert Heijn for hours—we felt like we'd *arrived*.

Amber Ruffin: Nothing made me more homesick than frigging Albert Heijn. I only ate there because that was the most convenient way to eat food. When people used to ask about my time in Amsterdam, I'd say, "I was cold and hungry for two years."

Pep Rosenfeld: Albert Heijn is where a new Boom actor's lack of Dutch-language skills hurts the most. Shopping for groceries should be comforting—an activity that grounds the actor and makes them feel at home. Alas, encountering a Dutch supermarket for the first time can make you feel dumb and confused. It *seems* like it should be easy. I mean, everything is global now, so lots of brands are the same as back home. Aquafresh is Aquafresh; Special K is Special K; Heinz remains, despite baked-in Dutch hatred for all things German, Heinz. But then you get confused. What's the name of the spice I want, *gember* or *kaneel*? Which cheese is *belegen*? Buying milk is a struggle, trying to tell *halfvol* from *magere*. And woe is the new actor who accidentally buys—and drinks—*karnemelk* before realizing they've guzzled a pint of sour-tasting buttermilk with a funny name. It's the little differences . . .

Holly Walker: Like the fact that there are only three different kinds of cereal in Holland—and two of them are muesli.

Amber Ruffin: For my husband, America was a bit of an adjustment—but now, every time we go to a Dutch supermarket, he's disappointed that there's not enough cereal choice. Yes! This was my only goal, and I succeeded. So my question for Mr. van Dalen is this: why do you only sell three kinds of breakfast cereal? What's the frigging point? Does no one in the Netherlands want anything else?

Pep Rosenfeld: Indeed, the biggest shock Amsterdam newbs encounter might be self-service bagging.

Nicole Parker: When I first went to Albert Heijn, I got to the cashier with all my groceries, and suddenly had to try to fit everything I was buying into this little bag you'd put, like, produce in. Everyone behind me was rolling their eyes, thinking, *Who's this thick American holding up the line?*

Pep Rosenfeld: Expats are like, *Wait, I have to bag this shit myself? And complete the bagging process—which I've never done before—before the next customer steps up? And if I don't, the checkout person pushes my groceries aside with that awful wooden thingy?* That's when Albert Heijn–related stress disorder can set in . . . Not even the quaint system of saving enough stickers to get a new teakettle can completely make it go away.

Jordan Peele: I was staying in a house with Joe Kelly, Randall Harr, and Dave Buckman. We were four guys who ate a lot, and that was an awful thing for locals to witness. One day, us four strapping American men went to Albert Heijn together. The Dutch woman ringing us up just started giggling so hard when she got to our ten enormous twelve-packs of toilet paper. We just stood there looking at them, slowly realizing, *Oh God, we're Americans—we eat more, so we're going to shit more too.*

Josh Meyers: This was perhaps the first time Jordan had ever visited a supermarket. I remember one day he was like, "What the fuck is up with everyone always doing errands all the time. Like, what are people doing when they run errands? What's an errand, exactly, anyway? Why are they so important?" I said, "You know, when you need to drop off your dry cleaning, or you go grocery shopping—those are errands, man." And Jordan just had this lost expression on his face, like, *Huh, okay* . . . So Joe asked him, "You don't ever run errands, Jordan?" And he was like, "Um, no."

Andrew Moskos: I'm with Jordan on this. Why shop when you can eat out? Restaurants in Amsterdam have come a long way. When I first moved here, there were Indonesian "rice table" places, some pizza and pasta joints, and that was about it. There was *the* Greek restaurant, *the* Italian, and *the* Chinese—as in, there was only one of each. All Chinese restaurants had the same menu; each pizza place had the same five topping options—margarita, four cheeses, salami, Hawaii, and tuna—none of which were unique to that restaurant. The Dutch thought of restaurants serving the cuisines of different, faraway lands like they did their dry cleaner or hardware store: you only needed one. There was no talk about which was the best Chinese restaurant—just eating *any* Chinese food was exotic enough.

Ike Barinholtz: For a fancy dinner, we'd go to an Argentinian steak place. For a normal meal, there was an all-you-can-eat spare ribs joint—we went there at least once a week. And there was this one *decent* Italian joint. And nothing was open late. Nothing.

Andrew Moskos: The restaurant scene is so much better now, and it's thanks to tourists. Oh, the Dutch love to hate on tourists—but hey, what are *you* when you travel to Greece or Istanbul,

Cloggie?[53] Let me guess: you're somehow sophisticated, and the local natives are dumb. *Check!*

In truth, Holland's current food and restaurant revolution is due to travel, foreign influences, and . . . tourists. Dutch people think that tourists eat badly, but that stereotype is a decade-plus out of date. Today's tourists are smart: they research restaurants, check out new places, and demand quality and authenticity. The best restaurants in Amsterdam are full of non–Dutch speakers. Who sits at home and rewatches the last *Voice of Holland* episode? Not tourists—tourists are going out on *Mondays*. They provide the extra 25 percent of revenue that makes restaurants profitable. If you want to see what life is like without tourists, go experience the culinary treasures of Almere. Bon appetit!

Pep Rosenfeld: It's not just tourists. Cooking shows on TV also raised the bar. As Dutch people grow more worldly, chefs have gotten more creative. Restaurants demand more from suppliers, and regular people demand more from their supermarket. Everything has become more international.

Greg Shapiro: Albert Heijn has certainly gotten a better selection over the years. In Amsterdam, Albert Heijn remains the great equalizer: everyone goes there. No matter what we're doing onstage, if we can swing a joke about Albert Heijn, audiences are going to laugh.

Pep Rosenfeld: It's the reference that always works. When new actors get to Boom, they always think, *Ah yes, these Dutch people will love my references to Alex Keaton from* Family Ties *or Derek Jeter's batting average just as much as they do back in the States.* But they never do. Why would they? Dutch people have their own references.

---

53 See? *Cloggie* doesn't work.

Greg Shapiro: I'm not sure those Alex Keaton bits are still going to work so well in the States, either.

Pep Rosenfeld: But then Albert Heijn quickly becomes a common reference point for Boom's new blood because they have to shop there too. New actors don't listen to K3—well, ever—but Albert Heijn on the other hand . . . It's a state of mind, really.

Greg Shapiro: Americans don't come to Boom with a built-in Dutch reference base. But after a week, they'll have shopped at Albert Heijn twice. Now they have something they can make a joke about.

Pep Rosenfeld: It's like our bit from "Trump Up the Volume" where we ask people where they think they'd live on the *Monopoly* board: the green squares, the yellow, and so on.

Greg Shapiro: We're basically asking them to admit their socio-economic status in public—which is a very un-Dutch thing to do. The Dutch will do *anything* before they start discussing how much money they have.

Pep Rosenfeld: Everyone was uncomfortable with this bit. You see, there's no class system here, supposedly. We've got low highs, and high lows: we're just all *normaal* here in Holland.

Greg Shapiro: But then we realized we could ask people to figure out where they live based on where they shop. That worked better.

From "Trump Up the Volume," 2018

> *Pep: Take a second and think about where you live. What color is your neighborhood in* Monopoly *terms?*

Greg: For example, who lives in the red and yellow squares? Let me put it this way: who goes shopping at Albert Heijn? That's basically middle class, just like the yellow and red neighborhoods in Monopoly. *You're red if you actually go to Albert Heijn. If you're yellow, Albert Heijn delivers groceries to you.*

Pep: Anyone live in the green neighborhood? You know you're green if, when you heard Greg mention Albert Heijn, you were like, "Oh, Gregory, I do not go to Albert Heijn. I shop at Marqt."

Greg: That's Marqt with a "q."

Pep: "And I don't buy coffee there, because I drink Nespresso with real pods." That's green.

Greg: Who's orange? Who likes shopping at Dirk van den Broek? Right? It's basically the same brands they have at Albert Heijn, but they're cheaper at Dirk. Yay! We're Dutch and we love discounts! That's why, if you shop at Dirk, you live in the orange neighborhood.

Pep: Who's purple? You know you're purple if you shop at Aldi. You're like, "Nespresso? Who needs Nespresso? This Senseo coffee still tastes good to me. Mmmm."

Greg: And if you shop at Lidl, you live in the dark browns. No time for coffee—just a no-name energy drink.

Pep Rosenfeld: If you want to discuss status among *Nederlanders*, it's better to come at it a bit sideways. In the US, rich people show off because being rich is the goal of *everything*. In the Netherlands, rich people like to pretend they're just middle class. Air France and British Airways, for example, offer a proper first class, whereas Dutch national airline KLM just has business class. First class? That's like being a tall tulip, and as we all learn at a young age, the tall tulip gets cut off.

This disturbingly phallic image is so ingrained that the Dutch language has many other expressions that mean the exact same thing. Take "The tall tree catches the most wind." Rich Dutch people don't like to catch wind. They communicate their wealth more subtly—driving a nice car, but still shopping at Hema. They're still "regular Dutch" like us. They eat *drop*.

Greg Shapiro: You still hate *drop*?

Pep Rosenfeld: Yeah. Do you actually like *drop*?

Greg Shapiro: I don't hate it.

Pep Rosenfeld: *Drop* and mayonnaise, two Dutch staples: I hate them both. But at least I used *drop* to make a political point in "Yankee Go Home."

From "Yankee Go Home," 2002

Greg: What do the Dutch love to eat? Dead fish, frikandel *. . . And what do they love more than anybody? Drop, which is made from gelatin, which is made from cow bones, cow hooves, and cow teeth.*

Pep: Right now, one of you Dutch people is like, "Wait a minute. Most of that was funny, okay. But . . . drop is great. It's delicious. It's lekker. You don't like drop because you are American." No, it's not just because I'm American. Because you know who else likes drop be-

sides Dutch people? NO ONE. Why? It's terrible. Drop is made of cow bones and it tastes like black licorice, the worst candy taste there is. The candy you throw away or give to your little sister when forced to share—that's the Dutch delicacy. It's like they were shooting for shit flavor . . . and missed the target.

You know what's weird? Americans get made fun of because when you walk into an American supermarket, it's like a sea of options. A wall of cereal, a sea of peanut butter—I mean, how many varieties of peanut butter can there be? And so many different kinds of bread, all of which are spongy and terrible. The Dutch, of course, don't have this kind of crazy selection—except for drop. *Oh boy, do you have a lot of* drop. *You've got the plain* drop, *you've got the* drop *with the salty white stuff on the back, you've got the* drop *with the sweet stuff on the back, you've got the* drop *with the red stuff on the back, you've got the* drop *sandwich—with white stuff on one side, and red stuff on the other. But here's the thing: they all taste like* drop. *It's like your political parties. Sure, they have platforms and different names, but when you mix up a handful of them, they all taste the same.*

Pep Rosenfeld: Like most supermarkets in the Netherlands, Albert Heijn has come a long way. In addition to excessive *drop* options, there's prepared food and even fresh sushi. But while Albert Heijn has changed over the years, it's still *onze eigen* Albert Heijn. We might scan our own groceries, or we might order online delivery, but Albert Heijn is still there, where we still can't get any bread after four p.m.

Andrew Moskos: And through all these changes, Mr. van Dalen was there, holding Holland's hand—but no longer: out with the old, just like the bread at four p.m. And if Albert Heijn ever needs an older, slightly nerdy manager to replace Mr. van Dalen on TV, remember—*onze eigen* Rob AndristPlourde is still interested, and we can put in a word with his people.

CHAPTER 22
2015

NOTHING INTERESTING HAPPENED THIS YEAR, BUT . . .

Honestly, nothing interesting happened in the year 2015. Therefore, we thought we'd fill the space by printing Pete Grosz's absolutely epic roast of Boom's founding fathers that he performed at a private event during our twenty-fifth-anniversary celebration.

It's a little inside *honkbal*, sure—but still probably the funniest, truest telling of the Boom Chicago origin story yet . . . Which is why we kept it, naturally, until nearly the end of the book. I mean, we can't have Pete Grosz outshine us *yet again!* It's our own fucking book, damn it!

"Boom Roast" by Peter Grosz

[A conversation that happened twenty-five years ago, somewhere on the North Side of Chicago . . .]

Pep: Hey, Andrew, what are you doing?

Andrew: Not much, Pep. Just going to Dennis' Place For Games on Belmont, beating teenagers at Galaga, then getting into fights with CTA employees. You know— livin' the dream. What about you?

Pep: Taking it easy, performing at Improv Olympic, and dating a girl for waaaay too long. She's cool, and I think she'll write for a show called House of Cards *one day starring Kevin Spacey.*

Andrew: Ooh, right. The guy from Glengarry Glen Ross *and* The Ref. *I like him. He's not creepy at all.*

Pep: I agree. Andrew, let's come up with an idea for what we should do with the next twenty-five years of our lives.

Andrew: Okay. But first let's get really high.

Pep: Yes, let's do that. Okay, cool. We just got high. Should we go to Amsterdam?

Andrew: Yes. Good idea.

Pep: Hey, now we're in Amsterdam.

Andrew: Cool. Let's get high again. [Inhales on joint.] Way ahead of you, Pep. Or Andrew. I lost track of which one of us is speaking.

Pep: Ha ha. Me too! That's how high I am.

Andrew: Now that we are so high that we don't know which one of us is which, let's plan our futures.

Pep: Hmmm . . . What if we abandoned our extremely successful careers of performing for free and antagonizing municipal employees—and opened an improv theater here in Amsterdam?

Andrew: That's a fantastic idea. I know a bar that will let us perform in the back for free. It's small, but it's also shitty.

Pep: Great! And we should definitely ask performers from Chicago to drop what they're doing, move here, and work for verrrrry little money while we all live in a single crappy Dutch apartment. Can we have people sleep on bunk beds in the kitchen of that apartment?

Andrew: Definitely. Because that's a true thing that will happen in our first year. Okay, I think we're really coming up with a great plan here, so I'd like to add another very good idea to the mix.

Pep: Okay. What is it?

Andrew: Well, I was thinking that we should force the people we hire as actors at our theater to also work twenty hours a week doing random meaningless things for the theater.

Pep: Let me get this straight. In addition to writing the show . . .

Andrew: Yes . . .

Pep: And acting in the show . . .

Andrew: Yes . . .

Pep: They should also perform mind-numbing tasks and manual labor?

Andrew: Yes! We are both extremely lazy and need the

people we hire to write and perform to also work twenty hours a week doing mind-numbing tasks and manual labor like regluing the legs to all the chairs in the theater. Another true thing that will happen.

Pep: When it comes to mind-numbing tasks, don't forget about passing out our homemade, mildly informative newspapers.[54]

Andrew: Ah, newspapers. They'll be around forever. Like Kevin Spacey! Before we open this improv theater, I feel that I should be honest and tell you something.

Pep: What is it, Andrew?

Andrew: I am a terrible improviser. Like, really bad.

Pep: How bad?

Andrew: You know how I am very bad at and know very little about sports?

Pep: Yes. You are physically very awkward, and a terrible athlete.

Andrew: Well, I am an even worse improviser.

Pep: Good God! I see what you mean. But Andrew, don't worry about being a terrible improviser. You've got me. I am a decent improviser. So we'll be fine.

---

54 While we're allowing ourselves to be demeaned so willingly, we might as well point out here that Boom alum Tami Sagher once wrote an essay explaining how the most demeaning job she ever had in her life was being asked to pass out Boom Chicago flyers in front of the Anne Frank House.

Andrew: Let's go over our strengths and what we each bring to the table. As previously stated, I am a bad improviser. I also like to take drugs.

Pep: Me too, Andrew! I also like drugs. Plus, I read the Economist, *so that means I'm good at business.*

Andrew: Wait a second . . . I also read the Economist. *This business is going to be a home dunk.*

Pep: You bet, Andrew. I got a good feeling.

Andrew: Why did you just say that?

Pep: I don't know, but I think I'm going to start saying it all the time.

Andrew: Okay, Pep, we've got a great plan in place. Now, what should we call the theater?

Pep: Good question. Well, we definitely don't want to pick a good name.

Andrew: You're right. A good name would be bad for our business.

Pep: So would a name that means something or makes sense.

Andrew: Absolutely. What about something with "Chicago" in the title?

Pep: Definitely. We are from Chicago and that would be appropriate.

Andrew: How about . . . oh, I don't know, I'm just picking this name at random here: Boom Chicago.

Pep: Perfect. I think Boom means "tree" in Dutch.

Andrew: Excellent. Naming our comedy theater Tree Chicago is sure to attract business.

Pep: Now that we have a name, can we write a sketch about two guys who get really high at a coffeeshop and crazy things happen?

Andrew: Wow. That is a very original and very funny comedy idea.

Pep: Thank you. But what should we call the sketch?

Andrew: What about a pun that means both friends AND is slang for marijuana?

Pep: I wish! Does such a magical word exist?

Andrew: It's got to. What about Bros?

Pep: Chums?

Andrew: Weeds?

Pep: Buds.

Andrew: Yes! Buds. That is as hilarious a name as the idea for this sketch is original.

Pep: As far as political sketches go, do you think it would be fun/informative/accurate for our actors to personify entire countries onstage?

Andrew: Yes, that would be a good way for people to easily understand what we are talking about.

Pep: One thing—how would we be able to indicate which actor is playing a country?

Andrew: Subtle acting choices?

Pep: Obviously not.

Andrew: Cleverly designed costumes?

Pep: Dear God, no.

Andrew: Big signs that just say what country each person is playing?

Pep: Yes. That will work perfectly. It's both not too subtle and not subtle at all. Right in the Tree Chicago sweet spot.

Andrew: Boom Chicago, you mean.

Pep: Ha ha. Yes. That's what I mean. What a great name. We are so high. I look forward to constantly doing drugs and allowing that to shape our decision-making.

Andrew: Yes. And I look forward to coming up with a bullshit credo about "buying half a plane ticket" that sounds profound but is really just a way to force people

*into doing more drugs than they want to—after which
they will find themselves in sexual situations that make
them feel uncomfortable.*

*Pep: I think that's very responsible. You are going to be
a good boss.*

Andrew: Yes. Like Kelly Leonard, or Charna Halpern.

Pep: The woman we both had sex with?

Andrew: Yes, the same woman.[55]

*Pep: Speaking of women, are we really sure we want to
move to Holland when there are tons of women from
America who want to marry us?*

*Andrew: Actually, the complete opposite of what you
said is true.*

*Pep: Right. I forgot that. We are not desirable. When it
comes to women, we are a total penalty ball.*

*Andrew: Foreign women are easy to trick into marriage.
Let's just marry Dutch women who don't know any better.*

*Pep: Yes. We will tell them we are the coolest guys from
America, and they will believe us because they will want
blue jeans and New Coke.*

---

55 For the record: neither Andrew nor Pep actually had sex with the longtime
owner of legendary Chicago improv institution iO. Pete Grosz wrote this, okay?
Talk to him.

Andrew: Well, I think that's it. One final question: should we grow our business exponentially, find true happiness in Amsterdam, start vibrant, amazing families, persist through ups and downs over the next twenty-five years, and launch the careers of countless actors, one late-night host, Oscar- and Emmy-winning writers, film directors, eccentric solo performers who like to show people their dongs, innovators who open their own improv theaters in cities across America, doughy male movie leads who can really only carry a movie if Jon Cena is in it[56]—and most importantly, one wildly successful commercial actor who will appear in TV's longest-running campaign of all time, even though he's immensely talented and quite capable of doing a wide range of work, both comedic AND dramatic?[57]

Pep: Yes, let's definitely do that. Let's be mentors—and more importantly friends—to everyone we hire, and give hundreds of people the unique experience of a lifetime, and our theater will be around forever. Just like Kevin Spacey . . .

Andrew Moskos: Wow! Reading that again, I hadn't remembered how mean it was.

Peter Grosz: Andrew, it's supposed to be mean. What part of "Dude, it's a fucking roast" do you not understand?

---

56 An Ike Barinholtz joke always goes down well with an insider Boom Chicago audience.

57 Pete Grosz starred in more than a hundred beloved commercials for the Southern hamburger chain Sonic. We think he probably substantially increased the acceptance and appreciation of Jews in American red states.

CHAPTER 23
2016

BOOM CHICAGO HIRED TO TEACH DUTCH PRIME MINISTER HOW TO BE FUNNY

2016 was a rough year in America for politics. With Donald Trump on the rise, smarts and civility in politics were vanishing exponentially, day by day. Trump was like a grotesque orange bowling ball, demolishing opponents and rules of decorum in one strike. He attacked the press. He claimned Mexico sent us their rapists. He lied so casually, about everything. Until Trump, the truth had always been a theoretical goal, if not always attained. Now, for so much of the American electorate, facts could easily be alternative, and news was suddenly fake. Meanwhile, fans of Bernie Sanders known as "Bernie Bros" weren't supporting Hillary Clinton enough to stop Trump. There was trolling on Twitter, and a steady stream of crazy propaganda planted by Russian hackers clogging our Facebook feeds.[58]

At Boom Chicago, the shocking developments of the mid-2010s couldn't help but make it into our shows. 2015's new arrivals—actors E.R. Fightmaster, Woody Fu, and Ian Owens, along with new artistic director/early Boom Chicago alumnus Sue Gillan—had seen the horror evolving stateside by the time they got to Boom. In 2016, new (old) artistic director Jim Woods and frosh cast members Karel Ebergen, Cené Hale, Else Soelling,

---

58 We assume similar things were happening on Instagram and Snapchat, but we're too old to actually know.

and Josh Rachford had escaped to Amsterdam just as Trump's political shitshow of a campaign had started to go positively nuclear.

In the wake of this unprecedented decline of Western civilization, Pep, Greg, and Andrew created a show, "Trump Up the Volume," that didn't stop until 2019. So with the mess exploding in the United States, you'd think that the last thing the Dutch would do is copy anything having to do with contemporary American politics. But lo and behold, 2016 was the year of the first Dutch Correspondents' Dinner—a fine tradition for Netherlands politics to borrow.

Founded in 1921, the White House Correspondents' Dinner has become an annual tradition (that is, until 2017, when Trump refused to participate). The event brings together the president of the United States and the reporters who cover the White House, where they lay down their gloves and have a civilized dinner—all while comedians brutally roast everyone in the room on national television. The president also gets up and does his own score-settling roast, with friendly and hostile press, political allies, and foes alike getting hilariously shanked. For one night, partisanship disappears into a boozy evening of quips and zings. It's a truce, really—kind of like in World War One when the English, French, and German troops held an unofficial ceasefire around Christmas to play football.

The person in the Netherlands who most wanted to make Holland's own version of the White House Correspondents' Dinner a reality was Twan Huys (pronounced "house"). A respected journalist and TV presenter, Huys had always been inspired by America since his days as a US correspondent. Indeed, he brought *College Tour*—a show based on American-style town hall meetings—to Dutch television. (Ironically, a one-hour deep-dive interview show featuring highbrow guests like *College Tour* is actually difficult to find on US networks.) Huys had been dreaming about a Dutch Correspondents' Dinner for some time. He'd even approached Mark Rutte, the prime minister of the Netherlands, not long after he'd been elected in 2010. Rutte seemed slightly interested in Huys's proposal, but remained noncommittal.

Then, in 2011, when Huys interviewed Prime Minister Rutte as a *College Tour* guest, Twan played him a video made by a previous *College Tour* guest, Seth Meyers. In it, Meyers challenged Rutte to step up and meet the press at a Dutch Correspondents' Dinner. Seth, who'd hosted a White House Correspondents' Dinner by then, was happy to help. This would be Rutte's chance, Seth teased, to show it was the Dutch, not the Germans, who had a sense of humor about themselves. The double-team attack of Twan and Seth finally convinced Rutte that there was no turning back. On camera, Rutte agreed to a Dutch Correspondents' Dinner; Twan quickly put out his hand to shake on the deal.

Alas, it would take years to make the Dutch Correspondents' Dinner a reality. First, a national election got in the way. Then there were another few years of slow responses and calendar conflicts from the man at the top. Rutte was getting, if not cold feet, chilled feet. Many in the press were skeptical, though Twan kept the idea alive. Finally, just before Christmas 2015, the stars aligned and a date was set for the following February.

Being an innate politics junkie, the son of renowned social scientist Charlie Moskos, and resident hustler of all things Boom Chicago, Andrew saw an angle to exploit. After all, Boom Chicago had already taught many authentic Dutch people what real funny is. Why not, pray tell, the prime minister himself? It was a great way to give back to the country he'd already given so much to.

Andrew sprang into action, approaching Rutte's people offering Boom's services to the prime minister. Andrew made his case to the RVD, the Dutch government's information service which serves as the official spokesbody representing the prime minister to the electorate. Andrew explained that he had the most experience with the actual US White House Correspondents' Dinner than, well . . . anyone else in the Netherlands. It was a funny thing to boast about, but he wasn't lying. Andrew had watched many Correspondents' Dinners, and was privy to Seth Meyers's preparations the year he hosted the event. Most significantly, Andrew had been in attendance at the most infamous White House Correspondents' Dinner in 2011—where Seth's and Barack Obama's brutal roasts of Donald Trump would go on to change history.

Just after Christmas, the RVD got back to Andrew. The answer was yes: he'd gotten the job, but on one condition. The prime minister insisted on paying for Andrew's services himself. He didn't think it was appropriate to spend taxpayer money on a *comedy* consultant. Seth found it hilarious that Boom Chicago would actually be sending the prime minister a bill.

Andrew Moskos: In 2011, when Seth hosted that year's White House Correspondents' Dinner (pro bono, I might add), he was given a table of ten seats. After his fiancée and family (including Josh Meyers) were taken care of, there were just a few open spots left. Seth called and said he wouldn't be at the White House Correspondents' Dinner at all if it wasn't for Boom Chicago, so he kindly offered Saskia and me two of the cherished seats. It was one of the best days of our lives—if ultimately one of the worst days for the world.

When we arrived in Washington, Seth was already in the hotel's business center, hard at work putting finishing touches on the night's material. He and some trusted writers from *SNL* had been working on it for weeks in New York. Still, Seth wasn't satisfied.

Seth Meyers: It was just about preparation and having really great writers writing stuff for me. We put a lot of time into it, and just wrote a ton of jokes until we walked out of that room with the feeling that it was going to work. You can't guarantee how jokes are going to go, but you can internally embarrass yourself that you couldn't have worked any harder.

Andrew Moskos: The hotel staff were impressed with Seth's diligence as well. "We didn't see Jay Leno here at the business center," a staff member observed dryly to Seth—an insider's zing about Leno's underwhelming Correspondents' Dinner performance in 2010.

Saskia Maas: Before dinner, we got to meet the Obamas. We were brought to a room with about a hundred other insiders to shake the Obamas' hands. When it was our turn, we were allotted thirty seconds of small talk with the president and his wife. I told them Seth got his start at our theater in Amsterdam. "Amsterdam?" Michelle said. "You did a great job with Seth," President Obama added. "Shall we get a picture?" The way Obama said it, it was like he wanted a picture with *us*, not the other way around. Then Andrew quickly discovered a problem. When you take a picture with the Obamas, what do you do with your hands? He thought it seemed wrong to put his arm around the president's back, so he left them hanging awkwardly at his side.

Andrew Moskos: Saskia, however, went right for Michelle's waist, and looked much more comfortable. After the photos were taken, Saskia and I headed with Josh and his parents to their table, while Seth headed to the stage to have dinner alongside Michelle Obama. After dinner, Obama was first to speak. That tradition came about so that the president didn't have to follow a professional comedian who may have anticipated his jokes and do them better. But Obama didn't need any help that night: he was *on*. This was his third Correspondents' Dinner: he knew what to do.

Seth Meyers: That night was *extra* as far as executing under pressure. Having to follow Obama was intimidating—I'm proud I was able to just hold my own. It's not like following George W. Bush or Bill Clinton: Obama is like an actual stand-up comedian.

Andrew Moskos: Obama had natural timing, good lines—and that night, really laid into Donald Trump. Obama had just released his birth certificate after trolling from Trump and his nativist "birther" movement. Clearly not a fan, Obama frequently had the fact-based press laughing it up at Trump's expense. He did a great, classy job of utterly ridiculing the idea that someone like Trump could ever hope to be president: "Recently, in an episode of *Celebrity Apprentice*, at the steak house, the men's cooking team did not impress the judges from Omaha Steaks. And there was a lot of blame to go around. But you, Mr. Trump, recognized that the real problem was a lack of leadership. And so ultimately, you didn't blame Lil Jon or Meatloaf—you fired *Gary Busey*. And these are the kind of decisions that would keep me up at night."

Good stuff. Funny stuff. Presidential stuff. Then Seth took his turn. I know we're biased, but just about every joke Seth did landed, and landed hard. Staring right at Obama two seats away, Seth jabbed humorously about how he'd aged since getting elected in 2008: "When you were sworn in, you looked like the guy from the Old Spice commercials. Now you look like Louis Gossett *Senior*. I've never said this to anyone before—but maybe you should start smoking again."

Pep Rosenfeld: Seth also made a joke that night about Osama bin Laden's whereabouts that got a big laugh from Obama. The next day, the world would learn that the president had just given the order to kill bin Laden.

Andrew Moskos: This was indeed more serious than any decision made on *Celebrity Apprentice*. As such, Seth leaned into his roast of Trump: "Donald Trump has been saying that he will run for president as a Republican—which is surprising, since I just assumed he was running as a joke." By lucky coincidence, a TV camera captured the perfect shot of Trump's stone-faced scowl while everyone in the room (and the world) laughed at his expense. It would only get worse from there.

"Donald Trump said recently he has a great relationship with the Blacks," Seth continued, repeating Trump's strange habit of saying "the Blacks." "But unless the Blacks are a family of white people, I bet he's mistaken." The crowd roared while Trump sat perfectly still, glaring at Seth: you could see him already planning his revenge for Obama and Seth's double-barreled humiliation. Although he denies it, it's been rumored that Trump's public shaming at that White House Correspondents' Dinner was what actually motivated him to run for real in 2016.

Pep Rosenfeld: Thanks a lot, Seth.

Seth Meyers: It was an awesome night. The profile of the event is always big—but then there was this weird situation with Trump, which is one reason the 2011 Correspondents' Dinner was so memorable. Trump was in the audience, and both Obama and myself realized that he was a deserving target. Obviously, how history turned out after that night makes it a little bit less fun to think about. But as comedians, we have to humiliate terrible people—that's the only thing they know. Moving forward, we can't stop making fun of bad people just because they might run for president.

Andrew Moskos: A few months later, I went to the Hague with Dutch comedian friend Wilko Terwijn to meet with the RVD about Rutte's speech. When we got there, officials handed us eight pages of jokes the civil servants had come up with themselves. Nervously, I read them . . . And actually, their jokes were good, and they had an insider perspective I didn't. Some of Rutte's best jokes of the night came from that official government document!

After Wilko and I spent some time coming up with our own set of jokes, we went back to the Hague to present them to Rutte himself. We arrived at our meeting at Het Torentje (the official office of the prime minister of Netherlands), which was super exciting: this was the Dutch equivalent of, you know, hanging out with the prez in the Oval Office. Het Torentje—in English, "The Little Tower," pronounced "tor-en-che"—is supposed to be small and unimpressive, but that's not true. It's a good size, and has an interestingly round layout, much like the Oval Office. Another good connection between the two countries.

As we presented our IDs to the guard, we both had shit-eating grins on our faces. Sitting in the waiting room, it settled in: *Wow, we're really here!* Soon, the prime minister welcomed us into his inner sanctum with a firm, welcoming handshake. Like Obama, Rutte displayed a true politician's ability to actually (seem to) care as he asked us questions. He apologized that he'd never been to Boom Chicago, but said he had heard great things about us. "And I liked your SpongeBob video," he continued—either having seen it, or having been briefed about it. *Whatever.* It all felt very genuine.

I remember vividly the prime minister reading aloud the jokes we'd prepared for him. "People say that I have no vision," Rutte intoned as he scanned our pages. "But I don't see it." First time through, he rushed, blowing the gag's timing. "Prime Minister Rutte . . ." I began. "Call me Mark," he interjected with such intense eye contact I got a little tingle. "So, Mark," I went on, "after you say, 'They say I have no vision,' you need to pause—then look up for a second like you're confused before delivering the next line. That's the way to make the joke hit." "Of course!" he responded. Sure enough, the second time through, he delivered it 100 percent better. I mean, Prime Minister Mark Rutte takes direction better than many Boom actors. Who knew?

The whole meeting went really well. Mark—my pal Mark, we were good friends now—was a natural, and wasn't scared of the harsher jokes. He understood the gig: be nice enough so that people didn't get too mad—but mean enough that people couldn't believe what he said. This was going to work!

We returned a week later for rehearsal. The RVD had set up a theater, with lights and a podium, inside the Hague's Binnenhof complex which houses the Dutch government. Before we started, however, we all dined on Indonesian food. When a staffer appeared with plastic bags full of takeout containers, the prime minister jumped up suddenly. "Wait, we need beer!" my homey Mark announced before disappearing into a top-secret room with a top-secret beer fridge. He returned with four perfectly frigid Heinekens—which he proceeded to open by slamming the bottle tops on the stately conference table's edge. Okay, that last bit didn't really happen, but Rutte did seem pretty at home in the Binnenhof with his secret beer fridge.

To follow the "I don't have any vision" bit, we wrote a patriotic, "This is what I believe . . ." speech—but with zero specifics. Coming after the previous joke, the gag here was about the lack of content, and therefore vision. When Rutte read it, however, it fell flat. "Mark, this is the part in *The West Wing* where the president finally connects with the American people with a perfect, inspiring speech," I noted. "You need to deliver it like it's the most important speech of your life—even though it's ridiculous."

One week later, it was showtime for the first-ever Dutch Correspondents' Dinner. The parliamentary press was there. Politicians who couldn't identify a celebrity were there. Celebrities who couldn't identify a politician were there. Dinner was served; wine was flowing. Wilko and I were seated at the RVD's table, joined by Pep and Saskia. Twan Huys took the stage and introduced the event. He played a video of great moments from the White House Correspondents' Dinner. There was Bill Clinton, gesturing with a closed fist; Bush, smiling with squinted eyes; Obama, doing classic Obama—and then next up was Seth's video from *College Tour* urging the prime minister to do his own correspondents' dinner. After Seth brought down the house, Twan introduced the guest of honor: "Ladies and gentlemen, Prime Minister Mark Rutte!"

Mark took the stage. "Tonight is an unusual business model," he said, setting up one of our jokes. "Journalists are being asked to pay to hear the prime minister speak, when on most days of the year, they can have that for free. It's kind of like asking people to pay for a newspaper." The media laughed especially hard because, unfortunately, it rang all too true.

As we say in "the business," Mark absolutely killed. The success of the event quickly made itself clear: three million people watched the Dutch Correspondents' Dinner, the ratings rivaling those of the Dutch football team playing in the World Cup. The press was gushing too, and Rutte's party actually went up three seats in the polls. Soon after, Mark wrote us a handwritten thank-you note—then transferred our payment to us from his own personal bank account.

Pep Rosenfeld: Somewhere, Seth was shaking his head . . .

Andrew Moskos: A few years earlier, Seth thanked us for helping him along in his journey to the White House Correspondents' Dinner. Now it was our turn to thank Seth for his role in getting us the Dutch Correspondents' Dinner. It felt like a new era for political comedy had arrived. Presidents and prime ministers had taken on the role of comedians, intentionally or otherwise, and late-night talk show hosts were replacing the traditional media in bringing news directly to the people. In the 2004 and 2008 elections, *SNL* proved especially influential, and a lot of that was due to the show's head writer, Seth. In 2004, *SNL* and Seth certainly influenced the volatile political conversation. I mean, Seth's impression of John Kerry portrayed him as wooden and boring, cementing that image in the minds of the show's nearly nine million viewers.

Pep Rosenfeld: To be fair, Kerry *also* portrayed himself that way.

Andrew Moskos: Then in 2008, the brilliant Tina Fey created her famous Sarah Palin character—also with a little help from her *SNL* colleague Seth. Looking and sounding exactly like the vice presidential candidate, Fey's Palin was sometimes indistinguishable from the real one. Her caricature, replayed tens of millions of times on YouTube, helped convince a nation that Palin was just too dumb to get anywhere near the Oval Office. *SNL*'s "Weekend Update" under Seth often shaped discussion around national issues. A piece by Seth Meyers or Stephen Colbert could now be more influential on public opinion than an op-ed piece in the *New York Times*.

Pep Rosenfeld: Of course, we loved watching Seth take on Trump, Palin, and other not-so-sacred cows on *SNL*. When Seth took over *Late Night* and got to finally host his own show, though, our excitement reached another level. We even went to New York to be there for his first taping of *Late Night*. It was fun to be back at NBC's 30 Rock: I hadn't been there since my time at *SNL*.

Andrew Moskos: Pep, did being at 30 Rock bring you back to your own *SNL* experience?

Pep Rosenfeld: Well, yeah. During the "Weekend Update" segment, I'd always go down to where the audience sat to hear how the jokes played in the room. It was there that I had my one and only chat with Lorne Michaels, *SNL*'s famed creator and executive producer. When I laughed at a joke during "Weekend Update"—I don't even think it was mine—suddenly I felt this hand on my shoulder. It was Lorne! Leaning in real close, he whispered two words quietly in my ear: "Be discreet." That was the sole conversation I ever had with Lorne Michaels during my time working at *SNL*.

Andrew Moskos: To be fair, you *do* have a super-loud laugh.

Pep Rosenfeld: So we're sitting there with Josh and Seth's parents when Seth says, "I'm so psyched to have my family here supporting me." We looked up at the studio monitor and all ten of us are on camera! Of course, my parents were watching too. I hadn't told them I was visiting the United States, and now they were pissed.

Seth Meyers: I would've never gotten onto *SNL* without Pep having been there first. And it was great having Andrew and Saskia at the Correspondents' Dinner. That's a night I'm particularly proud of. When I look back at the singular most important gigs in my life, there's always pressure, but you just prepare as much as possible and then commit to it—just like we did whenever we'd walk onstage at Boom Chicago.

CHAPTER 24
2017

TRUMP UP THE VOLUME: AMERICA EMBRACES FASCISM, NETHERLANDS REJECTS IT (SORT OF)

I f 2008 was the year we wish we could've seen an alternative time line, 2017 was the year that felt, at first, like it actually *was* an alternative time line. And not a good one. A bad one, like in *Back to the Future II*, where idiot bully–turned–casino magnate Biff Tannen has turned wholesome Hill Valley into a corrupt shithole.

Sound familiar? It should. Screenwriter Bob Gale admitted he'd based alternative-reality Biff on the lives-in-his-own-reality Donald Trump of the "greed decade" era. Yes, even back in the 1980s when the movie was written, Trump was a larger-than-life douche worthy of satire. Even more strange, in that movie Gale also predicted that the Chicago Cubs would finally win the World Series after a hundred years. And what happened the year that the world derailed into the dystopia of Trump's presidency? The Cubs actually won. I mean, the Cubs win the World Series *and* Trump wins the presidential election? Come on, guys. No audience would believe it!

But in the Netherlands circa 2017, Dutch people didn't fall for their country's homegrown Trump equivalents. Holland had a window to make *onze eigen* nationalist wingnut Geert Wilders prime minister. Thankfully, that alternative reality never became actual reality—though for a while there, it was touch and go. One of the most controversial figures in Dutch society, Wilders hit a nerve Holland would prefer not to admit it has with his relentless Islamophobia and vehement anti-EU stance. But then the whole world got to experience Trump in action as proof of concept. Seeing Trump's intolerant chaos, Dutch voters seemed to think, *Hang on a sec, maybe putting an insane populist into office is a bad idea.*

Comparing Wilders to then–prime minister Rutte, the nation let out a collective sigh and, being Dutch, found the correct answer in compromise: "Okay, we're not thrilled with Rutte—but we saw what happened when America ordered the weirdest thing on the menu. We'll stick with what we know, thank you, and have the potatoes. Next!" At Boom Chicago, we like to think the Dutch eventually put their support behind Rutte and his VVD party because he'd humanized himself so well during the Dutch Correspondents' Dinner the previous year. "I wonder which of my jokes was the tipping point that pushed voters over to Rutte's side and saved a nation?" Andrew would joke.

At Boom, we stayed the course amid the chaos of 2017, saving any big changes for the following year. That's when Brian Tjon Ajong departed, passing the theater's baton over to Emil Struijker-Boudier. Meanwhile, we'd hired Boom's first-ever British actors as cast members: Simon Lukacs, Tamar Broadbent, and Rhys Collier, joining the sole American addition, stage manager Lizz (Biddy) Kemery (who, staying on trend, was living in London at the time).

While big changes loomed on the horizon, maintaining the status quo in 2017 was tough enough. The world had gotten used to having the White House occupied by someone who made "Grab 'em by the pussy" a meme—whose desire to build a wall between America and Mexico seemed a bit, uh, Captain-Ahab-versus-Moby-Dickish (that is, if Moby Dick had been the Great *Brown* Whale, and with an emphasis on "dickish"). In response, worldwide movements coalesced—#MeToo, the Women's March, *Dear White People, The Handmaid's Tale, onze eigen*

Jordan Peele's *Get Out*—determined in art and activism to prevent white-male nationalism from becoming our new normal.

For comedy, Trump proved an insistent target. Making fun of Trump is like wiping your ass too early; you want to get everything, but the shit keeps coming. Seth Meyers's "A Closer Look" found its voice as the place to go for deep dives into the latest Trump outrage. Jimmy Kimmel grew passionate about health care on his show, while on *The Late Show*, Stephen Colbert found a new anger underneath his nightly monologue, which seemed to get longer and longer as he discovered his own anti-Trump groove. But perhaps the most biting Trump satire was Comedy Central's *The President Show*. It dared to ask the question on everyone's lips: what if comedian Anthony Atamanuik's deliciously troubled Donald Trump hosted a talk show from the Oval Office, with Boom alum Pete Grosz's milquetoast theocrat Mike Pence on second-banana sidekick duty (à la Andy Richter, Ed McMahon, and Tarik Davis)?

Watching Atamanuik and Grosz speak truth not *to* power, but *as* power, proved cathartic. Here in Amsterdam, Greg Shapiro—whose own epic Trump impression would go viral via his "Netherlands Second" video—offered up similar vibes in the live shows at Boom where he played the forty-fifth POTUS. In one scene, audiences were unleashed to ask Shapiro-as-Trump unscripted questions about politics, the news, or the president's personal life. The crowd got real satisfaction hearing Greg's scathingly truthful answers—but then again, truth really was stranger than fiction in those days.

Pep Rosenfeld: It's hard, really, trying to figure out the worst president of the United States. I mean, people forget how awful Bush was. Think about the Iraq War . . . The guy started a war because he was *cocky*. Dubya was really bad. And, of course, you gotta have Ronald Reagan in there. Trump, though, proved a quadruple threat—setting new standards for awful-conservative chic with his unforgettable mix of incompetence, narcissism, racism . . . and just being a goddamn crook!

Andrew Moskos: I put myself on Trump's mailing list for personal-research reasons. What he was sending to the MAGA faithful was worse than his tweets. I'm like, *Oh my God, you are really indoctrinating these idiots.*

Greg Shapiro: Trump is definitely the worst. Thankfully, he was often ineffective, but his presence alone was still bad for society.

Pep Rosenfeld: The uptick in hate crimes was real. What he did to the environment was real. What he did with tax cuts and net neutrality was real. And demonizing those who attacked him in the press and social media, that was fucking real.

Andrew Moskos: Interfering with the Justice Department, making tax policy to benefit himself, owning hotels on federal property . . . For foreign dignitaries, it became de rigueur to stay at Trump's hotel, or it was like an insult to the king. Hotels are the best money-laundering operation ever. Booking a $10,000-a-night hotel suite is like paying a bribe—but it's legal. They'll even give you a receipt. With everything that Trump did, the only goal was to benefit him and the rich people giving him money. And he was really lying about everything. To me, that's a different level of shitty. And don't get me started on January 6 . . . And who knows what has happened since this book has gone to print? But of course, I have to admit, Trump *is* a comedy gold mine!

Pep Rosenfeld: Boom Chicago's humor has always been topical, so we *love* tackling Trump.

Andrew Moskos: We started doing "Trump Up the Volume" in

2016. The initial plan was that the show would end on November 8, after Hillary inevitably won. Unfortunately, it didn't happen the way we'd planned it. But after a rewrite and relaunch following Trump's inauguration in January 2017, it's become one of our longest-running, most successful shows.

Pep Rosenfeld: Greg and I love doing "Trump Up the Volume." We come in early and bounce ideas off each other to write new jokes about whatever outrage Trump perpetuated that week. Then, hanging our heads in disgust, we share it all with the audience. It's like group therapy—except, you know, funny. Don't get me wrong: I'd rather have *not* done the show if it meant I could've instead spent these years struggling to find humor in the dull efficiency of President Hillary Clinton.

Andrew Moskos: Greg has gotten famous for his Trump impression in the show—it's astonishing. When Greg becomes Trump, he busts out in perfectly incoherent Trumpian cadence and syntax. It's so accurate, you can hear the audience gasp.

Pep Rosenfeld: Greg's able to make fun of Trump while *being* Trump. Political impressions have become a kind of mini industry for Greg—he's just a master of them. Greg did a great Bill Clinton, an excellent Obama, and a superb George W. Bush. They haven't been equally profitable, however. He was getting booked all the time for his Clinton impression. Everyone wanted a good Bill Clinton, so Greg became the Bill Clinton of Holland: he even played Bill in an insurance commercial, and in an ad for Amstel beer too. But then George Bush won the presidency, and even though Greg also does a great George Bush, his phone didn't ring once. Nobody wanted Dubya in their beer commercials. Then Obama happened, and it was back to the good ol' days . . . Now here we are with Trump.

Ike Barinholtz: Working at Boom Chicago, you learn about the world in different ways than your comedy-scene peers back home. You're living in a European country, traveling all the time: that affects your humor. I mean, when Seth started doing "Weekend Update" on *SNL*, with his global perspective, he sometimes came off like a real news anchor. Seth is a political junkie who understands the whole world better because he lived in Europe and experienced different perspectives. Comedians like Amber and Seth have more dimension *because* they made that choice to broaden their horizons. That choice gave them—and all of us—an even deeper, more objective perspective on what it means to be American as a global citizen. That's extended into Seth's political commentary during the Trump era too—that depth is what just makes him so good. Well, that, and he's funny.

Ruben van der Meer: I mean, my kids watch "A Closer Look with Seth Meyers" every Saturday morning instead of cartoons.

Pep Rosenfeld: I'm not sure if Seth will be psyched or horrified that "A Closer Look" is your kids' cartoon substitute: "Papa, we don't want to watch K3 videos—we want Seth Meyers!"

Andrew Moskos: It's the same with Pete Grosz and Allison Silverman and the groundbreaking work they did on *The Daily Show* and *The Colbert Report*. Their broader vision helped them make political comedy that stood out. Those were among the first comedic shows to put political commentary front and center like that. It's similar to what Jordan's doing now too. He and someone like Amber, they're these sort of philosophical, cultural lightning rods in the way that, say, Chris Rock and Richard Pryor were for earlier generations. Amber was amazing with what she did on *Late Night*. And Jordan making *Get Out* really moved the needle when we needed it moved the most. If you step outside of your comfort zone and come to Amsterdam, it's easier to see what America really looks like from the outside.

Peter Grosz: What's great about Boom Chicago is that you can make fun of Americans to an international crowd, which breaks you out of traditional ways of seeing politics and social satire. You get a chance to look at the world from an international outsider's perspective. That perspective doesn't exist at Second City. There's nothing you'd do on that stage about the way Dutch people feel about Belgians, or what we *really* think about the Germans. I mean, when I was at Boom, we'd do stuff about, like, Hong Kong returning to British rule as it was happening. In Chicago, you'd never do a sketch like that.

Suzi Barrett: That was always the cool thing about Boom Chicago: their model was, *Poke fun at everyone—as long as we poke fun at ourselves first.* So, let's spend the first part of the show just taking the piss out of Americans, out of our president, out of our political model, out of our imperialism. After that, everybody else is fair game. At the end of the day, the audience will have laughed at themselves *and* us—and then we can all have a beer together. It's the sort of thing that's necessary and healing for these times.

Andrew Moskos: Apart from Trump, probably the most significant event of that year for us was the release of *Get Out*. It was Jordan Peele's first movie as a director, and he absolutely killed it.

Pep Rosenfeld: *Get Out* was kind of perfect, because left-leaning America was like, "Trump's not *our* fault, he's *their* fault—them and their racism!" And Jordan's movie was like, "Yeah . . . but I kinda feel like there's still some racism on the left too."

In our Trump show, Greg and I do a bit about gerrymandering[59] where I say, "I love Obama, I voted for him twice. I would've voted for him a third time if I could." Then Jordan called out that phrase in *Get Out*. I actually met Obama in 2018 at an event in Finland. I shook his hand and told him that, if not for Jordan's movie, I'd be telling him I'd have voted for him a third time. He looked me in the eye, caught the reference, and gave me a full-on Obama laugh. Thanks, Jordan!

Heather Anne Campbell: At Boom, I'd be hanging out with Jordan, and he'd go, "Hey, have you seen *Martyrs*?" And I'd say, "Um, no." And then I'd end up watching the worst, most scary movie of my life. I'd always be like, "Fuck you, dude! Why did you do that to me?"

Josh Meyers: Jordan has been a student of horror and film in general for years, and paying so much attention is now paying dividends. Horror, sci-fi, war movies—like Kubrick, Jordan will eventually tackle every genre and put his own weird stamp on them.

Jordan Peele: Basically, I was going for what I've always been into. I loved how Kubrick movies never obeyed tone or genre—like *A Clockwork Orange* and *The Shining* are shocking and horrific, but they have these moments where you can't help but laugh. And Steven Spielberg too: stuff like *Poltergeist* was a complete inspiration. I just love that Spielberg was able to make movies that were so artfully entertaining. That really influenced me.

Andrew Moskos: *Get Out* became bigger than just a movie. It's amazing how it struck a chord and stayed relevant as part of the conversation. *Get Out* was like the Villa Volta of horror movies: seeing it altered how you see the world. And then people get on

---

59 The tradition of drawing political districts to particularly favor one party was actually named after a guy named Gerry—the first gerrymander-er, as it were.

the ride again and again. It was especially funny seeing people contorting themselves trying to figure out how to categorize it— like that whole controversy about how *Get Out* was nominated as "Best Comedy" for the Golden Globes instead of drama.

Ike Barinholtz: *Get Out* was always going to be funny. The great thing about it is that it's a true horror movie as well. It gives you everything you want from a horror movie—but because it's Jordan, of course it's funny and socially relevant. There's a huge message, all while totally subverting the expected genres.

Andrew Moskos: I was laughing all through *Get Out*. It's the kind of movie that makes you laugh because you're uncomfortable, which is so satisfying.

Ike Barinholtz: It was amazing watching the Golden Globes that year. I mean, Amber and Seth tackled #MeToo and Trump and everything totally correctly and astutely.

Jordan Peele: Amber and Seth were incredible. They hit all the right subversive, perceptive notes of the moment.

Andrew Moskos: So between Trump and all the shit Jordan pointed out . . . I mean, Amsterdam isn't perfect—but America at the end of the 2010s? Ugh, no thanks.

Pep Rosenfeld: Half a decade on, I don't see how it's getting better. The country's more divided than ever, and the politics seems ridiculously broken. Thirty percent of the country thinks evolution, global warming, and the front-page story of any day's *Washington Post* is a made-up fairy tale—but that Trump was a genius, and tax cuts for the rich really work!

You can actually plot the decline in American politics by the bits in the election shows we've done. In 2004, we were talking about hacked voting machines and attack ads. In 2008, it was racism and the fact that red states and blue states hate each other. In 2012, we ended the show with the red states and the blue states saying, "Fuck it, let's split up into two countries." We were, like, seven years early in predicting the split of the country. Sometimes it sucks being Nostradamus.

Greg Shapiro: We ended that 2012 show with dueling anthems for the two new countries, Redmerica and the BlueSA:

From "My Big Fat American Election," 2012

[To the tune of "The Star-Spangled Banner"]
Oh say, can you see? We are finally free
We're the Blue S of A! Intellectual and gay . . .

[To the tune of "America" from West Side Story*]*
We don't pay tax in Redmerica
Our jaws are slack in Redmerica
No one smokes crack in Redmerica.
Kick out the Blacks in Redmerica . . .

Pep Rosenfeld: Trump is like the cherry on the shit sundae that the Republican Party has been serving since the 1990s . . . or 1980s? Or would that be the '70s?

Greg Shapiro: The day Trump was sworn in, we showed his actual inauguration on the big screen while Pep and I did commentary. The idea was we would heckle and make jokes. Then we realized, "Hey, this isn't funny. It's heartbreaking."

Pep Rosenfeld: I'm a super nerd. In high school, Andrew and I were both "mathletes."

Andrew Moskos: A mathlete is a lot like being an athlete in that it uses many of the same letters.

Pep Rosenfeld: That's not just something Tina Fey made up for *Mean Girls*. That's a real thing at my high school. And I was pretty good! Not the best of the best, but I pulled my weight on the relay squad. And yes, there was a math relay squad.

So we explained that the election was like nerds versus jocks—and that unlike in the movies, jocks sometimes win. We kept saying that we shouldn't get too confident that Hillary will win, that Trump might win it . . .

Greg Shapiro: But we meant it as a joke. It was supposed to be a joke.

Pep Rosenfeld: It didn't turn out that way.

From "Angry White Men: Trump Up the Volume," 2016

Greg: Politics isn't a civilized exchange of points of view, and may the best idea win. No, it's a popularity contest. And you know who wins a popularity contest? The popular one. Like the suave bad boy . . .

Pep: Bill Clinton.

Greg: The handsome, intelligent stranger . . .

Pep: Barack Obama.

Greg: You know who doesn't win? The nerd in the classroom who reminds the teacher, "You forgot to assign us homework." Not very popular!

Pep: And Hillary is that nerd.

Greg Shapiro: Of course, we might do it loudest in the United States, but right-wing populism is definitely a thing right here in Holland as well.

From "Trump Up the Volume," 2018

Greg: Dutch people? You like laughing at Trump—this crazy right-wing populist with crazy hair could only happen in America, right? Oh, wait—here in the Netherlands, you've got Geert Wilders.

Pep: By the way, Dutch folks, there's another reason not to laugh at us about Trump. It's not just that Wilders came first. Though he did. It's more like—if you're honest with yourselves—you should look in the mirror and admit it: Donald Trump . . . he's your fault. I'm serious—Dutch people totally created Donald Trump. Hear me out. Donald Trump got rich by crooked real estate deals in Manhattan . . .

Greg: Just like Dutch people.

Pep: Donald Trump became a household name when he was a star of reality TV . . .

Greg: Which was created by Dutch people.

Pep: And Donald Trump plays on racism in America, which all goes back to when white people bought Black people . . .

Greg: From Dutch people. Dutch people created Donald

Trump! Why do you think he paints his face orange every day? He's like, "I'm constantly ready for King's Day!"

Pep Rosenfeld: While Trump continues to do his thing, Boom Chicago does ours: make fun of the situation—and yet hold the Dutch accountable for everything. For three decades, this approach seems to have worked out okay . . .

CHAPTER 25
2018–2023

BOOM TURNS TWENTY-FIVE—AND THEN
TED LASSO TAKES OVER THE WORLD

In 2018, Boom Chicago celebrated our twenty-fifth year with a blowout celebration—bringing back alumni from every era for two sold-out shows at Amsterdam's legendary Royal Theatre Carré.[60]

We're proud of our Rozentheater, where Boom had been happily ensconced for half a decade. But celebrating our silver anniversary at the glorious Carré—the classiest, most historic theater in town—meant we'd really arrived. It was an honor to play there. Bringing our show into that space made us think maybe we'd gone from being merely Boom Chicago to finally becoming Amsterdam's *onze eigen* Boom Chicago.

Seth Meyers opened the night with a riotously received stand-up set. Then over two more sets, the Carré stage was mobbed with Boom alums improvising together like old times. Joining Seth were Colton Dunn, Ike Barinholtz, Brendan Hunt, Kay Cannon, Lolu Ajayi, Ruben van der Meer, Josh Meyers, Horace Cohen, and seventy more of the brilliant actors who've graced our stages. Even Dutch comedy great Arjen Lubach was on hand. He freestyle rapped, though the Nickel Bag has nothing to worry about. Performing with these alums and friends was such a memorable way to ring in Boom Chicago's first quarter

---

60 The proceeds from our twenty-fifth-anniversary shows benefited InterActing, Boom's nonprofit program for teens with autism.

century of existence. It was the end of an era, and the beginning of a new one.

And then . . . something really weird happened. In the five years that have passed since Boom celebrated our twenty-fifth birthday, our alums soared to heights that we never could've predicted. Indeed, 2018 to 2023 brought forth an entirely new golden age of Boom Chicago—one that spans all generations and eras. I mean, we were high-fiving like crazy when Seth got on *SNL* and Ike and Josh launched their post-Boom careers on *MADtv*. But recent history proved a quantum leap for the ambitious talents who played with Boom from our Leidseplein days to the Rozentheater. Boomers weren't just having success, they were changing the game—carving out their own lanes with equal amounts of quality control and irreverence.

Seth continued to mine the most vital (and viral) political conversation with *Late Night* and "A Closer Look." Facing the constant assaults on democracy and hate-filled headwinds of a toxic Trump presidency unlike any other, Seth and his gifted *Late Night* crew took Johan Cruyff's adage "Every disadvantage has its advantage" to heart—producing their most trenchant, funniest work yet. Seth's POV provided the antidote when the world needed perspective on our bizarre new normal; if anything, tackling COVID seemed to give Seth even greater focus. Best of all, Seth created *Corrections*—the Emmy-nominated YouTube series where he hilariously "corrects" his show's mistakes that week.

Seth also championed crucial new voices during this period. He put his money where his mouth is, from *Late Night* and the much-discussed historic hire of *onze eigen* Amber Ruffin to his Sethmaker Shoemeyers Productions company—responsible for creating the ingenious *Documentary Now!* series, NBC's *A.P. Bio*, the amazing Netflix special *Seth Meyers: Lobby Baby*,[61] and

---

61 So named after the insane true story of Seth's wife Alexi giving birth in the lobby of their apartment building.

helping to develop—you guessed it—*The Amber Ruffin Show*.

Jordan, meanwhile, went from winning the Academy Award for Best Screenplay for *Get Out* at the 2018 Oscars to becoming a one-man cinematic industry unto himself. He followed up *Get Out* with the mindfuck horror of *Us* in 2019 and the Western-flavored sci-fi of *Nope* in 2022—both worldwide critical and box-office smashes endlessly debated and dissected across the Internet. Jordan is now a groundbreaking Tarantino-level auteur, his every new release a viral event—as well as an innovative mogul expanding his Monkeypaw Productions empire into a gusher of freakout must-see TV, from *Lovecraft Country* and his *Twilight Zone* reboot to the truly batshit Tracy Morgan vehicle *The Last O.G.*

Boom alumni are now producing their best work ever—simultaneously hilarious and meaningful in its commentary on our increasingly strange existence. Kay Cannon followed up her 2018 humanist comedy hit *Blockers* (and the standout performance she drew out of fellow Boomer Ike Barinholtz) with an inclusive twist on *Cinderella* in 2021. Heather Anne Campbell is now a writing-and-producing big shot on Adult Swim's mind-melting hit *Rick and Morty*. Holly Walker was nominated for an Emmy for her work on *A Black Lady Sketch Show*—which has led to her becoming a staff writer for *The Amber Ruffin Show*. Before Tarik Davis became Amber's cohost, he'd enjoyed his greatest professional triumph yet—starring in Lin-Manuel Miranda's innovative hip-hop-driven Broadway hit *Freestyle Love Supreme*.

We have watched with pride as Boom alums remake popular culture in their own idiosyncratic images. From Jordan's uncanny societal critiques to Seth's uncompromising satire and Amber's historic breakthroughs, Boom OGs are not just making people laugh, but opening their minds when the world is at its most divided. Expectations are high, and they are consistently surpassing them when we need them most. We couldn't have been more thrilled when we learned Boom's 2016 grad E.R. Fightmaster began starring in *Grey's Anatomy* as the series' first nonbinary doctor character. Aspiring to greatness, these goal-post movers and game changers' work has actually led to social change—improving our existence with their groundbreaking insights and outrages. And then . . .

Enter *Ted Lasso*.

Who knew that *Ted Lasso* would become the most-viewed show on Apple TV+ in, like, seventy countries? That success surprised even its cocreators, Jason Sudeikis, Brendan Hunt, and Joe Kelly. This trio took a shared passion for soccer spawned at Boom Chicago and developed *Ted Lasso* over nearly five years before it became a beloved, multiple-Emmy-winning, unstoppable-smash-hit cultural phenomenon. People love it so much, there has been backlash to the backlash. As we wait for season three to drop, *Ted Lasso* is fresh from scoring four new Emmy Awards for its second season: Jason Sudeikis for Outstanding Lead Actor in a Comedy Series, Brett Goldstein for Outstanding Supporting Actor in a Comedy Series, MJ Delaney for Outstanding Directing for a Comedy Series, and then that biggest of kahunas, Outstanding Comedy Series. Yeah, baby! And that's on top of the seven Emmys *Ted Lasso* earned in 2021 for its debut season.

This clearly isn't just another sports show or workplace dramedy. Instead, it has proven to be that rare American comedy able to transcend national borders with gusto—the freakin' *Star Wars* of fish-out-of-water-community-college-American-football-coach-incongruously-takes-over-struggling-British-football-club-without-knowing-anything-about-soccer-I-mean-football shows. People cannot get enough *Ted Lasso*, no matter how many extra episodes Apple+ orders. Funny, but also deep, *Ted Lasso* has ultimately touched a chord we didn't know needed touching.[62]

Most of all, though, the entire Boom Chicago community

---

62 Ew.

was just so fucking happy to see the world finally understand the undeniable talent of Brendan Hunt. Even more significantly, they got to see Brendan dance on camera. Lucky them, lucky us.

Hopefully, future generations of Boom talent will have their own golden ages that, like this current one, never stop pushing for laughs that make audiences reconsider their worldviews anew. Jordan always said he felt like he was playing among thoroughbreds at Boom. Well, their output of the last half decade proves it. We grew up learning life lessons from rebels with causes like Richard Pryor, Chris Rock, and Lenny Bruce; the OG *SNL* crowd were countercultural iconoclasts in their own right too. Steve Martin putting an absurdist fun-house mirror up to our existence subversively illuminated just how wild and crazy life could really be. And Monty Python, of course, was a total break with propriety—offering a twisted, surreal view of the world that was revolutionary in its gonzo absurdity. If you can have laughs and provoke minds, that's the comedy holy grail—and our people seem to be finding it on the reg. Laughs are always job one—but actually having them mean something is the best icing on our thirtieth-birthday cake there could ever be. So we thank you for making our lives so memorable, beloved Boom Chicago fellow travelers. We'll check in with you in another thirty years . . .

Seth Meyers: I was really looking forward to performing at Boom Chicago's twenty-fifth-reunion festivities. What I enjoyed most playing Boom again is that they still attract such a smart audience.

Ruben van der Meer: It was great to see Boom Chicago pack Carré. That's a special theater not only for Amsterdam, but for the Netherlands. They deserved it: Boom Chicago isn't just Amsterdam anymore. Now, Dutch people everywhere know Boom Chicago.

Kay Cannon: Playing with everyone, going to Efteling together—all that classic Boom Chicago stuff was an honor and a blast. Boom Chicago people are the best, and I'm so happy for everyone's successes.

Colton Dunn: Just feeling the vibe of Amsterdam and its sense memories, I had the same nostalgia someone would have at a college reunion. Seeing former cast members and old friends was cool, and I was also really excited to see the new actors.

Returning at that point in my career, I started thinking about all the things I'd come to rely on that I'd picked up at Boom. For every table read on *Superstore*, I didn't need the script in advance; I knew I could bring it alive from what we learned at Boom improvising onstage. One of my favorite things about coming back for the twenty-fifth was having the feeling of, *I made it*. When I left Boom, it was my dream to write and work in television comedy. Standing on those same streets where I had wanted that so much, knowing that I achieved those goals—it was so satisfying, and wouldn't have been possible without Boom Chicago.

Suzi Barrett: There's a Boom Chicago network now, but it's more than that. The people who I was with at Boom are my family. I would bail any one of them out of jail.

Peter Grosz: The Second City people who came up in the '90s really affected culture in a big way—Adam McKay, Tina Fey, Amy Poehler, Rachel Dratch, Horatio Sanz. Those people made a big impact, almost like the first wave of *Saturday Night Live* did, and they still pepper their way through TV, movies, podcasts, and other culture people enjoy. But there's something about Boom's late-'90s, early-2000s moment that has really come to fruition in the last few years. At Boom, you're creating something magical out of nothing, and that really is what you want in show business, in a way.

Tarik Davis: Everybody's just been busting their butts, and continue to. A lot of that happened because we were allowed to be our full selves. It's very profound, this moment. It feels surreal to be attached to these people who are going to be taught in classes. It's like being part of the Justice League.

Heather Anne Campbell: The cream of entertainment today is being made by people I know from Boom. It's a miracle! I feel like a jerk because it's impossible to not name-drop constantly and sound like an asshole: "Oh yeah, I know Jordan Peele and the *Ted Lasso* guys. We lunch every time we're in LA together." If I see Seth, we hug and have a lot to talk about. When Jordan won the Academy Award for *Get Out*, I was screaming and sobbing at the Oscar party I was at. These are just my good friends, and their success is so deserved.

Brendan Hunt: It's nuts—suddenly Boom has more than its share of people doing cool and prominent things. It was already an honor to be in this cohort, among both the ones people know about and the ones they don't. But now it's just even a little bit cooler.

Andrew Moskos: It got a little relentless and traumatic during Trump. When Boom Chicago alum Becky Drysdale left as head writer on *The Tonight Show* in 2020, in part she blamed Trump's toxic ubiquity. Becky posted this on Facebook explaining her decision:

> *Comedy is a powerful tool. I believe that it can handle anything, no matter how unfunny. I don't believe that making fun of this man, doing impressions of him, or*

making him silly is a good use of that power. It only adds to his. I am making the decision for myself to never work on, write, or be involved with another Trump sketch ever again. I have landed in several jobs and situations over the last few years, not just The Tonight Show, *where the project of making fun of Trump . . . has led to divided creative teams, anxiety, tears, and pain. I can't decide the outcome of this election, but I can make the choice for myself to vote him out of my creative life.*

Brendan Hunt: With *Ted Lasso* coming after the Trump moment, we actually wanted to remind the world that Americans don't have to suck. People needed light at the end of the tunnel.

Liz Cackowski: And when Seth had Josh on *Late Night* to do his California Governor Gavin Newsom impression—it's so good. He's like half surfer dude, half sommelier.

Pep Rosenfeld: In some ways, comedy shows became more vital than ever—in no small part due to the addition of *The Amber Ruffin Show* to that canon.

Andrew Moskos: That Seth was a mentor helping make that happen made it even more meaningful for us. Amber sometimes asks if she can do an old Boom Chicago improv game or scene on her show. I love to say yes. Even better if it also involves Tarik!

Tarik Davis: For real, I couldn't be happier that Amber made history. But it's a little bittersweet: why did it have to take that long? What really explains the success of her, Seth, Jordan, and Jason is they have a personal vision they see through all the way—you can only get what they do from them. Amber just perceives the world totally uniquely, and that voice and commentary is very, very necessary.

Peter Grosz: Amber's story is one of perseverance—her very existence in comedy is subversive.

Seth Meyers: The best people at Boom are self-starters. They don't wait for the assignment, they show up having done the homework a day early. Having seen Amber at Boom, I knew she'd be a great fit for *Late Night*. That said, I didn't know *how* good she'd be. She did something even better than fitting in: she took a conventional late-night show and shaped it to fit her.

Don't get me wrong, had Amber only written for me, she would have been terrific. But to write for herself, and to say the kinds of things that had been absent until her arrival, that's what makes her so special. Every time Amber was on camera, it was a perfect pilot for what she could do with more time and resources. And sure enough, when given the opportunity, she didn't have to set out to find writers—she had a list in her head, ready to go. Because she doesn't wait for the assignment.

I'd say Amber was born ready, but that undersells how hard she works to put herself in the position to succeed. She's like no one else I've ever worked with—both brightly optimistic and clear-eyed about what needs fixing.

Amber Ruffin: Boom Chicago has prepared me for literally every job I've had since. When I was on the mainstage at Second City, I was perfectly fine with changing things on the fly, memorizing sketches in a second, handling mess-ups. Boom really is a comedy boot camp. By the time you leave, you've done a thousand shows with no notice—in places people shouldn't be doing shows, for audiences who'd rather be at home—and you can do anything.

I mean, my sister Lacey and I wrote a book called *You'll*

Never Believe What Happened to Lacey, which is a list of all the racist things that have happened to her that are funny. We wrote down each story exactly like we would tell it; it reads like hanging out with us, which I can guarantee is fun. It's probably the easiest book anyone has ever written, and it became a *New York Times* best seller! I've also cowritten a Broadway musical version of *Some Like It Hot*, and I have a production company now too. We are working on a ton of projects at once, so things are fun over here. Really, it's all I've ever wanted. And everyone is doing such great things. I mean, that I even know Kay Cannon is hilarious to me. Like, she is truly doing king shit, and I can't believe I've ever even *talked* to her.

Ike Barinholtz: In 2000, Kay Cannon ate a space cake and I had to carry her home through the Leidseplein because she couldn't walk. Then in 2018, Kay directed me in a major studio movie, *Blockers*, which she helped write, and which I costarred in alongside Leslie Mann and John Cena. Not long after that, I directed my first feature film. That's how far we've all come together, and it all stems from Boom Chicago.

Kay Cannon: Ike is great in *Blockers*. There are actually a couple of scenes where he makes you cry—like real-emotional-tears cry. I'm so proud of him. We definitely had a shorthand on set. What I loved so much was that he made me cry-laugh when he got sprayed in the face in the butt-chugging scene—but then made me straight-up cry in the scene where his daughter comes out to him. Ike's evolved as a performer: he can now tap into that very real emotional side of his, and then a moment later undercut it with a joke.

Amber Ruffin: Kay's work is so complete, honest, and funny. Often, people write jokes without any humanity in them, but Kay never does. That allows you to fall in love with these people she creates whenever you watch her work.

Andrew Moskos: *Blockers* reinvented the teenage coming-of-age sex comedy into something that was richer and more inclusive— but still raunchy and dirty. It seems normal now, but we didn't always have such female-driven comedies: not rom-coms or chick flicks, but something specific and relatable from a female perspective.

Kay Cannon: Getting hired by Boom became a lifeline for a lot of people. If you were rejected by Second City (and most were), Boom was there to embrace you. Their openness to hire marginalized peeps—where getting a shot matters, stage time matters, and being able to fail without fear of being fired matters— helped us hone our skills and find our voices. So when we got back out there in that competitive world, we had the tools to crack the boys' club.

Heather Anne Campbell: Boom Chicago is not a male club. Sometimes in this industry being a woman matters to people, and I never felt like it mattered at Boom; it wasn't important in any way. I never felt like I was a *female* cast member there—I was a cast member. That's also because we were in Europe. Chicago comedy could be real macho. America has a specific masculinity that's defensive and self-protecting—whereas in Europe, it didn't feel like a toxic boys' club. You can be a dude wearing pastels, and nobody would give a shit.

Pep Rosenfeld: Exhibit A: Josh Meyers and his blue bonnet hat.

Heather Anne Campbell: Likewise, there's a really welcoming, loyal fraternity waiting for you when you get out that doesn't feel competitive or transactional. I'm always like, "Hey, do you want to meet with my manager?" When I sold an improv pilot for Fox, I hired Pep. When Jordan and I would hang out at Boom, often we'd talk about horror movies and genre films instead of comedy ideas. So when Jordan did the new *Twilight Zone*, he was like, "I've got a thing coming up you'd be perfect for. Remember we used to talk about crazy shit all the time? So, do you want to write on *Twilight Zone?*" It was the best dream come true, ever. Boom is my heart, and this is my family forever. You know it's a good place when everybody still wants to work with each other twenty years later.

Andrew Moskos: Outside of Boom Chicago's twenty-fifth anniversary, 2018's most significant event for me personally was Jordan winning an Oscar for *Get Out*.

Ike Barinholtz: I mean, Jordan made an actual classic, and on his first time up at bat. *Get Out* was the best movie that year. People just loved it: it spoke to them *and* entertained them. There just wasn't anything like it. Jordan took his two favorite things—horror movies and awkward white people—and turned them into one perfect piece of art. For those of us that know Jordan, it was like, "About time, motherfuckers!"

Colton Dunn: In the last five years, Jordan's become the Jordan Movement. He's become our Hitchcock: put his name on a poster and people go see that movie.

Nicole Parker: I knew Jordan would go supernova. I think back to all the things we talked about wanting to do: me wanting to do Broadway, him wanting to make films. To have actually achieved those dreams, that's pretty fucking cool.

Ike Barinholtz: Jordan's work has always had this ultra-psychological component. That comes from doing ten thousand hours of improv. Above all, Jordan wants a reaction from the audience, and in improv the work isn't complete without it. Jordan plays with you, teasing out the reaction he wants—usually one you didn't see coming at all. In another horror movie, Lil Rel's character in *Get Out*, Rod William, would just be comic relief—and definitely the first one killed off. So of course Jordan made him the linchpin of the movie. Fucking genius. He gives you everything you want from a horror movie—but because it's Jordan, it's funny *and* socially relevant. There's a huge message, all while totally subverting the expected genres.

Andrew Moskos: I loved it when Jordan tweeted out at one point, *Get Out isn't a horror movie or a comedy: it's a documentary.* He was like, *Hey, you can debate whether this was a drama or a comedy, but for a lot of people this shit is real.*

Ike Barinholtz: That's Jordan in a nutshell. The Golden Globes in 2018 was like home movies for Boom Chicago people: Seth hosting, Jordan nominated all over the place, Amber Ruffin killing it asking the audience questions Seth couldn't. Amber and Seth tackled #MeToo and Trump so totally correctly and astutely there.

Jordan Peele: It was so great to share that chapter with my Boom Chicago family there.

Pep Rosenfeld: We watched back in Holland like proud Jewish parents: "Our children, how they have gone out into the world and done so well for themselves!"

Andrew Moskos: We weren't the only *Joden* thinking this way. Jordan told me he got a call on his cell from a number he didn't recognize; he answered it, and the voice on the other line said, "Please hold for Steven Spielberg." Steven called just to talk and tell Jordan how much he liked his work—no big deal . . .

Jordan Peele: The *Get Out* ride exceeded anything I could've imagined. The year of the Oscars, Universal gave me the most incredible gift for my birthday. When I got to my office, I discovered they'd sent me a framed, original art-department architectural blueprint of Norman Bates's house from *Psycho*. I was like, *What? Really? Come on.* And while all this is going down, I'm trying to be there for my seven-month baby. I even promised my wife I'd stop smoking weed.

Pep Rosenfeld: Apart from Jordan claiming to be weed-free, the other seismic event in Boom Chicago's universe was *Ted Lasso*.

Liz Cackowski: When I saw how many kids dressed up as Ted Lasso and Coach Beard for Halloween, I was like, *Okay, something's happening . . .*

Andrew Moskos: If you measure a show's success by the amount of memes it spawns, *Ted Lasso*'s clearly the most successful show in television—uh, I mean streaming—history.

Brendan Hunt: My world couldn't be more different than it was at the last Boom Chicago anniversary. By 2018—also the year of the World Cup—*Ted Lasso* had been sold and we'd started writing, but it was not yet my full-time job. And basically, since the following January, it's just been nonstop writing, shooting, editing, and promoting *Ted Lasso*. It's wild: as of 2018, my mom had just passed, and my dad passed not long after my son was born. All this stuff was happening, but my parents weren't really there to see it.

Tarik Davis: What's amazing to me is that *Ted Lasso* successfully makes people laugh in countries that don't even speak English. That's just so Boom Chicago.

Ruben van der Meer: The whole premise of the series feels like an improv scene: "Hi, I am your new soccer coach." "But you are an American football coach." "Yes. Well, that shouldn't be a problem . . ." That's the creative mind of a good improv player: create a big, absurd problem, and then an even more absurd solution. That's Brendan—crazy and absurd.

John O'Brien: With *Ted Lasso*, it was finally my turn to be a fan. I called Brendan up after the first episode like, "Holy shit, dude, you guys nailed it! This show is totally you—this is what you were meant to do. You're the only people who could've made it happen so genuinely." Because of their passion and respect for the sport, the show is funny around football-culture stereotypes in a really insightful way. It's not like an outsider trying to do a soccer show.

As someone who lived it, I recognize the characters, the locker-room dynamic, all of it. The grumpy old-timer who's just bitter, angry, and right all the time like Roy Kent—I've definitely seen plenty of those. And then the African players who bring so much joy and love of the game to the team—those characterizations ring true as well. People take themselves so seriously in that competitive world, so it's great how that's played up.

I especially appreciate how they handle the stuff peripheral to the central team dynamic—the media, the marketing, the staff. I remember creating really meaningful relationships with staff because you had so much daily interaction with them. All that's a big part of players' existence, and they handle it so well. And then they throw in the quotes from Johan Cruyff, who was such an Ajax legend—classic stuff like, "Every disadvantage has its advantage."[63] With his Zen wisdom, Cruyff was the Yoda of the beautiful game.

---

63 You may recall from Chapter 3 that Brendan first put that bit of Cruyff wisdom into a Boom Chicago scene back in 2003. What can you say, dude loves Cruyff.

Pep Rosenfeld: "The Yoda of *Joden*"—finally, a legit way into that joke. Thanks for the assist, John!

Brendan Hunt: One time while Jason was at Boom, we both had the day off. We were like, "Great—let's take mushrooms." As we started walking around, I went off on a jag, exploring ideas for a show about the global context of soccer. This was inspired by a book called *Brilliant Orange: The Neurotic Genius of Dutch Football,* about how the character of a country is often represented in the successes and failures of its national football team.

So as I riffed on my tangent for a while, Jason listened patiently. Most people would have said, "Hey, can we move on to something else, please?" but he just listened. Finally, we reached the Spui,[64] and Jason turned to me and said, "So all that stuff you just said—that's stuff you believe?" "Yeah," I responded. We made a real connection that day, and there was a not-minor soccer element involved.

Nicole Parker: With Jason, Brendan, and Joe, it's very organic. *Ted Lasso* wouldn't exist if Brendan didn't know everything about soccer from his Boom era. Seth and Brendan were doing a show at Edinburgh in 2000 called "Ironic Yanks" which had a lot of stuff that became the groundwork of *Ted Lasso*. In "Ironic Yanks," Brendan explained everything about soccer to the audience—even doing impressions of his favorite football announcers, some of whom appear in *Ted Lasso*. To me, that was the real start of it all. When I saw those first *Ted Lasso* commercials, I was like, *Great, Brendan's finally able to use his "Ironic Yanks" stuff.*

Brendan Hunt: The stuff I was talking about with Jason on that

---

64 The Spui is one of Amsterdam's most mispronounced square names. It's nothing like "spewy," and more like "spow" (as in "pow").

magic mushroom–assisted day did end up in "Ironic Yanks." That was very encouraging, like, *Oh, maybe there's something here, because Jason thinks it's okay.* But one thing that's been overstated in the press is this notion that the character Ted Lasso and the idea for the show happened at Boom. That wasn't the case. Before Boom, I hadn't been into soccer at all, but then I always needed to know all the facts for the pub quiz that wasn't coming. The essential part of *Ted Lasso*'s DNA that *was* happening there was all three of us learning about soccer. It really all starts with me and Jason playing FIFA 2000 after I'd steeped myself in soccer lore. When Jason bought a PlayStation for the Shiny, I already knew all the classic teams and their context in football history, so I could translate soccer things for Jason: "Okay, in terms of Dutch team hierarchy, Ajax is comparable to the Showtime Lakers . . ." That translation was the kernel of the relationship between our characters on the show, and we definitely reproduced that dynamic in the first *Ted Lasso* commercials.

What is also directly related is how at Boom, you're trying to amuse audiences, but while simultaneously, invisibly explaining the joke to them. You've got to bring Dutch people into the American references, while bringing various tourists from everywhere into, like, Dutch politics. At some point, you realize that sometimes you'll get 90 percent of the crowd getting the jokes, but other times it'll only be 10 percent—but those 10 percent are laughing so hard that everyone else is like, *Wait, maybe I should start laughing too.*

On *Ted Lasso*, we talk all the time like, "Okay, that joke is not for everyone—but we like it, so it's staying in." We'll explain some jokes for the American audience, but then we'll leave some randoms in just for our English friends. You have to accept that you can't reach everyone, but you give it an honest try. That's Boom Chicago: the tram is moving to the next stop, and we will leave the door open, but we don't have time to grab everybody, you know?

Another huge Boom lesson is how *Ted Lasso* is a show very conscious of the perception of Americans in the world. That DNA reminds us to be aware of the context in which we exist, and what that perception is to those around us. We're writing for our American audience, but remain conscious of the world audience. The whole world gets the soccer part more than the Americans do, so there's a weird equalizer in play. Football is the construct, but there's something bigger beyond football. That approach is what we did at Boom too.

Anyways, after that one fateful day on mushrooms, eleven years go by. I'd been cast in one of Jason's movies, *We're the Millers*. I was stoked: I'd never been in a movie before. Several months later, around June 2013, I got a call from Jason: "So I have good news, and I have bad news. The bad news is your scenes were cut from *We're the Millers*. But the good news is there's this soccer thing . . ."

The "soccer thing" was a commercial NBC Sports was putting together. NBC was broadcasting the Premier League package that year, and they thought Jason was the way to promote it. Jason asked if I wanted to join him and Joe Kelly to write the spot, which was shooting two weeks later. We had to finish before soccer season began, so it came together extremely quickly. We were like, "Wow, we get to go to London for three whole days, and they're going to fly us out for a game!"

This ad agency, Brooklyn Brothers, came to us with three ideas, all involving Jason as a coach. Jason was like, "Let's go with the one where he's a college football coach who becomes a soccer coach. We'll call him 'Ted Lasso.' Thank you very much." We had bits we liked and the premise was good, so we went off and did it. In that first Ted Lasso ad, you see me doing exactly what I was doing with Jason playing FIFA in the Shiny thirteen years earlier: "Okay, this soccer team is kind of like the same thing as something in America that you'd understand . . ." Early on, Joe Kelly had a great suggestion. He realized that since

Ted was so loquacious, the proper balance would be for Coach Beard to talk as little as possible. Coach Beard didn't have a name yet, but I did have a beard at the time because I was doing a play I'd written, *Absolutely Filthy*, where I played a homeless person based on Pigpen from *Peanuts*.

That first commercial was super fun, and apparently went well, because the next year they asked, "Hey, can we do the Ted Lasso thing again? We don't have the budget for England, so we'll shoot in New York, okay?" The bit then becomes that Ted's not in England anymore and misses it; he's more curious now, with more of a tender side. We see Ted coaching a girls team and caring about the players more than before in the more cartoonish earlier version.

By then the spot had won a number of awards, and had become big in certain circles. Around that time, at some football illuminati event, this British media guy came up to us and said, "What's great about this Ted Lasso stuff is that you guys got everything wrong in exactly the right way." After the second commercial, talk shifted to, "Hmmm, there might be something else here. A TV show? A movie? Let's figure out what that is."

First we had to make sure Ted wasn't just a dummy, and make him more real. Jason had the foresight to realize Ted can't be like how he was in the commercials—you can't stretch that out for half an hour. The two commercials had also been 90 percent improvised. Jason said, "I don't want this to be improvised. Every word needs to be scripted." So me, Joe, and Jason met up at Jason's brownstone in Brooklyn. For a week, we pounded out the structure of an arc modeled after *The Office*—two six-episode seasons and a special, which has now become three seasons. Then we wrote the pilot.

Heather Anne Campbell: I read the *Ted Lasso* pilot before the show came out. I was like, *This is the best fucking pilot I've read in a decade.* And of course it was totally Boom Chicago.

Brendan Hunt: At that point, it was 2015. Jason and Joe then went and did other things for the next four years. Meanwhile, I was rotting on the vine. I'd gotten the odd role here and there, but was hanging on by my fingernails.

Kay Cannon: I'd been trying to make Brendan Hunt a household name for years. I cast him in an episode of *Girlboss* and wrote a role for him in a pilot that didn't go. Of course, Brendan didn't need my help in becoming successful; he did it all himself. But goddamnit if I didn't try.

Brendan Hunt: And then one day, Jason invited me to this rock and roll/comedy charity event in Kansas City—Wynonna Judd played, Fred Armisen hosted, and I did my lounge act, Elvis Prestello—a full-on Elvis Presley impersonator who only does Elvis Costello songs—which I'd actually debuted in Amsterdam. By the time we'd flown back to LAX, we'd hung out for seventy-two hours straight. We're waiting for our bags, and Jason says, "By the way, is that Ted Lasso stuff online somewhere?" Which was another way of saying, "Hey Brendan, I don't know how Google works . . ." I assured him that, indeed, those Ted Lasso spots were on YouTube for eternity. "Great, because I'm having lunch with Bill Lawrence[65] tomorrow," he continued. Bill was trying to get Jason to work on stuff, but what was getting pitched wasn't quite the right fit. So Jason said, "Well, I've got this soccer thing . . ." And Bill was like, "Oh yeah—I like that!"

So we took the pilot we wrote and filled it out, making it more of a TV show than just something we were tossing around. Suddenly, things started happening very quickly. We found out NBC wasn't interested in doing the show, and there was still

---

65 Bill Lawrence is a legendary TV comedy writer, showrunner, and director, known for creating or cocreating hits ranging from *Scrubs* and *Spin City* to *Cougar Town* before he got involved with *Ted Lasso*.

a bit of legal wrangle there. That's why *Based on characters owned by NBC Sports* is in the opening credits. So Bill and Jason pitched it to all the major streamers. We hoped for a bidding war, and didn't get one: Apple was the only place that bid. That was a bit nerve-racking. At the time, it was like, "Well, what is Apple TV+? What's *that* going to be like?" Ultimately, though, we wanted to go with streaming because if you're doing a soccer show set in London, it has to *sound* like London—that means way more cursing than network television allows. And Apple committed to the whole series, which was very, very cool.

To work on a project that incorporates my passion for soccer is really great. If I was working on *Yellowstone*, I'd have never looked a horse in the eye beforehand—it would be more, "All right, punching out. Bye, everybody." I realized this is about as close to the dream-come-true category as I get. I'm just grateful.

John O'Brien: While they put the show together, Brendan would ask me soccer-specific things—like the whole thing with Nate the kit man revealing his brilliant soccer brain. Brendan wanted to know what kind of play he'd come up with. We discussed how Richmond would have had to compensate for its playing style. As it's not a wealthy team, they don't have the best technical players, so any play would have to be a counter-attack move. What we came up with was Richmond using a decoy to free up space for someone else to take the ball. That was inspired from my time playing with FC Utrecht for a year. Utrecht is a mid-table team, whereas Richmond is more of a low-table team. Like Richmond, Utrecht wouldn't be attacking—but they're really good at working long wings and having overlapping runs.

Seth Meyers: *Ted Lasso* feels like a perfect Boom cast. Everyone on that show has a skill unique to them, and can make it work on their own or in concert with their fellow performers. There's never a second of that show where you wish someone else was on camera. And then there's Joe, Brendan, and Jason—again, three equally funny people who all bring something different to the process.

From previous collaborations, I know Joe to be a great master of premise, Brendan to be the king of the details, and Jason to have a unique ability to stand back and look at everything in the wide shot, making sure all the parts fit together. The worst writers' rooms are the ones where everyone shares the same strengths and weaknesses. Based on the results, that's obviously not the case with *Ted Lasso*.

Brendan Hunt: Seth's really on to something with that assignment of duties! Joe Kelly showed up at Boom at the end of 1999, and even then he was too good. Boy, could that guy work a crowd. Joe really understood how to keep the show moving along—that's one funny motherfucker. While we're all essential and do our part, Jason's the captain: he operates at a very high level, with a very clear sense of what the show is. The studio wanted things to zip along, but Jason stressed that we were going to be more English about it, taking our time to explore the grace notes. He sees things none of us see, because it's his heart and soul. And then Bill Lawrence comes in with these bombshell ideas.

There's a fine line between caring a lot about a subject and mansplaining—so whether I'm talking about soccer, the great German card game of Skat, or the curious legal situation of Amsterdam, I conversationally curate. On the show, we can't fit the whole history of soccer into each episode. We only explain what the audience needs to know. I locked into that early on in the writers' room. Other than me, Bill Wrubel,[66] and obviously Brett Goldstein,[67] none of these people know anything or care about

---

66 Another TV comedy legend, Bill Wrubel is also a writer and producer on *Ted Lasso*, known previously for his work on shows like *Modern Family*.
67 Brett Goldstein is the British comedian known for his writing on *Ted Lasso*

soccer, and I'm not going to get them into it. I'm just ready with what they need to know. One time I was endlessly explaining the process of relegation, and finally Bill Lawrence said, "If we're talking about relegation so much, why doesn't Richmond just get relegated?"

At the same time, Bill early on made clear, "This is not a soccer show: it's a workplace ensemble comedy." I thought, *That makes sense. The Office* isn't about paper, but the people working at a paper company. That was such a great insight by Bill, and it's carried us to where we are now. We honor the world of soccer because it's something we love, but it has to be about the relationships and emotions these people go through. Ultimately, we're just trying to make ourselves laugh—although what we really want is to make the crew laugh. If you can make an English crew laugh, you should feel pretty fucking good about yourself.

Amber Ruffin: Watching *Ted Lasso*, it's clear that a ton of people are named after Boom folks. That made me laugh so hard!

Nicole Parker: I like how they waited until the second season to put a Dutch player in, Jan Maas.

Brendan Hunt: It was actually Joe Kelly's idea to name the Dutch player after Saskia. I wanted a super-complicated Dutch name, because there's a history of that in football, like Jan Vennegor of Hesselink. In Dutch, "of" actually means "or": he came from a family that didn't want to choose between their last names, so they just used both. But Joe always looks for the simplest thing, and Jan Maas was pretty great. The first game of 2000 I watched was also the first time I went to Saskia's parents' house in Roosendaal, so the Maas family looms large with me

---

as well as his award-winning breakout performance as Richmond's chronically bitter captain and former star player Roy Kent.

and football. It was cool to honor not just Saskia, but Rien and Wilma Maas as well.

Saskia Maas: My dad, who's an enormous *Ted Lasso* fan, called me up right after he saw the episode introducing Jan. I said, "Dad, you know he's named after me, right?" When *60 Minutes* interviewed Jason Sudeikis, he singled me out as one of his mentors, explaining that's why Jan Maas was so named. Jan's brutally honest, so there are lots of hilarious moments for me as a Dutch person. It's such an honor—they actually gave me the jersey Jan Maas wears in the show.

Brendan Hunt: I'm still mad that Saskia hasn't framed that Jersey and put it up at Boom.

Saskia Maas: That's because I wear it too much.

Brendan Hunt: There's also a minor character on *Ted Lasso* named Anders Rosenfeldt. That name put Andrew and Pep in there, disguised as the name of a Swedish player. And there's also a pinball machine on the show, which has the high score attributed to *ACM*.

Andrew Moskos: I was delighted that the pinball grand champion that Ted Lasso tries to beat has *my* pinball initials. Now it's canon.

Jason Sudeikis: I hope *Ted Lasso* has a pinball machine someday. That would be dope.

Brendan Hunt: Those references show how much Amsterdam and Boom means. *Ted Lasso* would not exist if Pep, Andrew, and Ken hadn't gotten high in the back of Rookies and decided to move to Holland. It's cool to live inside that tapestry.

Saskia Maas: For the show's third season, *Ted Lasso* has an episode with Richmond playing Ajax. I love that they shot it authentically in Amsterdam. I never thought my home team would be on a TV show where a character is named after me. I mean, I scribbled *Ajax* on the cover of my school journal when I was eleven.

Ruben van der Meer: *Joden! Joden! Joden!*

John O'Brien: Taking *Ted Lasso* to Amsterdam really brings it full circle. That's got to be really fulfilling to go to the birthplace of the idea.

Brendan Hunt: It was pretty fucking cool to shoot a *Ted Lasso* episode in Amsterdam. Amsterdam is in the DNA of *Ted Lasso*. It's baked in, and to highlight that is just incredibly meaningful.

Saskia Maas: Brendan even hired our oldest son, Finn, to work on set as a production assistant.

Brendan Hunt: Bringing Finn along for the ride, I fully trusted he'd kick ass. It's the same as Jason hiring me—not just a buddy, but someone who will crush. And Finn crushed it.

Saskia Maas: After *Ted Lasso* finished shooting in Amsterdam, Brendan and Jason joined Boom Chicago's current cast for a "Shot of Improv" show. Then the entire crew and cast partied until early morning.

Brendan Hunt: It was thrilling to be up there on that stage again with Jason. It was also just great to be up there with that cast—the best cast Boom Chicago's had in fifteen years. It feels like Boom again. Boom works best when the cast is exposed to Andrew; there's just no better gateway to Amsterdam than him. Now it's all in place again, and that was so cool to experience.

Saskia Maas: At the *Ted Lasso* wrap party, I found the actor who plays Jan Maas and said, "I'm your mother!" It was as if I'd found my long-lost son. I wanted to be cast as his mother so the credits would say, *Saskia Maas as Saskia Maas*. I'd be even more brutally honest as a Dutch person, so it's clear he takes after his mom. They didn't go for it, but I'm waiting for another chance.

Jason Sudeikis: I've just been lucky to have Brendan in my life as an alpha-male mentor. He never ceases to impress, onstage and off—in support of his scene partner, coworker, or brother/sister in art. I couldn't say enough about him as an artistic soul.

Brendan Hunt: Props to Jason as well. I found out after we'd sold the show that at every pitch meeting for *Ted Lasso*, Jason said, "Coach Beard will be played by Brendan Hunt. If Brendan isn't involved, I'm not interested in doing this show with you." As nice as Apple has been—they send me presents on my birthday now, and when we're nominated for awards, there's always a new basket of cheese and champagne in my dressing room—three years ago, they weren't feeling good about my face on camera. That's all Jason—a Hall of Fame stand-up dude right there!

Andrew Moskos: One of my favorite *Ted Lasso* episodes is "Beard After Hours." It's definitely the craziest.

Brendan Hunt: The first episode of season one came out on a Thursday; by Monday, Apple picked us up for another season and was like, "Please add two more episodes." We sifted through our idea pile and came up with a Christmas show and "Beard After Hours."

Pep Rosenfeld: Totally unique among all *Ted Lasso* episodes, "Beard After Hours" features only one character from the main cast: Coach Beard. It's basically a solo Brendan Hunt jam session. The Hula-Hoop! And finally, the world got to see Brendan really dance his ass off.

Andrew Moskos: "Beard After Hours" is a totally surrealistic, dreamlike detour detached from the rest of *Ted Lasso*. In it, Coach Beard goes on a metaphysical journey through his soul, via crazy partying in London nightclubs. There are cinematic homages—*Fight Club*, the Martin Scorsese film *After Hours* alluded to in the title. But more than anything, it bubbles with the very recognizable abandon of Brendan Hunt. It's like peering into a fun-house mirror reflecting Brendan's id.

Pep Rosenfeld: It's so autobiographical, it's strange to find out that it wasn't written by Brendan, but by Brett Goldstein and Joe Kelly.

Brendan Hunt: They know what's up. The whole thing stemmed from an old memory. One Saturday at Boom when the show wasn't good, I got so bummed out I grabbed a beer and sat out on the terrace by myself. Boom's new bartender, Job (as in the Book of Job) came up to me and asked, "Brendan, would you like to go to an illegal beach party?" And I was like, "Yes, I would."

It was a sixty-guilder cab ride to these beach dunes in the middle of nowhere—just the perfect adventure I needed to lose myself in that moment. And of course the pants I wore in the episode were totally what I'd buy at Zipper or Club Warehouse if we were going dancing at Chemistry. There are definitely Boom Chicago Easter eggs in there.

Liz Cackowski: I'm pretty sure I have Boom-era pictures of Brendan in the pants he's wearing in "Beard After Hours."

Nicole Parker: The wardrobe designer copied those crazy pants *exactly*. That whole episode was a Brendan Hunt fever dream. I recognized so much. Partying at Club Vegas was 100 percent in "Beard After Hours." There were also references to Brendan's one-man theater shows like *Five Years in Amsterdam*, and the Hula-Hoop bit came from *Absolutely Filthy*. It's literally all Brendan Amsterdam memories.

John O'Brien: "Beard After Hours" is autobiographical in how Brendan's Amsterdam adventure fits with his own self-growth. And Brendan definitely likes going to weird places. That's a big part of his journey, that need to explore and be free. And then there's the dancing. At my bachelor party, Brendan got everyone going on the dance floor. He's *that* guy.

Heather Anne Campbell: You know what makes *Ted Lasso* incredible? Brendan was doing plays, honing his craft for years. And then, finally, the world was ready for what he wanted to write—and it hit bigger than anything. This was not a surprise.

Liz Cackowski: Brendan was meant for that Boom stage: he was its MVP—a Boom G.O.A.T. But he was also so supportive as a scene partner. He could do everything.

Peter Grosz: Brendan's later-in-life leap to fame is a story of perseverance. Jason needed to be the force driving *Ted Lasso*, but Brendan's just as uniquely suited to be a part of that brainchild.

Josie O'Reilly: Brendan was definitely in his own lane. His audition stands out strongly for me—he wore a suit to callbacks! He seemed in a rush to succeed, yet was incredibly patient waiting for his turn in the sun. I am so thrilled for what humility he brings to the whole thing.

Ike Barinholtz: If I had to pick one cast member who just constantly *killed*, it was him. He was just made for that stage on the Leidseplein; it became his métier. At the end of the day, Brendan's the best performer that's ever come through Boom.

Colton Dunn: Watching *Ted Lasso* made me feel like I was back in Amsterdam—and in Amsterdam, Brendan was *the man*. I'm like, *These people don't even know what they're in store for. They don't know where this guy can go.*

Suzi Barrett: I think it's fair to say that Brendan's the poster boy for the life-changing Boom Chicago experience. We all played in that sandbox, but nobody had the journey he did.

Jason Sudeikis: When I first met Brendan, he was living life. At that point, he was a living, breathing example of someone taking advantage of every artistic avenue in that town. This was clear in the way Brendan would laugh with castmates, and the sheer boldness of his wardrobe. He doesn't dance like nobody's watching, he dances like *everybody's* watching. I think that takes way more fucking bravery.

Brendan Hunt: I've learned that part of why it's taken me so long to get to something bigger was because of my certitude that TV was this faraway thing that I was not prepared to do. I thought maybe I didn't have the education or the experience that would allow me to contribute in a meaningful way. I convinced myself there was some missing thing that I didn't have. But doing this show, I've gone past giving this monkey on my back that power; instead, I've made him my nemesis. Of course I have a facility for this. I didn't suddenly become dog shit: I was putting myself in the doggy-poop bag. I'd been built on self-deprecation for a very long time.

At first *Ted Lasso* had no antagonist—the antagonists were internal. What was huge for me going to Amsterdam, of course, was finally living in a world where all that guilt and shame that a Catholic upbringing puts on you is, in fact, clearly a choice that you can throw away. But moving to LA, it all came back—especially when I was fucking broke. So *Ted Lasso* was just this great reminder that I'm still capable of contributing to something in a material way. We're not playing space aliens; we're doing versions of ourselves. We're doing something we really truly love, is close to our hearts, and doing it the way we always wanted to do it.

By the way, my last professional gig before *Ted Lasso* was doing an impression of Seth Meyers on *Animaniacs*. I had horrible guilt about it; it hadn't gone down the way I wanted it to. My agent told me *Animaniacs* was having trouble finding someone who can do an impression of Seth. I don't do impressions, but I was pretty sure I could do a passable Seth. I felt it was my duty, so I gave it a shot. I thought, *Man, being spoofed in* Animaniacs, *that's like fucking being in* Mad *magazine*. And it paid well too. Before *Ted Lasso*, I couldn't just turn down most gigs.

I hoped it would come out on TV not long after, and we'd have a laugh about it. And then it didn't come out for three years. I'd completely forgotten about it, and then someone brought it up in an interview! The part where Seth texts me and goes, *Hey, wait a minute, buddy* . . . hasn't happened. I still don't know if it was actually a horrible idea. So hey, Seth, I'm sorry I hadn't told you!

Tarik Davis: One of my earliest memories from Boom was Brendan Hunt introducing me to soccer. He took this love of his, and now he's made a huge explosion all over the planet with it.

You know, I think a lot about Brendan's success. It reminds

us that there's no age limit on any of this, no rules or limitations as to how this works out. That's a fundamental thing we learned at Boom. That's the correlation between all of us. Five years ago, I was doing theater pieces at the Brooklyn Museum, working with some talented writers and directors, finding my art in a different way—trying to make my small movies, booking a commercial here and there. Some of that stuff was incredible to work on, but I was also thinking my days being an improv rock star like we were on the Boom stage might be done.

Coming back to New York from Amsterdam was very grim. I'd grown up: I was twenty-three when I left for Boom, and twenty-eight returning to the US in 2007. Before Boom, I was unsure if I could even be an actor professionally—if I was even good. After Boom, those questions were gone: I knew I'd had moments where I was *great*. Back in the States post-Boom, I felt undeniable. Everyone thought I was insane: "What do you mean you can fly?" "Isn't that what everyone does? Here, I'll get onstage and show you . . ."

It was a trip. I'd returned fully into myself—aware, confident, and in love with who I was and what I could do. But then I found it very hard to reenter that world and flourish. Things are shifting now in the culture, but before that we were still supposed to be background. I don't want to talk out of pocket for Amber, but coming back from Europe, we'd have conversations about hitting that wall; it hits you really hard. And I didn't have a spot waiting for me on *MADtv*. So I started teaching in Brooklyn—using my skills to get through to the Black youth in Brownsville, Crown Heights, and Bed-Stuy. Then in 2019, I reconnected with Jamie Wright. He'd been Boom's video technician and was really someone who'd taken me under their wing when I was there.

Jamie was like, "Hey, Tarik, I'm going to see my buddy's show. You should come with me." And so Jamie took me to see *Freestyle Love Supreme* right before it went to Broadway.

Lin-Manuel Miranda was in the show. Seeing it, I was like, "Oh my God! Jamie—what they're doing is Boom!" It felt like a religious experience—like I'd traveled back in time and was sitting next to Pep again after getting off the airplane in Schiphol and seeing this pyrotechnic thing that I couldn't even figure out. Afterward, we hung out with the cast. Jamie was being very gracious, singing my praises—and then they asked me to audition.

I go in and there's James Monroe Iglehart, Anthony Veneziale, and Daveed Diggs, coming right off of the hugeness of *Hamilton*. I'd actually auditioned for *Hamilton* and almost got cast—the only reason being that I'd learned all the necessary things for the role at Boom. Tommy Kail was the director of *Hamilton* and also *Freestyle Love Supreme*. He remembered my *Hamilton* audition, and the connection through Jamie just solidified that bridge. I had a great experience. I felt like I'd traveled back in time to my Boom Chicago audition.

I got a callback. When I got there, Tommy was like, "So, what are you doing this weekend?" I ended up going to the Kennedy Center in Washington, DC, to do my first *Freestyle Love Supreme* shows. As I was leaving my hotel room, down the hall coming out of his hotel room was Wayne Brady. I'm trying not to get emotional, but when I first started doing improv at the beginning of college, he was the one Black guy doing it. I didn't know if there was a future for me, but then I saw Wayne Brady in *Whose Line Is It Anyway?* and thought, *Maybe I can do this.* And now we were doing shows together! In the elevator, I said, "You don't know me, but we're going to the same rehearsal—and you're the reason I'm here. I didn't know if I was good enough for this, but seeing you crush it kept me in the game—and now here we are, sharing the stage at the Kennedy Center."

Soon after, I made my Broadway debut in *Freestyle Love Supreme*—rapping onstage with Lin-Manuel Miranda, Daveed Diggs, and Wayne Brady, who all went on to become good friends. The whole time, I'm thinking, *The thing I was most*

afraid of doing at Boom was rapping—and now that skill is fi-
nally propelling me forward in my career.

The *Freestyle* crew had the same love and trust as Boom,
but this time my integration went much faster. As I was making this transition, Anthony Veneziale—one of the best people
I've ever met—said, "Hey, Tarik, is there anybody you want to
guest at an upcoming *Freestyle* show?" It was immediate who
that would be. I'd been seeing Amber a lot: she'd asked me to
come in and do sketches on *Late Night with Seth Meyers*. It just
made sense—I mean, that's my sister. I called Amber and told her
she had to do *Freestyle* because it's like Boom. She was nervous
about rapping onstage; she hadn't done it in years. I told her,
"It's going to be okay. Trust me, you're gonna be great. It's like
riding a bike. You're going to be incredible."

So Amber made her Broadway debut with *Freestyle Love
Supreme*, and it *was* incredible. She absolutely crushed it—just
like that moment when I saw the audience first fall in love with
her at Boom. When the show was finally over, we went out for
the curtain call and we got a standing ovation. Now, Amber's
always there 100 percent emotionally, but she still keeps her
cards very close—humor is really her love language. But when I
turned to look at her at that moment, she was crying, and then *I*
started crying. She said, "Tarik, you were right—this *is* Boom!"
We'd been through the hard times together, getting booed at bad
shows—and now we're on Broadway, holding hands onstage as
we receive a standing ovation. I love that lady, and I was so
happy I got to share that moment with her.

Then the pandemic happened, and we were like, "Will we
ever get back onstage again?" Almost a year after we did *Freestyle* together, Amber called. Very casually, she brought up that
she was hosting a new talk show on Peacock. And then she said,
"Do you want to do this show with me? There's no audience.
It'll be just you and me." And I said, "I'm on board—I'll always
have your back. When are we doing this?" And she responded,

"In two weeks. We're going to cowboy it." We were going to do something that had never been done. Because we'd been in the trenches together, there was nobody else she wanted to do it with—we'd grown up together doing this at Boom. It wasn't just a job that Amber gave me. She threw me into the deep end—jumping in right alongside me, not knowing what was on the bottom.

Amber wouldn't have given me that opportunity if not for what we'd done at Boom. She knew that I was able to fly on-stage, just like we did in Amsterdam. I felt assured again. Seeing where Amber has grown, being the captain of a ship, the first Black woman late-night writer now having her own show in this very competitive world? If that's not Darwinian, I don't know what is. And now, every time I walk into 30 Rock, I see Eddie Murphy's picture on the wall. You can't help but be very aware of the heritage of that building, but having grown used to walking on a tightrope at Boom, the pressure wasn't suffocating. It was energizing.

Amber Ruffin put me on a different platform in terms of exposure. Being comfortable with who we are, we can let the audience see how we joke together. I don't need to put on a mask; I don't need to put on airs. We're going to just show you what we do. We're going to let you inside like it's our living room, and we're going to hang out awhile. Doing that on that level, and being Black and being excellent, and seeing a brilliant Black woman captaining that ship—it definitely helped me. It gave me an appetite for what I can really do. It reignited something, you know?

The years after Boom were very hard—rewarding at times, but a lot of my successes were covert. So to be on that platform again, where people see you and your friend and feel the success of what you're doing together . . . We're still in this fight, and we still have a lot to do. But this lit up something a lot bigger than me, bigger than Amber, bigger than Jordan. We're part of something now, in new rooms where we're having conversations and getting things done.

Without *The Amber Ruffin Show*, I wouldn't have had that. Pushing that ball forward, the idea of what's possible . . . there's still a lot more elbow room that Black people need. If I have the great privilege to make just a smidgen of an impact, that's due to the path that I've been blessed to be on. Through Boom, through *Freestyle*, and now through Amber—that's the growth, scope, and vision those things gave me.

Boom remains a very profound place of change and growth for me—a chapter in my life from which so many important things have flowed, and I'm still moving forward. The work doesn't stop, and it doesn't get stale. It continues to evolve, and that's an incredible thing that Boom gave us.

Kay Cannon: My Boom Chicago experience shows up in all of my work. The jump-in, *Yes, and* . . . attitude that Andrew, Pep, Ken, and Saskia had in starting Boom really stuck with me. It's something that I carry along with me in everything I do.

Colton Dunn: With the success people have had, there's a kind of chess involved—a forethought that comes naturally to Boom Chicago people. Some of that might've come from Andrew in that he always has a plan. We'd be talking about developing the show, and Andrew would discuss the business angles on it too: "This is how we'll promote it to bring people in . . ." That sort of thing, which a lot of artistic people never want to talk about or accept. But Boom Chicago's professionalism and the fact that it was a business really had an impact. Someone like Jordan is not looking one step in front of him—he's looking at steps ten years into the future. I think that comes from Andrew's professionalism, making people like Jordan and Seth think, *Oh, I can have a plan for my career too.*

Brendan Hunt: Once things take off, it's something you've been unconsciously practicing for the whole time. Boom is a big step in that direction for all of us because across the board, it was everyone's first professional performing job, our first professional writing job. You learn the discipline and application you're going to need for real, as well as the liberty and privilege of letting a creative job take over your life. You're not pausing to wait tables—you're just doing it. Boom sent me down that path, so by the time all this happened with *Ted Lasso*, I knew I could roll with it.

Heather Anne Campbell: Boom Chicago is self-selecting for people who are adventurous. When I told people in LA that I was going to do Boom, nobody had heard of it. Groundlings specifically was like, "Are you out of your fucking mind? Don't go there. You'll ruin your career!" But a lot of creativity and potency goes hand in hand with being willing to uproot yourself and try out something else. That transfers into being able to think three-dimensionally in order to succeed.

That's why people from Boom are so interesting, deep, passionate, and talented. In committing to move to Amsterdam and creatively boil with these other people for years, they've already put up that filter. But yeah, they're fucking geniuses too. Boom doesn't just hire comedians—they hire people to make a family. That's why I have more lifelong friends from Boom Chicago than any other thing I've ever done. I don't talk to anybody from college or high school—but I talk to people from Boom weekly.

Carice van Houten: My time with Boom Chicago really has nourished me as much as any period of my life. There are so many funny anecdotes to talk about, but they were also such crucial moments. It really is a force!

Ike Barinholtz: It's funny what those years set in motion. There was a 0.0 chance I would have ever gotten hired on *MADtv* had I not been in Boom Chicago. I couldn't have been more ready and confident because I'd fucking opened for thousands of people at the Lowlands Festival with Boom. Whether it's 150 people or 1,500, Boom gives you the confidence to stand in front of a crowd.

Seth Meyers: Jordan has changed comedy; I think the estate of Boom Chicago has changed comedy. Look, Boom is incredibly important for me, obviously, but I also think it's true that in the intervening decades since Andrew and Pep started Boom, its influence and the influential people who came out of there—that's the proof.

Peter Grosz: Boom is Andrew, Pep, and Saskia's personalities combined, and all of us are in some ways their children. They built this place where all these people emerged from; that doesn't just happen. Obviously, people took mind-altering substances at Boom—but Boom itself is a mind-altering substance.

Josie O'Reilly: I still have somewhere a letter I wrote to my parents at the beginning of '97. In it, I said we had started rehearsals and I felt as though I was in the room with the American comedy greats of tomorrow. Turns out I was right.

BACKWORD
by Jordan Peele

I don't know if my quality of life has ever gotten close to the time I lived in Amsterdam as a Boom Chicago cast member. It's such a timeless world, with one foot in the past, one foot in the future. It's a great combination.

The biggest laughs I've ever been part of, or seen, were at Boom Chicago. Improv itself is such a special art form. When you combine that with the excitement of Amsterdam, the freedom of that environment, the letting loose . . . it's magic. What comes out of that combination is so prized: it's something you really cannot get anywhere else. It's like what Christopher Walken famously said: "When they need to hire a 'Christopher Walken type,' they have to call me." Amsterdam is the same: there's no substitute.

Going to Amsterdam actually gave me more experience as a writer and a performer and as a human being than I would've gotten anywhere else—and with no better people. My peers in the cast were motherfucking thoroughbreds, almost to an extreme. It's kind of crazy, the impact on culture so many Boom alums have had. In retrospect, we were on some "jamming with the Beatles in Hamburg" shit, Jimi Hendrix playing early shows at the Cafe Wha? in Greenwich Village, or an unknown Wu-Tang Clan MCing a Shaolin block party in high school. At the time, however, I was like, *These are just my friends and coworkers. Let's do this.*

Sure, we all knew there was something special going on. These children were not like the other children in the Midwestern comedy sandbox from which most of us had just arrived at

Schiphol. But once we were in Amsterdam, we were just living and working in the moment; we never stopped to ponder our future awesomeness. It was just the absolute right move for all of us in our lives to really learn our craft.

My origin story with Boom Chicago is similar to that of my peers. I'd moved from my hometown of New York to Chicago at the dawn of the millennium explicitly to get into the improv comedy scene there. In Chicago, I did everything I could to compete with hundreds of other people who were at the same stage of their careers. We all dreamed about the twelve primo paid slots for up-and-comers at Second City. Prestigious slots at Improv Olympic and ComedySportz didn't pay at all.

Twelve slots that paid enough to be a full-time improv actor—that's it. I figured if that was true, it's going to be at least three years of working at it, getting my reps, and paying my dues to get anywhere on the Chicago comedy scene. But was there a way to accelerate the process? The most valuable thing in comedy is the experience of actually doing it. The sooner you get in your Malcolm Gladwell ten thousand hours onstage, the sooner you're going to be good enough to deserve the attention and know what to do with it.

With Boom Chicago, the idea of getting paid to do what I always wanted to do in my career—and five to six nights a week, in one of the most beautiful cities in the world? It was like I'd received a golden ticket to the chocolate factory.

At Boom Chicago, you get to actually *do it*. Nothing is more valuable than getting to *do it* because learning to be an improviser is frustrating. You do a show and you suck, but you have to wait until your next show next week to try to dig out. In that time, you replay your mistakes in your mind, thinking of the things you could have done better, coming up with moves and lines that would have been funnier. It's a real mindfuck. But performing night after night onstage in Amsterdam? That's what really trained me for everything.

Being onstage with that kind of regularity, playing for audiences who may have never seen an improv show—that makes your boundaries fall away. Your entire world is just about getting the laugh. You commit to your choices. You explain your logic. And usually it works. But when it doesn't, then the audience really turns on you. It's a horrible feeling, but you get over it. Because the next night, you're going to have a completely new audience.

I can trace back my audience-pleasing sensibilities to this time. In Chicago, if you get a few people to laugh really hard, that's fine—but at Boom, you're always trying to get everybody in the room to laugh, so you're desperately locating all those things that make everybody tick. You have to be funny *and* accessible: true to the art form, but without sacrificing the hilarity of it.

Boom of course is a business, and the business is comedy. If you do well at a show, and you get your laughs, and you don't blow anything, then you get positive notes from the director. If you don't, you get negative notes.

Learning from your shows and interpreting those notes is its own training. It gives you more tools for your improv toolbox, without feeling like you blew it in front of a Second City big shot every time you bomb. Your shows are a continuum. At Boom, there is always another show tomorrow to improve for.

As you make Amsterdam your home away from home, you can't help but become more worldly. I mean, I come from New York City, a rather cosmopolitan place, but Amsterdam really broadened how I see the world. Being Black in the US meant I was sometimes an outsider. But in the Netherlands, I was an outsider in a different way. I was really able to get in touch with my identity as an American, but also as a global citizen.

That outside perspective is the value of living in Holland. It's fascinating to figure out what works and doesn't work onstage in that new context. Dutch people, expats, and tourists all come to see Boom shows. Not everybody in the audience speaks the same first language—but everybody has, at some point, a connection to that outsider feeling that we new actors feel in Amsterdam.

Those are the foundations of live comedy, and there's no better training ground than Boom Chicago. It was like an extension of university, that learning and growing experience for so many. For me personally, so much of my transformation at Boom Chicago was about becoming an artist and practicing my craft. It was about gaining confidence and knowledge that I couldn't get in any other environment. In Amsterdam, I became somebody who was capable of stepping up to the plate for any comedic challenge possible. Boom Chicago was where I became my best comedic self.

Now that you've read this book, maybe it will encourage you to study comedy and improvisation. And if you are an improviser, keep going. Play, perform, take classes, and grow. And if you have the chance to audition for Boom Chicago, or if they offer you a slot on their stage, take the opportunity. It will change your life.

Acknowledgments

Andrew Moskos

We would like to first thank the whole Boom Chicago crew—especially the actors who told their stories for this book, and all those who were part of those tales and memories. Our stories. Speaking of stories, thanks to Johnny Temple and everyone at Akashic Books for having the vision to take this project on and help shape it for the sensitive American literary palate . . .

I would like to thank my parents who were always very supportive of Boom Chicago, even if it meant me moving abroad. They learned Dutch (well, my mother did) and bought the apartment under us to be closer to their grandkids. They knew Amsterdam was home.

Thanks to Matt Diehl, who pushed for this book and led the charge. You have been a Boom supporter (and great writer) for years. Thanks to Boom Chicago's artistic director, Stacey Smith. It's not everyone I could give the keys to the car to . . . but you are the one! To the current cast—you guys are stars. It's not just Brendan who thinks so!

Thanks to Seth, Josh, Larry, and Hilary Meyers. That is one special family, and I am pleased that it gave us two very funny kids and great friendships that have lasted decades.

Thanks to my Boom Chicago partners and coauthors for cocreating this wonderful life. Saskia is CEO of Boom Chicago and my wife; let me say that, even in these #MeToo times, it's great to still sleep with the boss.

And finally to Pep, my best friend for forty years. We started this together, and it's still fun and exciting. We were on a corporate show with a keynote speaker who said that you stop laughing and trying new things at age forty-three. Not us. We are still trying new things and laughing a lot!

Pep Rosenfeld

First off, thanks and love to Andrew, my more-like-a-brother-than-friend. His confidence in us is what pushed us both to try to make a fun summer project work in 1993. And his confidence in me personally has pushed me to try what seemed untryable. Here's to many, many more guru gigs!

To Saskia and Ken for being great partners, great friends, and great teachers of the power of teamwork and *gezelligheid*. And you both say very nice things about me all the time; I hope you know the feelings are mutual.

To Rachel Dratch, who once introduced me at an LA party as a "political comedian," and who got my foot in the door at *Saturday Night Live*. Thank you!

To Matt Diehl: thanks for making this happen. Oh, and . . . CRUNK WINGS!

Thanks to Greg Shapiro (né Shapiro) for being a cowriter, coperformer, collaborator, makeup loaner, inexpensive therapist, and cookie provider/stealer for decades. Call time is always a pleasure, Shaps.

Thanks to my parents for (reluctantly) getting behind a crazy plan, for raising me right, and for being technically savvy enough that we've been in touch all the while. But Mom: put down that coffee and go to bed! And to Anne-Marijke and Richard, my *schoon*-parents. Not everyone is lucky enough to have a second set of supportive parents in their lives; and I doubt *anyone* has a mother-in-law who tries to get them drunk as often as Anne-Marijke tried to pour me wine at two p.m.

And finally to my wife, Tamara. It's not easy to juggle work, our two troublemaking boys, and my unpredictable schedule. And while I love my job, a cup of coffee with you while we walk the dog is still the reason I do it. I hope you know that. Oh, and Danté and Charlie: keep making trouble. What else is there?

Saskia Maas

Is it hard to run a business with your husband? No, it is not. It *is* both inspiring and challenging—so my thanks and love go to Andrew, whom I continue to look up to. My other business partner, Pep, I call my brother even though he isn't. Wow—reading these acknowledgments make us seem like a weird, incestuous bunch, though I still love working and hanging out with Pep as much as I can.

My family is incredibly important to me, and their continuous support makes me able to get through the hard patches, all while having them by my side for the fun ones too. My bonus family, the Meyers, have brought so many tears from laughter all these years. I am grateful that they are such a big part of my life.

People often ask me if it is it difficult to work with comedians. "Don't you have to be funny all the time?" Fortunately, all I have to do is laugh at their jokes and make sure the business runs smoothly. I think I'm pretty adept at both at this point. So I want to thank all the past and current cast members for coming up with all these jokes, sketches, and scenes. They make me a proud mama. And being mama to my two sons, Finn and Aidan—that's the best job of them all.

Matt Diehl

First of all, I'd like to thank the Boom Chicago actors and staff who spoke so wonderfully and candidly on the record. Their stories are what make this book significant. I feel honored to have seen so many of them on the Boom stage, before the wider world had yet to hear of Seth Meyers, Jordan Peele, or Amber Ruffin. I especially appreciate the efforts of Brendan Hunt, who gave so much to the project and was an essential cheerleader early on; the Meyers brothers always came through in a pinch too, I must say. I also want to thank the brilliant writers of the "Meet the Cast" section, Greg Shapiro and Rob AndristPlourde—great friends, and incredible talents and wits. They did what I could not, which is why I encouraged them to do their thing here. I appreciate y'all! Greg's also written many smart, funny books about life in Holland, which I truly recommend. And thank you above all to my family and their generous capacity to cope with a book as ambitious as this being written in their midst. And what a fun ride that was, collaborating with my dear friends Andrew, Pep, and Saskia—thank *you!* Thanks very much to Dave Prince for making me go to Amsterdam and see Boom Chicago in its natural habitat.

Lastly, thank you to Johnny Temple, Johanna Ingalls, Aaron Petrovich, and all at Akashic Books. Your integrity, ethics, taste, and collections of rare go-go vinyl are what authors dream of in an editor and publisher when they start writing.

Boom Chicago Alumni, 1993–2023

Lolu Ajayi (2007–2017)

Brian Tjon Ajong (2008–2018)

Rob AndristPlourde (1996–current)

Ryan Archibald (2004–2005, 2008)

Phill Arensberg (1997)

Dave Asher (1999–2002)

Ike Barinholtz (1999–2002)

Suzi Barrett (2003–2005, 2007)

Hilary Bauman (2006–2008)

Ally Beardsley (2014–2016)

Emilie Beck (1994)

Lesley Bevan (1995–1996)

Jennifer Bills (2000)

Liz Bolton (2008–2009)

Tamar Broadbent (2018–2019)

Jennifer Burton (2006–2008)

Dave Buckman (1999–2002)

Mark Burnell (1998)

Liz Cackowski (1999–2000)

Doreen Calderon (1993)

Heather Anne Campbell (2003–2005)

Joe Canale (1999–2000)

Kay Cannon (2000–2001)

Bumper Carroll (2000–2001)

Kristi Casey (2002)

Matt Castellvi (2019–current)

Matt Chapman (2006–2011)

Laura Chinn (2011–2012)

Horace Cohen (guest performer)

Rhys Collier (2018–2019)

Laurel Coppock (2005–2006)

Louie Cordon (2023–current)

Jez Cox (2000–2004)

Juliet Curry (1999–2000)

Lindley Curry (1993)

Tarik Davis (2004–2006)

Paddy Dawson (2001–2008)

Maurice de Hond (2010)

Michael Diederich (1993–current)

Tyrone Dierksen (2018–2020)

Lauren Dowden (2001–2002)

Colton Dunn (2002–2005)

Karel Ebergen (2016–2018)

E.R. Fightmaster (2015–2016)

Simon Feilder (2019–current)

Lauren Flans (2005–2008)

Lillian Frances (1995)

Woody Fu (2015–2016)

Sue Gillan (1996, 2015)

Ryan Gowland (2005–2006)

Tyler Groce (2019–2020)

Peter Grosz (1997)

Pam Gutteridge (1993–1994)

Cené Hale (2016–2019)

Randall Harr (2001–2002)

Bart Harvey (2000–2003)

Sacha Hoedemaker (2015–current)

Eleanor Hollingsworth (2013–2014)

Hans Holsen (2008–2009)

Jeremy Hornik (1996)

Brendan Hunt (1999–2005, 2006, 2008 . . . Brendan never really left)

Lisa Jolley (1997)

Matt Jones (2005–2006)

Scott Jones (1995)

Spencer Kayden (1996)

Joe Kelly (2000–2002, 2007)

Lizz Kemery (2018–2022)

James Kirkland (2007–2010)

Steve Labedz (2022–current)

Terrance Lamonte, Jr. (2022–2023)

Cari Leslie (2011–2013)

Ash Lim (2008–2009)

Jessica Lowe (2009–2011)

Simon Lukacs (2018–current)

Saskia Maas (1993–current)

Haley Mancini (2010–2011)

Ace Manning (2017)

Drew DiFonzo Marks (2011–2012)

Karin McKie (1996)

Neil McNamara (1993)

Jason Meyer (1996)

Josh Meyers (1998–2001)

Seth Meyers (1997–2001)

Rachel Miller (2001–2005)

Greg Mills (2015)

Marcy Minton (2012–2013)

Andrew Moskos (1993–current)

Becky Nelson (2006–2009)

Julie Nichols (2008–2009)

Katie Nixon (2022–current)

Jethro Nolen (1998–2000)

Kristy Entwistle Nolen (1997–2000)

Shane Oman (1996–1997, 2008–2013)

Josie O'Reilly (1994, 1996–2000)

Michael Orton-Toliver (2006–2012, 2018)

Dan Oster (2005–2007, 2016)

Ian Owens (2015–2016)

Raquel Palmas (2023–current)

Nicole Parker (2000–2002)

Sue Peale (1998)

Jordan Peele (2000–2004, 2009)

Cathal Power (2016)

Josh Rachford (2016–2018)

Dave Razowsky (2000, 2002)

Pep Rosenfeld (1993–1998, 2001–current)

Amber Ruffin (2004–2005, 2008–2011)

Tami Sagher (1995)

Ken Schaefle (1993–2006)

Jon Schickedanz (1998)

David Schmoll (2003–2013)

Greg Shapiro (1994–current)

Dani Sher (2002–2003)

Allison Silverman (1997)

Sid Singh (2019–2020)

Stacey Smith (2019–current)

Tim Sniffen (2004–2005, 2018)

Else Soelling (2017–2018)

John Stoops (1998)

Emil Struijker-Boudier (2015–current)

Jason Sudeikis (2000)

Anděl Sudik (2007–2009)

Sam Super (2012–2014)

Steven Svymbersky (1998–2016)

Carl Tart (2014)

Miriam Tolan (1993)

Neil Towsey (2008–2010)

Ruben van der Meer (guest performer)

Gerbrand van Kolck (1999–2003)

Holly Walker (1998–2001)

Ron West (2002)

James Winder (2010–2012)

Jim Woods (2003–2005, 2007, 2011–2017)

Jamie Wright (2000–2006)

About the Authors

Andrew Moskos is a cofounder of Boom Chicago. He works on various creative projects, major business events, and cowrote Dutch Prime Minister Mark Rutte's "most successful speech ever." Mark calls him Andrew.

Pep Rosenfeld is a cofounder of Boom Chicago. He is a sought-after event host, keynote speaker, and trainer who helps organizations see how humor can make their businesses better. Pep received an Emmy nomination for his writing on *Saturday Night Live's* 2000–2001 season, and he once got a laugh out of Barack Obama.

Matt Diehl is a journalist and author renowned for his contributions to the *New York Times, Rolling Stone*, the *Washington Post*, the *Los Angeles Times*, and *Interview*, among others. Diehl has also written/coauthored nonfiction books such as *Notorious C.O.P.* (with Derrick Parker), *Drinking with Strangers* (with Butch Walker), and *My So-Called Punk*, as well as publishing essays in anthologies spanning *The VIBE History of Hip Hop* to *The Rolling Stone Album Guide*.

Saskia Maas is CEO of Boom Chicago. In that role she is responsible for business development, production of global corporate programs, strategy, and finance. She also has her hands full keeping Pep and Andrew in line. In addition, Saskia is cofounder of InterActing, a program for teenagers with autism that teaches them social understanding and skills through improvisation.